Eric D. Miller, Editor

STORIES *of*

Complicated Grief

A Critical Anthology

NASW PRESS

National Association of Social Workers
Washington, DC

Jeane W. Anastas, PhD, LMSW, *President*
Angelo McClain, PhD, LICSW, *Chief Executive Officer*

Cheryl Y. Bradley, *Publisher*
Sarah Lowman, *Project Manager*
Wayson Jones, *Copyeditor*
Cara Schumacher, *Proofreader*
Bernice Eisen, *Indexer*

Cover by Metadog Design Group
Interior design and composition by Rick Soldin
Printed and bound by Sheridan Books, Inc.

© 2014 by the NASW Press

Library of Congress Cataloging-in-Publication Data

Stories of complicated grief : a critical anthology / Eric D. Miller, editor.
     pages cm
  Includes bibliographical references and index.
  ISBN 978-0-87101-448-1
1. Grief. 2. Bereavement. 3. Adjustment (Psychology) I. Miller, Eric D., 1972-
  BF575.G7S763 2013
  155.9'37—dc23   2013032009

Printed in the United States of America

To those who have found the courage to write about
their grief so that others may learn from their experiences

Contents

v

PART 3
The Death or Physical Loss of One's Child: Everlasting or Pathological Grief?

PART 4
The Effects of Intergenerational Grief

Preface

An Introduction to Complicated Grief and the Nature of This Book

I consider myself to be quite fortunate to have come across the call for book proposals from NASW Press that included an interest in the study of loss and grief. As an academic psychologist who studies and writes about grief, loss, and adjustment to adverse life events, I find the question about how to understand complicated grief to be one that has profound academic, clinical, practical, and personal implications for most individuals. Psychology and related fields, such as social work, have long considered how "best" to construe grief. Initially, the inability to move on from grief was widely thought of as pathological. Particularly in the latter decades of the 20th century, there has been a backlash of sorts against this perspective that sought to understand grief as a more normal part of the natural life cycle. However, concurrently, there has been more of a focus on the nature of complicated grief. For an excellent overview of this history, I would especially refer readers to chapter 2 of this anthology.

Complicated grief (which is sometimes known as prolonged grief disorder) is generally viewed as a form of grief that affects a subset of those who have lost a loved one. Such individuals tend to have more severe grief reactions, such as intense yearning and longing for the deceased; not accepting the death; feeling numb, angry, bleak, or agitated about oneself or life; and not trusting others (for example, Prigerson & Maciejewski, 2005). Simon and colleagues (2011) suggested that a commonly used measure of complicated grief, the Inventory of Complicated Grief scale, appears to have six distinct components: yearning and preoccupation with the deceased, anger and bitterness, shock and disbelief, estrangement from others, hallucinations of the deceased, and distinct behavioral changes within the individual.

Although there is not an absolute consensus about this point, some scholars and clinicians believe that this form of grief should be recognized as its own unique mental disorder in the *Diagnostic and Statistical Manual of*

Mental Disorders (*DSM*). In fact, at the time of this writing, the American Psychiatric Association (APA) is proposing the inclusion of complicated grief as a disorder in the *DSM-5*. If included, this disorder would be marked by the following symptoms, according to APA (2012):

A. The development of emotional or behavioral symptoms in response to an identifiable stressor(s) occurring within three months of the onset of the stressor(s). In the case of the Related to Bereavement Subtype, 12 months of symptoms (or six months for children) are required after the death of a close family member or close friend.

B. These symptoms or behaviors are clinically significant, as evidenced by one or both of the following:

 1. marked distress that is in excess of what would be proportionate to the stressor, taking into account the external context and the cultural factors that might influence symptom severity and presentation

 2. significant impairment in social, occupational, or other important areas of functioning

C. The stress-related disturbance does not meet the criteria for another mental disorder and is not merely an exacerbation of a pre-existing mental disorder.

D. Once the stressor, or its consequences, has terminated, the symptoms do not persist for more than an additional six months.

Indeed, there is a growing chorus of scholars, researchers, and clinicians who have been arguing that considerable evidence has been building over the past several decades indicating that complicated grief truly is associated with a unique symptomatology that requires its own particular clinical intervention (for example, Neimeyer, 2005/2006; Shear & Frank, 2006). Though this research question continues as the *DSM-5* is set to be released in 2013, there is also growing evidence that complicated grief appears not to be synonymous with the well-established disorders of depression and posttraumatic stress disorder (for example, Bonanno et al., 2007). Even if we assume that complicated grief is a unique condition, Lobb et al. (2010) add that there are many factors, such as one's psychiatric history, previous exposure to loss and trauma, and circumstances surrounding the nature of the death itself (for example, whether it was violent) and the relationship the bereaved had with their deceased loved one (for example, the level of closeness), that might predict the likelihood of its occurrence.

However, there are serious ramifications to the debate surrounding the nature of complicated grief and whether it should be formally recognized as a psychological or psychiatric disorder. On one hand, there is growing evidence that some individuals truly do suffer more psychological distress after a major loss. And, indeed, it is also known that all losses have their own unique qualities depending on the nature of the individuals involved and their social–environmental contexts. Sociologist and death studies scholar Tony Walter (2006) very nicely summarized this sentiment by noting:

> Complicated grief is a multidimensional phenomenon that exists within and is negotiated through the power relationships that link researchers, clinicians, reimbursers, clients, and families. Grief—like madness, trauma, homicide, sexuality, and homosexuality—exists, but how we normalize and pathologize it is a social construct. Homosexuality, for example, has been seen as sin, as disease, and as personal choice. Grief too has been seen in a variety of ways. Complicated grief is one way; it is a social construct, and a highly complicated one! … [T]he roots of complicated grief lie not just in the individual mourner's psyche, but also in the concern of family and friends to reduce suffering, to get the mourner back to autonomy and happiness, to reduce their own inconvenience and worry, to replace chaos and guilt with order and predictability. Without such concern, there would be no concept of complicated grief. There are other roots in normalizing psychiatry and the organizational needs of bereavement agencies. It is such things that lead us to see some grief as uncomplicated, and some as complicated. Complicated grief is a function of our concern as much as of the mourner's psychology, and can be understood only as an interaction between the two. (pp. 77–78)

In essence, Walter (2006) highlighted and cautioned that grief, much less complicated grief, is at least somewhat understood by what society views as advantageous or detrimental to our well-being. Certainly, there can be little argument that society should work to help those who are suffering in trying to cope with loss. However, there is a larger question of the broader consequences of recognizing complicated grief as a form of pathology.

Dennis Saleebey's (2011) work on the strengths perspective has had much impact on the field of social work, in particular. In brief, this perspective holds that individuals, clinicians, and society should work to highlight personal strengths and to adopt a resilient spirit even in the wake of personal setbacks and adversity. This view seeks to de-emphasize the role of pathology and emphasize the role of normalcy of life experiences. Interestingly, the field of psychology has seen the rise of a similar perspective with the development of the positive psychology movement (for example, Seligman & Csikszentmihalyi, 2000). An important related—though subtle—theme that has been previously advanced is that it is possible to showcase personal strength in the wake of (or maybe even due to) adversity and loss (for example, Miller & Harvey, 2001). In fact, there is some evidence that a lifetime history replete with a moderate level of adversity may benefit mental health and well-being more so than very little exposure to such life challenges (Seery, Holman, & Silver, 2010).

Readers of this anthology will quickly discover that virtually all of the chapters detail personal accounts and stories from individuals who poignantly discuss how their experiences of loss and grief—with particular emphasis on the ability to give voice to these narratives through writing—allowed for some degree of personal growth and betterment. In doing so, these accounts definitely should raise questions regarding the wisdom of labeling complicated grief as pathological. If one's grief is so severe that one is considering, for instance, suicide, it is hard to defend a view that some form of psychological or psychiatric intervention is not really necessary. However, the possibility that individuals may look at life-altering adverse events as a means to allow for insights and growth that otherwise may not have been possible should not be ignored. Readers of this volume will find that many authors have eloquently argued that it is almost impossible (and perhaps even undesirable) to detach experiences of loss and grief from the self.

This preface opened with an acknowledgment that grief has been largely thought of as an abnormal reaction and something to move on from as swiftly as possible. Since at least the 1980s, several scholars have chipped away at this notion by exposing various common (and largely incorrect) societal myths of loss (for example, Wortman & Silver, 1989). In some ways, the basic question of whether complicated grief will be viewed as a mental disorder by APA may be irrelevant. A more significant question to entertain is whether mental health fields return to the earlier aforesaid view of grief. Such a return to this theoretical perspective truly would be a loss. There is a voluminous literature that highlights how society still holds many stigmas against the mentally ill, who, in turn, often internalize these negative attitudes (for example, Rüsch, Corrigan, Todd, & Bodenhausen, 2010). It bears to reason that new categories of mental illness associated with grief may further exacerbate related stigmas. Doka (1989, 2002) established that grief can be disenfranchised such that society (in general) does not recognize one's loss as such; for instance, there is evidence that certain forms of bereavement, such as suicide, are more likely to carry a sense of stigma (for example, Feigelman, Gorman, & Jordan, 2009).

Given these very real concerns, it is unclear whether complicated grief is to be viewed as a form of mental illness and whether this will make individuals even less likely to share their stories of loss and grief. Perhaps bereaved individuals may develop a sense that only troubled individuals feel grief. Clearly, much work has been done, particularly in the 1990s, to establish how experiences of loss and grief should be viewed as a normative life experience (for instance, Klass, Silverman, & Nickman, 1996). Although much care and latitude should be allowed in the expression of grief, it is also understandable that we might try to mitigate personal suffering associated with a given loss. Looking ahead, the challenge will be how to allow for the realization of these two (often conflicting) goals.

The General Nature and Organization of This Book

I did not want this book to be a mere discussion about the nature of complicated grief among scholars who primarily research this issue. Although such a project would be a noble endeavor, I wanted to collect stories from individuals—mostly academics—who were willing to write about their own stories of complicated grief while also giving some larger academic and theoretical background to the issues contained in their respective chapters. In order to allow for this book to be a success, I knew that I would require many quality proposals from scholars who had the two aforementioned basic characteristics. Although I had a couple of possible contributors in mind when I proposed this book, I also knew that I required a much larger pool of possible chapters. Further, I wanted to feature accounts from individuals from a wide array of academic disciplines. To that end, I posted a call for contributors on the Web site H-Net: Humanities and Social Sciences Online (http://www.h-net.org). The precise wording used was as follows (and please note that I explicitly invited and encouraged development on a wide variety of topics):

> I am looking for personal accounts from individuals who may have experienced various forms of complicated grief and are willing to write a chapter about their experience. Ideally, potential contributors will be able to draw from some academic literature in areas such as psychology,

social work, and other related fields in their papers. However, particularly powerful accounts from those outside psychology and related fields will most certainly be considered. Papers that can offer a creative synthesis of personal narratives with an academic tone are especially encouraged. Clinical accounts will also be considered.

Papers that highlight a wide swath and diversity of topics are sought. Such examples can include, but are not limited to, complicated grief due to or related to: either an extremely close, poor, or conflicting relationship with the deceased, loss due to various forms of violence, complex situations or dynamics surrounding the death, previous losses contributing to challenges of bereavement, regrets over actions (or inactions) taken prior to the loss, or other sudden or expected losses. I would also welcome papers from those who may have experienced potentially difficult aspects of a grief experience and did not show severe grief symptoms.

Once more, I knew that for this proposed book to be a success, I would need to have several high-quality abstracts from individuals who were willing and able to write about their own losses while still maintaining an academic tone (or at least had a willingness to explore academic issues within the body of their respective papers). I was overwhelmed with the number of high-quality abstracts I received. Less than one month after posting my call for contributors, I felt that I had sufficient material to proceed with a proposal for this anthology.

I would suggest that the ability to write an account about one's own experiences with loss (particularly complicated or traumatic loss) is extremely challenging and admirable in its own right. There is a very lengthy and important literature that highlights the significance and functions, including great physiological and psychological benefits, of writing stories and offering one's accounts; many chapters in this anthology further discuss and elaborate on this point. If nothing else, the accounts featured in this collection have the potential to offer more clinical and practical insight on the nature of (complicated) grief for practitioners, researchers, and laypeople alike. Again though, these stories—as powerful and moving as they are in their own right—are unique in that they all attempt to highlight academic issues regarding the nature of loss and grief. It is hoped that this anthology will help to shed some additional light on what it means to experience complicated grief by presenting the stories of those who have endured such losses. Each chapter also weaves in many other related topics (for example, cultural differences, stigma and shame, and loss or trauma other than death).

Readers of this anthology will find six distinct sections. Before each section, I have offered some brief commentary designed to introduce both the nature of the section itself and an abstract of each of the chapters contained within each respective section. The first section of this book is titled "When and How Is Grief 'Complicated'?" and is designed to introduce some basic issues about grief, complicated grief, and the use of writing as a means of coping with loss. The next three sections, all in their own unique ways, make a clear case for why and how grief is often a lifelong process that becomes enmeshed with one's sense of self. The second section, "Unresolved and Long-Lasting Grief," explores many accounts of grief that, for a number of disparate reasons, has never really abated with the passage of time. The third section, "The Death or Physical Loss of One's Child: Everlasting or Pathological Grief?" illuminates this aforementioned theme with a focus on a form of loss that is commonly construed as one of the most profoundly devastating events that one can experience. The fourth section, "The Effects of Intergenerational Grief," explores how grief can be transmitted across generations within families. The fifth section, titled "Cultural and Societal Constraints and Complications of Grief," examines a number of cultural and societal factors that can make grief complicated. Taken together, these chapters raise some serious questions about the rationale and consequences of viewing complicated grief as a form of mental disorder. The final section is titled "Concluding Thoughts," by John H. Harvey. Harvey has helped immensely to shape and direct our understanding of loss by stressing both its everyday and applied importance to the lives of individuals during the lifespan as well as the healing role of writing and sharing accounts as a means of making sense of one's loss (for example, Harvey, 2000). His instructive comments and analysis of these chapters should be of great value to readers of this book.

Let me offer some comments to prospective readers of this book. This book should have a natural appeal for those in psychology and social work. I am very mindful of the fact that, as an academic psychologist, I am writing this book in conjunction with NASW Press, which is a division of the National Association of Social Workers. Given that NASW Press strives to incorporate scholarship across the social sciences, I felt very comfortable publishing this work with this particular publisher because this anthology bridges many disparate fields. In fact, I am very proud of the very strong interdisciplinary (or multidisciplinary) flavor of this book. The diversity of academic backgrounds and general perspectives from the included contributors further helps to underscore the very strong multidisciplinary components of this book.

Even so, let me address any readers from the field of social work who might question how or why this book, edited by an academic psychologist, could represent the field of social work fairly. Zastrow (2009) suggested that there are five basic goals of social work:

> (1) Enhance the problem-solving, coping, and developmental capacities of people; (2) link people with systems that provide them with resources, services, and opportunities; (3) promote the effectiveness and humane operation of systems that provide people with resources and services; (4) develop and improve social policy; and (5) promote human and community well-being. (p. 38)

I would suggest that this basic topic and this anthology (more specifically) address all five of these goals. Clearly, most of these chapters involve a consideration of coping methods (goal 1) and how to achieve well-being from either an individual or community level (goal 5). Many of them also give serious consideration to and analysis of various societal systems that can either facilitate or worsen grief (goals 2 and 3). Finally, the larger question of the consequences of viewing complicated grief as a form of mental illness will certainly affect social policies related to this issue (goal 4). There may be different interpretations of the nature (or existence of) complicated grief across the major mental health fields (for example, social work, psychology, psychiatry). However, all of these fields should necessarily be concerned with how individuals tell their stories of (complicated) grief, in part, as a means of understanding the nature of such grief.

Let me add that this book could be of great interest to those in other social and health science fields, such as communication, sociology, and nursing. Given the very strong use of narratives, I suspect that those in humanities-based fields will also find much potential merit in this collection. I am proud of the very strong applied aspect of this book: After all, this book fundamentally is about the stories contained within it. Anyone who has an interest in grief and loss—including those who have personally endured such experiences—may find this book personally helpful. It is hoped that this book will also find a larger, more general (lay) audience of readers as well. Further, this book could be used as a primary or secondary text in a number of undergraduate, graduate, or professional programs or classes (for example, courses pertaining to death and dying, grief, narrative writing, and mental health).

To the best of my knowledge, I am unaware of any books with the particular focus of this anthology. Although there are some books that feature a single author's reflection on his or her own (complicated) grief, there are fewer that seek to highlight select narratives conducted by researchers who primarily use them to showcase broader themes of loss or grief. Furthermore, there are few books primarily authored by scholars who have personally experienced complicated, difficult, or protracted grief and are willing to openly write about their experiences while also placing their stories into a larger academic context. Frankly, I believe that a book of this nature—that is, a critical anthology—helps to fill a significant void in the academic, clinical, and general literature.

I would like to conclude by again thanking all of the authors in this anthology for submitting their works and giving me the honor of editing their works. Throughout this process, I never lost sight of the fact that this book was much more than a mere collection of theories, intellectual debates, and sets of data. I was entrusted to help to tell all of the stories contained within this book. I hope that this book gives these courageous stories the just forum that they all deserve. I suspect that there may be readers of this book who at some point may find solace in their own grief—complicated or not—after reading some of these stories. Perhaps these stories can help to teach such individuals that it is possible to experience great loss and to survive it, and perhaps even give voice to it through writing.

Eric D. Miller
October 2012

References

American Psychiatric Association. (2012). Proposed revisions/trauma and stressor related disorders/g 04 adjustment disorders. *American Psychiatric Association DSM-5 Development.* Retrieved from http://www.dsm5.org/ProposedRevision/Pages/proposedrevision.aspx?rid=367#

Bonanno, G. A., Neria, Y., Mancini, A., Coifman, K. G., Litz, B., & Insel, B. (2007). Is there more to complicated grief than depression and posttraumatic stress disorder? A test of incremental validity. *Journal of Abnormal Psychology, 116,* 342–351.

Doka, K. (Ed.). (1989). *Disenfranchised grief: Recognizing hidden sorrow.* Lexington, MA: Lexington.

Doka, K. (Ed.). (2002). *Disenfranchised grief: New directions, challenges, and strategies for practice.* Champaign, IL: Research Press.

Feigelman, W., Gorman, B. S., & Jordan, J. R. (2009). Stigmatization and suicide bereavement. *Death Studies, 33,* 591–608.

Harvey, J. H. (2000). *Give sorrow words: Perspectives on loss and trauma.* Philadelphia, PA: Brunner/Mazel.

Lobb, E. A., Kristjanson, L. J., Aoun, S. M., Monterosso, L., Halkett, G. K. B., & Davies, A. (2010). Predictors of complicated grief: A systematic review of empirical studies. *Death Studies, 34,* 673–698.

Klass, D., Silverman, P. R., & Nickman, S. L. (Eds.). (1996). *Continuing bonds: New understandings of grief.* Philadelphia: Taylor & Francis.

Miller, E. D., & Harvey, J. H. (2001). The interface of positive psychology with a psychology of loss: A brave new world? *American Journal of Psychotherapy, 55,* 313–322.

Neimeyer, R. A. (2005/2006). Complicated grief and the quest for meaning: A constructivist contribution. *Omega: Journal of Death and Dying, 52,* 37–52.

Prigerson, H., & Maciejewski, P. (2005). A call for sound empirical testing and evaluation of criteria for complicated grief proposed for DSM-V. *Omega: The Journal of Death and Dying, 52,* 9–19.

Rüsch, N., Corrigan, P. W. Todd, A. R., & Bodenhausen, G. V. (2010). Implicit self-stigma in people with mental illness. *Journal of Nervous and Mental Disease, 198,* 150–153.

Saleebey, D. (2011). Some basic ideas about the strengths perspective. In F. J. Turner (Ed.), *Social work treatment: Interlocking theoretical approaches* (pp. 477–485). Oxford, England: Oxford University Press.

Seery, M. D., Holman, E. A., & Silver, R. C. (2010). Whatever does not kill us: Cumulative lifetime adversity, vulnerability, and resilience. *Journal of Personality and Social Psychology, 99,* 1025–1041.

Seligman, M. E. P., & Csikszentmihalyi, M. (2000). Positive psychology: An introduction. *American Psychologist, 55,* 5–14.

Shear, K., & Frank, E. (2006). Treatment of complicated grief: Integrating cognitive-behavioral methods with other treatment approaches. In V. C. Follette & J. I. Ruzek (Eds.), *Cognitive–behavioral therapies for trauma* (2nd ed., pp. 290–320). New York: Guilford.

Simon, N. M., Wall, M. M., Keshaviah, A., Dryman, M. T., LeBlanc, N. J., & Shear, M. K. (2011). Informing the symptom profile of complicated grief. *Depression and Anxiety, 28,* 118–126.

Walter, T. (2006). What is complicated grief? A social constructionist answer. *Omega: The Journal of Death and Dying, 52,* 71–79.

Wortman, C. B., & Silver, R. C. (1989). The myths of coping with loss. *Journal of Consulting and Clinical Psychology, 57,* 349–357.

Zastrow, C. (2009). *The practice of social work: A comprehensive worktext* (9th ed.). Belmont, CA: Brooks/Cole.

Postscript

I have written this postscript just a couple of months after finishing my preface to the book. Frankly, this postscript is one that I would have rather not had to write insomuch as it reflects on a horrific event: the mass shootings that occurred on December 14, 2012, in Newtown, Connecticut, at the Sandy Hook Elementary School. Although the investigation of these shootings was ongoing at the time of this writing, a heavily armed gunman shot his way into this elementary school on that day; once inside, 20 first-graders and six school staff members and teachers were senselessly murdered within minutes.

There is almost an unspeakable aspect to this tragedy in that the trauma associated with it became palpable to the world. All of these deaths are tragic—and almost beyond words. However, there is one death from this tragedy that I would like to briefly highlight: the death of six-year-old Noah Pozner. The deaths of all of these children are unimaginably shocking—but there were some aspects about Noah's death that seemed particularly haunting to me. Perhaps it was that Noah was the youngest of all the victims. I considered that he seemed to share similar personal attributes with my own sons (particularly when they were around Noah's age). Ultimately, there is the very troubling and unsettling way that Noah died. Although all of these deaths are beyond disturbing, it has not gone unnoticed that Noah was shot the most times of all of the victims, 11 in all, and at close range. In an interview that Noah's mother, Veronique Pozner, gave with *The Jewish Daily Forward* reporter Naomi Zeveloff ("Wrestling With Details of Noah Pozner's Killing," 2013), it was revealed that Noah's "jaw and his left hand were mostly gone." In the article, Zeveloff revealed her reluctance to first publish Ms. Pozner's account of viewing her son's body. But, ultimately, she said the decision to do so was consistent with Ms. Pozner's wishes. Veronique Pozner was quoted as saying:

"We all saw how beautiful he was. He had thick, shiny hair, beautiful long eyelashes that rested on his cheeks. He looked like he was sleeping. But the reality of it was under the cloth he had covering his mouth; there was no mouth left. His jaw was blown away. I just want people to know the ugliness of it so we don't talk about it abstractly, like these little angels just went to heaven. No. They were butchered. They were brutalized. And that is what haunts me at night."

Soon after this tragedy, many important issues were highlighted by the popular press, political figures, and public health experts—chief among them were questions about access to guns and general mental health care. Although these are indeed important debates to have, the Sandy Hook killings also suggest how difficult it is for society to honestly look at the rawness and cruelty of death, as noted in Ms. Pozner's account. It also again highlights how difficult it can be to grasp the difference between complicated grief and trauma and depression. It is almost incomprehensible to imagine sending a young child to school and later finding out that he or she is dead, and then to view and bury that child hours or days later. One could say that the "normal" reaction in such a case might be symptoms associated with complicated grief. The trauma associated with the Sandy Hook shootings, particularly among the families most directly affected by the tragedy, underscores the urgency and relevance of the conversations highlighted in this book.

References

Zeveloff, N. (2013, January 3). Wrestling with details of Noah Pozner's killing. *The Jewish Daily Forward*. Retrieved from http://blogs.forward.com/forward-thinking/168707/wrestling with-details-of-noah-pozners-killing/

Acknowledgments

There are many individuals to whom I would like to express my sincerest appreciation. There are many wonderful individuals at NASW Press that I would like to acknowledge. First and foremost, I owe much gratitude to Lisa O'Hearn for her incredible encouragement and support in bringing my book from just a germinal idea into a full-fledged book project. I would also like to acknowlege the helpful guidance given by John Cassels during the time period after the book's signing up until the commencement of the copyediting process. I would like to state my immense appreciation to Wayson Jones for his thorough, detailed, and thoughtful copyediting. I strongly believe that his edits and related suggestions to all authors have greatly strengthened the quality of this book. I am also thankful for the fine work and efforts exhibited by many others at NASW Press, such as Cheryl Bradley, Sharon Fletcher, and Sarah Lowman, who further assisted with the book. I would also like to thank anonymous reviewers for their input and suggestions as well.

Of course, this edited book would never have existed if it were not for the incredible contributions contained within this volume. I would like to thank each and every one of the chapter authors for either contacting me and/or accepting my request to contribute to this collection. Ultimately, it is their respective works that I believe have made this book a great success and one that will be read by academics, practitioners, and laypersons for years to come. I would also like to thank several others who contacted me with prospective interests in this book; though I could not include all manuscript abstracts for this volume, this interest was appreciated, too.

I would like to express my appreciation to my wife, Jennifer, and my children, Zachary and Joshua, for their ongoing support and patience while I worked to assemble and edit this very important book. I tried to take much care in helping to bring all of these very solemn stories to print. In my view, it was critical to bring these stories together into one volume. However, the vibrant spirits of my family also provided me with a much-needed larger perspective that aided my completion of this edited work.

PART 1

When and How Is
Grief "Complicated"?

*T*his first set of readings offers an excellent overview to the question of when and how grief is "complicate"—or whether such a term is appropriate. In many ways, Carolyn Ellis's chapter (chapter 1) causes us to seriously question whether holding onto and writing about the death of one's loved one is pathological or "complicated" in any way. Ellis makes a powerful and poignant case that it can be quite healing to cope with the death of a loved one in the long term by telling stories that become part of the survivor's sense of self and deepen her life. Instead of desiring to get rid of these emotions, Ellis argues that her memories of her brother, Rex, who died in the 1982 Air Florida 90 plane crash, allow her to keep him alive in her memory. Ellis has written extensively about her loss and reflects on many of these writings in her chapter. However, she offers some new insights upon her realization that her brother has now been dead longer than he had been alive and that the crash took place more than 30 years ago. She acknowledges this, in part, by focusing on the positive results for aviation safety that came from learning about the factors that precipitated that crash. Even so, her memories of Rex's life continue on.

Next, in chapter 2, Leeat Granek offers an outstanding review of historical debate as how to define grief and mourning. Granek opens her chapter with some discussion about her own recent experience of losing many close others—in particular, her mother—all within a year's time. Even with her extensive professional and personal experiences, Granek concedes that it is difficult to clearly discern "normal" versus "abnormal" grief reactions. She notes that, historically, grief has been conceptualized as a process to quickly recover from in order to return to "normal" (presumably, pre-loss) functioning. Granek does a superb job of highlighting how the push to pathologize grief in recent years came to be; yet, she adds that there still lacks a clear consensus on what is complicated grief (or whether it should exist at all). Granek cautions that the sheer act of the pathologization of grief can profoundly influence how one sees oneself and has great implications for the creation of a sort of "grief industry." Granek concludes her chapter with discussion of data she collected highlighting the fairly commonly symptoms that the public often experiences due to grief that some may term "complicated." In doing so, Granek's piece also raises some very important questions about the wisdom of creating an absolute classification of complicated grief symptoms.

In chapter 3, Laura Kerr makes some fascinating observations that seek to understand how grief sometimes can best be understood in phases or stages and, often, only with the passage of time and perspective. Her analysis considers the role of attachment theory and how the bereaved cannot fully accept the reality of death or the possibility of new ways of relating to the deceased. Much of Kerr's chapter documents her own recollections of how her mother reacted to the death of her maternal grandfather when she (Kerr) was a child. Kerr discusses that while her mother was still responsive and loving after the death of her maternal grandfather, she couldn't quite understand why she often seemed absent—until Kerr herself had to contend with the death of her mother as an adult decades later. Though Kerr suggests that her mother was clinically depressed and suffering from complicated grief, she suggests that she also felt "frozen" at times after her mother's passing and found it difficult to fully process what had happened. Kerr suggests that it can be healing to not view grief as "unspoken" and to try to acknowledge how it alters one's sense of self. In doing so, the bereaved still can have a healthy, attached relationship with the deceased.

The last chapter of this section by Trish Staples (chapter 4) also offers some intriguing insights that challenge some assumptions about the negative qualities of complicated grief. After suffering through an unhappy marriage, Staples discusses how she found a new love in life who died suddenly and inexplicably soon after her remarriage. Staples candidly discusses her hospitalization due to depression and suicidal ideation. But, she also notes the importance of journaling as a means of noting her thoughts and perhaps keeping some sort of connection with her late husband. Though she believes that she likely would have met the criteria for complicated grief, she also believes that her grief allowed her stories to be told. In doing so, she suggests that she gained a sense of emotional, physical, and spiritual growth that likely would not have occurred had it not been for her suffering and grief. Staples's article suggests the larger issue of how to weigh the potential benefits (for example, treating depression and preventing suicide) and the costs (for example, personal growth) of treating complicated grief.

Chapter One

Seeking My Brother's Voice
Holding onto Long-Term Grief through Photographs, Stories, and Reflections

Carolyn Ellis

> *Death ends a life, but it does not end the relationship, which struggles on in the survivor's mind toward some final resolution, some clear meaning, which it perhaps never finds.* (Anderson, 1968, p. 281)

> *As we cherish memories, we return to freshen and deepen our understanding of those who died, attend to them again, bring them closer, embrace them in their absence, reconnect with some of the best in life, feel grateful, feel the warmth of our love for them, sense that they are grateful for our remembering, and feel the warmth of their love for us.*
> (Attig, 2001, p. 48)

*I*t has been 30 years since my brother Rex died in a commercial airplane crash on his way to visit me. I recall the phone call, TV images of people floundering in the Potomac, searing pain and overwhelming sadness that nothing could relieve, the hope and then the anguish when the reality of loss sunk in. The details and feelings are vivid still, although I don't live in them anymore, and they no longer live in me. Still, sometimes it feels like the accident happened yesterday. At the same time, I now have trouble calling up an image of my brother's face; hearing the sounds of his voice; or telling stories about him, other than how he died.

My purpose in this chapter is to consider the lived experience of long-term grief by examining how I feel about and cope with the death of my brother. I introduce readers to the initial story I wrote about losing my brother (Ellis, 1993) and to the reflections I wrote 25 years after his death (Ellis, 2009). These provide background to the story I tell now about my continuing efforts to maintain a connection with my brother. I write and reflect again through photos and stories to remember my brother and continue my relationship with him, and to add to the academic conversation about continuing bonds with lost loved ones (Klass, Silverman, & Nickman, 1996). Stories about long-term grief are rare. My hope is that this story shows how grief can change over time and that it opens a conversation about the different ways the process of grieving might be experienced over a lifetime.

Until the 1990s, most of the literature about grief of a long-term duration referred to these feelings as pathological, complicated, or unresolved.[1] Counselors and researchers advised grieving people to detach from grief and get on with life within a reasonable amount of time. The goal was to recognize that you no longer had a relationship with your lost loved one and that it was time to turn attention to other living people. Sooner or later, according to this view, the time comes to move on.

Beginning around the turn of the 21st century, some authors and practitioners began to turn from detachment theory toward maintaining continuing bonds with deceased loved ones (Klass et al., 1996; Valentine, 2008) and the value of holding onto grief (Hedtke & Winslade, 2004). These writers are more likely than detachment theorists to examine grief over a longer period of time. For example, Silverman and Klass (1996) discussed grief that occurs over a lifetime, and Rosenblatt (1996, p. 50) described loss as a "sequence, perhaps extending over our lifetime, of new losses or new realizations of loss." Others have questioned our need for and love affair with "closure." For example, Berns (2011) raised the possibility that you do not need closure to live again after loss and that remembrance itself might help you heal.

Certainly, intense grief of long duration that keeps you from living your life fully can be a problem that sometimes warrants professional care. Moreover, terms such as *pathological grief* or *complicated grief* can be important for suffering people who need to justify receiving funded care from professionals. Moreover, for some, there might be benefit to leaving well enough alone or using repression and denial as strategies to move on with life once loss has occurred. Nevertheless, I suggest that for many it can be healthy to hold on to grief as a way to maintain a relationship with a person who has died. Why should it be necessary to demand that those coping with the loss

---

[1] For example, see articles in (Stroebe, Stroebe, & Hansson, 1993) that summarize pathological and normal grief. Stroebe et al. (2000) discuss the complications and need for "greater accuracy" in identifying grief as pathological. However, they say that there is "fair consensus" in terms of pathology "about grief that has gone on 'too long'" (p. 68).

of a loved one's physical presence also detach from their feelings of love and need for the deceased (see also Hedtke & Winslade, 2004)?

The risk in writing a personal narrative focusing on long-term grief is that readers may think that grief has taken over my life. That is far from the case. Episodic and fragmented, these feelings are fleeting, are often connected to anniversary dates, such as my brother's birthday or the day he died, or they occur in the context of more recent losses, discussions of death in my classes, rereading stories I have written about him, or visiting with family. My memories occur along with—rather than in place of—my joy in and passion for living and relating to those currently in my life. The complex emotions attached to my brother become part of my self and deepen my experience of living. The stories I tell help keep him alive in my memory. When others read my stories, my brother becomes someone readers and I have in common—he becomes a part of what they and I share. Thus, I do not experience my grief as pathological or unresolved, or something I desire to get rid of.

Re-membering My Brother through Photographs[2]

I have written so much about my loss of Rex that I wonder what more I have to say. How do I write about someone who has been dead for so long? Though he has continued to live with me all these years in my writing and memories, I feel him fading away, and I wonder if there are ways to "work on" our relationship. Is it possible, at this stage, to learn more about him?

I start by gathering the few photos I have of Rex from around my home study, where I display them. Most of our family photos were destroyed in a flood in my sister's home in Mississippi during a hurricane, and a bag of old photos I had are now lost somewhere in the bowels of my paper-and-book-stuffed home.

I stare closely at the first photo, a four-by-six, protected by a glass frame. In it, Rex looks to be seven or eight years old. Crouched on his knees, he poses in front of a watermelon, his hand resting on top and eyes squinting as though he is looking into the sun. As I think about the large garden we always had as kids, I wonder if he grew the melon himself. He's clearly proud, probably because of the watermelon's large size. I remember how we always

---

[2]Following Hedke and Winslade (2004), "re-member" is hyphenated to indicate that we not only remember then, but also re-member now in that we include the dead as members in our lives.

complained about working in the garden and didn't think much about the fresh food we had every summer. Now I love flower gardening and look forward to the home-grown vegetables neighbors always share.

I continue examining the photo, looking first at one part, then the other. If I look deep enough, perhaps the photo will reveal more stories and memories of Rex. Suddenly pain ripples through my chest and sits in my gut. Then my mind takes over, remembering, remembering, the day of the crash. I am not an observer now. I feel an emptiness, an absence; I sigh. The strength of my reaction, 30 years later, surprises me. How could that little boy in the photo be dead?

My desire to describe what I feel brings me out of my feeling. I admire Rex's blond hair, short on the sides with the strands on top hanging almost to his eyebrows. "Put a roach in your hair," I can hear my dad demanding, meaning to add Brylcream or Vitalis so that the longer hair could be combed into a wave, sort of a modified short James Dean pompadour. A smile breaks out on my face, as I remember when Rex shaved his head as a teenager. As usual, my father had been after him to cut his hair short. Like the other kids, Rex wanted to grow it longer, but my father would have none of that. Insisting it was time for my brother to get his biweekly haircut, he gave Rex money and took him to the barbershop. When Rex came home, he strutted and showed off his shaven head, which fit my father's specifications—it was short. My father took it all in good cheer, as I recall, and left Rex alone about his hair after that. The family got plenty of laughs out of how Rex had outsmarted Father, and this event became a frequently told family story.

Now come other memories. The ones that rise first to my awareness are those I included in a story I wrote about Rex a few years after he died. I recall again how we used to fight, although our fights were short-lived, and we were friends afterwards. I think fighting was just a way to expel our kid energy. Often I would sit on top of him and hold his arms spread-eagle above his head. Then I would put my face close to his and threaten him with the spittle dangling from my lips, sucking it in just before it escaped. We never hurt each other. Well, except one time when he accidentally blackened my eye with a baseball bat. He cried when he saw my eye turn red, then purple. I made sure my parents understood it had been an accident so they wouldn't punish him. Another time I pretended I couldn't find a switch for my father who was going to spank Rex for swimming in the pond in winter, and he escaped the threatened spanking. We had a bond and could be counted on to protect each other.

I also loved to play tricks on Rex. I once borrowed his bike after he had failed to lock it securely. I told him I had picked the lock, so then he stopped locking it. Instead, he often offered to let me ride it. Another time, when I was washing my hair in a washbasin in the bathroom, Rex called my name. When I didn't answer, he came into the bathroom to check on me. I let my head hang listlessly in the water. When he peered under my hair to see if I was breathing, I opened my eyes and said, "Boo." I felt bad when I saw the concern on his face. Of course, he immediately tried to hide his worry by hitting me—but only lightly.

These stories, among many that came to me quickly and vividly when I first wrote them many years ago, are now stamped on my memory, making it hard to access other stories that might lie beneath them. That's the thing about stories. You remember the story you wrote, which stands between you and the experience, which you can never really access again. The story becomes the experience.

I think photos have the same function. You remember a photo you have seen, and your mind plays tricks, making you believe you actually recall the experience you saw in the photo. Once I argued with my sister-in law Barbara that I had been present when my older brother Art gave her an engagement ring. Later, I ran into a photo my mom had of Barbara opening the many boxes inside of boxes that eventually held her ring, and I realized that I had remembered the photo and the stories that were told about this event, not the event itself.

Maybe that's what is happening here, as I look at this photo of Rex and "remember" him shaving his head. I search among the few old family photos I have on my computer, and there it is: a black-and-white photo of Rex pretending to comb his very white and bald head while looking in the mirror. He is all smiles. Even if I do remember the event—which now I am not sure of—the photo has helped sear the details of the stories I heard about it into my memory.

Intrigued, I return now to the photo of young Rex with the watermelon. Though I know full well that the result of "memory work" always "involves some transformation" (Bochner, 2007, p. 200), I seek to create the experience behind the photos, behind the stories I have written before. Here come some memories now to the forefront, events long ago silenced and put away. Once a minister held me down while Rex kissed my face over and over, then he held down Rex while I kissed his face over and over. We laughed and laughed, forgetting whatever we had been fighting about. I think I can feel those wet, slobbery kisses even now.

These specific memories are flooded with more general memories: keeping secrets from our parents; building playhouses, running over the piles of sand and lumber; playing ball—basketball, football, softball—climbing trees; catching lightning bugs in jars; and playing games like hide-and-seek, "mother, may I," and "red light/green light." I imagine Rex in motion, running as fast as he can. Everyone used to say we looked alike. We acted alike too—high energy, always moving quickly, smiling and cheerful, passionate and intense. I often wondered if I caused my parents more pain after Rex died because I looked and acted so much like him.

Rex and I also were different. I excelled in academics. Two years behind me in school, Rex stood out as well, but more as an athlete, jokester, and musician. People loved his common-sense approach to life, charm, good nature, and seemingly unself-conscious ability to have fun no matter what. I have sometimes wished I had had a son because he might have looked like Rex and shared some of his ways.

Coming into view now, I see in my mind photos of many Christmases, Rex and his toy guns, my last doll—a bride doll; birthdays with decorated cakes and lit candles; family members in hospitals surrounded by family. Among the imagined photos, Rex appears now in real life, in his early teens, standing up to my father, who is threatening my mother. I close my eyes and listen carefully. I want to hear his voice, remember his mannerisms—how he walked, whistled, winked, scratched his nose, shook hands. I want to hear his laughter. But I can't.

I pick up the second photo now, a five-by-seven. Oh, there's that shit-eating grin, squinting yet crinkling eyes, big indented dimples, and strong square chin. A cap covers his hair, which hangs to his eyebrows and covers his ears. I would guess he is in his late teens, though I don't know for sure. He is heavier now, the size of a fullback, I think, which makes me recall how much he loved playing football in high school. "If you needed a few yards on third down, you always gave the ball to Rex," the high school coach said at the dedication of a field house named after Rex. During the games, I played in the band and in my senior year was the homecoming queen, no doubt partly due to Rex, the captain of the team, influencing his teammates to vote for me.

The flannel work shirt Rex wears in this photo reminds me of how he took over my father's construction business a few years before he died. He would line up little bottles of different size gravel so the older ladies could see the kind he was recommending for their driveways. Ah, they loved him, the older women. So did the younger ones.

I'm not sure, but it may be that Rex had imbibed a few drinks in this photo. Given how much he loved to party, it wouldn't surprise me. Later, my sister Judi will say he had been drinking—she remembered the day in the photo—without my mentioning the possibility. I laugh as I think about the time we all got high on moonshine in a friend's cabin. Rex was dancing like a madman, and when I said I didn't want to dance with him because he was sweaty, he got miffed. Why do I remember that now? What is the significance? I think I've felt guilty all these years that I rejected him because of his sweat. If I could only dance with him now—and feel and smell his sweat.

Suddenly I can hear him. He has had a few drinks and is singing at the top of his lungs in a band. It's interesting that I can hear his singing voice but not his speaking one. He might not have been the best singer, but he was good enough, and his enthusiasm and wild abandonment were catching as he traced out the steps of the Temptations with his friends. I know I've seen a photo of him on stage, the band members in matching outfits. Am I really remembering him singing or am I recalling the photo? Does it matter? Either way, the image is vivid.

I fast-forward to a day when he scared all of us. He wrecked my red convertible. I was at college and can remember getting the call on the hall telephone, and crying when I heard the news. I don't remember who called. Fortunately, my hometown boyfriend was visiting me and offered comfort, even to take me home if I wanted to go. I didn't care about the car, just Rex, that he had battery acid in his eyes and might not see again.

Suddenly I remember something else. When my sister was cleaning out my mother's house, she found a story Rex had written about the accident. Knowing how much I like stories, she gave it to me. It is somewhere in my house. I look and I look, for hours, through the stacks of dust-covered papers that haven't been moved for years. I vow to clean up and throw away what I don't need. Days later I look again for hours. How could I have lost this precious document, his words, the only writing of his I have? I am sad that I must go on without it, just as I must go on without many photos—and without his physical presence.

I pick up the third photo, a small three-by-five. In this side view, he is older, mid-20s maybe, handsome still and very thoughtful and serious. He sports a mustache—which I never liked—and his hair is darker than before, a "dirty blonde," as my mother called it. His hair is the same color as mine is now (though mine has thinned and is mingled with grey). His eyes are deep set, almost closed, squinty even, his brows bushy. The photo has been cropped to portray only his face. But it doesn't matter. I remember the larger scene well. We were at my parents' home; I had come to visit from graduate school with a new 35-mm camera. I remember taking this photo of Rex sitting outside at a picnic table where we had just eaten grilled hamburgers and hotdogs, all of us enjoying being together as a family. Everyone lingered and talked, unlike when we were growing up and left the table in a hurry to go our separate ways.

Rex's short hair in this photo reminds me that he was in the Marines. Where is the photo of him in his uniform? It was a big one, 8" × 12". I know I have it somewhere, but it was never one of my favorites. Anyway, when Rex came home after being discharged, he bought a Corvette and a motorcycle. I was scared to ride with him on the motorcycle, but did after he promised he wouldn't scare me.

We're riding fast up the mountains. I can feel the wind. I hold on tight. "Are you scared?" he asks. When I say yes, he slows down. Then, "just a little faster," he encourages, and I nod and loosen my grip. Soon, we are flying up the mountain, and I'm not frightened at all. I remember that event because it was so much fun and because he so much wanted me to enjoy the adventure with no fear, perhaps feel what he felt. He always looked out for me.

I pick up the fourth and last photo, an 8" × 10". Rex is holding his dog, Buffy, in his arms. On his back, Buffy is completely relaxed; Rex stares lovingly at her. I am mesmerized by the gentle way he holds his dog. Seeing him so loving makes me feel loving. I call my dogs Zen and Buddha to my side and pet them. Rex loved Buffy, in the same way I love my dogs. "She is my child," he used to say. I often say the same thing about mine.

Rex is dressed in tight-legged jeans over brown leather boots. I smile as I remember the time he visited me in New York in the late 1970s while I was a graduate student there. We drive into the city, his first time. As we walk in Greenwich Village, gay men eye him up and down. "It's because of your short military style haircut," I explain, wanting him to be comfortable, "and your tight narrow-legged pants, tight shirt, and leather boots. You're dressed like they are, not like the rest of us hippies with our long hair and bell-bottomed jeans." Gay men are always ahead of the curve, their fashion leading the way for the rest of us. Rex, from a small town in the mountains, was behind the curve. Interesting that at that moment the two groups intersected. I was surprised by how open Rex was to the stares of the men, especially since he was a small-town boy who had only rarely been out of the Virginia mountains. As I recall stories about how he used to meet tourists in town and invite them to dinner and to spend the night, I am reminded that Rex never met a stranger.

I pick up each photo again. This time I wipe the dust off the glass with the end of my shirt, trying to get a better look, hoping that the photos will reveal something more. I take the photos out of their frames, to see if there are dates on the backs, but no luck. I stare; I sigh. Thirty years. Where did the time go? He would have been close to 59 now. Instead he will always be seven, or 17, or 27, or whatever age he is in the few photos I have, whatever age he is in our memories of him and his short life on earth—while we all continue to age.

I load the photos on the computer and move back and forth between them. On my screen, they are bigger and more brilliant than in hard copy. It's that smile, I think; it gets me every time. And his sensitivity, how tuned in to others he could be. I feel warmth in my heart. The absence is still there, but is filled now with thoughts of and affection for Rex.

I admire his hands in several of the photos and compare them with mine. My fingers are longer and narrower, with more veins showing. (Perhaps because my hands are so much older than his?) I wonder about the ring on his little finger, which I had not noticed before. Had that been Daddy's? Mom gave Daddy's old wedding band to Rex, and he had it resized to fit his little finger. I think of how close Rex was to Daddy and how hard he tried to please him when he took over the construction business. Sensitive to my father's needs, Rex paid Daddy to run errands and continue to be a part of the business. Once Rex died, my father tried to restart the business, but his heart was no longer in it.

I hit "I'm feeling lucky" in the Picasa editing program, and Rex's face comes in clearer and brighter on the screen. I am feeling lucky, lucky for having known Rex. I like remembering him, the details of our time together. It feels pleasant to experience these feelings, even the intense grief. These feelings bring him closer to me and reinforce that he still is part of my life. The closeness I feel takes over any pain that is still present.

Re-membering My Brother through Stories: "There Are Survivors"

Finally, I put away the photos and pick up "There Are Survivors," a story I published in 1993 about Rex's death (Ellis, 1993). Rex had been on his way to visit me in Tampa when his plane crashed into the Potomac River. We were becoming close adult friends who wanted to spend time together, and I had been so excited to see him. I read quickly through my description of that day, jumping from scene to scene, my memory of the words I wrote filling in the storyline I skip. I know this version of the story by heart.

Scene One: *The Crash*[3]

Rex was scheduled to arrive today, Friday, January 13, 1982. Although I was supposed to meet him at 4:30, his plane was just ready for takeoff from Washington when I called the airline at 3:45. Since I had invited several friends to dinner, I was glad for the extra time.

"Hey, what you doing?" my older brother Art asks when I pick up the ringing phone. I am surprised to hear from him, and, in spite of the lightness of his words, I detect worry in his voice. Rather quickly, he asks, "Has Rex gotten there yet?"

"No, his plane has been delayed. Why?" Already I feel alarmed.

"Oh, someone called Mom and said a plane had crashed, and she thought they said something about Tampa. I just want to reassure her that Rex is okay. You know how she worries."

Although he says this nonchalantly, I tense up because I feel how hard he is working to normalize this conversation. Then I speak from inside a numb fog, "Where did they say the plane was headed?"

"Well, she thought they said it was coming from Tampa to Washington."

"Then that can't be it," I respond too quickly, adrenalin now starting to pump. We breathe.

Into the silence my brother says, "But there was confusion because they said it was Flight 90."

"That's his flight number, but Mom probably just got the number wrong." Yes, that's the explanation, I assure myself.

"No," he says. "I just heard the number myself on the radio."

"Did they say Air Florida?"

"I don't know, just that it had crashed into the Potomac."

"Oh, God, I'll call the airline and call you right back."

Flashes of lightning go off behind my eyes. My breathing speeds up, yet I am suffocating. As I dial, my hands shake, and I say aloud over and over, "No, please, God." Struck by the triviality of my everyday concerns, I remember how rushed I had felt getting ready for Rex's arrival and how important that had seemed. Now, if he is only alive, nothing else will matter. Of course he is,

---

[3] This section includes excerpts from Ellis, 1993, pp. 711–730.

I admonish myself. Calm down. Mom has this all messed up. But then how did Art hear the same flight number?

I get a busy signal a couple of times before an Air Florida agent responds, "Air Florida, may I help you?"

The familiar greeting comforts me. See, there's nothing wrong, I reassure myself. "Yes, I want information on an arrival time."

"Certainly. What is the flight number?" he asks cheerfully.

"Flight 90."

Now his voice takes on a businesslike quality as he quickly replies, "We cannot give out information on that flight."

"What do you mean you 'can't give out information on that flight'?"

"We can't give out information on that flight," he repeats.

My heart pounds as I calmly ask, "Did an Air Florida plane crash today?"

"Yes."

"Was it going from Washington to Tampa?"

"Yes," he says, seeming relieved to answer my questions.

"How many flights do you have going from Washington to Tampa today?"

"Two."

"When were they scheduled?"

"One this morning. One this afternoon."

"Did the one this morning make it?"

"Yes."

"Thank you very much," I say softly and hang up the phone, my heart pounding.

Art answers on the first ring. "There was a crash," I say. "And it sounds like it was Rex's plane."

"They are saying now there are survivors," says my brother, and I feel hope. He continues, "I'm going to Mom and Dad's. They're pretty upset. They're going to be more upset."

"Okay, yes, go. We'll keep in touch."

Now I am alone, in shock, adrenalin rushing through my body. Numb on the outside, my insides are overstimulated. I tumble slowly through blank space. "Please, God, no," I hear myself moaning deeply from my gut. I move quickly to turn on the television. "Flight 90 crashes," it rings in my ears. "There are survivors in the water being rescued. Look, another head." This is not a movie, or an instant replay. I sit, my arms wrapped around my body, and sway back and forth 12 inches from the TV, breathing deeply and groaning. My eyes are glued to the rescue of the victims from the Potomac, and I search frantically for Rex. "He has to be there," I say out loud. In a daze, I am conscious of myself watching the TV as part of the scene. Reality becomes hazy, and more multilayered and boundary-less than usual.

A car approaches and I know from the familiar sound that it is Gene, my partner, and Beth, his daughter, home from shopping. When I rush to the door, the fog lifts suddenly and the slow motion scene I am in slips into fast forward. "What's wrong, honey?" Gene asks as he steps through the door, drops his packages to the floor, and embraces me.

Quietly and desperately, I say, "My brother's plane crashed."

"Oh, my God," he says calmly. Do something, I want to yell. Make it okay. But I say nothing. His body quivers; his embrace tightens. It feels good to be held and to have told someone. Not just someone. Gene, my anchor. He will know what to do and how to think about what has happened. My body slumps against his. "Oh, my God," he says again.

"It doesn't seem real," I say.

"Death never does," he replies. "But it is." Death? Why is he talking about death? It's just a crash. I cry quietly.

Then like a shot, I remember, "The TV. I've got to get back to the TV. There are survivors," and I break free from his embrace. That's right, he doesn't know there are survivors. That's why he's talking about death. "I'll see Rex being pulled from the river," I say loudly, fists clenched in the air. "Then I'll know he's all right. He had to make it. He's tough. There are survivors," I repeat.

Beth and Gene don't watch the instant replays of the people floundering in the icy water. Why do they sit silently at the kitchen table? They should be helping me look for Rex. They must not believe me. But they don't know him like I do. He can get himself out of anything. Any minute his head will appear. I continue rocking back and forth with my hands clasped together, periodically putting my face against the television screen to get a closer view. But I cannot find my brother in the Monet-like dots and lines. Hope and desperation alternate—hope when a new survivor is sighted, desperation when it is not Rex. There must be more survivors. "Rex, pop up out of the fucking water," I scream.

The announcers talk about the hero who just died saving others. "That must be Rex," I say, feeling proud. "He would do that. That's what he was like." Was? Why am I using the past tense? "He's not dead," I say. "I know he isn't." But if he has to be dead, I want him to be the hero. But then I will be angry that he could have saved himself and didn't. Why aren't Gene and Beth responding to me? They sit, silent, sad, watching me. He's not dead. Quit acting like he's dead. Of course, he's not dead. Not my brother.

I keep my eyes peeled to what are now the same instant replays of the same people being pulled out of the same river. Twelve people have survived. Then they announce seven. Then there are five. And one dead hero.

Scene Two: *Small-Town Grief*

What will it be like to see my parents? I take a deep breath, my head swims, and I walk into the house. My dad cries and holds onto me. Already in my caretaker role, I have no tears. My mom's body is rigid in response to my hug. "It's going to be okay," I say. "We'll talk."

"It won't be okay," she says angrily. "He's dead. He's not coming back." I am silenced by the truth of her response.

I ignore the two local ministers I don't know and hug Barbara, my sister-in-law, who whispers into my ear, "They found his body."

"Thank God," I say, feeling great relief and then wonder why. "When?"

"They called an hour ago."

My brother Art and I hug each other tightly. The atmosphere feels like death. When the town sheriff and the funeral director stop on their way to Washington to identify and bring back my brother's body, my mother sobs, "Bring my boy home." My grief for her then, and for myself, threatens to take me over. Afraid, I choke it down.

"A mother's pain is the worst there is," my mother says, leaving me no place to share my grief. The only time I had for myself was when I showered. I loved feeling the hot water run over my body. As I cried and relaxed, the pain would break through my numbness and a moan from deep in my being would escape. Amazed at the intensity of the pain, I pushed it down. I can't deal with you now. Would I ever be able to? I talked out loud to Rex, telling him how much I already missed him. "Rex, help me deal with this. Help me comfort Mom and Dad." It was a close, peaceful feeing.

"I am communicating with Rex," I tell my mom, thinking she will like that I am being "religious," even though it doesn't fit into her Lutheran doctrine.

"What kind of religion do you have anyway? You can't talk to the dead," she replies, and I shrug.

The people came. Three to four hundred of them. They occupied my parents and validated for me how important Rex had been. I became the greeter, letting them in, hugging, listening to them marvel at how I had changed, and then directing them to my parents, who sat side by side in their La-Z-Boy chairs. Offering their sympathies, men looked sad and stoically held my father's hand and kissed my mother. Women were more likely to cry openly with my mother and often with my father, sometimes falling in sobs into my parents' arms. Older people comforted, while the younger ones stammered about not knowing what to say. That would come with experience. My mother cried continually and my father wiped tears constantly. I was the dry-eyed director, who craved and feared collapsing into my parents' embrace.

The next day, Monday, is the funeral. The funeral parade leaves from our house. A town policeman, my eighth-grade boyfriend, holds up traffic, so we can enter the main road. Now he stands, with rigid posture and hat held over his chest, crying openly.

At the funeral home, the curtain is drawn before we approach the casket so that the crowd cannot see the family's grief. But it is impossible to keep it hidden. Mom screams when she sees the casket, and Art holds on tightly as she breaks out into loud sobs. The rest of us cry softly, staring at the casket draped by the American flag, surrounded by the flowers that people weren't supposed to send. I am removed. This isn't what I want. I kiss the casket.

When the curtain is opened, I see that the funeral home is packed. I am glad that hundreds of people stand in the hall and outside in below-zero weather, while others wait in their cars to go to the cemetery. Rex is here, watching with me, like Tom Sawyer. How he relishes all these people. You ham. You would have loved all the media coverage of your death. I smile. And just think, Rex, you lucky stiff, you will never have to suffer through the death of loved ones.

Scene Three: *Letting Go/Holding On*

Rex's friends organize a party. "A better way to remember him," we say. But it isn't what we want either. We want Rex. Okay, the joke is over, Rex, come out of hiding. "If the boy would just send me a sign that he's okay, I would feel better," a friend says. "He left so suddenly." "Yeah, have a drink in Heaven and tell us how it is." But our gayness keeps switching back to serious talk. I have a Scotch, and my feeling breaks through, my sobs catching me by surprise. "I am tired of supporting everyone, including myself," I say to Rex's friends who gather around me. "I don't know why I feel I have to be so strong."

"You don't. Let go," I hear, and I feel a bond with the people who embrace me as I sob.

Now it would be happening, a few seconds after take-off. There is the bridge it hit. Here is how his head snapped forward. Boom. I let my head fall into the seat in front of me. The vivid picture of the gash in Rex's head helps me reenact the scene—this time and every time I fly into or out of Washington, DC.

Re-membering My Brother Through Reflections in Writing and Teaching[4]

I first wrote "There Are Survivors" as part of a larger project, *Final Negotiations,* which told the story of losing my partner Gene in 1985 (Ellis, 1995). The chapter about my brother was so intense that some readers advised me to take it out of the book and publish it on its own, which I did (Ellis, 1993).

Writing about this experience was my first venture into autoethnography, where I focused on my personal experience to understand life sociologically. I also wrote to get through the experience, to make it into something I could live in and with, to become a survivor of what had happened. I wrote because I hoped that my story would offer companionship to others going through similar losses. I wrote to memorialize my brother and to stay connected to him, though I didn't know that at the time.

I have revisited this story many times. Writing in 2006, I included it as part of my book, *Revision* (Ellis, 2009), which was slated to be a collection of my previously published stories. But when I started with "There are Survivors," I felt too much had happened in the 15 years since I had published this story, and I began to think about how I might narrate this loss now, 25 years after the event. I wondered how my feelings of long-term grief were different from what I had experienced shortly after Rex's death.

I reflected on what had happened, examining my feelings, how readers had responded to the story (see, for example, Bochner 2005; Kleinman, 1993), and the critiques of my personal narrative approach to writing about grief. My goal became to turn the narrative snapshots I had written in the past into a form more akin to a video—a text in motion—one in which I dragged and dropped in new experiences as well as revised interpretations of old storylines, then reordered and restoried them. The storyline about my brother involved my long-term experience of grief and the effect that writing about it and using the story in classes had on my experience.

Living, writing, and publishing this story about the loss of my brother changed how I live and think. It increased my appreciation for the qualities of caring, love, vulnerability, and relational connection. For me, these

---

[4] Portions of this section are a condensed and edited adaption of Ellis, 2009, pp. 152–154.

characteristics are part of the core of what makes us human, and I want to express them in my writing. Writing this story has helped me survive the loss of my brother (and perhaps subsequent losses) and understand the value of writing in overcoming trauma (Pennebaker, 1990).

None of these positive sentiments mean I am free from the pain of loss. Every time I reread this story I shed tears, even now, 25 years after Rex's death. Though the pain is not as intense as it was shortly after he died, the powerful way it descends on my life still rattles me. When Rex died, the acute pain and shock took over my life. That sense of being overwhelmed has been muted by the passing of time. But in its place is a consistent gnawing hole of long-term grief that sometimes feels like it is trying to ingest my very being. I don't feel grief all the time, nor is the sensation always intense. But its presence reminds me that I will lose others and that I surely will die. Every time I experience a new loss, I feel that it also contains renewed grief over losing Rex (see Rosenblatt, 1996). Rex was my first significant loss—a loss that showed me I had no control over death, made me realize my own mortality since we were close in age, and led to the loss of innocence I experienced earlier in life when death stayed out of my conscious awareness (Rosenblatt, 1996). Perhaps this loss hits me so strongly because Rex was so young and his death was so sudden; though inconsistent, the majority of studies describe sudden loss as leading to more intense, distressing, and prolonged grief than does anticipated loss.[5] It also was a loss of someone whose role in my life would not be replaced, a loss of someone who knew me from childhood and had he lived would have known me for most of my life.

Since I experience sadness and grief whenever I assign, reread, and discuss "There Are Survivors" in my classes, workshops, and lectures, I often wonder about the value of continual exposure to this story and reading and writing loss narratives in general. Does my exposure to this story make my grief more frequent and deeply felt than otherwise might happen? Perhaps reentering the experience as I do every time I read this story does bring up those sharp signifiers of loss that generate the "gnawing hole" feeling (as other remembrances do as well). Does that mean it might be better not to expose myself time and again to this story? Might it be better to "just move on"?

Some of the feelings of loss I experience on revisiting this story are intentional on my part. When I reread this story, I seek to place myself in an

---

[5] See, for example, Lehman, Wortman, and Williams (1987); Sanders (1982); and the literature review in Carr, House, Wortman, Nesse, and Kessler (2001).

emotional space of grief so that I might better talk about what happened; thus I expect to feel grief. Yet I also distance myself so that I might analyze from afar and not break down emotionally as I speak about what happened; thus the feelings are controlled to an extent. The acute effects of relived grief are short term, halted by the responsibility of leading seminars and helping students comfortably discuss loss and grief—their own as well as mine—and by the need to continue on with the day's activities and demands once class is over.

Frequent exposure to this story also brings its own rewards. I have come to feel that grieving well can (or must) include revisiting loss. Reading and remembering enhance the attachment I continue to have with my brother. As Arthur Frank (1991, p. 41) says: "To grieve well is to value what you have lost. When you value even the feeling of loss, you value life itself, and you begin to live again."

In spite of my mother's protestations that you can't talk to the dead, I continue to have conversations with Rex in my mind and with my students and workshop colleagues about him. I appreciate the gift of stories: that Rex can be a topic of conversation and memory for me and that I can keep him present for myself and introduce my relationship to him to many people. Narrative then has a memorial function (Bochner, 2007). In this way, instead of "letting go," which is the conventional wisdom offered by most grief counseling, I can continue "holding on" (Hedtke & Winslade, 2004).

Rereading this story and having these feelings remind me to be compassionate and caring rather than critical and judgmental. My feelings of vulnerability make me more sensitive to others' vulnerabilities and our common plights. When people react to this story out of their own grief or empathy for mine, I feel part of a community of caring people. That belonging gives me comfort and makes me want to comfort others, to feel we are not alone in our grief. In the process, I feel human and alive.

Readers, including students, who respond to my writing say they appreciate the anticipatory socialization into feeling and coping with grief that my stories provide. Those who have experienced grief welcome the companionship and the opportunity to feel from an aesthetic distance about the experience. Comparing their grief to mine helps them feel less alone. Many express that what I write gives them permission to tell their stories. I believe that writing and reading stories such as these has the potential to help us all be more empathic.

Sometimes when I read this story, I pretend I am reading someone else's story. Then I feel for Rex's siblings, who try to cope and often stifle their own grief to help their parents through theirs; for this family, who has suffered the ultimate interruption and whose lives will never be the same; for this little town, represented by the policeman who cries as the family drives by on their way to the funeral. I feel for Carolyn: the young woman whose world has fallen apart and whose world view has been disrupted, her optimism shredded by the reality of loss; the young woman who tries to be strong, hoping that somehow strength and control might ward off her grief and vulnerability. I wonder about the confusion she experiences when she can't connect with her mother, a person she needs to touch and love, and be loved back, to release her own grief.

Further Reflections: Re-membering My Brother in 2011

On the day I began writing this chapter, I had assigned "There Are Survivors" to my Communicating Grief and Loss class. I like for them to read it early in the semester because it breaks the ice and gets students talking. I can feel the students' eyes on me when I come to class that day. They see me differently now; they are different with each other; I am different with them. We no longer are teacher and students who don't know each other; now we are human beings sharing our pain.

"I feel I am introducing Rex to you. Your responses, my feelings, our conversation makes him come alive in my life," I explain. I tell them how I cried when I reread the story for class. I tell them about this chapter I am writing and I pass around the photos of Rex, which they reverently examine and return to me.

I talk then about the circle of life/death, and most of the students seem to be with me. When I ask one male student, squirming in his seat, what he is thinking, he says, "I don't like to think about death. So I don't. Maybe that's because I'm young." "I'll be glad when we get to happiness," says a second male. "We've been talking about happiness," I say, interrupting the women who are complaining that men can't deal with their feelings. "We talk about death and loss to remind us of our common humanity and to live the best life we can. This course is a celebration of life."

I recognize that students' resistance to, even denial of, death allows them to maintain some distance, providing an effective coping mechanism at least in the short term. I try not to take their defenses from them, understanding that their resistance gives them a reprieve and allows them to live free of the angst of mortality. Because of my age and experience with loss, I no longer have the same luxury of forgetting and delaying. My goal is to give students an opportunity to recognize that life is finite and consider taking that fact into account as they figure out how to live.

"I have not lived—and do not want to live—inundated by death, but I want to be aware of it," I say. "Staying aware of loss reminds me of the dialectic of vitality and mortality; this consciousness helps me incorporate absence into my life and sensitivities and, at the same time, strive to live a vital life. I try 'to live as though [I'll] live forever, yet be prepared to die tomorrow' (Shames & Barton, 2004, p. 7). When I keep death on my shoulder, my day-to-day world also is filled with happiness, satisfaction, passion, and engagement, in spite of (because of?) the losses I have experienced and the ones I know will be there again someday. Part of this good feeling for me comes from writing from the heart and rewriting myself and my intimate relationships."

In many ways, what I try to do for myself and what I advocate in the classroom is a form of the resilience and strengths-based practice now popular among social workers and social support groups. I partner with students to assist them in managing the impossible, "imagining the possible," and thinking of themselves as agents "able to effect some change in [their lives], having *goals* that not only have promise but also pathways to their accomplishment—pathways that may be short or long, full of ruts or smooth, well-lit or darkened" (Saleebey, 2000, p.133). Together we imagine and then enact the possible through listening and telling, and then writing and rewriting.

As I walk back to my office from my classroom, I note that my grief feels gentler and comes less often now than it did five years ago when I wrote about my brother in *Revision*. Even with the photos, the memories and feelings are more distant, and I have to search harder to find them. I wonder, are there other ways to remember my brother?

Re-membering in Difficult Places: Trying out Family Conversations and Media Coverage, October 2011

I am excited to visit Art and Barbara, my older brother and his wife, who moved into my mother's home in Luray, Virginia after she died in 2002. My sister Judi and her husband Ron also are joining us there, and bringing their daughter, her husband, and their four-year-old daughter. It will be nice to have a reunion, our first in four years, and to see each other in a context that doesn't involve death. I wonder whether we will talk about Rex. Will he be a presence or just be an empty chair at the table? Before I arrive, I e-mail the four photos of Rex to my siblings and ask them to think about the memories the photos stimulate.

Upon arriving in Luray, I am greeted by Art's announcement that he can't remember the past. He refuses to talk when I turn on the tape recorder, and he rushes out of the room when Barbara and I look at the photos. I think he is afraid of breaking down, or feeling sad, but later Barbara says, "I asked him why he won't look at the photos. He said it's because he really doesn't remember anything about them." Yet later in the day, he talks briefly about not recognizing Rex after he got his head shaved and he remembers the name of Rex's dog. Then after a few drinks, he tells me funny stories about Rex, usually involving heavy drinking and acting out in some way. He tells them quickly, laughing, then leaves the room.

"He does not think to look deeply into each photo," Barbara says. "He would not be comfortable doing that." Barbara and I do look closely at the photos, discussing how old Rex is in each one and where and when it took place. As we look at the photo where he might have been drinking, her memory goes to the times when my two brothers were partying together. "Rex was 15 years younger," she says, "and my husband was acting like he was Rex's age, instead of being the older brother."

"You know," she says, "Rex used to say he didn't want to grow old. I think of that sometimes."

When Judi looks at the photos, she talks in general about how sensitive our brother was. "Look how thoughtful he is in that photo," she says. "He was so handsome. Look at how sweet he is with his dog."

"Yes," I respond, "it's interesting that all four of us siblings are so crazy about dogs."

"Especially since we didn't have dogs when we were kids," Judi says.

We approach the task enthusiastically, but there are many silences and few details. It feels as though we are trying too hard to remember. So much time has passed; there doesn't seem to be much to say.

When we stop for dinner, my sister gives the blessing and lovingly mentions our mother, who died nine years before, but not our father, who died 24 years before. And not Rex. I am disappointed. It is my mom's birthday that day and this is her home we are in, so I understand. But still … why isn't our father here? Why isn't Rex? I want to add something, but no words come to me. I am afraid I will break down if I speak, and I don't want to do that on this occasion when we are all so happy to be together.

Later, I decide to go to the graves of my brother, mother, father, and aunt. Art volunteers to go with me. We are very goal oriented, replacing the artificial white lilies with flowers of autumn orange and yellow, checking to see if the Styrofoam in the vases needs replacing. Fearing I will make my brother uncomfortable, I don't say anything about our dead relatives or linger at the graves. Recalling how keeping up the graves was very important to our mom, I am pleased we are able to do this together.

Afterward, I visit the mother of a good friend of Rex's. "If Rex had lived, this community would have been different. He would have shaken it up," she says. "Yes, he was always a community person," I respond, "and he cared greatly about this little town." Our short conversation about Rex reminds me of how important he was to this community.

After being back in Tampa a while, I again pick up this chapter. I note that it is October 25, 2011, Rex's 59th birthday, and that he has now been dead longer than he lived. Still seeking information, I look up my brother's plane crash online, something I have never done before. I am surprised when I find videos and first-hand, detailed, emotional, and vivid descriptions of the crash site as well as audios of the pilots' last words synchronized with an illustration of the crash and stories of pilot error. "Why couldn't his pilot have been Sully, who landed a plane safely on the Hudson?" I ask myself, though I know this is a dead-end question.

"You could hear the screams of the survivors," I read in a Wikipedia article ("Air Florida," n.d.). I am overcome with thoughts of Rex struggling for life. Then "According to the coroner, Williams [the hero] was the only passenger to die by downing." There it is. So that's how he died. I imagine his head hitting the seat, and I am there beside him, feeling the impact.

I watch a video of the survivors being rescued, a man swimming out and risking his life to save a female passenger. My mind screams, "My brother is in that water!"

Suddenly, my body rebels. My face flashes hot, my stomach quivers, I feel icy cold. I gulp, take deep breaths, and I know—for sure—that this is not working as a way to remember. There are limits to what I want to know and remember. I go outside for some fresh air.

When I return to my desk, I concentrate on an article that discusses in detail the good that came out of this crash. "While most air disasters quickly become historical footnotes, aviation safety experts say few crashes have left a legacy as sweeping as Air Florida Flight 90" (Wilber, 2007, para. 4). Along with lessons about communication and management skills, this crash also became a case study for training pilots and rescue crews, an impetus for reforms in pilot training and regulations and for the development of an improved rescue harness for use in helicopter recoveries, as well as for improvements in many other industries. The vice chairman of the National Transportation Safety Board said, "This accident was ingrained in the minds of the entire world, and we watched the recovery efforts as they happened. I don't know of any other accident that has had this amount of impact on aviation but also in other industries" (Wilber, 2007, para. 5). I had no idea of the importance this crash had, and I feel proud that something good came from Rex's death. Still, that does not erase my loss.

Finding Rex's Voice

If only I could hear Rex's voice, I think, then I might feel that I had found the connection I am seeking. I hunt again for the story Rex wrote about his car accident. Maybe there I will find clues about who he was, things I have forgotten or never knew. Obsessed, I look through piles of yellowed papers and flip through files that have been unopened for decades. Surely I have put it somewhere safe; it has to be here. Just as I tell myself I must give up, I see a large scrapbook on the bottom shelf of my bookcase. Tucked inside, among all the newspaper clippings my mom kept of weddings and accolades of local people she knew, are nine lined pages torn out of a notebook. Cursive handwriting covers the front and back of each one. Rex's cursive leans to the right, yet it is a free-style, undisciplined, just as he was. Someone has written a few comments in response in the margins and put check plus marks at the top of each two-page segment. Though a continuous story about the accident, it is clear that the nine two-page segments were written at different times; the ink is different shades of blue, the responder uses different colors to write the remarks on each of the sections, and Rex ends each part with a sentence about what he will talk about next time. Perhaps this was a school assignment.

I read his text hungrily, looking for what I can't find in the photos, stories, newspapers, and family conversations. He writes in detail about the car accident, which happened on the day of his 17th birthday, as he was on his way to pick up his girlfriend for a homecoming dance. Writing from his perspective more than a year later, he details the aftermath of the accident as well. The accident was not his fault, and the other man's insurance paid all the bills. As I had recalled, he got battery acid in his eyes and couldn't see for days. He is not afraid of writing about how he cried out of fear and was lonely in the hospital, or how scared he was a year later driving down the same road again to a homecoming dance to pick up the same girl, so frightened he stopped the car and got out to make sure no other car was coming, or how on his birthday he "just started crying" because he was so "happy to be home and well." His biggest concern, next to not seeing, was that he wouldn't be able to play football. During recovery, as he was watching a game being played, he wrote,

> As the game went on I became sick. I wanted to play so bad I actually got sick on my stomach. The boy that had taken my place wasn't doing the job and we were getting killed. I'm not saying that I was that good of player, but when you are used to playing with a certain eleven players and one is missing it really throws the timing of your plays off. Anyway Strasberg beat us pretty bad.

He convinces the doctor to let him play the next week. He is modest about his abilities in terms of catching the ball. He wrote,

> One thing that stands out in my mind about the game was when I caught a pass. It was fourth down and about five yards for the first down. Usually we would have punted, but this time we decided to pass and try to get the first down. We still lined up in punt formation to make them think we were going to punt. When the ball was snapped there were two men covering the other receiver and there were none on me. I remember running down the field about ten yards and cutting to the outside. Then I remember seeing a brown blob coming toward me. I didn't think they were throwing a pass to me because I didn't have very good hands and there weren't many passes thrown to me. But sure enough it was a pass to me, and by luck I caught if for a first down. I know it was luck because I didn't really see the ball.

On page 16, he concludes with: "I feel like God let me keep my sight for some reason and one of these days I'm going to find out." I wonder then if he ever did.

The last story details what football meant to him.

> Fridays during football season is a very bad day for me. Because Friday is the day that the football game is played. I have trouble keeping my mind on anything but football. I especially have trouble concentrating when I hear the band practicing for the game that night.

On Thursday night I usually go to bed with butterflies and I keep the butterflies until the game starts. Butterflies affect different people in different ways. Butterflies make me feel like before I give an oral book report only about ten times worse. I sometimes think instead of butterflies in my stomach, there are vultures or something down there.

During the summer weeks of practice I sometimes wonder why I'm out there running, sweating and literally getting the "hell" BEAT out of me, when I could be somewhere swimming, drinking Pepsi colas (or something else) and having a good time. When school finally starts and the day of the first game comes and there's the pep rally and the cheerleaders and fans yelling for me and the team, I then know that it was worth the effort.

When Friday comes I'm one of the most cocky and proudest persons in school. When I put that jersey on I'm really proud. The reason I'm like this is because I know I'm one out of thirty-some guys that could make the football team, and to me that is something to be proud of. No one can imagine how hard it is to play football, unless they have played themselves.

Friday comes, then the football game passes and it is now Saturday morning. You wake up and feel like you have been run over by a Mack truck. If we won, the aches and pains don't matter, but if you lost, the aches and pains hurt a little more.

I definitely believe football helps build you into a man. Football teaches you that just because you are behind, that is no reason to give up. Just keep trying and if you try hard enough you'll win in the game of football and in the game of life.

Reading my brother's words brings alive his spirit, energy, emotionality, and passion for life in ways that photos, our memories and storytelling, and my writing do not. His words bring him here to me now, in ways I haven't imagined before. Though I don't have his corporeal presence, his presence in my memory is comforting. I have enjoyed our visit, our time together, and feel that my relationship with my brother has grown and changed. I wonder if I'll still feel this closeness tomorrow? or next week? or next year? I put the photos back in their proper places, my books and papers I've written about Rex back on the shelf, and his words back into my mom's scrapbook, vowing that this time I won't forget where they are.

Anniversaries

On Friday, January 13, 2012, the 30th anniversary of my brother's death, I send e-mails to my siblings that say, "Thinking of our dear brother today. Love, Carolyn."

"Are you focusing on this anniversary day?" asks my partner Art, when the crash flashes on the TV news program we watch later that day.

"Not nearly as much as I'm thinking about our wedding anniversary tomorrow, January 14th. Do you believe we've been married now 17 years and together for 22?"

"Don't make any plans tomorrow," says Art. "I have a surprise planned for you."

Dream Coda: February 29, 2012

I wake up from a rare dream about Rex. In it, I am at our childhood home, waiting for Rex, who is coming home after a long time away. When a car arrives in the middle of the night, I know it is Rex and I get up to greet him. A woman comes through the door, but not Rex. "He has taken a very sick friend to the hospital," she says. "It doesn't look good." Disappointed, I stay up to wait for his return, wondering if we will be as close as we used to be, or if he will be distant as he was the last time I saw him. When he arrives, I approach him with open arms, eager to touch and hug him, but he holds me back with an outstretched arm. "I am too sweaty," he says. As I slowly awaken, he gradually disappears.

References

Air Florida Flight 90. (n.d.). Retrieved from http://en.wikipedia.org/wiki/Air_Florida_Flight_90

Anderson, R. (1968). I never sang for my father. In O. Guernsey, Jr. (Ed.), *The best plays of 1967–1968* (pp. 277–298). New York: Dodd, Mead.

Attig, T. (2001). Relearning the world: Making meaning and finding meanings. In R. Neimeyer (Ed.), *Meaning reconstruction & the experience of loss* (pp. 33–54). Washington, DC: American Psychological Association.

Berns, N. (2011). *Closure: The rush to end grief and what it costs us*. Philadelphia: Temple University Press.

Bochner, A. P. (2005). Surviving autoethnography. *Studies in Symbolic Interaction, 28,* 51–58.

Bochner, A. P. (2007). Notes toward an ethics of memory in autoethnography. In N. Denzin & M. Giardina (Eds.), *Ethical futures in qualitative research: Decolonizing the politics of knowledge* (pp. 197–208). Walnut Creek, CA: Left Coast Press.

Carr, D., House, J., Wortman, C., Nesse, R., & Kessler, R. (2001). Psychological adjustment to sudden and anticipated spousal loss among older widowed persons. *Journals of Gerontology Series B: Psychological Sciences and Social Sciences, 56,* S237–S248.

Ellis, C. (1993). "There are survivors": Telling a story of sudden death. *Sociological Quarterly, 34,* 711–730.

Ellis, C. (1995). *Final negotiations: A story of love, loss, and chronic illness.* Philadelphia: Temple University Press.

Ellis, C. (2009). *Revision: Autoethnographic reflections on life and work.* Walnut Creek, CA: Left Coast Press.

Frank, A. (1991). *At the will of the body: Reflections on illness.* Boston: Houghton Mifflin.

Hedtke, L., & Winslade, J. (2004). *Re-membering lives: Conversations with the dying and the bereaved.* Amityville, NY: Baywood.

Klass, D., Silverman, D., & Nickman, S. (Eds.). (1996). *Continuing bonds: New understanding of grief.* London: Taylor and Francis Group.

Kleinman, S. (1993). Culturally speaking: Carolyn Ellis' "There are survivors." *Sociological Quarterly, 34,* 731–733.

Lehman, D., Wortman, C., & Williams, A. (1987). Long-term effects of losing a spouse or child in a motor vehicle crash. *Journal of Personality & Social Psychology, 52,* 218–231.

Pennebaker, J. (1990). *Opening up: The healing power of expressing emotions.* New York: Guilford Press.

Rosenblatt, P. (1996). Grief that does not end. In D. Klass, D. Silverman, & S. Nickman (Eds.), *Continuing bonds: New understanding of grief* (pp. 5–58). London: Taylor and Francis Group.

Sanders, C. M. (1982). Effects of sudden vs. chronic illness death on bereavement outcome. *Omega: Journal of Death & Dying, 13,* 227–241.

Saleebey, D. (2000). Power in the people: Strengths and hope. *Advances in Social Work, 1*(2), 127–138.

Shames, L., & Barton, P. (2004). *Not fade Away: A short life well lived.* New York: Harper Perennial.

Silverman, P. R., & Klass, D. (1996). Introduction: What's the problem? In D. Klass, D. Silverman, & S. Nickman (Eds.), *Continuing bonds: New understanding of grief* (pp. 3–30). London: Taylor and Francis Group.

Stroebe, M., Stroebe, W., & Hansson, R. (1993). *Handbook of bereavement: Theory, research, & intervention.* Cambridge, England: Cambridge University Press.

Stroebe, M., van Son, M., Stroebe, W., Kleber, R., Schut, H., & van den Bout, J. (2000). On the classification and diagnosis of pathological grief. *Clinical Psychology Review, 20*(1), 57–75.

Valentine, C. (2008). *Bereavement narratives: Continuing bonds in the twenty-first century.* New York: Routledge.

Wilber, D. Q. (2007, January 12). "A crash's improbable impact." *Washington Post.* Retrieved from at http://www.washingtonpost.com/wp-dyn/content/article/2007/01/11/AR2007011102220.html

Chapter Two

The Complications of Grief
The Battle to Define Modern Mourning

Leeat Granek

Mourning Has Broken

In 2005, all the women died. At least that's how it felt to me. My mother, to whom I was exceptionally close, died after living with metastatic breast cancer for 18 years. In the same year, I also lost an aunt, a close family friend, a woman who was my mother's "chemo partner," and a cherished professor. I was 25 years old.

These were my first experiences with grief, and they shocked me. One of the things that I found most distressing about grieving was how shameful it felt to express my sadness in public. I often had the sense that I was doing something wrong or taboo when I appeared (feeling rather) unhinged in public. Aries (1981) argued that dying and mourning have been constructed as scandalous in Western culture. We have, according to Aries, "eliminated [death's] character of public ceremony, and made it a private act, and on the other hand, associated with this privatization of death was the second great milestone in the contemporary history of death: the rejection and elimination of mourning" (p. 575). This was true to my own experience. I often felt ashamed, embarrassed, and regretful for my sadness, and I was sorry for burdening others with my pain.

After the shock came the curiosity. As a grieving health psychologist, I began to notice how many inconsistencies there were between what I was experiencing and what I had learned to be true about bereavement. One example of this contradiction was the matter of the duration of grief. While I was in the "acute" phase of grieving, which lasted well over a year, I often thought my suffering would never end. I longed for the pain to abate and would have done anything to make it stop. While this was happening, I was getting the message from those around me that it was "time to move on." I did not know yet that bereavement was listed in the appendix of the *Diagnostic and Statistical Manual of Mental Disorders* (*DSM*) (American Psychiatric Association [APA], 2013) or that there was a category called complicated grief (CG) that was widely used by psychology and psychiatry professionals and would become a hotly contested psychological diagnosis in the years to come.

Several years later, I had become a scholar and "expert" on grief. I put expert in quotation marks because although I have intimately experienced grief, have devoted years to its study, have heard from thousands of mourners about their experiences, and have published in the field, I still know little about what the grief process is, does, and transforms in us. I am still not certain about what is normal or abnormal; indeed, it appears from my extensive research on the topic that all grief is complicated in some capacity.

In this chapter, I dive into this ambiguity and uncertainty about grief. I begin by examining grief in its social and historical context and continue by addressing the psychological imperative to gain control over mourning by trying to define the parameters around what is normal and abnormal in expressions of grief. In the second half of the chapter, I explore the implications of this pathologization and the contemporary attempts to manage grief with psychotherapy and pharmaceuticals. In the fourth and final section, I explore what the public seems to wants when it comes to grief and how community support may be a particularly powerful antidote to the pathologization narrative.

Grief in Context: Modernism, the Individual, Death, and Grief

The emergence of grief as a psychological, scientific object of study is an early 20th-century invention (Granek, 2010a). While most of my research has focused on the contributions of the psychological and psychiatric disciplines in constructing cultural expectations about what is deemed normal or abnormal with regard to acceptable mourning practices, it is paramount to understand that the psychologization and pathologization of grief are situated within several other cultural and historical movements that have been part of the shifting understanding of mourning. These contexts includes the rise of modernism, the focus on the psychological self as a site of meaning, and the subsequent fear of death and grief (Becker, 1973; Kellehear, 2007; Seale, 1998); the proliferating role of therapeutic experts in managing everyday life (Illouz, 2008); and an adherence to a progress narrative that emphasizes happiness, innovation, and a forward-moving mentality while denying sadness and mourning (Cable, 1998; Gorer, 1967). Contemporary culture does not like to look in the rearview mirror when it comes to pain, loss, or grief.

The main tenets of modernism are an emphasis on scientific rationality, reason, the self, observation, and a belief in continuous progress. Modern life emphasizes goal directedness, functionality, rationality, and efficiency in all areas of living (Gergen, 1991, 1992). Science values empirical evidence and believes only what it can see and prove (Bordo, 1987). As such, modernism has developed in tandem with a decline in religion and a belief in science instead of God (Bauman, 1992; Gorer, 1967). This "desacralisation of social life" has meant a focus on the self as a site for meaning and identity, and in this process, a revisioning of the way people conceive of and understand death and grief (Mellor & Shilling, 1993, p. 413). Mellor and Shilling (1993) noted that whereas death used to be a disruption to the social body, it has become instead a disruption to the dying individual and the bereaved family. Whereas it used to be the case that religion and traditional societies offered social processes around mourning that ascribed rituals and practices to deal with death, and subsequently grief, the modernist focus on the self has left people bereft of meaning, community, and structure with which to manage grief.

These massive changes happening around death, dying, and grieving in the 20th and 21st centuries represent shifts in ideology and culture that have left an open space for psychologists to step in and provide guidance amid this uncertainty and ambiguity surrounding mourning (Illouz, 2008). Seale (1998) suggested that psychology has replaced religious institutions in giving explanations and rituals for dealing with death and grief. When applied to grief, this paradigm assumes that

> People need to recover from their state of intense emotionality and return to normal functioning and effectiveness as quickly and efficiently as possible. Modernist theories of grief and related therapeutic interventions encourage people who have experienced loss to respond in just this way. Grieving, a debilitating emotional response, is seen as a troublesome inter-ference with daily routines, and should be 'worked through' … Such grief work typically consists of a number of tasks that have to be confronted and systematically attended to before normality is reinstated. Reducing atten-tion to the loss is critical, and good adjustment is often viewed as breaking of ties between the bereaved and the dead. (Stroebe, Gergen, Gergen, & Stroebe, 1992, p. 1206)

Grief within this frame is constructed as a potentially pathological condition necessitating psychological intervention for people to heal as quickly as possible. Indeed, this view is so widely held that (as of this writing) grief was being considered for inclusion in the fifth edition of the *Diagnostic and Statistical Manual of Mental Disorders* (APA, 2010).

The "Grief Police": The Pathologization and Psychologization of Grief

The grief police emerged in my own life before my mother had even died. Although she had been sick for close to two decades, the last few months of her life were shocking. A new form of cancer had developed, and it was extremely aggressive. One Friday, we had spent the day shopping. It was a day spent in slow motion; we walked, ate, talked, and traveled more slowly than we had ever done because she was so ill. On Sunday, she slow danced with my father at a family friend's wedding. On Tuesday, she started talking gibberish. (We would later find out that the tumors had spread to her brain, causing confusion and speech problems.) On Thursday, she was admitted to the hospital, and on the following Tuesday, she took her last breath. Punctuated in between doctor appointments, worried conversations with family members and friends, scans and tests, phone calls to relatives overseas, and vigilantly sitting by my mother's, side, I had conversations about work, teaching, and taking time off. Many had chimed in and urged me not give up my work *even as my mother was dying.* The pressure to maintain my normal routine while in the throes of terrible anticipatory grief was a form of grief policing by well-meaning and well-intentioned family and friends who were having a hard time coming to grips with my mother's impending end. It was hard for all of us (Granek, 2010b). Policing affect, especially grief with its rogue and unpredictable nature, is one way to try to gain control over that which is essentially uncontrollable. The attempt to police grief or to get a harness around it is the core of the contemporary psychological imperative to normalize some expressions of grief while pathologizing others.

Grief has always been policed in one form or another (Holst-Warhaft, 2000; Walter, 2000). In every society, grieving has been regulated in terms of duration, modes of expression, and rituals and traditions around how to mark and mourn a death (Gilbert, 2006). As with my own community and their concern about my returning to work, this policing is perceived to be in the service of care. In other words, the policing of grief is more complicated than it first appears because it is delivered with genuinely good intentions and in the service of what is perceived to be best for the mourner, making it particularly challenging to contest when it does not suit one's needs. This has become even more salient in the modernist context, in which the individual is held responsible for his or her self-care and functioning. As noted in the introduction, the policing of contemporary grief has grown in tandem with the modernist rejection of religious authority and community in favor of a focus on the individual situated within a therapeutic culture that prizes rationality and autonomy. In this context, psychologists, psychiatrists, and other mental health professionals reign as experts and have stepped in to provide the dictates around what constitutes normal mourning. Turning to psychological services to cope with grief is a prime example of how the scientific paradigm deals with grief. Walter (2005–2006) noted:

> The distinction between the normal and the pathological is the central intellectual device of psychiatric medicine, so once grief became medicalised and psychiatrized, it was inevitable either that all grief would be seen as mental illness, or that distinctions between normal and abnormal grief would be made and elaborated. Overwhelmingly, it is the latter that has occurred over the past forty years. (p. 73)

In other words, *all* grief has become potentially pathological in 21st-century North America. By virtue of its inclusion as a psychological object of study, what was once considered to be a natural reaction to death has fallen under the purview of psychology, psychiatry, and other mental health professionals and has therefore become monitored, understood, and experienced in a way that previous generations could not have conceptualized (Granek, 2010a). As with other psychological diagnoses in recent years (for example, social anxiety disorder, see Lane, 2007; Scott, 2006), the specific criteria of what constitutes pathology are less important than the notion that one can evaluate oneself on a continuum of normality–abnormality at all. Regardless of how grief has become pathologized within the discipline, the very inclusion of it as a psychological–psychiatric subject has had a drastic effect on the way people understand their experience of bereavement (Granek, 2008, 2010; Granek & O'Rourke, 2012).

Pathological Grief, Traumatic Grief, and CG

What exactly is pathological grief? There are quite a few debates on the matter. (For recent reviews, see Lobb et al., 2010; Mancini, Griffin & Bonanno, 2012; Wittouck, Van Autreve, De Jaegere, Portzky & van Heeringen, 2011.) In a frame in which all grief is considered potentially pathological, some grief is described as excessive, a disease, out of the norm, and a mental disorder (Forstmeier & Maercker, 2007; Goodkin et al., 2005–2006; Hogan, Worden, & Schmidt, 2005–2006; Horowitz, 2005–2006; Prigerson et al., 2009; Prigerson & Jacobs, 2001; Shear & Frank, 2006; Shear et al., 2011).

Bereavement is listed in the DSM-IV text revision as a V code, which indicates that it is a disorder that needs further research and clinical attention (APA, 2000). The extreme end of pathologizing grief is the diagnosis of CG, sometimes referred as *traumatic grief, prolonged grief,* or *pathological grief* (Stroebe & Schut, 2005–2006). CG (at the time of this writing) is a proposed diagnostic category for the DSM-5 (Forstmeier & Maercker, 2007; Goodkin et al., 2005–2006; Horowitz, Siegel, Holen, & Bonanno, 1997; Prigerson et al., 1995; Prigerson, Shear, Bierhals, et al., 1997; Prigerson, Shear, Frank, et al., 1997; Shear et al., 2011). Although CG is not an official diagnosis, it is widely used by researchers and clinicians.

The determination of the prevalence of CG depends on the definition, for which there is currently no professional consensus. One study that used one set of criteria for CG found the prevalence rate of the pathology to be 41 percent in a sample of bereaved people (Horowitz et al., 1997), whereas another study that used a different set of CG criteria found that prevalence to be anywhere from 20 to 57 percent, depending on how much time had passed since the death of the loved one (Prigerson, Shear, Frank, et al., 1997). Another review indicated that approximately 40 percent of the bereaved met criteria for grief-related major depression a month after the loss and another 15 percent met the criteria after one year (Hensley, 2006a, 2006b). According to the DSM-IV, a diagnosis of major depressive disorder (MDD) can be given to a bereaved person two months after a loss (APA, 1994). In the new edition of the DSM-5, this bereavement exclusion will be removed and an MDD diagnosis can be given two weeks after a loss. Pathological grief has been identified as being inhibited (absent or minimal grief; Jacobs, 1999); delayed (characterized by late onset and severe intensity; Parkes, 1988); and prolonged, or chronic (Parkes & Weiss, 1983).

The leading proponents of including CG in the DSM-5 are Prigerson and her colleagues, the majority of whom are affiliated with the Department of Psychiatry at the Yale Medical School (Prigerson et al., 1995; Prigerson & Jacobs, 2001; Prigerson, Shear, Bierhals, et al., 1997; Prigerson, Shear, Frank, et al., 1997). In their view, the main diagnostic components of CG include the following: (A) "chronic yearning, pining and longing for the deceased"; (B) the presence of four out of eight symptoms such as "inability to trust others," "uneasy about moving on," "numbness/detachment," "bleak future," and "agitation"; (C) marked and persistent dysfunction in the social and occupational domain caused by grief symptoms; (D) a symptom disturbance of at least six months duration (Prigerson et al., 1995; Prigerson & Jacobs, 2001; Prigerson, Shear, Bierhals, et al., 1997; Prigerson, Shear, Frank, et al., 1997). In order for CG to be diagnosed, all criteria must be met. When challenged about how CG differs from normal grief, the authors wrote:

> The issue is not whether the symptoms themselves fit into seemingly pathological versus seemingly normal symptom clusters. What our results demonstrate is that the set of CG symptoms that we have identified, at persistent (beyond six months post-loss) and severe (marked intensity or frequency, such as several times daily) levels, are predictive of many negative outcomes and that is the basis for distinguishing them from normal grief symptoms. (Prigerson & Maciejewski, 2005–2006, p. 15)

Horowitz et al. (1997) also proposed criteria for the DSM-5 and differentiated between three categories of symptoms, including (A) intrusion, such as unbidden memories, emotional spells, and strong yearnings for the deceased; (B) avoidance, such as avoiding places that are reminders of the deceased and emotional numbness toward others; and (C) failure to adapt symptoms, such as feeling lonely or empty and having trouble sleeping. The main differences between Horowitz et al. (1997) and Prigerson and Maciejewski (2005–2006) are the criteria for duration and the number of symptoms necessary for diagnosis. Although Prigerson stipulated that a diagnosis can be made six months post loss, she also indicated that all four criteria categories must be met. Horowitz, on the other hand, proposed that diagnosis should be made 14 months after loss; he also proposed that fewer criteria had to be met in order to be diagnosed.

More recently, Shear et al. (2011) have come forth with a new set of criteria for CG. As with Prigerson, Shear, et al. suggested that there is little difference between the symptoms of acute grief and CG but that it is the duration and intensity of the symptoms that distinguish pathology. She notes that grief becomes complicated when the symptoms of acute grief last for longer than six months and therefore become persistent. According to Shear et al. (2011), CG includes (A) persistent, intense yearning or longing for the person who has died; (B) frequent intense feelings of loneliness; (C) recurrent thoughts that it is unfair, meaningless, or unbearable to have lived when the loved one has died and; (D) preoccupying thoughts about the person who has died. In addition, she included a range of other symptoms in which two of the following criteria are necessary for diagnosis: rumination, disbelief about the death, shock, feeling dazed, emotionally numb, anger, bitterness about the death, difficulty trusting or caring about people, feeling envious of others who haven't experienced a loss, having intense physical responses to memories of the deceased, changing behaviors as a result of the loss (that is, refraining from going places or doing things that remind a person of the loss), and hearing voices or having visions of the deceased among others (Shear et al., 2011).

The theme in all of these understandings of CG is the trend toward inclusiveness and pathologization, and labeling even the mildly impaired patient as diseased. Most proponents of CG as a disease category concede that there is a fuzzy line between normal grief and pathological grief but argue that this is not significant in making a diagnosis of CG. Researchers in the field claim that although normal grief and pathological grief *look* the same, *it is a matter of duration and intensity that marks the distinction between them,* and furthermore, that psychologists and psychiatrists should err on the side of caution by overdiagnosing rather than missing a case.

One difficulty with this conclusion is that it is hard to determine what is dysfunctional or complicated in relation to grieving. For some people, taking a year off from work to grieve a major loss is normal and culturally appropriate. For others, taking more than a few days off to grieve would be considered dysfunctional and suggest a need for professional help. What qualifies as disordered seems laden with value judgments, and although some theorists have argued that these distinctions are made on the basis of cultural context (that is, Horwitz, 2002), I suggest that psychologists and psychiatrists have an active role in constructing cultural expectations about what is deemed normal or abnormal. In the case of grief, psychologists and psychiatrists have determined what is supposedly too long, too short, too intense, or too absent with regard to grief.

The Grief Industry:
The Impact of Pathologization
and Grief Interventions

The pathlogization of grief has had an effect on how mourning is understood and managed in day-to-day life. The vocabulary of grief has been thoroughly psychologized. Terms such as "coping," "recovery," "healing," "denial," and "grief work" or "grief process" are all constructions of psychology, psychiatry and the mental health professions, and today psychotherapy and medication are common ways in which grieving is dealt with. For example, the treatment of both large-scale grief (events such as 9/11, school shootings, other acts of terrorism) and small-scale grief (individual responses to death) has become the province of psychology and psychiatry (for examples of psychologists intervening and providing grief counseling, see Brown & Goodman, 2005; Metcalf, 2005; Rosenblatt, 2005; Welt Betensky, 2007). Groopman (2004) called this phenomenon "the grief industry" and stated that it is led by professionals who claim that all bereavement requires intervention in order to avoid CG reactions. Whether it is for individuals or groups experiencing loss, the idea is that grief counselors are needed to help initiate the so-called grief work that enables people to express their feelings and begin the process of healing.

Despite the fact that the evidence for grief counseling is questionable (Groopman, 2004; Jordan & Neimeyer, 2003; Neimeyer, 2000; Mancini et al., 2012; Schut, Stroebe, van den Bout, & Terheggen, 2001), research on grief, grieving, and bereavement counseling continues to proliferate.

Psychological Counseling

Depending on how CG is defined, as many as 80 percent of people who are bereaved require counseling (Genevro, Marshall, Miller, & Center for the Advancement of Health, 2004). Although there is little evidence that grief counseling helps people cope specifically with grief (Allumbaugh & Hoyt, 1999; Jordan & Neimeyer, 2003; Kato & Mann, 1999; Schut et al., 2001), this has not stopped the publication of numerous articles on the efficacy of interventions. Various bereaved populations have been targeted, including all people who have experienced a loss through death; those bereaved in specific groups, such as widows or bereaved parents; and those with CG (Genevro et al., 2004). The evidence for counseling those at risk for CG is inconsistent. Some research has shown that cognitive–behavioral therapy is moderately effective for certain symptoms of CG, such as intrusion (intrusive thoughts), avoidance, and failure to adapt; however, the researchers also noted that

> The percentage of patients who experienced reliable change was highest for intrusion and failure to adapt, but a considerable number of patients in the control group [who received no treatment] also showed reliable changes and low to moderate effect sizes. This replicates previous findings of natural declines in bereavement-related symptoms. (Wagner, Knaevelsrud, & Maercker, 2006, p. 447)

Other studies have shown the potential, but minimal, benefits of using cognitive–behavioral therapy to treat CG (Ehlers, 2006; Matthews & Marwit, 2004). However, another study looking at interpersonal psychotherapy for treating depression-related bereavement showed that the intervention was no better than a placebo in treating traumatic grief (Hensley, 2006a).

Finally, Currier, Neimeyer, and Berman (2008) conducted a meta-analysis examining the efficacy of grief counseling. In this ambitious study, the authors examined 61 randomized outcome studies of bereavement interventions (that is, psychological counseling, professionally organized support groups, crisis intervention, writing therapy, and formal visiting service) that were reported in 64 academic articles. The authors concluded that

> Bereavement interventions have a small but statistically significant effect immediately following intervention but that therapeutic outcomes failed to differ reliably from zero to later follow up assessments … On average, recipients of bereavement interventions are not appreciably less distressed when compared to those who do not receive any formalized help. (p. 23)

Although it would seem from this evidence that overall the effectiveness of grief counseling is questionable, professionals working in the field have explained this by arguing that grief counseling may not work in the form in which it is delivered in research studies, and that the positive effects of grief counseling are most likely masked by poor methodology and a need for different design and implementation of treatment (Jordan & Neimeyer, 2003; Schut et al., 2001). Even more striking, Jordan and Neimeyer's (2003) suggestion that psychologists focus their energies on those who are at risk for CG means that everyone who is bereaved comes under the purview of psychological research and intervention, because everyone who is grieving is potentially at risk for CG. This tautological logic stipulates that if the interventions don't work, more research is necessary to find a good treatment for grieving; if the treatments do work, then it is evidence of the necessity of psychological intervention to aid in the grieving process.

Pharmaceutical Industry

The development of psychiatric categorization in the *DSM* has had a powerful effect on the perception of mental disorders as medical problems to be solved. Moreover, the development of drugs to treat mental disorders further increased the perception that mental disorders are akin to diseases.

The data regarding the use of pharmaceutical drugs to treat mental disorders are staggering. In 2007, sales of Paxil, an antidepressant–antianxiety drug, exceeded 2.7 billion dollars worldwide. In 2005, eight out of the 20 of the most prescribed medications (for all medical conditions, not just mental disorders) in the United States were antidepressants or anti-anxiety medications, with Paxil topping the list (RX List, 2007). In 2006, 227 million antidepressant prescriptions were written in the United States (Barber, 2008). Estimates of the efficacy of antidepressants and anti-anxiety drugs are controversial and range from 15 percent to 45 percent in treating symptoms of depression and anxiety (Barber, 2008; Breggin, 1991, 1998, 2001; Glenmullen, 2000; Healy, 1997, 2003; Solomon, 2002; Stoppard, 2000). Despite the controversy over the efficacy of these drugs, and despite the clear evidence that placebos are often as effective as antidepressants, the drugs are still widely used and are the most common treatment for disorders like depression and anxiety (Barber, 2008; Healy, 2003).

The treatment of grief has been no exception to this trend. The number of people who are given pharmaceuticals to treat their grief is difficult to measure. Even though complicated, pathological, prolonged, or traumatic grief are not official disorders, some psychiatrists have explicitly prescribed medications to treat grief and, as with counseling, have had questionable results. Although these psychiatrists have focused specifically on grief treatment, countless other bereaved people have been prescribed antidepressants and anti-anxiety medications to treat MDD. The diagnostic system is decontextual, making it impossible to determine why people are depressed and prescribed antidepressants (Horwitz & Wakefield, 2007). It is highly plausible that many of the millions of patients put on antidepressants could have been suffering from context-specific depression that may have had to do with a loss.

For example, Wakefield, Schmitz, First, and Horwitz (2007) looked at a U.S. comorbidity survey of 8,098 people ages 15 to 54 years. Of those who were diagnosed and treated for MDD, 90 percent attributed their depression to either a bereavement-related loss or another type of loss, such as losing a job or a relationship. The authors used these data to advocate for more stringent criteria for MDD that take into account the social context of why people are depressed before making a diagnosis, and their research is relevant to this argument. The authors found that those who were grieving looked almost identical in terms of symptom presentation (that is, appetite and weight problems, sleep problems, lack of energy, and so on) to those who were depressed for other reasons. The conflation of grief with MDD is a significant problem, as one is context-specific and should not be pathologized, whereas the other is a clinical diagnosis and is considered to be a pathology.

The conflation of grief and depression and the overuse of medications to treat grief make it significantly more likely that a grieving person will be given an antidepressant to deal with their sadness. The treatment of bereavement-related depression with medications and the new trials to test antidepressants for CG are the extreme result of the medicalization of grief (see Jacobs, Nelson, & Zisook, 1987; Pasternak, Reynolds, Schlernitzauer, & Hoch, 1991; Reynolds et al., 1999; Zisook & Shuchter, 2001; Zygmont et al., 1998).

The pharmaceutical industry—and the psychiatrists who are dependent on it for their funding—have a vested interest in turning grief into a pathological condition. Medicating people who are grieving not only puts them at serious physical risk, including increased suicidal thoughts (Barber, 2008; Healy, 2003), sexual dysfunction (Modell, Katholi, Modell, & DePalma, 1997; Montejo-Gonzalez et al., 1997; Patterson, 1993), medication dependence, and withdrawal symptoms (Frost & Lal, 1995; Giakas & Davis, 1997; Kent & Laidlaw, 1995; Keuthen et al., 1994; Lejoyeux & Ades, 1997; Pyke, 1995), but also affects their self-understanding and how they make sense of their grieving experience.

The pathologization of grief does not represent merely a diagnosis, it is a constructed narrative in which people learn how to understand themselves and, in the process, experience their grief in a new way. The pathologization narrative is a prime example of a shift from understanding grief within a religious, existential, and communal frame to understanding it within a psychological, individual, and private one.

The People Have Spoken:
The Impact on the Public

In a critical reflection on the grief literature in psychology, Breen and O'Conner (2007) concluded, "There is a plethora of research on grief, including the descriptions of 'symptoms', 'risk' factors, and outcomes, without significant attendance to the context of the bereavement itself on the resulting grief experience" (p. 209). Kellehear (2007) wrote, "Notwithstanding the genuine value of psychological grief theories there are several rather startling features of them that make those theories appear socially irrelevant, medically abnormal, and publicly bizarre" (p. 75). He goes on to state,

> The main contemporary response to grief—however defined—is to view this as a mental health problem requiring *individual therapeutic intervention.* Grief is a problem of the emotions. Little academic or professional attention and energy has been spent understanding grief as a relationship and social context matter that requires a relationship and social context response. (p. 75)

Indeed, as grief has steadily slipped into the net of the psychological domain, it has also simultaneously moved out of the public communities that once housed its rituals and traditions. When examined in the context of the public's experiences of grief, these psychological theories do appear to be highly disconnected from what people yearn for when it comes to dealing with their grief.

This conclusion came to me with jarring force as a result of an informal survey I conducted with the writer Meghan O'Rourke for the online magazine *Slate.com* (Granek & O'Rourke, 2011; O'Rourke & Granek, 2011). Within a week of mounting a survey asking about people's experiences of grief, we had received nearly 8,000 responses; what respondents had to say was surprising, touching, and fascinating. There were three major themes that arose repeatedly in this survey.

The first was that there was a tremendous variation in people's lived experiences of grief that significantly challenges contemporary psychological definitions of what grief should look and feel like, and more important, how long it should last. For example, 60 percent of our respondents (4,629 of $n = 7,715$[1]) had dreams of the deceased, and 20 percent reported imagining they

---

[1] The sample size refers to the total number of people who answered the specific question on which I am reporting the data. Some participants skipped some of the questions. For each of the findings I report on in this chapter, I provide the total n who answered the question.

had seen the deceased alive: "symptoms" that some health care professionals consider an indicator of CG (Shear et al., 2011). See Table 2-1 for a list of grief symptoms reported by our participants in the context of CG criteria.

In terms of duration, 27 percent of our respondents ($n = 7{,}081$) reported that they never went back to feeling like themselves after their loss, and another 27 percent said they felt normal only one to two years after the loss. Whereas complicated, pathological, or prolonged grief can be diagnosed six months after a loss, our respondents reported that recovering from the death of a loved one can take a year or several years, and 27 percent indicated that it may never happen at all. Indeed, a mere 11 percent of our sample reported feeling normal or symptom free again six months post-loss.

Table 2-1: Results of Slate.com Survey of Grief Symptoms (N = 7,715)

Answer Options	Response (%)
Sorrow	81[a]
Overwhelming sadness	72[a]
Yearning or nostalgia	72[a,b,c]
Trouble sleeping or insomnia	57[b]
Trouble concentrating	63
Dreams of the deceased	60
Longing	57[a,c]
Frequent crying	56
Guilt	55[c]
Loneliness	55[c]
Anger	49[a,c]
Disbelief about the loss	49[a,c]
Anxiety	48[c]
Anguish	46
Overeating or trouble eating	40
Self-pity	37
Sense of disorganization	39[c]
Feeling run down or prone to illness	35
Forgetfulness	32
Physical pain or physical tension	30

Answer Options	Response (%)
Feeling of emptiness in stomach	30
Confusion	29[a]
Tightness in throat	29
Agitation or a jittery, jumpy feeling	26[a,c]
Relief	25
Frequent sighing	25
Imagining you see the deceased alive	20[c]
Shortness of breath	17
Physical illness	12
Muscle weakness	11
Searching for the deceased	9[a,b,c]
Chills	6
Tremors	5
Hallucinations	4[c]

Note: The *a,b,c* indicates which of these response options are considered criteria for complicated grief according to three theorists.

[a]Prigerson's criteria must be met six months postbereavement.

[b]Horowitz's criteria must be met 14 months postbereavement.

[c]Shear's criteria must be met six months postbereavement.

The second major finding from our survey addressed what I have been suggesting throughout this chapter: that the process of psychologizing grief has inadvertently created a kind of public culture around mourning in which grievers feel embarrassed, uncomfortable, and unsure about whether their grief is normal or not. For example, our survey found that 40 percent of respondents ($n = 7,616$) said they felt pressured to "get over it," "move on with their grief," or "stop talking about it" some of the time. More distressing, 23 percent of respondents ($n = 7,616$) said they felt pressured to move on about their grief most or all of the time.

Finally, and perhaps most important, people seemed most of all to want a community in which to grieve but often felt alone with their mourning. Thirty percent of our sample ($n = 7,563$) reported being strongly encouraged to seek professional help by their families and friends, and 35 percent ($n = 7,683$) turned to a therapist or another professional to deal with their grief. Interestingly, half the sample ($n = 7,283$) reported a desire for more social support and more public and collective ritual around grief and loss.

The grief literature has yielded similar findings regarding the benefits of social support. *Social support* refers to emotional, economic, and practical help or information that family members, friends, neighbors, and coworkers provide to those in need (House & Kahn, 1985). Diamond, Lund, and Caserta (1987) conducted a longitudinal study with bereaved spouses and found that the size and quality of one's social network was associated with lower depression and higher levels of coping and life satisfaction. Goldberg, Comstock, and Harlow (1988) found that larger social networks, particularly friends who the bereaved contacted frequently, were associated with a reduced risk of emotional distress. Research in the field has reported the importance of social support in reducing the intensity of grief and helping the bereaved cope with their loss (Saranson, Saranson, & Gurung, 1997). The value of emotional and practical support from close family, friends, and work colleagues has also been stressed by the bereaved as particularly important to them. They cite comfort, practical help, and physical and social stimulation as being pivotal to their coping with grief (Cohen, 1988; Dyregrov, 2003–2004; Johnson, 1991; Sherkat & Reed, 1992; Thuen, 1997).

Community is therefore a particularly critical resource for the bereaved. The evidence for the effectiveness of the community in providing social support for grievers seems more convincing and more robustly indicated than the evidence for the effectiveness of grief counseling and medications. In agreement with the need for more communal support rather than psychological intervention, Kellehear (2007) argued that we must return to an organized community of compassion to support the bereaved. Judging from the evidence on social support and grief outcomes, this seems like an excellent direction to pursue.

Mourning Madness? A Conclusion of Sorts

The loss of protocol around how to grieve and how to help or support a mourner has left those grieving bereft not only of their loved ones, but also of any community in which to understand, mediate, and express their sadness. This is situated within a larger modernist cultural framework that fears and denies death, and believes that one should be perpetually happy and upbeat. Moreover, mental health professionals are not solely responsible for the disappearance of traditional grief practices in North America, and as outlined in the introduction, have replaced religious authority to become the regulators of grief and loss. In many ways, these professions have filled the need of the listener and the supporter for the bereaved, and one could claim that this has aided sufferers from falling into deeper, more incapacitating depressions. Illouz (2008) noted that psychological ideas become particularly popular during times of upheaval and uncertainty:

> What has made psychologists the arbitrators and guides of the soul in so many institutional manifestations is that they have performed massive "cultural work," a vague term that includes such diverse phenomena as the collapse of traditional social roles and role uncertainty, the demise of established patterns of life, the multiplication of values, and the intensification of social anxiety and fear, all of which can explain why individuals search for ways to explain the behavior of others and shape their own behavior. (p. 57)

Grief is a good example of this cultural work. The mental health sciences have been successful in drawing this area of human life into their purview because they provide a framework for how to manage grief in an era of uncertainty, anxiety, and fear around dying and mourning. In this sense, the pathologization of grief can be considered a positive outcome, for it has provided a feeling of orderliness around an area of life that is filled with chaos and insecurity for a lot of people.

At the same time, research has suggested that the boundary around pathological grief is ambiguous and therefore inclusive of almost anyone who is grieving. There is very little qualitative difference between what is deemed normal versus pathological grief, and it seems from the literature that the diagnosis of CG is arbitrary and based on the clinician's or researcher's determination of what she or he defines as normal. This ultimately suggests that the particulars of what defines pathology are less relevant than the idea itself that grief can be evaluated on a normal–abnormal continuum. The introduction of grief as psychological object has a symbolic value whereby one does not need to be diagnosed to be affected by the diagnostic classification of mental disorder. The self-consciousness around grief is one example of this. In addition to the sorrow and depression that often accompany bereavement, contemporary mourners are also faced with a distinctively modern anxiety about whether they are doing their grief work properly and whether they are on track with their progress. This new self-consciousness often comes with a sense of shame and embarrassment about mourning that has become part of the experience of the modern griever.

References

Allumbaugh, D. L., & Hoyt, W. T. (1999). Effectiveness of grief therapy: A meta-analysis. *Journal of Counseling Psychology, 46,* 370–380.

American Psychiatric Association. (1994). *Diagnostic and statistical manual of mental disorders, fourth edition (DSM-IV).* Washington, DC: Author.

American Psychiatric Association. (2000). *Diagnostic and statistical manual of mental disorders, Fourth edition, text revision (DSM-IV-TR).* Washington, DC: Author.

American Psychiatric Association. (2010). *DSM-5 development.* Retrieved from http://www.dsm5.org/ProposedRevisions/Pages/Conditions ProposedbyOutsideSources.aspx

American Psychiatric Association. (2013). *Diagnostic and statistical manual of mental disorders* (5th ed.). Arlington, VA: Author.

Aries, P. (1981). *The hour of our death.* New York: Knopf.

Barber, C. (2008). *Comfortably numb: How psychiatry is medicating a nation.* New York: Pantheon Books.

Bauman, Z. (1992). *Mortality, immortality and other life strategies.* Cambridge, United Kingdom: Polity Press.

Becker, E. (1973). *The denial of death.* New York: Free Press.

Bordo, S. (1987). *The flight to objectivity: Essays on Cartesianism and culture.* New York: SUNY Press.

Breen, L. J., & O'Connor, M. (2007). The fundamental paradox in grief literature: A critical reflection. *Omega: Journal of Death and Dying, 55,* 199–218.

Breggin, P. R. (1991). *Toxic psychiatry: Why therapy, empathy, and love must replace the drugs, electroshock, and biochemical theories of the "new psychiatry."* New York: St. Martin's Press.

Breggin, P. R. (1998). *Talking back to Ritalin: What doctors aren't telling you about stimulants for children.* Monroe, ME: Common Courage Press.

Breggin, P. R. (2001). *The antidepressant fact book: What doctors won't tell you about Prozac, Zoloft, Paxil, Celexa, and Luvox.* Cambridge, MA: Perseus Publishing.

Brown, E. J., & Goodman, R. F. (2005). Childhood traumatic grief: An exploration of the construct in children bereaved on September 11. *Journal of Clinical Child & Adolescent Psychology, 34,* 248–259.

Cable, D. C. (1998). Grief in American culture. In K. J. Doka & J. C. Davidson (Eds.), *Living with grief: Who we are, how we grieve* (pp. 61–70). Washington, DC: Hospice Foundation of America/Brunner/Mazel.

Cohen, S. (1988). Psychosocial models of social support in the etiology of physical disease. *Health Psychology, 7,* 267–297.

Currier, J. M., Neimeyer, R. A., & Berman, J. S. (2008). The effectiveness of psychotherapeutic interventions for the bereaved: A comprehensive quantitative review. *Psychological Bulletin, 134,* 648–661.

Diamond, M. F., Lund, D. A., & Caserta, M. S. (1987). The role of social support in the first two years of bereavement in an elderly sample. *Gerontologist, 27,* 599–604.

Dyregrov, K. (2003–2004). Micro-sociological analysis of social support following traumatic bereavement: Unhelpful and avoidant responses from the community. *Omega: Journal of Death and Dying, 48,* 23–44.

Ehlers, A. (2006). Understanding and treating complicated grief: What can we learn from posttraumatic stress disorder? *Clinical Psychology: Science and Practice, 13,* 135–140.

Forstmeier, S., & Maercker, A. (2007). Comparison of two diagnostic systems for complicated grief. *Journal of Affective Disorders, 99,* 203–211.

Frost, L., & Lal, F. (1995). Shock-like sensations after discontinuation of selective serotonin reuptake inhibitors [Letter to the editor]. *American Journal of Psychiatry, 152,* 810.

Genevro, J. L., Marshall, T., Miller, T., & Center for the Advancement of Health. (2004). Report on bereavement and grief research. *Death Studies. Special Issue: Report on Bereavement and Grief Research by the Center for the Advancement of Health, 28,* 491–491.

Gergen, K. J. (1991). *The saturated self: Dilemmas of identity in contemporary life.* New York: Basic Books.

Gergen, K. J. (1992). *The social constructionist movement in modern psychology.* Washington, DC: American Psychological Association.

Giakas, W. J., & Davis, J. M. (1997). Intractable withdrawal from venlafaxine treated with fluoxetine. *Psychiatric Annals, 27,* 85–92.

Gilbert, S. (2006). *Death's door: Modern dying and the ways we grieve.* New York: W. W. Norton.

Glenmullen, J. (2000). *Prozac backlash: Overcoming the dangers of Prozac, Zoloft, Paxil, and other antidepressants with safe, effective alternatives.* New York: Simon & Schuster.

Goldberg, E. L., Comstock, G. W., & Harlow, S. D. (1988). Emotional problems and widowhood. *Journal of Gerontology, 43,* 5206–5208.

Goodkin, K., Lee, D., Frasca, A., Molina, R., Zheng, W., O'Mellan, S., et al. (2005–2006). Complicated bereavement: A commentary on its state of evolution. *Omega: Journal of Death and Dying, 52,* 99–105.

Gorer, G. (1967). *Death, grief, and mourning* (1st ed.). Garden City, NJ: Doubleday.

Granek, L. (2008). *Bottled tears: The pathologization, psychologization, and privatization of grief.* Unpublished doctoral dissertation.

Granek, L. (2010a). Grief as pathology: The evolution of grief theory in psychology from Freud to the present. *History of Psychology, 13,* 46–73.

Granek, L. (2010b). "The cracks are where the light shines in": Grief in the classroom. *Feminist Teacher, 20,* 42–49.

Granek, L., & O'Rourke M. (2011, Spring). What is grief really like: Analyzing the results of the Slate survey on loss. *Slate.* Retrieved from http://www.slate.com/id/2292126/

Granek, L., & O'Rourke, M. (2012, March 12). Is mourning madness? *Slate Magazine.* Retrieved from http://www.slate.com/articles/life/grieving/2012/03/complicated_grief_and_the_dsm_the_wrong headed_movement_to_list_mourning_as_a_mental_disorder_. html#comments

Groopman, J. (2004, January 26). The grief industry. *New Yorker,* pp. 30–39.

Healy, D. (1997). *The antidepressant era.* Cambridge, MA: Harvard University Press.

Healy, D. (2003). *Let them eat Prozac.* Toronto: Lorimer.

Hensley, P. L. (2006a). A review of bereavement-related depression and complicated grief. *Psychiatric Annals, 36,* 619–626.

Hensley, P. L. (2006b). Treatment of bereavement-related depression and traumatic grief. *Journal of Affective Disorders, 92,* 117–124.

Hogan, N. S., Worden, J. W., & Schmidt, L. A. (2005–2006). Considerations in conceptualizing complicated grief. *Omega: Journal of Death and Dying, 52,* 81–85.

Holst-Warhaft, G. (2000). *Grief and its political uses.* Cambridge, MA: Harvard University Press.

Horowitz, M. (2005–2006). Meditating on complicated grief disorder as a diagnosis. *Omega: Journal of Death and Dying, 52,* 87–89.

Horowitz, M. J., Siegel, B., Holen, A., & Bonanno, G. A. (1997). Diagnostic criteria for complicated grief disorder. *American Journal of Psychiatry, 154,* 904–910.

Horwitz, A. V. (2002). *Creating mental illness.* Chicago: University of Chicago Press.

Horwitz, A. V., & Wakefield, J. C. (2007). *The loss of sadness: How psychiatry transformed normal sorrow into depressive disorder.* New York: Oxford University Press.

House, J. S. & Kahn, R. L. (1985). Measures and concepts of social support. In S. Cohen & S. L. Syme (Eds.), *Social support and health* (pp. 83–108). Orlando, FL: Academic Press.

Illouz, E. (2008). *Saving the modern soul: Therapy, emotions, and the culture of self-help.* Berkeley, CA: University of California Press.

Jacobs, S. C. (1999). *Traumatic grief: Diagnosis, treatment, and prevention.* Philadelphia: Brunner/Mazel.

Jacobs, S. C., Nelson, J. C., & Zisook, S. (1987). Treating depression of bereavement with antidepressants: A pilot study. *Psychiatric Clinics of North America, 10,* 501–510.

Johnson, T. P. (1991). Mental health, social relations, and social selection: A longitudinal analysis. *Journal of Health and Social Behavior, 32,* 408–423.

Jordan, J. R., & Neimeyer, R. A. (2003). Does grief counseling work? *Death Studies, 27,* 765–786.

Kato, P. M., & Mann, T. (1999). A synthesis of psychological interventions for the bereaved. *Clinical Psychology Review, 19,* 275–296.

Kellehear, A. (2007). The end of death in late modernity: An emerging public health challenge. *Critical Public Health, 17,* 71–79.

Kent, L. S. W., & Laidlaw, J. D. D. (1995). Suspected congenital Setraline dependence. *British Journal of Psychiatry, 167,* 412–413.

Keuthen, N. J., Cyr, P., Ricciardi, J. A., Minichiello, W. E., Buttolph, M. L., & Jenike, M. A. (1994). Medication withdrawal symptoms in obsessive–compulsive disorder patients treated with paroxetine. *Journal of Clinical Psychopharmacology, 14,* 206–207.

Lane, C. (2007). *Shyness: How normal behavior became a sickness.* New Haven, CT: Yale University Press.

Lejoyeux, M., & Ades, J. (1997). Antidepressants discontinuation: A literature review. *Journal of Clinical Psychiatry, 58,* 11–17.

Lobb, E. A., Kristjanson, L. J., Aoun, S. M., Monterosso, L., Halkett, G. K., & Davies, A. (2010). Predictors of complicated grief: A systematic review of empirical studies. *Death Studies, 34,* 673–698.

Mancini, A. D., Griffin, P. & Bonanno, G. A. (2012). Recent trends in the treatment of prolonged grief. *Current Opinion Psychiatry, 25,* 46–51.

Matthews, L. T., & Marwit, S. J. (2004). Complicated grief and the trend toward cognitive–behavioral therapy. *Death Studies, 28,* 849–863.

Mellor, P. A., & Shilling, C. (1993). Modernity, self-identity and the sequestration of death. *Sociology, 27,* 411– 431.

Metcalf, P. (2005). *"A passion of grief and fear exasperates us": Death, bereavement, and mourning—What we have learned a year after 9/11*. New Brunswick, NJ: Transaction Publishers.

Modell, J. G., Katholi, C. R., Modell, J. D., & DePalma, R. L. (1997). Comparative sexual side effects of bupropion, fluoxetine, paroxetine, and sertraline. *Clinical Pharmacology and Therapeutics, 61,* 476–487.

Montejo-Gonzalez, A. L., Llorca, G., Izquierdo, J. A., Ledesma, A., Bousonon, M., Calcedo, A., et al. (1997). SSRI-induced sexual dysfunction: Fluoxetine, paroxetine, sertraline, and fluvoxamine in a prospective, multicenter, and descriptive clinical study out of 344 patients. *Journal of Sex and Marital Therapy, 23,* 176–194.

Neimeyer, R. A. (2000). Grief therapy and research as essential tensions: Prescriptions for a progressive partnership. *Death Studies, 24,* 603–610.

O'Rourke, M., & Granek, L. (2011). How to help friends in mourning: Condolence notes? Casseroles? What our grief survey revealed Slate. Retrieved from http://www.slate.com/id/2300735/

Parkes, C. M. (1988). Bereavement as a psychosocial transition: Processes of adaptation to change. *Journal of Social Issues, 44,* 53–65.

Parkes, C. M., & Weiss, R. S. (1983). *Recovery from bereavement.* New York: Basic Books.

Pasternak, R. E., Reynolds, C. F., Schlernitzauer, M., & Hoch, C. C. (1991). Acute open-trial nortriptyline therapy of bereavement-related depression in late life. *Journal of Clinical Psychiatry, 52,* 307–310.

Patterson, W. M. (1993). Fluoxetine-induced sexual dysfunction. *Journal of Clinical Psychiatry, 54,* 71.

Prigerson, H. G., & Jacobs, S. C. (2001). *Traumatic grief as a distinct disorder: A rationale, consensus criteria, and a preliminary empirical test.* Washington, DC: American Psychological Association.

Prigerson, H. G., Horwitz, M. J., Jacobs, S. C., Parkes, C. P., Aslan, M., Goodkin, K., et al. (2009). Prolonged grief disorder: Validation criteria proposed for DSM-V and ICD-11. *PLoS Med, 6*(8), e10000121.

Prigerson, H. G., & Maciejewski, P. K. (2005–2006). A call for sound empirical testing and evaluation of criteria for complicated grief proposed for DSM-V. *Omega: Journal of Death and Dying, 52,* 9–19.

Prigerson, H. G., Maciejewski, P. K., Reynolds, C. F., Bierhals, A. J., Newsom, J. T., Fasiczka, A., et al. (1995). Inventory of complicated grief: A scale to measure maladaptive symptoms of loss. *Psychiatry Research, 59,* 65–79.

Prigerson, H. G., Shear, M. K., Bierhals, A. J., Pilkonis, P. A., Wolfson, L., Hall, M., et al. (1997). Case histories of traumatic grief. *Omega: Journal of Death and Dying, 35,* 9–24.

Prigerson, H. G., Shear, M. K., Frank, E., & Beery, L. C. (1997). Traumatic grief: A case of loss-induced trauma. *American Journal of Psychiatry, 154,* 1003–1009.

Pyke, R. E. (1995). Paroxetine withdrawal symptoms. *American Journal of Psychiatry, 152,* 149–150.

Reynolds, C. F., Miller, M. D., Pasternak, R. E., Frank, E., Perel, J. M., Cornes, C., et al. (1999). Treatment of bereavement-related major depressive episodes in later life: A controlled study of acute and continuation treatment with nortriptyline and interpersonal psychotherapy. *American Journal of Psychiatry, 156,* 202–208.

Rosenblatt, P. C. (2005). *Grieving families and the 9/11 disaster.* New Brunswick, NJ: Transaction Publishers.

RX list. (2007). *The Internet drug index for prescription drugs and medications.* Retrieved from http://www.rxlist.com/script/main/hp.asp

Saranson, B. R., Saranson, I. G., & Gurung, R. A. R. (1997). Close personal relationships and health outcomes: A key to the role of social support. In S. Duck (Ed.), *Handbook of personal relationships: Theory, research and interventions* (pp. 547–573). New York: John Wiley & Sons.

Schut, H., Stroebe, M. S., van den Bout, J., & Terheggen, M. (2001). *The efficacy of bereavement interventions: Determining who benefits.* Washington, DC: American Psychological Association.

Scott, S. (2006). The medicalisation of shyness: From social misfits to social fitness. *Sociology of Health & Illness, 28,* 133–153.

Seale, C. (1998). *Constructing death: The sociology of dying and bereavement.* Cambridge, United Kingdom: Cambridge University Press.

Shear, K., & Frank, E. (2006). *Treatment of complicated grief: Integrating cognitive–behavioral methods with other treatment approaches.* New York: Guilford Press.

Shear, M. K., Simon, N., Wall, M., Zisook, S., Neimeyer, R., Duan, N., et al. (2011). Complicated grief and related bereavement issues for DSM-5. *Depression and Anxiety, 28,* 103–117.

Sherkat, D. E., & Reed, M. D. (1992). The effects of religion and social support on self-esteem and depression among the suddenly bereaved. *Social Indicators Research, 26,* 259–275.

Solomon, A. (2002). *The noonday demon: An atlas of depression.* New York: Simon & Schuster.

Stoppard, J. M. (2000). *Understanding depression: Feminist social constructionist approaches.* London, New York: Routledge.

Stroebe, M., Gergen, M. M., Gergen, K. J., & Stroebe, W. (1992). Broken hearts or broken bonds: Love and death in historical perspective. *American Psychologist, 47,* 1205–1212.

Stroebe, M., & Schut, H. (2005–2006). Complicated grief: A conceptual analysis of the field. *Omega: Journal of Death and Dying, 52,* 53–70.

Thuen, F. (1997). Social support after the loss of an infant child: A long-term perspective. *Scandinavian Journal of Psychology, 38,* 103–110.

Wagner, B., Knaevelsrud, C., & Maercker, A. (2006). Internet-based cognitive-behavioral therapy for complicated grief: A randomized controlled trial. *Death Studies, 30,* 429–453.

Wakefield, J. C., Schmitz, M. F., First, M. B., & Horwitz, A.V. (2007). Extending the bereavement exclusion for major depression to other losses: Evidence from the National Comorbidity Survey. *Archives of General Psychiatry, 64,* 433–440.

Walter, T. (2000). Grief narratives: The role of medicine in the contemporary policing of grief. *Anthropology & Medicine, 7,* 97–114.

Walter, T. (2005–2006). What is complicated grief? A social constructionist perspective. *Omega: Journal of Death and Dying, 52,* 71–79.

Welt Betensky, J. L. (2007). The R.A.F.T.: Recovery after family trauma. A manual for a group psychotherapy intervention for children and families experiencing traumatic grief. *Dissertation Abstracts International: Section B: The Sciences and Engineering, 67* (9-B).

Wittouck, C., Van Autreve, S., De Jaegere, E., Portzky, G., & van Heeringen, K. (2011). The prevention and treatment of complicated grief: A meta-analysis. *Clinical Psychology Review, 31,* 69–78.

Zisook, S., & Shuchter, S. R. (2001). Treatment of the depressions of bereavement. *American Behavioral Scientist. Special Issue: New Directions in Bereavement Research and Theory, 44,* 782–792.

Zygmont, M., Prigerson, H. G., Houck, P. R., Miller, M. D., Shear, M. K., Jacobs, S., et al. (1998). A post hoc comparison of paroxetine and nortriptyline for symptoms of traumatic grief. *Journal of Clinical Psychiatry, 59,* 241–245.

Chapter Three

The Betrayal That Was Love

Laura K. Kerr

Every childhood is more or less traumatic, none is without wounding,
and the pleasure of being alive is to discover how to get over it—by
first getting under it and feeling our vulnerability.
Ginette Paris, *Heartbreak* (2011, p. 103)

The death of a loved one, and the grief that follows, may be one of life's greatest initiations into the transformative power of love. Few natural occurrences are as radically disorienting and cause as much despair as grief. Acute states of grief have all the features of madness, which ironically, are often present when falling in love: labile, rapidly changing emotions; intense longing; time lost to reverie; pangs of insecurity; and preoccupation to the point of life-threatening distraction. Grief is palpable; it alters the biochemistry of the body and dulls the senses, hijacking imagination, thoughts, and emotions—in effect, changing the very nature, if not identity, of the person grieving (Worden, 2009).

Psychologist John Bowlby (1977), who pioneered the study of attachment, saw grief as an effort to remain attached to the deceased person. This makes sense, particularly when attachment is acknowledged as a key component of human survival. Instinctively, we fear abandonment. To be abandoned as an infant is to risk death. Similarly, death was almost a forgone conclusion for early humans who had been ostracized by their tribe (Fabrega, 2002). The centrality of attachment to survival dictates the very nature of grieving: Healthy grieving is not about "getting over" the lost loved one, but rather grief continues the attachment bond, albeit through remembering, rituals, and reverie. As psychiatrist M. Katherine Shear (2003) asserted, "Grief is a permanent state. You don't really resolve grief. Rather, you change the relationship with the deceased." According to Shear, instead of stages of grief, there are surges of grief that reemerge throughout life. Especially around holidays and anniversaries, sadness returns as we continue relating to those we love, even after their deaths.

Although grieving is a natural part of life, getting stuck in grief is relatively common. When grief becomes complicated, rather than transforming the relationship with the deceased, the bereaved often has difficulty accepting the death and growing into new ways of relating. Ironically, the deceased is "too dead," and the mourner becomes frozen in grief and the former relationship. The signs of complicated (or traumatic) grief include alternatively being preoccupied with the deceased or avoiding all reminders, as well as suffering from intrusive thoughts and images associated with the lost loved one—much like the cardinal symptoms of posttraumatic stress disorder (Shear, 2003).

When complicated grief is perceived through the lens of attachment, it is more similar to separation anxiety disorder, a diagnosis given to children who show excessive distress when separated from their primary caregiver (Schupp, 2003). Risk factors for developing complicated grief as an adult include the traumatic, unexpected loss of a loved one. Complicated grief, however, can also be the outcome of a history of childhood abuse or neglect, a history of childhood separation anxiety, or an insecure attachment style that emerged from growing up with a depressed caregiver (Prigerson, Vanderwerker, & Maciejewski, 2007). When first attachments are compromised or unhealthy, they can be experienced as failures to love. Life seems to begin with heartbreak, and this unmourned loss is brought to future relationships. Because of the instinctual drive to attach, many attempt to make do with a broken heart, intuiting that more attempts at love will eventually overcome their initial, unhealthy attachments. Such a strategy is not in vain; research in neuroscience and attachment theory reveals the healing power of love and the possibility of "earning" secure attachment through later healthy, loving relationships (Wallin, 2007).

I believe most of us love the best we can. Yet when a child receives inadequate nurturing during the first years of life, the initial learned ways of relating typically resurface in later relationships. Without grieving the first failures at loving and being loved, it is more likely that the past will be recreated. Learning to break old attachment patterns requires identifying ways out of futile reenactments of prior dynamics. Complicated grief thus becomes an opportunity to find new ways of loving. Like many of life's major lessons, the power of complicated grief lies in the pain it causes, which grabs attention, spotlighting the futility of unhealthy attachment patterns. Complicated grief seized me after the death of my mother, initiating two bleak years of life, yet it also started a deeper, more soulful connection with her, a shift that affected all my relationships and led to a long-overdue self-transformation.

I feel as if I lost my mother twice to death—first when I was almost two years old and again when I was 41. The first loss occurred when her father died; the second and final loss happened when she passed away unexpectedly. My grandfather's death insinuated feelings of betrayal into the mix of love and dependency I felt toward my mother. Her death set the stage for confrontation with this painful emotional mix, as well as an opportunity for its renunciation. Each death was characterized by deep longing and a sense of being stuck in feelings and reverie from which there was no escape. Both deaths were complicated, even traumatic. Yet with the second death, I was finally secure enough to appreciate the wisdom of a broken heart. What follows is my story of complicated grief.

My Maternal Grandfather's Death

My mom was 30 years old when her father died, but I suspect she was very young for her age. Whenever I considered my mother as a person separate from her role as my caregiver, she seemed to me like a child in need of rescue. Whether this was the outcome of her father's death or of her own early life losses, I cannot say. I doubt any of us are ever really prepared for the loss of a loved one, especially when the death was as gruesome as my grandfather's.

I am told my grandfather was a man committed to doing good and being good, a man who saw order and rules as the path to salvation. He was a God-fearing man, a deacon in his Baptist church, who valued hard labor and the Scripture. For him, a commitment was something that was fulfilled, even if it was an arbitrary pledge made to oneself. Sloth was a sin, and a messy lawn was a sign of sloth. So, on the day of his death, despite family pleas and inclement weather, my grandfather trudged to the edge of his yard to cut down branches broken by a recent storm. This was how he planned to spend his day, and nothing would stop him.

Autumn's dry leaves covered his East Texas lawn as he strode to his day's work, chainsaw in hand. A gas leak in the chainsaw provided fuel for the inferno that would engulf him. Sparks ignited droplets of gasoline, spreading fire quickly to the kindling strewn about the yard. The flames nearly swallowed him; 80 percent of his body was covered with burns. He was given morphine and died that day. In many ways, so did my mother.

I have looked at photographs of my mom before and after her father's death. From the "before" shots, I have two favorites. In one, my mom holds my brother and me like two sacks of groceries, each of us securely in place. She looks into the camera lens; a relaxed smile frames her beautiful face. In the other photo, she holds an album cover in her hand. With rapt attention and that same sweet smile, she watches me dance.

My next photos of us together were not taken until two years after my grandfather's death. My mother's face is still lovely, but it seems frozen and nonresponsive. Her eyes are always diverted from the camera. Mechanically, she decorates birthday cakes or dips Easter eggs in dye. She no doubt takes care of us, but that other key nourishment, affection, is noticeably absent.

I also changed. Like many children who lose the love of a parent, I alternated between being excessively endearing, a smile pasted on my face, and self-reliant, trying to grow up too soon. Both strategies were perhaps innate responses to diminished opportunities for attachment in childhood (Wallin, 2007). Although I was not aware at the time, I was gaining life lessons for how to deal (or not deal) with grief. I learned that some wounds never completely heal, and that the measure of a self is often the resilience mustered against unbearable pain. This is a lesson my mother and I learned together—that grief does not really end, but perspectives change, and the heart hardens to feelings of loss and longing.

No doubt my mother was clinically depressed and suffering from complicated grief. Mental illness and complicated grief often occur together. One study found that 77 percent of psychiatric inpatients in a California facility suffered from complicated grief (Schupp, 2003). Bowlby (1980) believed the majority of mental disorders were actually manifestations of pathological mourning. About two years after my grandfather's death— plenty of time for my mother to recover, but she had not—I sat on my aunt's knee at my grandmother's kitchen table, its specks of gold and silver encased in Formica. My aunt said "Now you be a good girl for your mother, Laura." She didn't have to tell me why she said this. Everyone was somber. We had already had to deal with losing my grandfather, and we were not ready to watch as my mother slowly disappeared from us as well.

When an infant or toddler has to deal with separation from or loss of a parent, she develops a style of attaching that allows her to cope with this loss with the least amount of distress. The outcome can be what attachment theorist Mary Ainsworth described as an "avoidant attachment" style (Wallin, 2007, p. 19). Although the child may feel distressed when the caregiver is absent or emotionally unavailable, she does not reveal her distress, because she does not expect her emotional needs will be met. This was certainly the scenario I experienced with my mother. Her depression and grief consumed the emotions otherwise available for my siblings and me. Fortunately, I had the benefit of frequent visits by my paternal grandmother, a very loving woman, and a nanny, Miss Marie, who I loved more that life itself. I learned to love in sips and gulps, alternating feelings of safety and love with feelings of neglect and aloneness. Like the love I received (and failed to receive), my attachment style developed into one of alternating between seeking closeness and avoiding connection.

The evolutionary role of attachment is to ensure that a child seeks safety when there is danger or threat. A young child must feel her caregiver is trustworthy and reliable and believe that efforts at connection will actually increase safety. A reliable caregiver becomes a safe base from which a child ventures into the world, knowing that if danger is encountered, there is refuge nearby.

My mother's complicated grief and depression challenged my sense of her as dependable, not only because she was emotionally unavailable much of the time. My mom's distraction by her inconceivable loss also meant I lost protection from my sometimes violent father. Violence, like complicated grief, is another family legacy. Both my paternal and maternal grandfathers used corporal punishment to disciple my parents and their siblings. Both followed the adage "spare the rod, spoil the child." My mother once shared with me a time when as a young girl her father beat her so hard her aunts needed to pull him away. She told me similarly brutal stories about the whippings my father received when he was a child. My mom also told me a story about how as a toddler I desperately tried to turn the front doorknob in an effort to escape one of my father's beatings.

The psychoanalyst Sándor Ferenczi (1949/1988) is remembered for his analysis of how persons who are subjected to cruelty by an abuser will actually identify with the aggressor as a way to maintain some semblance of attachment. Ferenczi saw this psychological defense as a source of internal splitting and dissociation. By identifying with the aggressor, an abused child can dampen the fears of abandonment that abuse invariably causes. In particular, Ferenczi believed the child internalized the abuser's feelings of guilt and culpability, in effect becoming "bad" so that the abuser could still be a "good" attachment figure worthy of the child's continual efforts to receive love (p. 202). Yet, this leaves the child with a split-off part of the self that is experienced as bad and shameful, which the child might also want to rid himself of by projecting his negative affects onto another person, or even an entire population (Miller, 1998). In extreme cases, identifying with the aggressor can lead to the child developing into a bully or an abuser.

Internal splits caused by abuse impede growth, integration, and healthy attachment (Van der Hart, Nijenhuis, & Steele, 2006). Children who psychologically divide in response to abuse believe that only parts of themselves are lovable. One of grief's most redeeming functions, despite the suffering it produces, may be its capacity to heal internal divisions caused by such traumatic experiences. The sorrow and overwhelming emotions felt during grief have a way of upturning the precarious ordering of self that abuse requires. Grief leaves none of the self untouched and thus may be a natural crucible for healing internal ruptures. Consider the following four stages of grieving identified by Bowlby (1980): (1) an initial numbing phase, (2) a yearning phase, (3) a phase of disorganization, and (4) a final phase of reorganization. The processes of disorganization and reorganization are perhaps just the conditions that can lead to reintegration of split-off parts of the self. At the very least, when grief becomes complicated, one becomes unable to continue one's life course unimpeded by emotional pain. To regain momentum, attention must be given to worn-out psychological defenses; with luck, an integrated and authentic sense of self develops.

How could I not split, given that both my parents and my environment— Texas in the 1960s—condoned corporal punishment? Gender also plays a role in how psychological defenses are constructed. I took to heart my aunt's admonishment that I needed to be good for my grieving mother, along with all the other messages that taught me that being aggressive was not something a good girl did. Identifying with the aggressor is just one way of avoiding feeling the loss of a safe attachment. Research on betrayal can also account for the ambivalence I once felt towards love. As Bowlby pointed out, attachment to a caregiver has "a key survival function of its own, namely protection" (1988, p. 121). When that protection is not forthcoming, feelings of betrayal can emerge in response to an instinctual awareness that trust has been violated. As claimed by proponents of betrayal trauma theory, "survivors of interpersonal trauma may remain unaware of betrayal in order to maintain a necessary attachment" (Kaehler & Freyd, 2009, p. 261).

Betrayal is a painful emotion marked by fear, rage, and revenge—feelings too big for a child to safely feel on her own, let alone express to caregivers unwilling or unable to consider the effect of their behaviors. One primary role of attachment figures is to help a child learn how to emotionally regulate and tolerate seemingly overwhelming affects (Wallin, 2007). Who can a child turn to when her caretakers are the reason she feels betrayed? Rather than risk abandonment, a child (including the child I was) remains unaware of overwhelming feelings, splitting them off from conscious awareness, much like Ferenczi's split. In effect, a child dissociates the offending thoughts, feelings, and body sensations related to the awareness of betrayal.

For a young child, survival needs dominate, and love is as vital as food, water, air, and shelter. Jungian psychologist Ginette Paris correctly observed, "A child can only express: 'Love me! If need be, I'll betray myself to please you. I'll deny, repress and overlook abuse'" (2011, p. 99). This is what I did to feel loved. Despite all the chaos in my childhood home, all the unacknowledged feelings of betrayal, I continued to try to please, alternating these efforts with avoiding my family altogether. I learned very early one of love's greatest challenges: the need for love conflicts with the need for freedom. In my case, this conflict was experienced as the lack of freedom to openly express both parts of me—the angry girl who felt betrayed and the sweet child who knew how to please. Paris saw such conflicts at the root of all love:

> No one escapes a measure of neurosis around love, because we all have a need for love which conflicts with our need for freedom. Because of that conflict, our need for love (an instinctual one) is necessarily mixed with fear. That fear is felt as a tension between opposites: the fear of losing love and the fear of loving, because love may restrict the freedom necessary to discover one's own identity. (p. 59)

It would take nearly four decades, and lots of living and loving, for me to learn that the fear I felt as a child—and *not* the love I experienced—led to hiding feelings of betrayal.

A Good Life Made Complicated by Grief

It was only natural that my mother's death was surrounded by the unpredictable and the tragic, because my initial loss of her occurred under a similar state. The day my mother died, my husband and I were in the midst of putting our house up for sale. Open house was scheduled for the next day—a necessity, as we had already purchased another home (a dubious strategy even in a seller's market). It was no surprise that it didn't really register when my sister called in a panic after finding my mother dead on her bedroom floor. Stress from selling and buying a home had already frayed my nerves. The most I could do was add her death to my mental "to-do" list: *mop kitchen, call*

Danny and let him know mom died, plant curbside flowers, get flight to Texas, order a funeral wreath, install new shower curtain, pack black dress. It never occurred to me that perhaps we could put off the open house, or even moving. I was stunned and unable to make major decisions. The sense of swirling down the drain of unstoppable chaos felt too normal for me to question whether there could be a different, more nurturing, approach to the end of a life.

The funeral was jarring. A month prior, my sister had told me my mother was doing great—"better than ever." When I looked at my mom in the casket, she looked too real, still alive. I felt lost and dizzy. The week before, she had called to congratulate us on our new home. I was elated to get her message; my mom rarely gave me praise. I fantasized about her coming to visit us in our new home. Foolishly, I put off calling her back; I was too busy. I planned to call her Sunday when we would be forced to vacate our home to prospective buyers. She died the day before.

The days after the funeral were as task-driven as the days preceding it, as I helped my sister find a new place to live. (She had been living with my mother.) My sister was rattled by my mom's death, still shocked by her memory of my mom's dead body on the floor. I quickly jumped into action, helping my bereft sister find a new home, playing the good-girl role I knew so well. I was starting to become comfortable not feeling. Working off my to-do list, I inhabited only a corner of my mind—a place absent of emotions yet filled with tasks and distractions. I simply could not face her death, or at least part of me couldn't—the part that hoped she would have been different, *happier*, the part that fantasized about us being happy *together*, sharing a different kind of love that always seemed out of reach.

After a week with my sister, I left Texas and went to New York for my husband's conference before returning home to pack for a move we would make in six weeks, to start a new life I was quickly forgetting why I had ever wanted. I was beginning to doubt my good fortune. I felt plagued by survivor's guilt. This guilt started to take on a shadowy presence over my entire existence. No matter how irrational I knew this feeling was, it seemed to have its own internal drive and direction that was beyond my conscious control. It couldn't be pushed away by a stream of endless commitments.

Before our scheduled move date, I had two professional lectures scheduled, one in South Africa and the other in Oxford. There was talk of me canceling; I did not want to be so far from my sister during *her* time of grief. I felt afraid to leave the safety of my home, which, oddly, only propelled me forward. Much like when I was a child, I split off this fear, not believing I could protect myself from perceived danger.

While in South Africa, one of my dental fillings cracked, beginning two weeks of throbbing pain. I continued to march forward, presenting a paper and visiting historic sites and traumatized populations as planned. I have two photos of myself from that time, both taken by my husband. In the first photo, I am looking out from a ferry as we approach Robben Island. My face looks frozen, much like my mother's did after her father died. In the second photo, my husband has captured my attention. I smile like the good girl I had learned to become.

It was these two parts of me—and their different approaches to attachment—that I believe also complicated my experience of grief. One part expressed authentic emotions, whereas the other always pushed forward, putting on a face others likely found soothing. Such splitting is a common reaction to ongoing childhood abuse. Alternate personalities can emerge, ways of being that are so radically distinct the person is oblivious to how the self contorts to survive conditions of cruelty and neglect (Van der Hart et al., 2006). However, I knew the splits of my psyche, how I had learned to be one person when it was safe to authentically express my desires and needs, and how survival in the face of threat meant submitting to the desires and needs of others. Missing were the time, space, and supportive relationships to grieve the lack of unconditional love and protection that should be every child's birthright. Unresolved, complicated grief is an often-unacknowledged outcome of adverse childhood experiences. Healing these early wounds requires attention to grieving, much like the care ideally given to those suffering the loss of a loved one.

I left South Africa with increasing mouth pain and a virus I caught while there. I went to Oxford anyway, and my husband returned to the States. I continued to feel lousy and slept in the morning after the conference. Before I left Oxford for London, departing later than planned, three suicide bombs exploded in the London Underground. I have wondered what my fate would have been had I left even 20 minutes earlier; I would have been on one of the trains that exploded.

My husband frantically tried to get me to take the next plane home. I told him other people needed the plane seats more than me. When he queried who these people might be, I replied those who had just lost someone they loved. I still couldn't fully situate myself in that category, one I had denied belonging to since the initial loss of my mother 39 years earlier.

The day after I returned home, I went to the dentist and had a temporary filling made. I left his office for the final cleaning and clearing of our soon-to-be old home, marking the end of the moving process. My husband

and I had planned to camp in our sleeping bags in the den that night as a proper goodbye to our first home. Heading to the house, I started to believe all the pain was behind me, including the tragedy, grief, and guilt I felt for surviving. With my guard down, I walked directly into a ceiling lamp that was no longer protected by a well-placed dining table. I split open my forehead, requiring about 20 stitches. The doctor ordered me to just *sit*—no unpacking or moving boxes. I had lost my ability to run.

That Which Does Not Kill Us...

When I look back on those six weeks following my mother's death, I see an old pattern at hand: an inability to take care of or even protect myself, as if waiting for divine intervention. I can now identify a belief driving my blind propulsion forward, a belief that had been walled off with the feelings of betrayal, but which also organized my experiences and the choices I made. I believed: "If I suffer enough, it will bring her back to me." As a child, there never was an opportunity to feel the pain of losing my mom to her grief. And grief itself is filled with feelings of betrayal. As Buddhist psychologist Jack Kornfield (2008) observed, "When we grieve we allow ourselves to feel the truth of our pain, the measure of betrayal or tragedy in our life. By our willingness to mourn, we slowly acknowledge, integrate, and accept the truth of our losses" (p. 135).

I wonder if I also inherited my mom's feelings of betrayal, those she could not feel because she was emotionally dependent on her father yet also afraid of his violent temper. During the first years of life, children feel their caregiver's emotions as if they were their own. A young child cannot discriminate between what she feels and what her primary caregiver feels. Through this emotional symbiosis, children implicitly learn from their caregivers feelings that will be recognized, feelings that are not safe to feel, and feelings that must be dissociated from awareness. Despite all the betrayals in my family, feelings of betrayal were rarely expressed, if at all. Betrayal became part of the unspoken family legacy, along with the unresolved grief that kept my family stuck in sorrow, while at the same time walled off from its expression.

Betrayal is a hateful, destructive emotion, one that I believe can inspire survivor's guilt, especially when directed toward a parent. How can any child fathom wanting to destroy the person she loves most in the world? Deep feelings of guilt seem inevitable, if only as a defense against acting in ways that might threaten survival.

Like many people after the loss of a parent, I felt like an orphan after my mom's death. Mantras of gratitude and staying busy (my old remedies for a broken heart) failed me. It was as if being the good girl had run its course and I was living the other part of me—the hidden away, unloved part that never connected with mom because of the denied hurt that stood in the way. I was sad, immobile, irritable, only seeing things in grayscale. I literally developed tunnel vision; more than once I hit my head. The outside world existed on the edges of my conscious awareness. At the time, I did not know that the likelihood of accidental death increases greatly the first year after the loss of a loved one (Neeld, 2003).

My dream life felt the most real, and it became a respite from sorrow. I often dreamed of my mother, and I took those dreams as signs of how she was doing and how we were doing as mother and daughter. I could not break the connection and did not know how to make sense of us in my waking life. Although I felt unsteady and lost without her, I was determined not to notice the real-world effect of my loss. Nevertheless, I physically ached for her. I would have given anything to hold her once more.

Her death and our separation became sources of distress and numbness. As a child and adolescent, I had often tried to shore my mother up against depression. In her death, I did the same. Yet this time, I ruminated over ways I could have saved her and how her death was a sign of how I had failed her. I could swing from being completely preoccupied with such beliefs to going days or weeks without even a thought of her—mimicking the avoidant attachment dance we began so early in my life.

With time, a sense of aloneness emerged, which although discomforting, seemed to shift something in me. I started to become aware of my swinging between avoidance and preoccupation. I witnessed how this dynamic had a life of its own, seemingly independent of any external influences. I started to observe how my states of preoccupation and avoidance left little room for being present with the actual conditions of my existence and the supportive relationships I had formed as an adult. After a year of frantically trying to regain my footing and return to my so-called normal life—what I associated with who I was before my mom's death—I finally started letting go. The tension could no longer hold. The split was becoming a worn-out divide that no longer made sense. The threat that drove the split in the first place was long gone.

Letting go was not a conscious process. I connect the transformation with changes in my dreams, and the unconscious aspects of my psyche that stayed out of awareness yet influenced how I organized my experiences and my sense of self. After the shock of my mother's death wore off, I started to have dreams of just being with my mother, doing the kinds of things I imagined happy mothers and daughters did together—going to movies, getting pedicures, linking arms while strolling in parks, lounging on sun-drenched beaches. In these dreams, we were delighted to be together. Invariably I would wake from my mental oases resisting opening my eyes. Sometimes I would cry. I never wanted these dreams to end. For the first time, I was grieving the mother I lost as a little girl.

Eventually, I had the following lucid dream: *I am sitting in my bed next to my future self. I look at this other me and notice how much larger she is. She is also strong and calm, and she looks at me with compassion. I look at her and think to myself, "How the hell is that going to come about?"* After this dream, I began to mourn the loss of self I had experienced with the loss of my mother as a child. I stopped telling myself the old story about our hopeless relationship and started weaving a new tale, filled with hardship and dark emotions, but also resilience, strength, and courage. I became more myself, more integrated, and less afraid of heartbreak and betrayal. I began appreciating grief (although never liking it) and seeing it as an initiation into loving and living more fully.

Lasting Thoughts

Depth psychologist C. G. Jung (1989) described the life course as a teleological process, which through millions of years of adaptation lies dormant in the human psyche and soma, waiting for the corrective experiences that activate the next state of development. This model of human growth underscores how the "stuckness" of complicated grief does not have to be seen as an impediment to living, or even a disorder, but may signify a need to look deeper, differently, or longer to create conditions for healing and a return to growth. Paris (2011) connected heartbreak and mourning with the *individuation process*—the name Jung gave to the teleological drive of life. Through grief, we have the potential to further our individuation, becoming more our authentic selves, unfettered by psychological defenses developed as a child. Through individuation, Paris remarked, "the pain of heartbreak brings about a new conscious standpoint, one that transcends the previous opposition between love and hate, security and freedom" (2011, p. 64). She added, "The process of individuation is like a quest for wisdom, a life-long fascinating adventure, a process of withdrawal of more and more projections, a continuous recognition of more contradictory impulses within oneself, leading to ever-increasing levels of consciousness" (p. 64). My individuation involved gaining a new understanding of heartbreak, one that did not involve splitting off parts of myself to survive the hurt. My emerging sense of heartbreak meant no longer seeing grief and love as opposites, but rather as complimentary emotions, each needing the other for validation and worth. Paris identified a similar relationship between joy and sorrow:

> Joy and Sorrow are the two priestesses that meet us at the gate of the rich inner city called "*me.*" The priestess by the name of Joy greets us with these words: "I am Joy. I defend the eternal principle of Love no matter what, because if Love were to die, I too would die, and humans would not survive the catastrophe." Joy stands side by side with her unavoidable twin sister, the priestess by the name of Sorrow, who has this to say: "I too defend Love, which cannot exist without me. I am Sorrow, who creates the need for Love." As I entered their territory, they said in unison: "Take it all, or leave it all." (2011, p. 252)

When we resist grief, we also unwittingly resist love. This is a societal problem as well as an individual one. Collectively, we focus on the emotional stages of grief—the anger, denial, guilt, and feelings of hopelessness—as if grief were just another checklist, something endured rather than part of the life course and a potentially transformative experience. In our modern world, what detracts from progress is quickly pathologized. According to the *Diagnostic and Statistical Manual of Mental Disorders* (American Psychiatric Association, 1994), grief can be diagnosed as major depressive disorder as early as two months after the death of a loved one. This suggests to me the discomfort generally felt in the United States when suffering (or any intense emotion) is prolonged.

The transformative power of complicated grief may be its capacity to stop the modern preoccupation with progress and productivity by seizing the bereaved, demanding that heartache and love finally be given their due. Perhaps complicated grief is at least in part "complicated" because of the strains it places on us not only as individuals, but also as communities and as a society. If attachment and grief were honored as inescapable bookends of life—that is, *birth* and *death*—perhaps we could honor these inevitable stages with the creation of conditions that would lead to healthy attachments in the first place, thereby setting the stage for healthy grief reactions when the time comes to grieve those we have lost.

References

American Psychiatric Association. (1994). *DSM-IV: Diagnostic and statistical manual of mental disorders* (4th ed.). Washington, DC: Author.

Bowlby, J. (1977). The making and breaking of affectional bonds. *British Journal of Psychiatry, 130,* 201–210.

Bowlby, J. (1980). *Attachment and loss: Loss, sadness and depression* (Vol. III). New York: Basic Books.

Bowlby, J. (1988). *A secure base: Parent–child attachment and healthy human development.* New York: Basic Books.

Fabrega, H. (2002). *Origins of psychopathology: The phylogenetic and cultural basis of mental illness.* New Brunswick, NJ: Rutgers University Press.

Ferenczi, S. (1949/1988). Confusion of tongues between adults and the child: The language of tenderness and passion. *Contemporary Psychoanalysis, 24,* 196–206.

Jung, C. (1989). *Memories, dreams, reflections* (R. Winston & C. Winston, Trans.). New York: Vintage Books.

Kaehler, L. A., & Freyd, J. J. (2009). Borderline personality characteristics: A betrayal trauma approach. *Psychological Trauma: Theory, Research, Practice, and Policy, 1,* 261–268.

Kornfield, J. (2008). *The wise heart: A guide to the universal teachings of Buddhist psychology.* New York: Bantam Books.

Miller, A. (1998). The political consequences of child abuse. *Journal of Psychohistory, 26,* 573–585.

Neeld, E. H. (2003). *Seven choices: Finding daylight after loss shatters your world.* New York: Warner Books.

Paris, G. (2011). *Heartbreak: Recovering from lost love and mourning.* Minneapolis: Mill City Press.

Prigerson, H. G., Vanderwerker, L. C., & Maciejewski, P. K. (2007). A case for inclusion of prolonged grief disorder in *DSM-V.* In M. S. Stroebe, R. O. Hansson, H. Schut, & W. Stroebe (Eds.), *Handbook of bereavement research and practice: Advances in theory and intervention* (pp. 165–186). Washington, DC: American Psychological Association.

Schupp, L. J. (2003). *Grief: Normal, complicated, traumatic.* Eau Claire, WI: Pesi.

Shear, M. K. (2003, December 8). *Traumatic grief: An overview* [DVD]. (Produced by South Central Mental Illness Research, Education, and Clinical Center and Department of Veterans Affairs Employee Education System.)

Van der Hart, O., Nijenhuis, E.R.S., & Steele, K. (2006). *The haunted self: Structural dissociation and the treatment of chronic traumatization.* New York: W.W. Norton.

Wallin, D.J. (2007). *Attachment in psychotherapy.* New York: Guilford Press.

Worden, J.W. (2009). *Grief counseling and grief therapy: A handbook for the mental health practitioner* (4th ed.). New York: Springer.

Chapter Four

Tears and Tattoos
Complex Grief Revisited

Trish Staples

Introduction

My husband Paul was 36 years old when he died in November 1997. Having married him only seven months earlier, I felt my world implode. I was suicidal, depressed, and considered enough of a danger to myself a few months later to necessitate inpatient psychiatric care. If the proposed *Diagnostic and Statistical Manual of Mental Disorders, Fifth Edition* (DSM-5) category of complicated grief, or prolonged grief disorder (Prigerson et al., 2009), had existed at the time, my behavior over the following years would have almost certainly made me an ideal candidate for such a diagnosis.

Several years after Paul's death, I returned to university to undertake counselor training, with the intention of specializing in the field of bereavement and grief. Life, events, experiences, and providence have thus led to my involvement with this book and the opportunity to write on the basis of an abundance of reflections, theory, and knowledge. I do not profess to be an expert in any particular field, though elements of sociology, psychology, psychiatry, medicine, philosophy, and literature are interspersed throughout my writing. I am, however, the only authority on my grief. In writing this chapter, I hope to frame my position regarding the potential inclusion of complicated grief as a category in the DSM-5 within the parameters of the aforementioned combination of lived experience and academic theory.

In "The Wounded Storyteller" (1995), Arthur W. Frank defined postmodern autobiographical writing as multilayered, interrupted stories operating as different selves. In this sense, I am writing in the here and now not only as a person who has experienced significant bereavement, but also as a woman, a mental health services user, and a qualified and experienced teacher and counselor. I hope my writing will develop into reflection within a structured academic context, but this can only be achieved by first recounting my personal chaos narrative, reminding readers that my story can only ever be a illustration of my experience, for "those who are living the chaos cannot tell in words" (p. 98).

The Impact of Earlier Losses

While acknowledging the relevance of childhood loss experiences, I believe the following descriptions of my adult losses hold the key to unlocking the idiosyncrasies of my grief. The shattering of so many elements of my previous assumptive world (Janoff-Bulman, 1992), and the subsequent psychosocial transition and reorientation required to remain functioning after Paul died (Parkes, 2006), overwhelmed me. I further purport that my grief was the *only possible thing* that could have happened to me capable of instigating such immense personal, physiological, and psychological transformation, though it was many years before I was able to admit this.

In 1989, I was 35 and extremely happy working as a primary school teacher, specializing in physical education. I was physically fit and healthy—a dancer, skater, and tennis player. After years of incorrect treatments for chronic back pain, I was diagnosed with endometriosis, which eventually required a full hysterectomy. Childless at the time—a class of 32 children allowed me to satisfy emerging maternal needs—the operation evoked a knee-jerk reaction that left me bereft of children I would never have. I threw myself back into teaching too quickly, really. A year later, tests for mysterious neurological symptoms and debilitating fatigue led to a conclusive diagnosis of multiple sclerosis (MS). I deteriorated rapidly and was reliant on a wheelchair within the year, resulting in early retirement from my career in education.

I had been married seven years. Indications that my husband had a cruel streak magnified once I became, as he described me, "a useless cripple," worthy only of being put out of misery. Later, I often wondered whether his abusive behaviour was somehow linked to my illness: "Illness becomes the body's vehicle of communication, forcing us to stop and examine unprocessed trauma and change the way we live our lives" (Etherington, 2003, p. 15). The following few years saw an escalation of boredom after such a full and active life, feeling trapped by my illness and an emotionally abusive husband and, ultimately, a lengthy period of intense reactive depression.

Writing was one of my few pleasures, and I attended creative writing classes each week. I was amazed at my ability to express how I felt about my illness and my marriage, to describe my depression, to feel I had some control over events. As Philips, Linington, and Penman (1999) stated,

> The particular advantage of writing is that participants can choose to write whatever they want—the production of something beautiful or useful has not been demanded, and difficult and unacceptable ideas can be transformed into a form that can be appreciated and explored. (p. 13)

I developed dysarthria[1] and was unable to talk in anything but a whisper. Now, I couldn't walk, talk (live?) anymore. Writing a villanelle[2] at my writing group one day, all I produced was, "I feel so bad that I could cry, oh, how I wish that I could die." I was also transfixed by a scribbled rearrangement of the word *depression* that resulted in my desperate plea, "press 0, I end." The next morning, I was unable to communicate with anyone or to stop sobbing. I was so desperate to die, it hurt. After visits from my general practitioner, a psychiatrist, and a social worker, I accepted voluntary admission to an acute psychiatric ward. Liberated from the confines of my marriage, I quickly summoned up enough inner strength to divorce my husband.

Every Ending Is a New Beginning

While in the hospital, I met and fell in love with Paul, a fellow inpatient suffering from severe depression and epilepsy. For the first time in more than 10 years, I was in the company of a man who loved me unconditionally, whose humanity helped silence the self-deprecating messages I had internalized from my first husband's relentless bitterness. Mine and Paul's was not a popular alliance, though. Embarrassment had conformingly prevented me from disclosing that I was a target of domestic emotional abuse, so seeking a divorce was a huge shock to everyone. Our families worried about our emotional capacity to form a relationship, and psychiatric hospital personnel notoriously, and understandably, frown on such things (Dein & Williams, 2008).

---

[1] Characteristically slurred, slow speech that is difficult to produce and for others to understand
[2] A villanelle is a 19-line rhyming poem.

Paul and I believed we were the exception. We were soul mates, our relationship intense and passionate. It was as if we had both found something we had been searching for all our lives. Bearing in mind our circumstances when we met, we still bore heavy baggage and deep emotional scars when we left hospital. Alone, separated, we were still vulnerable, anxious. Together we felt invincible and able to overcome anything life threw at us.

Because we were one another's constant caregivers, the primary obstacles to our survival were health related. Despite no real prior knowledge or experience of epilepsy, I soon recognized signs indicating Paul was going to have a seizure. His warning auras involved bizarre hallucinations in which he became deeply immersed. What he called "come-go men" were just one example of this curious alternative reality, in which Paul gazed fixedly at nonthreatening little men in red and green clothes who appeared and disappeared through our lounge living room wall. Challenging the truth of Paul's visions made him distressed and agitated, so accompanying him into his world to ensure his safety was imperative. Being with Paul during his preictal states was my first, and most critical, introduction to what I refer to as "serendempathy."[3] The arrival of his seizures was almost a relief. I could at last feel more in control of the situation, putting Paul into the recovery position, administering rectal Diazepam, and phoning for an ambulance each time he went into status epilepticus.

Paul and I married in March 1997, on his 36th birthday. A few months later, after our holiday abroad, he went missing. This was completely out of character. My reaction was one of unbearable dread, and I spent the next few days desperate and confused, searching for him. Where is he? Is he still alive? Over the next few days, police helicopters circled the area near our flat, Paul's picture was displayed at bus and railways stations across the United Kingdom, and local newspapers sought assistance in tracking him down. In spite of my limited mobility, I searched nearby graveyards, parks, and other areas of wasteland, concerned for his safety; his epileptic auras, hallucinations, and seizures not only left him physically drained and vulnerable, but also affected his cognitive functioning and awareness.

After three agonizing days and nights, I answered the phone one evening to hear Paul's voice. It was soon apparent that his memory and comprehension were seriously compromised. He'd found a phone number in his wallet and decided to ring it, but he didn't know who, or where, I was. The police were with me when Paul phoned, and between us we ascertained

---

[3] Serendempathy: (n) spontaneous empathy occurring in unanticipated situations

his location and made arrangements to get him home. Medically assessed as being in a dissociative fugue state, Paul was admitted to a psychiatric ward for a few weeks. He improved slowly, gradually recognizing people again but struggling to understand his relationship with them, or to experience emotion. Hearing him say, "I *know* I love you, I just don't feel anything inside," broke my heart. Once we were home, however, we began to rebuild our life together, and—although he was clearly traumatized by his experience—each day marked another milestone in Paul's recovery.

Death Entered and Time Halted

Two months later, my MS symptoms exacerbated by the stress of Paul's disappearance, I was admitted to hospital for intravenous steroid treatment. Paul seemed well enough to be alone for a week. For the following six days, Paul walked to the hospital to see me, and we talked each night on the phone. The night before I was due to be discharged, Paul died. Just like that. Suddenly, cruelly, out of the blue, and with no apparent reason or cause. My brother discovered Paul's body the next day, sitting in our hall, next to the phone. I convinced myself Paul died, without any pain, immediately after we had talked. It was the only version of the time of his death I could, or would, accept.

No one ever told me Paul was dead. I had been trying to contact him for several hours to let him know I'd been discharged. I phoned him again, one last time. My brother answered the phone. He sounded uncommonly awkward with me, simply saying, "Is there a Sister there?" I dropped the phone receiver and hobbled away on my crutches, muttering repeatedly, "Don't tell me, don't tell me, I don't want to hear it." I knew Paul was dead, though. I think I'd known since I'd woke up that morning after a distressing nightmare, and my fears were confirmed when he didn't answer that first phone call. The ward staff had obviously been informed already and led me into a small room to offer the customary tea and clichés.

My father and sister collected me from the hospital and took me home. My brother was still there. The police had broken the door down, the ambulance service had attempted and failed to resuscitate Paul, and the doctor had attended to certify Paul's death. The flat seemed still, almost serene. I longed yet was afraid to see Paul. I'm not sure what I imagined, but any initial feelings of shock or sadness that he was dead were temporarily overwhelmed by gut-wrenching fear. The police had placed Paul's body on our bed. I tentatively crept into the room, almost as if not to wake him. I need not have been scared. He looked so peaceful, so beautiful. I lay down on the bed next to his icy cold body and held him tight. I'm not sure how long I stayed there, but eventually the funeral directors requested to move him. For some strange reason, I stayed in my lounge and didn't see them carrying Paul out in the body bag. Maybe I wanted to think he left of his own volition.

An Idiosyncratic Grief Model

At first I seemed to react as if Paul was missing again and would eventually return or be found. When reality hit, my reaction was extreme, endless, narcissistic, obsessive, and bizarre. Enmeshed by a phenomenon identifiable in a wider social context as grief, but known to me at that time as the only possible way to be, I had no way of knowing whether how I was behaving and feeling was any different from anyone else after a sudden death. I never thought once in terms of personal survival or coping; I simply experienced my grief, unconditionally.

Where to start? A roller coaster, tunnel, black hole, thick fog; all these oft-used metaphors seem relevant yet somehow inadequate and universally lacking in uniqueness. The day after Paul died, there were early suggestions that my grief would be complex when I phoned the policeman dealing with the case and asked him out. He was professional and experienced enough to gently suggest I might like to concentrate on spending time with my friends and family. Regular visits to be with Paul's body at the Medico-Legal Centre were followed by practically taking up residence at the funeral director's, again reinforcing the idiosyncratic and often extreme nature of my grief. These were not actions or decisions I chose to take; rather, they reflected a physical need, sated only by actually being with Paul.

I spent many hours alone with Paul's body during the nine days between his death and his funeral. My family were concerned at the amount of time I devoted to my mourning. I remember it as if it were yesterday. It had nothing to do with denial; it was more an inability to comprehend. I had briefly encountered death before, but never the death of someone I was so intimately close to. I talked to Paul. I touched his cold body constantly. I gazed endlessly at his mask-like face. I stroked his soft, curly blond hair. It was as if I was comforting him, reassuring him, taking care of him, while simultaneously struggling to grasp the reality of what had happened.

And I was strangely curious about this dead body in the room with me: "If someone else's body can become nothing, so can your own" (Fisher, 2009, p. 8). But how *did* someone just stop breathing? Could *I* just stop breathing if I wanted to? What did the pathologist do to Paul at the autopsy? Did they put everything back where it belonged? Did rigor mortis mean Paul had an erection? I took numerous photos of Paul and coerced my brother to take more of me standing with Paul's corpse. There was such urgency in my decisions and actions. I knew I would be unable to stay with Paul much longer, so it was important that I make the best of the time I had left.

During the time I spent away from Paul's body, I wrote prolifically, not random chaotic scribbling, but neatly written poems focusing on aspects of what I was witnessing, such as "Decomposition," a graphic investigation of the curious physical deterioration of Paul's body: "The black stain continues to grow, moving down his hand and into his arm, until I realise he really is dead." Writing seemed the only way of expressing myself and of connecting with Paul. Louise DeSalvo (1999) identified how healing narratives allow us to reflect on events and connect a particularly traumatic experience to other experiences in our lives. David Aberbach (1990) astutely observed how creativity is enhanced by its similarities with the process of mourning, the desperation, searching, longing, and discovery experienced and documented by writers often symbolically imitating manifestations of grief.

The funeral came and went. I planned every detail meticulously, ever the consummate perfectionist. I needed some control over what happened, who came, the music, what was said. I felt my greatest triumph was preventing the removal of the coffin until after I had physically left. But I don't remember ever emotionally leaving Paul. A few hours after the funeral, while I was staying at my parents' home, my flat was burglarized. My brother and I disturbed the intruder in Paul's and my bedroom. I was incensed. How dare someone invade our home and obliterate my last memory of lying with Paul on our bed after he died? I think this was probably my breaking point.

Madness

Not unexpectedly, a few months after Paul's death I was once again admitted to an acute psychiatric ward suffering from reactive depression and suicidal ideation. I went willingly, at that time feeling so desperate to die that I believed I would be able to go through with my suicide once I was away from my family. This was the "stop the world, I want to get off" element of my grief.

I had lengthy—and what I believed were quite rational and measured—talks with ward staff about wanting to die, and I remained on suicide watch for several weeks. I remember thinking how little I was bothered by this invasion of my privacy; I knew if I behaved they would increase the intervals between observations, and I would finally find an opportunity to escape their scrutiny long enough to perform the deed. That was as far as my thinking went. I had no definite plans, though I had considered simply throwing myself in front of a bus or off a high building. I deliberately use the word *simply* here. In my confused state, I believed it would be easy to kill myself.

My parents and siblings took it in turns to visit me every day. I so resented their persistent presence. How could I kill myself when they cared so much? I couldn't understand why they cared about me anyway. Didn't they realize they didn't matter? Why could nobody understand, and accept, that the only person that mattered to me was Paul? Why was everyone so eager to keep me alive, to show me how much I had to live for? "Suicidal thoughts in response to loss … usually grow out of a sense in that person that their feeling-world cannot be understood by anybody else" (Lendrum & Syme, 1992, p. 144). I felt not only lost, but also judged, marginalized. Surely my rationale made sense. Paul and I were soul mates, and as I saw it, when one soul mate died, the other naturally followed. It was impossible to function alone as a soul mate if the other one was no longer there. Cowardice or some other weakness (or perhaps a will to live, though I refused to accept that possibility at the time) continued to prevent me from killing myself, and repetitive self-harm with a sharp blade proved a helpful alternative.

I was visited in hospital by a bereavement counselor who told me I was still young and had plenty of skills and a lot to live for. The irony was unbearable. I wanted to scream at her—actually, no, I wanted to kill her. I was disabled, with no children, no career, and no husband. I believed I had nothing to live for and, more important, I didn't *want* anything to live for. And there you have it, I suppose (but more of this later).

Connecting

Before admittance to hospital, I had become obsessed with writing to Paul, forcing myself to stay awake each night to keep a journal. Sometimes I was so tired I wrote while asleep, waking to read the gibberish I had produced. Guided by a need to prolong my connection to Paul, I got several tattoos depicting aspects of our relationship, and obsessively collected hundreds of tiny words from newspapers and magazines to create a portrait-sized collage poem dedicated to Paul.

Once discharged from hospital, I encountered another feature of my grief, perhaps best described as childlike, egocentric magical thinking. I was convinced I would be reunited with Paul if only I could die too. The popular media seemed to conspire to reassure me that Paul understood how I felt and was waiting for me, song lyrics encouraging me to contact him, or suggesting he was angry with me for taking so long, or that he would come and fetch me.[4] Newly released films conveyed similar messages; "Titanic" (1997) and "What Dreams May Come" (1998) were just two at that time that portrayed soul mates joined again in death.

After a while, older films reappeared, with different messages; "Ghost" and "Truly, Madly, Deeply" depicted how immeasurable love facilitated the return of the dead partner. I visited Spiritualist Churches and mediums to make contact with Paul, but he never made contact with me, and he certainly never came back. I became angry and disillusioned, wondering if he had ever really loved me. At this point, I cognitively made the shift from wishing him back to finding out how he had died in the first place. It was never really about why; after my MS diagnosis, incessant "why me?" questioning and the lack of apposite answers had led me to alter my philosophy to "why not me?" No real answers there, admittedly, but less damaging to my soul.

Investigating

Thus began the "morbid curiosity" component of my grief. Actually, *curiosity* is too mild a word for the all-encompassing obsession with death and mortality in which I immersed myself in, but it will suffice. I read numerous books, watched anything on television with even the most innocuous of connections, and switched from writing *to* Paul to writing *about* his death. There was nothing I avoided: "If death was sudden and unexpected, and the bereaved person was not present when it happened, an overriding need may be felt for detailed information" (Stroebe & Stroebe, 1987, p. 241). I revelled in knowledge extracted from TV documentaries about coroners and the role of the undertaker; at last I could comprehend what caused the black stains on Paul's dead hands, why a sheet covered him up to his chin after his autopsy, the mechanics of his body being burned by fire.

Increasing use of the Internet also led me to Epilepsy Bereaved, a relatively new organization campaigning for awareness and prevention of

---

[4] For example, "Never Ever" (All Saints), "Theme from Titanic" (Celine Dion), and "Post-card from Heaven" (Lighthouse Family).

Sudden Unexpected Death in Epilepsy, where I discovered, "SUDEP is considered to be more common in young adults, in people with epilepsy who are not seizure free, and in people who have seizures at night" (Epilepsy Bereaved, 2011). Paul matched this profile perfectly—he was in his thirties, his seizures were usually at night—so it seemed my searching had finally paid off. I suddenly felt in a position of power, believing I could finally get evidence that would allow me to challenge individuals and agencies I judged instrumental in allowing Paul's death.

Culpability

And so began months of fighting—the "retribution" phase of my grief—compounded several months after Paul's death by the coroner's recording of an open verdict. Exactly how could these so-called professional people have missed the fact that Paul would die? Neurologists were, in my mind, guilty of either misdiagnosing Paul's epilepsy, underestimating its severity, or—and I was adamant about this—prescribing him the wrong drugs and killing him with a lethal cocktail of inappropriate and ineffective medicines.

Perceiving some sort of conspiracy, I believed psychiatrists must also have played their part. Paul had attempted to provide detailed accounts of his experiences

> I never realised that I've been like this since I was six, not just for the past four years as I thought before. Doing strange things, seeing things at night when I was a child—bricks coming at me out of the ceiling. (personal communication with P. Staples, Sheffield, England, September 8, 1997)

However, I was convinced that everyone had consistently missed the connection between Paul's depression and his epilepsy. As I saw it, the experts had failed to correctly diagnose Paul throughout his life, prescribing yet more drugs that must surely prove to have compromised his chances of survival. Nobody escaped my scrutiny and judgment. Social workers, art therapists, nurses, counselors; I was sure their incompetence *must* have contributed to Paul's death.

Determined to prove a case of gross medical negligence against someone—anyone—and to ensure that somebody was held accountable, I hired an attorney and spent a considerable amount of money obtaining Paul's medical notes, and an even longer time reading and trying to make sense of them. This mission was doomed to fail. First, I ran out of money.

Second, and most important, there was no case. Much as I hated admitting defeat, the fact was that from his developing symptoms of epilepsy as a child to his subsequent mental health difficulties, Paul's treatment and care had been exemplary. The case was dropped, the anger was abandoned, and the need for reprisal disappeared as quickly as it had arrived.

Isolation

About 18 months after Paul's death, I found myself in an abyss. Until then, I had not only focused all of my attention and energy on getting Paul back, joining him, or punishing someone for what they had done to him, I had also failed to take any notice of the world around me. Out of hospital, with only tears and tattoos for company, and nobody left to attack or blame, I was left with the problems of being me, being alone, and living without Paul. Thus began the "who am I now" part of my grief.

Inexperienced as I was with death, bereavement, and grief, I stumbled clumsily through the next months and years. I clung to Paul desperately. I continued writing to him daily, displayed numerous photos of him in every room of the flat, and played his favorite music around the clock. My obsessive pedestal-placing of Paul gathered momentum, propelling me disturbingly close to becoming a modern-day version of Queen Victoria or *David Copperfield's* Miss Havisham. I uncharacteristically started wearing jewelry, and anything turquoise—like my engagement ring, or a Celtic knot representing the eternal life I *knew* Paul and I would have together—was avariciously and obsessively purchased. I rallied vehemently against change, and although I was able to control my immediate surroundings, the world outside my flat seemed less cooperative. Shops changed owners, houses were painted different colors, flowers in the garden died. How could the world *possibly* carry on as if nothing had happened? Didn't everyone *know*?

The need to self-harm continued, and many tumultuous nights were spent sitting on my bedroom floor, ritualistically scoring my wrists until the compensatory physical relief was achieved. Compulsive spending became a hobby, as did gambling, the acquisition of credit cards, inappropriate relation-ships, and an overriding desire to destroy myself. A few close family members understood my torment and respected my decisions; other people let me know in no uncertain terms that my actions were unacceptable. Some indi-viduals insisted they knew how I felt, while fervently predicting a positive future for me. I don't know which response angered me most. In general, the world seemed unable to tolerate the manifestations of my grief.

Newness

I have no idea when or how things began to change, but almost impercep-
tibly, they did. The first indication of transformation manifested as a craving
for mental stimulation, and my physical health improved sufficiently to
enable me to become involved in something not too demanding of my time
or energy. A few years after Paul's death saw my return to the psychiatric
sector, not as a patient this time, but facilitating creative writing classes at
the local branch of MIND, a leading mental health charity in the United
Kingdom. I also became a service user representative with Sheffield Care
Trust, collaborating in a project designed to improve medication management in a psychiatric setting (Turner, Gardner, Staples, & Chapman, 2007).
I attended creative writing classes again, and though my work was perhaps
morbid and introspective, my writing facilitated reflection and learning. I
subsequently returned to university to train to become a counselor, and
became a volunteer with a bereavement organization and at a local hospice.

Still very lost at times, and with a lot of grieving left to do, my ability to
care about others increased. A major turning point in my grief was meeting
my current husband, over three years after Paul's death: "Despite our doubts,
love, the ultimate cushion against disaster, goes on" (Parkes, 2006, p. 148).
He was getting over his own divorce, and we both longed for companionship; anything more was a bonus. He understood my need for emotional
space and more importantly, and generously, accepted my need to maintain
ongoing links with Paul.

Theoretical Considerations

Earlier potentially prescriptive and time-limited stage, phase, or process
bereavement models of grief (Kübler-Ross, 1969; Parkes, 1975; Worden, 2002)
are increasingly being challenged. Supplementary and alternative models are
being introduced that not only reflect heightened understanding of how
people grieve, but also highlight perspectives that validate the diversity of
grief's manifestations and recognize the importance of a continuing relationship with the deceased (Klass, Silverman, & Nickman, 1996; Neimeyer, 2001;
Stroebe & Schut, 1999; Walter, 1996). Perhaps the most significant features of
all of these models are their emphasis on the uniqueness of individual grief,
and the avoidance of generalization. I believe my narrative reflects this uniqueness, at the same time conveying some important messages relating to a wider
understanding of the process of grief and how it can become complicated.

Running alongside bereavement theory is the *DSM* (or psychiatric "bible") (Kutchins & Kirk, 1997), first introduced in 1952 by the APA, and constantly under revision. Since its inception, the manual has been censured for its Western bias and subsequent ethnocentricity, its omission of aetiology for specific mental disorders (Shorter, 1997), and its ever increasing number of new disorders.

Complicated grief has not until recently been thought to merit its own exclusive diagnostic category in the DSM and was present in earlier versions only as an exclusion criterion for diagnoses of major depression. This exclusion was subsequently rejected in DSM-IV because of a "lack of empirical work on its constituent symptoms" (Horowitz et al., 1997, p. 904). Despite the APA's reassurance that "the goal of DSM is to establish clear criteria for diagnosing mental disorders, not to create medical conditions out of the full range of human behavior and emotions" (APA, 2011), this amendment prompted concerns that bereaved people may in the future risk being incorrectly diagnosed as experiencing major depressive disorder. Kenneth Kendler (2010) presented the view of the APA Mood Disorder Work Group, arguing that because research studies had found only negligible differences between reactions to bereavement and to other stressful life events, isolating grief as an exclusive exception in the DSM risked marginalizing grief while simultaneously devaluing the significance of different forms of abuse; loss of relationships, home, health or employment, and many other examples of personal and sociocultural adversity.

Since the publication of DSM-IV in 1994, several quantitative research studies have concurred that some complications of grief might reflect trauma responses representing a clinical disorder distinguishable from other bereavement-related depression and anxiety disorders (Boelen & van den Bout, 2005; Boelen, van den Bout, & de Keijser, 2003; Horowitz et al., 1997; Latham & Prigerson, 2004; Ogrodniczuk et al., 2003; Prigerson et al., 1996; Prigerson, Frank, et al., 1995; Prigerson, Maciejewski, et al., 1995; Prigerson, Vanderwerker, & Maciejewski, 2007). Yet proposals for the inclusion of a new singular diagnostic category of complicated grief in DSM-5, and suggested complementary treatment strategies (Castonguay, Goldfried, Wiser, Raue, & Hayes, 1996; Currier, Neimeyer, & Berman, 2008; Kersting, 2004), continue to generate ongoing debate: "Issues identified with diagnosis of individuals with CG include concerns about misuse of the term, distinctions between normal and complicated grief, fears regarding stigmatisation and health insurance funding issues associated with potential *DSM-V* classification of CG" (Kristjanson, Lobb, Aoun, & Monterosso, 2006, p. 30).

Although recommendations favoring one term over another have been made (Maciejewski, Zhang, Brock, & Prigerson, 2007), efforts to accurately define the disorder to be included in the DSM-5 persist, not helped by an absence of established terminology: According to Kristjanson et al., "adjectives include absent, abnormal, complicated, distorted, morbid, maladaptive, atypical, intensified and prolonged, unresolved, neurotic, dysfunctional, chronic, delayed, and inhibited" (2006, p. 20). In 2011, the APA announced, "Currently, there is insufficient evidence to propose a specific Bereavement-Related Disorder in the *DSM-5*, although such a diagnosis has been proposed for the appendix" (APA, 2011). Thus, the discourse continues.

Hypothetically

Let's suppose my life had been delayed 20 years; that agreement regarding terminology, assessment criteria, and treatment had been reached; and that in 2013 a complicated grief diagnosis had finally been accepted as a mental disorder in DSM-5. Still experiencing extreme grief reactions six months after Paul's death, I would probably have been assessed by a psychiatrist. On the basis of results gleaned from the "Inventory of Complicated Grief" (Prigerson, Maciejewski, et al., 1995), I might have been diagnosed as suffering from complicated grief (or prolonged grief disorder) and prescribed a combination of antidepressant medication and cognitive grief treatment. Cognitive grief treatment is a customized version of techniques used in interpersonal psychotherapy that incorporates cognitive–behavioral therapy interventions to explore responses to trauma and loss and find strategies for moving on (Shear, Frank, Houck, & Reynolds, 2005). For approximately 16 weeks, and in keeping with the motivational interviewing (MI) approach (Miller & Rollnick, 2002) of cognitive grief treatment, my sessions might have included keeping a grief diary, imaginal revisiting, and "waving a magic wand" (Shear, 2010, p. 13). By the time the first anniversary of Paul's death arrived, I would have been discharged, hopefully with goals and optimism for the future and the intention of forming new satisfactory relationships.

Discussion

Bereaved individuals actively seeking support should undoubtedly have access to appropriate professional care and, despite the possibility that the goal of recovery or return to normality may be difficult to achieve, a diagnostic label might indeed prove reassuring for some. However, the proposed treatment of complicated grief, its quick-fix ideology, and its substantial focus on the bereaved person's supposedly faulty cognitions concern me to some degree. The implications of supporting bereaved people using cognitive therapy are far reaching; not only might they be informed that the way they think about the death is faulty, but also they are less likely to have their stories heard. Furthermore, the therapeutic relationship is at risk of being compromised by the therapist's focus on the depressive impact of the client's distorted thinking, thus becoming counterproductive to treatment (Castonguay et al., 1996). Robert Neimeyer suggested that professionals should be cautious of standardizing cognitive therapy, as a great deal can be learned from simply "finding the silver lining in loss and from fully experiencing the process of grieving." Kersting (2004) added, "Understanding how ... people are successful in coping with loss and developing constructive methods for continuing their lives will help psychologists guide those who are more likely to struggle" (p. 51).

My main objection to this proposed categorization, however, relates to the universality and inference of the initial analysis, of including *any* form of grief under the remit of a mental disorder or condition. Surely, any proposed generic diagnosis of grief (normal or complicated) is somewhat incongruous with the now widely accepted remit that grief is idiosyncratic. Arthur W. Frank suggested that society's lack of empathy, combined with a historical insistence on diagnosis, labeling, and curing, has created a world incapable of respecting personal choice and action, thereby focusing on a portrayal of individual deviance. In keeping with Frank's statement that "denial of chaos only makes its horror worse" (Frank, 1995, p. 112), I am mindful of the clichés and euphemisms directed at bereaved people, appeasing the speaker yet simultaneously failing to indicate any attempt to understand the grieving individual's reality. Granek (2010) also expressed concern that the proposed DSM-5 diagnosis will potentially formalize this inappropriate response to bereavement and grief, and that it will be easier for people in general to be intolerant of manifestations of grief in everyday life.

Dorothy Rowe (1997) similarly highlighted the potential disservice of any DSM-driven diagnoses of mental disorders that are based only on interpreting an individual's unusual or strange behavior but fail to identify the actual lived world of the person. She asserted that many of these supposedly pathological behaviors are probably "well within the range of most people's experience" (p. xvii). As a society, have we become too formulaic with regard to human emotion, too obsessed with so-called normality, too eager to categorize each and every response to life events? How difficult is it for an individual to think, behave, and feel the way he or she needs or wants to without some well-intentioned onlooker or, even worse, a professional, telling them there *is* a better way, it *can* be easier, you don't *need* to suffer.

I have a somewhat radical theory. I doubt many will agree with it, but I believe it possesses an element of harsh reality. Some bereaved people don't *want* a better way, or for grief and life to be easier. Some bereaved people believe they need to suffer, and feel absolutely justified in their responses. Some bereaved people find it difficult to understand why others need to categorize, help, and guide them just because their behavior is difficult to observe without intervening. Rather than making assumptions about others, or ostracizing and avoiding, would it really be so difficult for society to accept and honor these individuals who choose—as I did—to opt out of life for a while, to live in chaos, or to suffer willingly in order to gain emotional, physical, and spiritual growth? From a different perspective, though, the luxury of pursuing such an introspective grieving style surely depends on the grieving individual's circumstances. I can only surmise (and hope) that however difficult it may have been, my grief would have needed to accommodate other responsibilities had I been healthy, a parent of young children, or in employment.

Grief's diverse manifestations can be horrendous, cruel, and relentless. They can linger, confuse, surprise, and devastate. But, however complex they are, they are nearly always normal responses to bereavement *for that person*. Many bereaved people already think they are going mad, a diagnosis subliminally imposed on them by others—family, friends, colleagues—whose comments and responses convey the message that the person's responses to bereavement are abnormal, that the way they are grieving is somehow not right. Surely diagnosing the person as having a mental disorder will reinforce this belief.

Attitudes adopted by professionals in their work with bereaved people can either enhance or sabotage the therapeutic relationship and clinical progress. I was not helped at all by a psychiatric nurse who suggested I see a clairvoyant, or by the social worker who told me bone meal was good for the garden when he discovered I had scattered Paul's ashes in my garden. What bereaved people often need most is an "exquisite witness" (Jeffreys, 2005), someone who will listen, over and over again if necessary, and accept and respect, how they feel. Professional practice therefore needs to be grounded in the core conditions of empathy, acceptance, and genuineness (Rogers, 1951), and a willingness to trust in the bereaved person's ability to survive their grief, to 'believe the client and *believe in* the client' (Saleebey, 2000, p. 133).

Closing Thoughts

My views on grief have been colored by my own experiences and learning. I have been impressed and reassured by several powerful analogies and metaphors, especially the powerful 'Circles of Grief' model (Tonkin, 1996), illustrating how life grows around grief, and Richard Wilson's "Whirlpool of Grief" (Hindmarch, 2000), which, while offering a simplistic but honest appraisal of grief's turbulence, also allows the bereaved person to see that life can never be as it was before the death. We can stay (grieving) in the whirlpool, or we can carry on down the river (live again). But we can *never* go back up a waterfall.

But my greatest learning came from succumbing to and experiencing my grief. Paul's death was, and always will be, the most significant event of my life. If personality is a determinant of grieving style, or at least plays a significant part, then my obstinate, imaginative, obsessive, perfectionist, and analytical tendencies, to name but a few, facilitated my journey through, and beyond, my complex grief experience. I became a 'responsible rebel,' questioning and challenging bereavement models in order to discover my own (Wolfelt, 2007). I created theories and fantasies, "grief and suffering seen through rose-coloured spectacles" (Ironside, 1996, p. 163), which protected me until I was strong enough to withstand honest reality. Only when I discovered anything to be gained from my experiences—strengths, qualities, skills, and characteristics I could rescue from the ashes of my life and use again, just in different ways—was I able to acknowledge I actually *did* have something to offer, that previously elusive "something to live for."

As I mentioned earlier, Paul died in 1997. I qualified as a counselor in 2002 and completed a master's degree in 2010. I belong to various groups in mental health and voluntary sectors, and regularly speak at conferences or facilitate training courses. My physical health fluctuates, but that is the nature of MS. My mental health is more robust, but I never take it for granted. Further education, reading, research and, most importantly, life, have all provided me with coping strategies and techniques when difficulties arise, and I believe I have at last learned how to relax.

I am grateful for the opportunity to write my story, now "our" story (Frank, 1995). Knowing at least one more person will hear it enables me to leave some of the impact of my experience in the public domain, a sort of "ceremonial sharing" (DeSalvo, 1999). Please take care of it.

References

American Psychiatric Association. (2011), *DSM-5 Development*. Retrieved from http://www.dsm5.org/ProposedRevision/Pages/proposedrevision.aspx?rid=367

Aberbach, D. (1990). *Surviving trauma: Loss, literature, and psychoanalysis*. New Haven, CT: Yale University Press.

Boelen, P. A., & van den Bout, J. (2005). Complicated grief, depression, and anxiety as distinct post-loss syndromes: A confirmatory factor analysis study. *American Journal of Psychiatry, 162,* 2175–2177.

Boelen, P. A., van den Bout, J., & de Keijser, J. (2003). Traumatic grief as a disorder distinct from bereavement-related depression and anxiety: A replication study with bereaved mental health care patients. *American Journal of Psychiatry, 160,* 1339–1341.

Bly, R. (1990). *Iron John: A book about men*. Reading, MA: Addison Wesley.

Castonguay, L. G., Goldfried, M. R., Wiser, S., Raue, P., & Hayes, A. M. (1996). Predicting the effect of cognitive therapy for depression: A study of unique and common factors. *Journal of Consulting and Clinical Psychology, 64,* 497–504.

Currier, J., Neimeyer, R., & Berman, J. (2008). Effectiveness of psychotherapeutic interventions for bereaved persons: A comprehensive qualitative review. *Psychological Bulletin, 134,* 648–661.

Dein, K., & Williams, P. S. (2008). Relationships between residents in secure psychiatric units: are safety and sensitivity really incompatible? *Psychiatric Bulletin, 32,* 284–287.

DeSalvo, L. (1999). *Writing as a way of healing*. Boston: Beacon Press.

Epilepsy bereaved. (2011). Retrieved from http://www.sudep.org

Etherington, K. (2003). *Trauma, the body, and transformation*. London: Jessica Kingsley.

Fisher, S. (2009). Motionless body. In S. Earle, C. Komaromy, & C. Bartholomew (Eds.), *Death and dying: A reader* (pp. 7–11). Chicago: Sage Publications.

Frank, A. W. (1995). *The wounded storyteller: Body, illness, and ethics*. London: University of Chicago Press.

Granek, L. (2010). Grief as pathology: The evolution of grief theory in psychology from Freud to the present. *History of Psychology, 13*(1), 46–73.

Hindmarch, C. (2000). *On the death of a child*. Abingdon, England: Radcliffe Medical Press Ltd.

Horowitz, M. J., Siegel, B., Holen, A., Bonanno, G. A., Milbrath, C., & Stinson, C. H. (1997). Diagnostic criteria for complicated grief disorder. *American Journal of Psychiatry, 154,* 904–910.

Ironside, V. (1996). *You'll get over it*. London: Penguin Books.

Janoff-Bulman, R. (1992). *Shattered assumptions: Towards a new psychology of trauma*. New York: Free Press.

Jeffreys, J. S. (2005). *Helping grieving people: When tears are not enough*. London: Brunner-Routledge.

Kendler, K. (2010). *Mood disorder work group*. Retrieved from http://www.dsm5.org/about/Documents/grief%20exclusion_Kendler.pdf

Kersting, K. (2004). A new approach to complicated grief. *Monitor on Psychology, 35*(10), 51. Retrieved from http://www.apa.org/monitor/nov04/grief.aspx

Klass, D., Silverman, P. R., & Nickman, S. L. (Eds.). (1996). *Continuing bonds: New understandings of grief*. London: Taylor & Francis.

Kristjanson, L., Lobb, L., Aoun, S., & Monterosso, L. (2006). *A systematic review of the literature on complicated grief*. Perth: Commonwealth of Australia Department of Health and Ageing Care.

Kübler-Ross, E. (1969). *On death and dying*. New York: Touchstone.

Kutchins, H., & Kirk, S. A. (1997). *Making us crazy: DSM—The psychiatric bible and the creation of mental disorders*. London: Constable.

Latham, A. E., & Prigerson, H. G. (2004). Suicidality and bereavement: Complicated grief as psychiatric disorder presenting greatest risk for suicidality. *Suicide and Life Threatening Behavior, 34*, 350–362.

Lendrum, S., & Syme, G. (1992). *Gift of tears: practical approach to loss and bereavement counselling*. London: Routledge.

Maciejewski, P. K., Zhang, B., Block, S. D., & Prigerson, H. G. (2007). An empirical examination of the stage theory of grief. *JAMA, 297*, 716–723.

Miller, W., & Rollnick, S. (2002) *Motivational Interviewing*. New York: Guildford Press.

Neimeyer, R. (Ed.). (2001). *Meaning reconstruction and the experience of loss*. Washington, DC: American Psychological Association.

Ogrodniczuk, J. S., Piper, W. E., Joyce, A. S., Weideman, R., McCallum, M., Azim, H. F., & Rosie, J. S. (2003). Differentiating symptoms of complicated grief and depression among psychiatric outpatients. *Canadian Journal of Psychiatry, 48*, 87–93.

Parkes, C. M. (1975). *Bereavement: Studies of grief in adult life*. London: Penguin.

Parkes, C. M. (2006). *Love and loss: The roots of grief and its complications*. London: Routledge.

Philips, D., Linington, L., & Penman, D. (1999). *Writing well*. London: Jessica Kingsley.

Prigerson, H. G., Bierhals, A. J., Kasl, S. V., Reynolds, C. F. III., Shear, M. K., & Newsom, J. T. (1996). Complicated grief as a disorder distinct from bereavement-related depression and anxiety: A replication study. *American Journal of Psychiatry, 153,* 1484–1486.

Prigerson, H. G., Frank, E., Kasl, S. V., Reynolds, C. F III., Anderson, B., Zubenko, G. S., et al. (1995). Complicated grief and bereavement-related depression as distinct disorders: Preliminary empirical validation in elderly bereaved spouses. *American Journal of Psychiatry, 152*(1), 22–30.

Prigerson, H. G., Horowitz, M. J., Jacobs, S. C., Parkes, C. M., Aslan, M., Goodkin, A., et al. (2009). Prolonged grief disorder: Psychometric validation of criteria proposed for *DSM-V* and *ICD-11. PLoS Med 6*(8), e1000121. doi:10.1371/journal.pmed.1000121

Prigerson, H. G., Maciejewski, P. K., Reynolds, C. F., Bierhals, A. J., Newsom, J. T., & Jacobs, S. (1995). Inventory of complicated grief: A scale to measure maladaptive symptoms of loss. *Psychiatry Research, 59,* 65–79.

Prigerson, H. G., Vanderwerker, L. C., & Maciejewski, P. K. (2007). Prolonged grief disorder as a mental disorder: Inclusion in DSM. In M. S. Stroebe, R. O. Hansson, W. Stroebe, & H. A. Schut (Eds.), *Handbook of bereavement research and practice: 21st century perspectives* (pp. 165–186). Washington, DC: American Psychological Association.

Rogers, C. (1951). *Client-centered therapy: Its current practice, implications, and theory.* Chicago: Houghton Mifflin.

Rowe, D. (1997). Introduction. In H. Kutchins & S. A. Kirk (Eds.), *Making us crazy: DSM—The psychiatric bible and the creation of mental disorders.* London: Constable.

Saleebey, D. (2000). Power in the people: Strengths and hope. *Advances in Social Work, 1*(2), 127–136.

Shear, M. K., Frank, E., Houck, P. R., & Reynolds, C. F III. (2005). Treatment of complicated grief: A randomized controlled trial. *JAMA, 293,* 2601–2608.

Shear M. K. (2010). Complicated grief treatment. *Bereavement Care, 29*(3), 10–14.

Shorter, E. (1997). *A history of psychiatry.* New York: John Wiley & Sons.

Stroebe, M., & Schut, H. (1999). The dual process model of coping with bereavement: Rationale and description. *Death Studies, 23,* 197–224.

Stroebe, W., & Stroebe, M. S. (1987). *Bereavement and health.* Cambridge, England: Cambridge University Press.

Tonkin, L. (1996). Growing around grief. *Bereavement Care, 15*(1), 10.

Turner, J., Gardner, B., Staples, T., & Chapman, J. (2007). Medicines with respect: Developing an integrated collaborative approach to medication management. *Mental Health Nursing, 27*(6), 16–19.

Walter, T. (1996). A new model of grief: Bereavement and biography. *Mortality, 1*(1), 7–25.

Wolfelt, A. D. (2007). *Companioning the bereaved: An introduction.* Fort Collins, CO: Companion Press. Retrieved from http://www.centerforloss.com

Worden, J. W. (2002). *Grief counselling and grief therapy* (3rd ed.). London: Routledge.

Part 2

Unresolved and Long-Lasting Grief

The previous section considered whether it is sensible to have a construct of complicated grief that includes labeling it as a mental disorder. These chapters help to cement the point that grief oftentimes can remain unresolved and be long lasting—perhaps lasting throughout one's entire life. In chapter 5, Mary Lynn Navarro presents a powerful case of how difficult it can be to finally come to terms with the death of a loved one with whom one regularly had strained or poor relations. Specifically, Navarro recounts her difficult relationship with her brother and her reaction to his death from cancer. While she suggests that there was not a "rational explanation" per se for their relationship, Navarro makes it clear that writing and metaphor can greatly assist in the healing process. Such writing may help to define the nature of certain situations, including those for which they are no easy and clear resolutions.

Rose Richards's piece (chapter 6) extends several of these themes by questioning whether complicated grief may very well be a "reasonable reaction to extraordinary circumstances." Richards documents the sudden death of her mother and the torrent of conflicting (though largely negative) emotions that it brought. She also discusses her decision to finally scatter her mother's ashes, 10 years after her passing. In doing so, Richards highlights how complicated grief often takes on a developmental trajectory in which the passage of time may be necessary to gain perspective on one's loss. She further suggests that it is nearly impossible (and perhaps unrealistic) to think that one will (or should) "get over" or "ignore" one's loss. While Richards's chapter clearly showcases the role of personal strengths and writing in coping, it just as clearly makes the point that extraordinary circumstances sometimes thrust "normal" people into extraordinary circumstances.

In chapter 7, Vanessa Russell furthers this theme that grief can sometimes become more complicated as a result of extenuating circumstances. Russell discusses how she was struggling with (or perhaps avoiding) the death of her father for a couple of years when she encountered a new crisis: physical and psychological abuse by her ex-boyfriend. In an attempt to shelter herself and her newborn son from this violence, Russell details how she had to flee her then-country of residence; in doing so, however, her ex-boyfriend tried to have Russell branded as a kidnapper. Russell raises several important points about complicated grief. First, she questions whether or how it can be distinguished from posttraumatic stress disorder given their commonality of symptoms. She further questions whether some may attempt to make the concept of complicated grief so broad that any experience of loss becomes complicated grief. Ultimately though, Russell suggests that therapy, support, and writing allowed her to stop avoiding acceptance of her father's death and her subsequent trauma.

Elisabeth Hanscombe causes us to consider how we should make sense of experiences that could effectively be viewed as a lifetime (or near lifetime) replete with events and circumstances that effectively cause complicated grief for individuals in chapter 8. Much of Hanscombe's narrative focuses on a pile-up of losses throughout her life: dysfunctional familial interactions, sexual abuse, and her dismissal from psychoanalytic training. Hanscombe contends that death need not precipitate a sense of complicated grief. Rather, multiple or continued losses can become so entrenched in one's life that they are effectively one and the same with one's lived experience. She further suggests, though, that such experiences help to define who we are and represent stories in need of telling, rather than disease in need of treatment.

Chapter Five

The Rhetoric of Grief
When a Loved One You Have Never Loved Is Dying

Mary Lynn Navarro

I hate him! I hate him! I hate him!" These words I shouted routinely as a child best sum up my childhood relationship with my older brother Jack. Yet when I found out that Jack was dying of cancer, I was stunned. Misdiagnosed for two years, Jack underwent surgery, which revealed that the disease had already spread to the lymph nodes and the liver. Given a terminal prognosis, he survived for one more year but died a month before the wedding of his daughter, Meghan, whom he had hoped to be able to walk down the aisle.

Had he even made it that far, he would have been too frail, though his dire condition was kept secret until nearly the end. Jack did not tell me that he was dying. I was at my café when I received the call from my brother Michael, who, over a scratchy cell phone, broke the news with such sublime simplicity it sent shock waves. The truth served up coldly is the most impressive. Yet as sad as I was to hear this, contrasting emotions—one frozen cold, another heartbroken—only obscured my guilt and shame about how much I had hated Jack throughout and beyond childhood. I had long given up thinking that eventually we would warm up to each other like the toasty warm TV commercials we grew up watching, life imitating artifice. I knew if I were going to have any kind of conversation before he passed, I would have to be the one to make initial contact. The only other time in my life I telephoned him was when I implored him to sign the do-not-resuscitate order for our father, who was brain dead. Jack resisted on religious grounds. Now it was Jack who was dying. I waited two full weeks after hearing the news just to phone him, risking that he might pass at any moment. When I finally did call, only in an awkward moment did he mention that his chances for recovery were nil. We talked as if it were the beginning of what could have been our relationship. I visited him once at his home—he was already enfeebled—then at the hospital right before he died.

My parents raised us to be stoical, withhold all emotion, and put up a good appearance, no matter the reality. As children of the Great Depression, my father—a World War II Marine veteran—and my mother—born in Greenwich Village in a close-knit Irish community—both envisioned a picture-perfect family and strived to uphold that image. They had met on a beach in Staten Island, where my father was a lifeguard, and when they were young, people said that their lives were charmed. The perfect couple, they epitomized the modern American family of the mid 20th century and looked model perfect, both of them. Dad was tall, broad, and handsome with a light brown complexion, almond eyes, and a wide smile. Mom was a brown-haired, blue-eyed natural beauty. Both loved each other dearly.

My father got his first job as a lineman the New York Telephone Company, "Ma Bell," and worked his way up the corporate ladder by attending Brooklyn College part-time at night. He was a diligent worker, and continuous promotions resulted in a senior management position. He refused all offers, including a lucrative one to install telephony in Saudi Arabia that would have raised our living standard; instead, we stayed in our same home in Midland Beach. More blue collar than white, where modest homes lined one side of town and summer shacks left over from the 1940s resort era lined the other poorer side, this mixed community defied social mobility. Our town confronted major drug traffic after the Verrazano bridge was built, connecting more worlds than imagined. The 1960s and 1970s saw many neighborhood youths embroiled in drugs and petty crime, culminating in early deaths and tragedy.

Mom, with her work as a Catholic religion volunteer teacher, and Dad with his severe authority, together invoked strict rules, religiosity, and swift punishments to keep us in line. But they were also community givers: Mom volunteered for anything she could and, after Dad's retirement, she became his secretary to help him achieve the impossible, the completion of a new community center for our fractured neighborhood. In short, they were our role models and raised us in the best way they knew.

My father was also ingenious. Before I was born, he spotted a house in a 1957 Sears catalogue, as a do-it-yourself kit, and envisioned its possibilities. The house was shipped in pieces with instructions, and Dad swiftly built our home. By himself, he dug a huge hole that became our built-in pool;

he constructed the deck and planted a garden. And for his entire life he was always building something new, tearing something down; kitchen renovations, a closet turned into a bedroom and then a bathroom, and a tacked-on back porch are a few examples. Our house—like our family, in a way—was perennially unfinished. He rigged electricity with copper telephone wire that I liked to make into jewelry. Dad got the latest telephone models and devised a room-to-room intercom system that never quite worked and was laughable, considering that we all were within an earshot of each other. Our TV room—or den, as my father referred to it—was a small room, with a bookshelf mostly housing his books on World War II, and two recliner chairs with a little space in between to squeeze in one small person, and that TV.

My father captured the early years of family life though photographic slides; our childhood was splendidly rendered in Kodachrome. The carousel clicked, flashing each picture of our growing-up years: birthdays, family cookouts, First Communions and graduations, summers at Lavallette, New Jersey. Each season, new imprints. Our American Dream was a composite of those constructed images, and in time, both the images and the dream warped. After we grew up, the carousel became a broken piece of obsolete equipment; the slides faded and corroded. The accumulated images of those years, kept in a box in the basement of (ironically) Jack's house, were all thrown out. Only in my memory do they exist. I try to outline our figures; I see the negatives. I review the images, filling in the Kodak color, reconstructing our shapes: me skinny, Mike small, Jack big, and Robert the baby.

As with many of our generation, the American Dream was defined by the influence of TV shows and commercials. Pop-Tarts began our day, Skippy peanut butter in the middle, and evenings with Shake 'N Bake chicken, topped off with Devil Dogs or Sara Lee. My mother, a convenience-is-everything cook, faltered on nutrition, but to our delight, we swallowed the American Dream whole, happy for a few short years. Struggling to be generous, our parents filled Christmas with things wanted and not always needed, until the day my mother said, "You know, Santa Claus is not free. We have to pay him." And thus I prayed to God to get Santa Claus to cut my mother a fair deal.

TV shows like "Father Knows Best," "The Donna Reed Show," and "Leave It to Beaver" depicted the "perfect" nuclear family, and our parents bought into the corny, fake reality. After our childhood years, they were deeply disappointed that we children were all so removed from their efforts to be what they saw in those photos and the TV life we learned to pretend to have. Appearances were everything; thoughts and feelings had no place in our home.

Jack was perhaps the only one of the family that I never pretended to love, and with whom I never put on the "we're the perfect children" show for my parents. Simply put, Jack hated me from the start. It is not only me who has said that; everyone in the family joked about it. One of the old photos shows me as an infant in my mother's arms and Jack, at five years old, making one his scrunched, angry faces at me; he was my personal torturer from the beginning. My family, by their complicity with his cruelty, all assumed the roles of "perpetrator, accomplice, bystander" (Herman, 1997, p. 217).

Jack and I were not responsible for our shattered relationship. We children, from parents who scripted specific roles and established a social hierarchy, were born to realize the parents' dreams, to become the badge of their success that hid deep insecurities and fears. Threatened by my individuality, they made every effort to quash it. Jack inadvertently assisted them. I needed to write about this!

I am a teacher of composition-rhetoric and I have taught a variety of classes; one writing course involves self-exploration and psychological healing. Writing would lead to a new understanding about the complicated relationship with Jack, I thought. However, in exposing the ugly side of our family life, I violated my parents' fierce code of silence. Nevertheless, this process was long overdue. It was difficult to write. What I preached to my students about the liberating and healing experience proved to be an onerous weight.

My students have lifted themselves from their "heavy weights." As I struggled, I reread some of their work: 16-year-old Josmine blamed her mother's untimely death on her neglectful father. In writing through her pain, she produced a book of poetry that transported her to another place of consciousness and acceptance. After witnessing his friend's murder, Dezo wrote a play exploring gang violence, and Pane wrote poetry. I have also taught adult students who write narrative essays called "My Turning Point," a topic that explores harrowing ordeals that have led to transformation and growth. HIV/AIDS, drug use and rehabilitation, mental suffering, wrongful incarceration, and racism are not just abstract phenomena; they all happen to people with faces and names. In naming your pain, telling a story as a "healing narrative" (DeSalvo, 1992), you can honor, "pain, loss and grief" (DeSalvo, 1999). Recently, one of my former students contacted me to thank me; he completed a memoir that began with the "My Turning Point" assignment.

Witing to heal can address trauma (Herman, 1997), but writing for a "cure" can be antithetical to discovery and truth. As the Greek word *pharmakon* suggests, writing might indeed be a healer of emotional ills, but one that poisons as it purges (Neel, 1988). In Greek, the meaning of *pharmakon* is quite complex and includes narcotic, charm, curse, and seducer. I wanted to write from the heart, and also utilize my knowledge of rhetoric. I considered deeply the following questions: Is there a rhetoric of pain, an actual emotional, psychological, or affective state that does not merely arise from words but is actually embedded within syntax and semantics? Conversely, could there also be a pathological state of grief that a person experiences with no relief, for which there are either no words or only a *pharmakon*? Given both scenarios, how is it possible then to liberate grief through language and rhetoric?

Writing through Grief: My Backward History with Jack

Never revealing that his cancer was terminal, Jack emulated my father, who also never discussed the gravity of his illness. Jack accepted his misfortune—the life before him cut short. When I saw him for the last time at Memorial Sloan-Kettering, where the nurses assured us, "We are only making him comfortable now," Jack appeared in control of his emotional state. He thanked the doctors, nurses, and aides, and after receiving last rites, the priest. My curiosity as to the nature of the experience of death, which was stronger than any love for one another, was a callous thought, I know. I wanted to ask Jack if he saw "death at the gate," opening as he lay in wait. (Any visions? Mom or Dad ready to embrace you? Jesus, even … ?). I remained silent as I watched. In cruel honesty I have to say that I shed more tears over the death of my beloved cat, Pasha, than I did for Jack. But if had had time alone with him, could I ever have confronted him? Probably not. I'd have done the same thing—remain silent.

I was a silent invader. There I was to witness the most intimate of moments with Jack's family: his girls, not mine, for I had long given up feeling that any of his were mine. This humiliating intimacy permitted me to see what people share at the time of death, people who, in this case, happened to be related to me. I watched Sheila, Jack's wife, tending to him as if by her power of will; she too, had acquiesced, and all was well. At one lucid moment, Jack whispered, "Lotta people here."

I was standing in front of Jack's gaze, really by accident, when his daughter, Katie broke down sobbing on my shoulder as I embraced her. His looked pierced me; I though he might just ask me, "Hey what the heck are *you* doing here, as if you belong?" But instead, "You watching the Yankees?" he eked out, weakly, almost inaudibly, totally throwing me off guard. Mike adjusted the TV to get the game on. "Yeah," I said, "the game hasn't yet started. Andy Pettitte is being interviewed. I think he's cute," I joked. A slight smile waned on Jack's lips. He looked at me—I hesitate to say—almost lovingly. This was not the Jack I grew up with.

Although now a fan, growing up with an older brother who dominated everything—including that one little rabbit-eared TV we had—I had no allegiance to the Yankees as a child. Jack always got what he wanted, and sports were a priority. He was an adorable child, with a wide smile punctuated by large dimples. I see a photo of him, from memory: a five-year-old driving a red-hot toy racing car, truly a Kodachrome color. His devilish smile says something like, "Get in my way and I'll run you down!"

In contrast, a pale, wan girl—all legs, arms, and a head that housed a really bad attitude—was what he had for a little sister. A photograph that I also see from memory is one of me in a puffy dress, my stick-straight hair curled into a head of miniature Slinkys; my mother was going for a Shirley Temple look but it got amped up. My dress, something akin to a wedding cake, has tiers of frills all held up underneath by rubber tubing—an inflatable slip—and its circumference was a circular tire. My mother blew this up. After an hour or so, the skirt would begin to deflate; my curls uncoiled as if by their own decision. My mother would pay attention to the slip, saying, "Come over here dear," and I knew I had to get reinflated. No matter where we were, she would lift my skirt and blow up that rubber tube. Besieged by my hair, she used chemical permanent-wave formula, but it ultimately burned whatever hair was left so that she had to cut it practically bald. As a "pixie" cut, it was a success; with both of us finally happy, she called it a day. Still, I learned what I was supposed to look like, not what I was, not as I was. It became a skill to negotiate the performance of the little "girlie girl" against my need for freedom. Inevitably, I learned to be female by these kinds of moments.

Jack learned how to be male in very different way. The stand-out memories of Jack all involve our fights, with me in tears running to my mother for help. "He's a boy," she'd say, "what do you expect?" I soon learned that boys were different from girls, not just by anatomy, but more like Freud's assertion that "anatomy is destiny." When I was relegated to washing dishes, I gave up asking about what he might be doing. Jack had full reign of the house, being the firstborn male—he reigned in his superiority. Film and linguistic theorist Kaja Silverman stated, in *The Subject of Semiotics* (1983),

> What is at issue … is not the female subject's biological inferiority, but
> her symbolic exclusion or lack—her isolation, that is, from those cultural
> privileges which define the male subject as potent and sufficient. (p. 142)

I experienced the symbolic and social order of male privilege. As a boy,
Jack had full permission to tease, taunt, and torture; in short, bully. Though
he pushed me around, Jack didn't need to be violent because his size, at five
years my senior, was overpowering. But I did. I recall the decisive moment
I had had enough; my mother was of no use to stop him, so I took matters
into my own hands. I took a big, wood handle brush and cracked the wood
side over his head with the intention to kill him. I then ran into my room,
locking my door, leaving his screams behind, and shaking from my own rage.
At that moment, our bitter enmity was sealed. I was seven.

"Hysterical," Jack called me, to which my father added, "and too
sensitive." My mother's response to whisk me to the church confessional
came with instructions: "Tell the priest you hate your brother." Confession,
between God, the sinner, and the priest only by proxy, was a disciplinary
means to a submissive end. Every Catholic school kid growing up during the
20th century learned about the chalked soul. Enter Sister Patrick: a medieval
tower, black-robed, face like crumpled paper, my first-grade instructor in
Fear. Frozen at our desks, hands folded, nary a peep, we watched as Sister
Patrick marked venial sins with the small spots of chalk marks on this amorphous circle, the soul. An unforgivable mortal sin was vigorously colored
along with the fire of eternity. Hell. To hate your own brother must surely be
more than just venial sin.

I hadn't yet murdered my brother (mortal sin), but hating him was close
enough to warrant the penance of one long rosary. Thus, I confessed the
same sins, my stock "sins on file." "Bless me father,". . . the confession goes.
"This week I had a fight with my brother, and I disobeyed my mother.
Once." Bored with the routine and certain that the priest must have been
even more bored, I'd alter once in a while to, "I lied to my mother. Once."
The truth was that the most lying I was doing was in the confessional. I
did, however, learn how to lie for the sake of appearances and swallow my
emotions in one big gulp. I dreamed of running away—where's that circus
when you need one?

Jack stayed at home until he was 27 and then got married. I left home
like a hurricane. He attended mass every Sunday, whereas I rejected my faith,
much to my mother's resistance. She once charged, "We did everything to
make you this way." I joke that I am now a practicing atheist, but few get it, so

then I have to say, I am a devout atheist. My parents found out I was ditching Sunday Mass when I came home once smelling of cigarette smoke, carrying a *New York Times.* I hung out until the mass was well over, and Mike and Jack ratted on me that I was nowhere near church. Many severe punishments followed. Again, the unfairness of my situation was clear: Jack could just show up for noon mass with a huge hangover and sleep through service, whereas I actually thought about the existence of God and acted upon my beliefs. He was free while I was jailed, though very lucky to have books to comfort me. Words. Sometimes I scrawled my feelings on paper; "bad poetry," I called it. I tore them to little pieces; I'd even burn them. My life, miserable until I left behind a clipped-winged life, needed new wings. But I kept at writing about it; I had no choice. I wrote about my own "wings of desire."

My status in the family did not improve with time, and I held bitterness toward Jack for his treatment of me, carrying our feud into full adulthood. He relished his power to still intimidate, embarrass, or offend me. "Stupid and weird" were words I got used to hearing. Steeling myself against his inevitable sarcasm, I ignored his existence. I would not even say hello to him at family gatherings and made sure to avoid any eye contact. When both my parents died rather suddenly, as executor of the will, Jack sold our parent's home, solidifying the deal with my other siblings, and never even told me. I then "outed" him to old friends as the bad brother. I subsequently felt really embarrassed. The truth was that Jack was still laughing behind my back, my outrage another indication of my "hysteria."

Yet all of this family melodrama played on my guilt as I watched Jack pass. If I hadn't seen it myself, I would never have believed that he could have left this earth so humbled. His arrogance, his sense of entitlement—all evaporating as his body withered—dissipated in front of me. At the end, it was as if I were already seeing a person more in the next world than this one, an ethereal, gentle being, completely vulnerable; his face sallow, yet awash in a glow, emanating like circles, like that of a stone thrown into a lake. A halo? This was definitely *not* the Jack I grew up with.

Deeper Learning, Deeper Healing

I discovered new truths about my childhood, but in all my writings, no relief was found; instead, grief endured. There was a sense of hopelessness; the lure of *pharmakon* persisted. I contemplated on these things: Language is a gift and our birthright, and it is an entirely, fully human experience. Words are what we have to name what it is that makes us ill, thereby giving our pain its own life and likewise its own release. I revised my questions: If words carry a marker of pain, can words release the pain from the somatic experience to become a heightened sense of understanding? How can one consciously use words to release pain and to begin healing? It is painful to think that I never loved my brother, but it is more painful to withhold the words both of love lost and deep disappointment, as if the unstated thoughts scab the raw, naked body of emotions. I clearly had some serious and deep thinking to do if I were to use language toward my own healing.

When I teach, I often ask students to go deep, think critically and write with the intention to awaken the intellect and the senses. Recently, I was reading about a concept called the *deeper learning principle* (Wickersham & McGee, 2008) that emphasizes thinking beyond critical analysis. Though this idea is not new, I thought about ways a fresher understanding of critical thinking could apply to the discovery of healing. As suggested by Weigel (2002), reflective thinking is an art, and one learns by tapping into the reservoir of curiosity and setting a course for discovery. This comes with risk. Playing it safe through denial, escapism, delusion, and holding onto false consciousness for the sake of being comfortable is not healing; rather, it perpetuates grief and sickness. In digging deep for the truth and telling it boldly, writing in earnest, *pharmakon*, that poisons as it purges, is facing painful truth. As we live with the pain, let it sit in the body and not try to 'fix' it right away, or at all, we let our deeper thinking guide our emotion, a fusing of an affective state with intellect.

Anderson, in interpreting Lacan, states that as a result, we are "in a constant state of being victimized by the other, whose discourse creates positions and controls our subjectivity" (2000, p. 60). To use this analogy in my own life, I can assert that my hatred for Jack was a discursive position that could be attained by only difference; for example, Jack as the masculine subject versus me as the feminine object, both socially circumscribed discursive positions of power. But entering into discourse is our deepest desire for meaning, so much so that "we will take it at any price, even with the fullest knowledge of what it entails—passive assertions into pre-existing discursive positions ... threatened losses and false recoveries and subordination" (Silverman, 1983, p. 199; see also Anderson, 2000, p. 61).

Jack didn't ask for privilege, and he was never instructed to behave otherwise or to cherish a sister, especially when he, in his own development as a male, learned his behavior from the father figure, the patriarchal symbol of socially constructed power. Moreover, if Jack had been mean to me, I was mean back. I was mean to other children, even a bully at one point; I exacted similar justice on others as my father had exacted on me. I learned subservience, but I thus also learned aggression and power. Our most painful lessons are often learned from those who are supposed to love us: our family. Jack, the quiet, church-going, good-looking boy who also excelled at school (he was skipped a class level, considered superior in intelligence) secured their beliefs, whereas a female who rebelled, asserted her own ideas, and rejected their ways was clearly a threat. And thus they allowed this power play; they staged it themselves. If they thought that Jack was a safer bet than I, they were surely wrong. For Jack was never really close to anyone, never really communicated, cruelly made fun of people who suffered, and had a sarcastic laugh that was not reserved just for me. He was socially awkward and only really engaged in conversation about sports, but he was a "genius" at his job. To my parents, Jack looked good, and that's what counted. Honestly, knowing what I do now, I think he might have been on the autism spectrum.

In thinking more deeply about Jack, I came around to the memory of my baby brother, Robert, who died as an infant when I was about seven years old. I had a "eureka" moment about how the loss affected my parents, and I realized that his death made them become even more overly protective, angry, and stifling. They suppressed our grief, as well; they forbid it. To this day, thinking about Robert ushers in feelings of utter sadness.

Quite unexpectedly, my brother Michael, who had no idea that I was writing about any of this no less thinking about Robert, broached the subject of Robert's death. Michael and I, a year apart in age—like twins really—had drifted apart, but we have never forgotten our childhood bond that was sealed by Robert's death. In this conversation, Mike confirmed the feelings: "You got the worst of it." But he also suggested what I had never dared to mention. Michael explained that my mother might have blamed me, especially, for Robert's death, not consciously, of course. As she enabled Jack to be mean spirited, she condoned his behavior.

The impact of Jack's death penetrated into my deepest memories of Robert's death. The baby was sleeping in his stroller. I was minding him when I saw that the entire left side of his face had turned blue. Our neighbor, a fireman, was immediately summoned and tried to resuscitate him, but he had suffocated and was already dead. My feeling for that baby brother, the first sibling whose death I experienced, cast new light on complicated grief. I loved that baby with all my being.

Michael reminded me also that our mother had sternly warned us not to cry at the funeral mass for Robert. She said, do not embarrass us, Mike emphasized; remarkably, we did as she had ordered, like little toy soldiers. Embarrassment was what she cared about! I imagined horrible things happening to my family, all of them dying in a car accident, leaving me alone and happy without them. I fantasized drowning my father in the bathroom sink, an incredible shrinking man swallowed by the drain. Funny now, but horrific then.

We never communicated directly but read into each other's thoughts and responded in ways that eluded words, a hidden kinetic language, stripped of emotion. The wooden brush incident was a breaking point. Within the parameters of the social and symbolic order, I acted out on what was wrong in me. The confessional became the punishment and cure for the stigma of being different. Confessing also keeps the stigma alive as much as it is supposed to cure it. The stigma reveals shame through its mark, a permanent scarlet letter tattooed on one's psyche. Mine was on the soul.

Jack's discursive agency, as the firstborn male, though clearly privileged came with its own encompassed codes of silence, learned from my father, passed as silently as his bond. Dad never knew his true heritage or discussed his shame. Born to an Italian unwed teenage mother, he never once saw his father—said to be a Spanish merchant marine—but we never talked about any of that. (I dug for records; whatever the case, it's still a mystery.) Jack's discourse embodied all the silence that I railed against by my rage, and now through writing, knowingly breaking the codes around family secrecy; in this way we were diametrically and discursively polar opposites.

Anderson et al. (2000) discussed discourse that controls, violates, and silences. Through our stories, sites of pain, longing, confusion, and loss become the symbolic strands that connect memory and being with the "larger web of human experience" (p. 61). I too felt that my sense of self was suffocated, silenced, but I would not be annihilated. I wasn't going away quietly. "The symbolic strands," the words we reach out for, connect us to pain, loss, and recovery. One must participate in life by growing, receding, stepping out again to risk loss and failure, breaking down, stitching up life's pieces and moving on, a process Anderson et al. (2000) described as "suturing," in applying a complex theory of Jacques Lacan. Simply put, we identify ourselves through discourse by "fastening" ourselves in the subject position, creating a "discursive" self, for example, as in identifying with the protagonist of a story. A writer can create many discursive selves as subjects, either in fiction, nonfiction, or any genre. "[O]ne discursive self might intentionally work on another ... to bring into being ... a subjectivity capable of healing itself by ordering, transforming and fully overcoming stigma" (p. 77).

So through writing out these "discursive selves" in the family, all the roles we played, I used a healing principle. "New wings" was the image and metaphor I had always retained in my mind and released through my writing, freeing myself of past dogma and dictates. Trying to heal complicated grief encompasses a range of modalities and professional treatment. But I am convinced that using writing and metaphor can assist on many levels. Naming gives value to the pain, the stigma, and therefore, gives value to your life. Lakoff and Johnson (1980), in their iconic work, *Metaphors We Live By,* stated, "[M]etaphor is pervasive in everyday life, not just in language but in thought and action. ... Our concepts structure what we perceive, how we get around in the world, and how we relate to other people" (p. 3).

Psychotherapist and educator Lefki Lolis, both in her own life and in her counseling practice, uses metaphor as a powerful tool. She states, "Once you articulate the feeling of grief, name it, and consciously transport it from the somatic experience to new level of consciousness, it opens a pathway for healing." Usually, one will uncover other related emotions underlining complicated grief. For example, I discovered that guilt, shame, and anger were at the core of my feelings. I entered into the site of pain—guilt, shame, anger—I can feel that pain in my body. When able to endure pain, one connects the mind to the body through the metaphor. Because the metaphor provides an image that is attached to feeling and in language, it is then marked in syntax and semantics. Linguistically, as language moves us in thought to communication, we can experience movement from the site of pain.

A victim of a near-fatal accident, Lolis put her shattered life back to together slowly. As she worked on her own physical, mental, and emotional rehabilitation, she began to write to heal herself. Her complicated grief is recognizing that the life she lost was her own. A young woman, on the path of a successful life, Lolis lost it all and forced herself to build a new life and purpose for living. Her poem from her work, *Journey through Time: Emotional Change through Healing Metaphors* (Lolis, 2012) captures this:

Escaping into Monet's Water Lilies

Running to escape the fears from the pain, there is no salvation from this moment's reality. Is there an escape? Can anyone help? Is there anywhere to run to? Of course the edge of insanity knocks on my shoulder inviting me into a tornado where a world of darkness is only an insult upon the heartfelt pains and injuries. Can you hear me God? And right as the answer was coming there I was floating into the scene of water lilies of Claude Monet. The path of water lilies leads to a world that is serene.

> Peaceful and magical filled with healing colors of azure blue earth
> tone greens, pretty dark pinks and water lilies surrounded by slow moving
> cool water. Details aren't important—only lilies in water huge puffy white
> clouds and there I am surrounded by nature enveloping itself around me.
> Soft, serene nature sounds remind me of the peace my body can heal with.
> As I lie there I think back…. what was it you were telling me Dear God?

Lolis explained in conversation that "movement comes from within.
Once the mental image is in place, you can make a shift in consciousness.
You can use the metaphor to take yourself to a new place. The pain may not
go away—and may never go away—but you can choose to work with it and
become free."

Although I had worked with students, I was not wont to attempt poetry;
it is not my forte. Lolis affirmed that being a good poet is not necessary
for writing poetry and healing metaphors, and believes that we all tap into
collective unconscious when we experience pain. I see this as the universal
experience of life, what we all share in humanity. One metaphor I use is a
wall of ice. I see the big ice cube on Jack's eye and forehead where I had
pummeled him with the brush, wrapped in a cloth that my mother applied.
That ice formed the beginning of that wall, a solid-as-brick ice wall that
separated me from my family. Ice can be a protection, too. But now my
purpose has deepened, to remove protection to feel the pain in order to heal,
and to determine whether writing this piece presents such opportunity. I
chose the title of this chapter deliberately. The phrase "a loved one" is ironic.
It is the standard one refers to when thinking of a family member. Yet Jack
and I were never loved ones to each other. Jack was never truly close to
anyone, except, I think, his daughters.

The love Jack had for his daughters and they had for him filled the
hospital room at the last moments of his life. "I love you, Dad." I bore witness
to words I could never say to Jack. Jack gave a slight nod. Sheila said, "Jack,
Chrissy just said she loves you, tell her you love her back." Jack nodded his
head, but he did not say the words. He could not. "Well, that's all you're gonna
get Chris," said Sheila. We all laughed while entrenched in a painful end.

This surreal moment is now memory, and I sit with metaphors, meaning
connected to image, to feeling, to idea, to enlightening—could the wall of ice
turn into melted floes? I thought about writing a letter to Jack, one he'd never
read of course, like a school assignment. But what came was comic relief,
something like, "Dear Jack, I'm sorry for trying to kill you with that hard
brush…. The rest is history." Switching gears entirely, I turned to art, images I

love to look at. I began with an image of a nonspecific Mondrian painting—color blocks of red and blue. There was no logic to this; I just had the image of Jack when he was little, in that photo of him in the red car. So that image became a metaphor. Robert was soft and blue; that's what I connected to him. I began a poem "prototype." I started it with an image of blue and red:

> A poem for two brothers
> One—a tiny little ball dropped into my lap
> Bright and blue, soft as a pillow
> Blue from the sky
> Blue from his eyes
> Blue in rays in his face/ sad blue
> The other is
> red and hard. Stands above me then beneath
> Hammered with a brush with death
> Always in some other plane of existence

This was just a beginning. It gave me no sense of healing or resolution, so I worked with the images more and found myself back at the "deeper thinking" stage all over again. I asked myself: Can Jack or I be blamed for the lack of words over the years, or any of what happened to us as kids? He was not my loved one, but his family deeply loved him. In was what was to be my last conversation with Jack, three weeks before he passed, I said more to him than then I had in all our years. I actually told him about my life, and he listened and responded, no sarcasm, but encouragement and real happiness for my success. Still no emotional outpouring; nothing could be fixed. I wrestled with the question of Robert. Robert became an object of love that I craved; throughout these years, I had thought of him as belonging to me. The truth is this: a little loveable being died, and I was stuck with two brothers—one who abandoned me and the Other. For forgiveness and recovery, I needed to see that the love I felt for Robert was real but was displaced love, for the lack of acceptance from Jack and all my family. Could I come to love Jack in this way?

I had a dream. Jack was in a business suit, carrying a briefcase, walking by smiling. He looked like an Escher, man against a surreal blue sky. He smiled lovingly. I revised my poem with this image. I admitted that writing bad poetry was not fulfilling. Lolis advised me to work more explicitly with what I feel as I compose: the *healing* metaphor. So I wrote with the sense of happiness I found in my dream, still keeping the Mondrian:

Two Brothers/ Red and Blue

One, a tiny ball
Dropped from azure skies
into my lap
Supple little pillow
—blue
soft, sad, true blue

bundled in endless ribbons/joy flowed
tethered to me, longing to cherish to love to
protect you.
Severed from me,
My soul, a wound
you left/ribbons afloat, billowing air
rising to source,
back to blue.

The other/ mean/
Red/hard. Stands above then
hammered by a brush with death.
—below
Rage
Sore loser red, no love of you
Searing red
But what might have been—crimson red

But then again, in kodachrome
Funny, these memories of red
Enliven you
the dimpled smile, daredevil
in your hotrod racing car red
Speeding past all that was gifted to you.
—And is it really true
you'd run me down?

Little prince, who knew you found your way in life
family love
a blush of rose,
halo light
Surrounding you in your honor, their devotion
—I never knew…

> I saw you
> in my dream last night
> you walked by me, suitcase in hand,
> your smile big as sky
> back to blue
> as you passed by
>
> Waving your hand
> Illumined in azure
> perhaps you wanted to say
> Goodbye
> or hello?
> Or a silent smile only
> as my dreams paint
>
> You both
>
> in kodachrome
> landscapes of indigo

Somehow it still feels unfinished, for now, perhaps forever, but it renders a greater truth. Truth does not, however, conclude with a metaphor. The search for truth, the examination of discourse, the entrance into deeper thinking and deeper healing is ongoing. I don't love the poem, the staccato sound, the clipped language, like my wings! I do, however, like the way I feel when I read it—peace, closure with Robert—and for Jack? Well, that will remain as it is.

References

Anderson, C. M. (with Holt, K., & McGady, M.). (2000). Suture, stigma and the pages that heal. In C. M. Anderson & M. M. MacCurdy (Eds.), *Writing and healing: Toward an informed practice* (pp. 58–82). Urbana, IL: NCTE.

DeSalvo, L. (1999). *Writing as a way of healing: How telling our stories transforms our lives*. Boston: Beacon Press.

Herman, J. (1997). *Trauma and recovery: The aftermath of violence—from domestic abuse to political terror*. New York: Basic Books.

Lakoff, G., & Johnson, M. (1980). *Metaphors we live by*. Chicago: University of Chicago Press.

Lolis, L. (2012). *Journey through time: Emotional change through healing metaphors.* Unpublished manuscript.

Neel, J. (1988). *Plato, Derrida, and writing.* Carbondale: Southern Illinois University Press.

Silverman, K. (1983). *The subject of semiotics.* New York: Oxford University Press.

Weigel, V. B. (2002). *Deep learning for a digital age: Technology's untapped potential to reach higher education.* San Francisco: Jossey-Bass.

Wickersham, L. E., & McGee, P. (2008). Perceptions of satisfaction and deeper learning in an online course. *Quarterly Review of Distance Education, 9*(1), 73–83.

Chapter Six

Luvandwar and Letting Go

Rose Richards

Introduction

Grief is complicated, especially when one is mourning the death of a parent. My mother died unexpectedly and in front of me in February 1998, in the wake of years of medical crises, financial crises, and family deaths. I was 28; she was 59. In the years that followed, I had to work through many emotions about her life and death. These included shock, horror, despair, powerlessness, rage, guilt (at my newfound freedom, at my sense of responsibility), sorrow, and fear. After her death, I had to cope with being left financially vulnerable after a lengthy, serious illness of my own. Also, after my mother's death, my immediate family was gone. I still have relatives, but I no longer have a family, and I have never attempted to form one of my own.

As the only other person present when my mother died, I blamed myself for her death for a long time until I discovered that the forensic doctor who handled her case did not blame me and that my mother had a terminal medical condition that she knew about but had not discussed with me. That was when the full force of my fury erupted. I wrote about my grief and its socially unacceptable associated states in a short story and in journals. I talked about it with friends. But it took me 10 years to scatter her ashes. Even now, years later, I find it hard to remember my mother with love and appreciation. In some ways, I feel I have never recovered from the abandonment, betrayal, and financial mess. I have never moved, literally or symbolically, from the house we shared.

In writing this chapter, I have a renewed appreciation for how complicated grief can be. I set out in my twenties to describe my own grief reactions at the unexpected and untimely death of my mother. Thirteen years later, I returned to my story to write this chapter, and I found as I wrote the narrative parts of it that I was mourning not only her death, but a whole series of deaths, some of them metaphorical. And I noticed that my family has a strange way of dealing with grief: We never talk about it. Our unresolved grief goes back generations, and each fresh episode of loss adds another layer to our familial bereavement.

Most of this chapter takes the form of narrative fragments, written in different periods in my life after my mother's death. Arranging the chapter like this allowed me to see changes and patterns. It also made me see some reasons for the complicated nature of my grief. The length of the pieces included here corresponds to the intensity of the experiences. They are also not chronologically arranged. Grief shatters things, and one of those things is one's experience of time. Sometimes the past seems more real than the present. Sometimes, certain events that were quite short seem to last a very long time, especially if one relives them over and over or if they were intensely painful. Some events are forgotten completely and others recalled in agonizing detail. Some events recall other events to which they at first appear unrelated.

After the narrative sections, I draw together some of the themes and briefly discuss them in the context of some of the research into complicated grief and strengths-based work. I do not think complicated grief should necessarily be viewed as a mental illness. Instead, I have found that it may be the reasonable reaction to extraordinary circumstances. In my case, I see it as a struggle with the meaning of a lengthy series of profound losses and with unhelpful familial patterns of learned behavior concerning grief. Despite my best efforts to move on and not dwell on the past, I had few resources for behaving differently. My intention is that the following bits of narrative will explain my ambivalence about being identified as suffering from complicated grief. After all, is a normal reaction to an abnormal situation a disorder, or is it an attempt to reorder a shattered world?

The Diary of Luvandwar

A year after my mother's death, I wrote a short story called "Luvandwar" in the hope of being able finish my exhausting grieving process and move on. The following is part of the ending:

> I see angels where I used to see spaces, but not wearing curls and frilly nightdresses. My angels' lion faces are ringed with fire, and their wings are ardent flame. Their pugmarks are around my heart. They soar incandescent in the face of luvandwar and the word that roars out of their furnace hearts

is not 'reconciliation.' It is resurrection. Lightning claws the sky open. The hidden stars fall down as icy meteors of rain. (Richards, 1999, p. 35)

I should have realized that my story had not achieved the therapeutic goal for which I had longed. It was packed with cataclysmic, not to say apocalyptic, imagery, and anyone who read it commented on how sad it made them feel.

But I could not then afford to see that it was not about the cathartic experience of resolving grief so much as the need to memorialize the grief and to contain it. In some senses, the story, far from ending, had only just begun. In the following 13 years I attempted to work through and shrug off the grief that continued to haunt me, by writing, by talking, by clutter-clearing, by symbolic gestures. I was only ever partly successful, and I find myself perturbed that although I have worked so hard on this for so long, I am still in many ways literally and figuratively where I started: living in her house and sleeping in her bed.

June 27, 2011: *The Present Day*

I am tired. I have been fighting for almost a year to get medical and legal assistance to a woman who, like me, has undergone kidney failure and transplantation. Unlike me, she has lost her transplant and is too poor to afford medical insurance. I am doing this because this woman needs help and because she has the same medical condition as me. Something, like a half-forgotten dream, nags at me as I drive home on a crisp and sunny winter's evening. Traffic is relatively quiet because of the school and university holidays, and this gives me time to think.

I am driving down the main road of my hometown when I suddenly realize something, and the realization is so painful that it brings tears to my eyes. My fellow transplant recipient is not the only person I have ever tried to save. Of course she isn't. How did I manage to block this memory out?

I know *why* I blocked it out. I desperately want to put it behind me and move on. I want very badly to get over it. And 13 years later, I suspect that I never shall.

February 6, 1998: *The Day My Mother Died*

It is a hot, smoky summer evening. The weather is so hot that the milk has gone sour in the fridge, and along the roadside dry fynbos spontaneously catches alight. The mountain behind us is burning, and it smells as if something is burning in our street. For some reason, my mother has cooked fried chicken livers in peri-peri sauce for supper. They are incredibly rich. Sitting at the stinkwood dining room table, she and I eat all of them and sop up the sauce with white rice. We are barefoot and sweating in our T-shirts and cotton trousers.

We fought all morning before I went to work about something silly. It was really a power struggle. I am growing up belatedly since my transplant, and my mother is afraid of that. She is used to my being ill and vulnerable, dependent on her for everything. She does not know what will become of her when I am gone. She also fears I will not be able to look after myself and will die, leaving her bereft. She cannot bear either of these options. She phoned me at work to make amends, but she pretended she was checking on what I had planned for lunch.

For some reason, this evening while she's watching her soap opera before she starts cooking supper, I come up to her as she sits on the couch and tell her I'm sorry for the mean things I said this morning. We are not in the habit of apologizing. She waves off my apology and says it's not necessary, before returning to the nefarious doings of the glamorous. She likes a good story.

After supper, she washes up and we sit on the couch to watch the news at eight. She prefers the English news, so we watch that. At about a quarter past eight she complains of having a tight chest and asks me to fetch her Ventolin spray and her cortisone inhaler. I bring them to her quickly. I wish she'd take better care of her asthma. She's had several crises in the last few years and has refused to be hospitalized. I am also convinced that she doesn't take her medication as regularly as she should. In fact she's doing exactly what her younger brother did, what she always fought about with him—and made me swear I wouldn't do to her: she's neglecting her condition.

My mother loved her baby brother as much as she loved her own children. His early death from asthma left her shattered, so much so that she developed asthma herself, shortly afterwards, in her fifties. His death left me numb; I barely wept. He died when I was nearly dying myself, on dialysis, waiting for a transplant. He was only 18 years older than me and was like the elder brother I had always wanted. I had assumed he'd be there long after everyone else was gone. He died when I was 21, three weeks before my grandfather, with whom my mother, my brother, and I lived, after years of financial abuse by my father, after the acrimonious divorce, after we lost everything else: two homes, our social status, our social circle, our self-esteem.

Her inhalers are not working, and I feel a growing sense of panic and anger. Now I'll have to spend all night trying to convince her to go to hospital. The later we leave it, the less chance there will be that a neighbor can drive her there. Clearly, she can't drive herself. And I don't have a driving license because she won't let me practice driving in her car. She fears I will wreck it, and I can't afford driving lessons. She asks me to make her some hot black tea.

When I bring her the tea, she can barely swallow it. I tell her we must get her to hospital immediately. Naturally she argues with me, short of breath as she is. Then she grabs my arm and tells me her chest is getting tighter. I can't reach my neighbor by phone, so I have to go over to his house to tell him that we have an emergency, and he agrees to fetch his car out of the garage. I rush back to our house; I am going to save her.

June 27, 2011: *The Present Day*

Other than a stolen CD player, I have never managed to replace anything I have ever lost. It is not for want of trying. When something's gone, it's gone.

February 6, 1998: *The Day My Mother Died*

My mother died in the garden. She had tried to follow me out of the house and had collapsed at the garden gate. I found her barely breathing but no longer conscious. Our neighbor called the ambulance and other neighbors. Some of the men tried to move her so they could lift her into a car, but they could not. The ambulance came, and the paramedics worked on her. The neighbors prayed; I did not. As much as I wanted my mother to live, I knew at the age of 28 that if she did I would never be able to get away and have a life of my own. She barely let me out of her sight. I even had to watch TV with her, and I hated soap operas.

After my uncle's widow had moved to the Cape, we had left Johannesburg too and followed her. Mom had wanted to be near her nephews and the sea. I had wanted to stay in Johannesburg and get on with my life. I had a network of friends and associates working and studying in the same field as me. But she told me that if I did not come with her she would suffer and die on her own and it would be my fault. If I stayed I would deny her a last chance at happiness—and more to that effect. So I abandoned my life for her. And now this.

The paramedics were unable to revive her and pronounced her dead. I accompanied them to the hospital (I remember one of them was drinking Sprite Lite from a can with a straw), where the doctor on duty agreed that she was dead but refused to sign the death certificate because he could not determine the cause of death. The nurses flocked together whispering that they did not know what to do, as "Doctor" (they treated his title as a first name) would not sign it. Here they glanced surreptitiously at me. They seemed sympathetic and attempted to comfort me with hot milky tea and what appeared to be half a Valium. I declined it.

The doctor passed by occasionally. He did not approach me but scowled at me from a distance. He seemed angry with me, but I did not know why. "I don't even know how long she's been dead," he said loudly at some point, staring at me from across the emergency room. Why didn't he ask me? Or why not ask the paramedics? She had died while they were working on her. The nurses covered her with a blanket that was too short and did not extend over her face. I moved it up and it exposed her bare, dusty feet. They pulled it down; I pulled it up. And so it went on until my aunt arrived to take me home. When I started calling relatives to tell them the news, my nose started bleeding. I hadn't had a nosebleed in years.

February 7, 1998: *The Day After*

A friend's father, who lived in the area, took me to the funeral parlor to arrange the funeral. I did not have enough money even to pay for a coffin, and the death certificate still had to be signed. I wasn't sure we were allowed to bury her without one and worried about what to do next. My elder uncle offered to pay for the funeral. It turned out that because the doctor refused to sign the death certificate, there had to be a police inquest into her death. The police interviewed me at the funeral parlor. My friend's father thought this would be better because it would not make the neighbors uncomfortable.

I had to give the police a statement explaining what had happened, and they asked me more questions. Their questions seemed to concern whether or not I had anything to do with her death. I told them several times how I had tried to fetch help. I wondered how long I'd go to prison for if I was found guilty of matricide. I could not afford a lawyer. I wondered if I would be able to get my transplant medication in prison and how long I could survive without it. Eventually I asked the inspector if he thought I was guilty of killing my mother. He said he did not. I hoped his point of view counted for something.

February 8, 1998: *And the Day After That*

A close relative arrived and so, fortunately, did a school friend from Johannesburg. The relative was a medical student and had done a CPR course. He made me tell him over and over again what had happened on the night my mother died. At last he started screaming at me, red in the face, that I had let her die and that I could have saved her. He shouted so loudly that my friend came out of the house to see what was going on and swept me back inside, locking him out to rant at us through the windows that I should have done CPR on Mom.

The relative refused to help with any of the funeral arrangements or to help notify any of my mother's friends or relatives. He wouldn't even stay to sort through her belongings and decide what to do with them. He said he was too upset. So I took care of everything.

June 1998: *Some Months Later*

I was not arrested for matricide or sent to prison. The police investigation showed I was not responsible for my mother's death. The forensic report described a massive heart attack. Now people started saying those cheery things that they tend to reserve for the bereaved: you'll get over it, that's life, I am sure she would have wanted it this way, perhaps it's all for the best, and so on. Friends lectured me on taking care of myself and not blaming myself for what I could not control. I still felt responsible for her death, however. Eventually, I hunted down the name and contact number of the doctor who had done the postmortem and insisted he tell me everything, although I had read the report.

He told me that I was not to blame myself for her death and that she died almost instantly. His elderly mother had done the same, and he—a doctor with years of experience—had not been able to save her, so he would never have expected me to have saved my mother. He even said it was better that she had not survived because the damage to her system would have been immense. I told my relative, but he refused to discuss it with me.

June 1998 to December 2000: *The Next Couple of Years*

For months after my mother's death, I would wake in a panic at four in the morning, unable to breathe. I became convinced that I was dying. It took me eight months before I could face Friday evenings at eight thirty again without a creeping feeling of dread and helplessness. It was so bad that I used to start pacing without being aware of what I was doing. My whole body would go stiff, and my legs would just start walking and walking and walking. I couldn't stop it. For two years, I made sure I worked the Friday evening shift at the bookshop every single week, so I didn't have to be home where she'd died at that time.

My guilt, loss, pain, and fear possessed me, but these feelings were gradually replaced by a burning fury at the predicament in which I found myself: marooned and barely employed in a foreign part of the country, with an estate to settle, debts to pay, and secrets to cope with. The secrets were worse than everything else put together. Among other things, it turned out that my mother had known for some time that she had a terminal heart condition. She had told none of the remaining family members nor her friends. This did not make up for her not telling me.

Somewhere in the middle of this I began trying to purge myself of the overwhelming sadness and loss that had taken possession of me. Purging myself of what had happened became a project that was to preoccupy me for many years, but I did not know it then. At the time, I thought it would be over within a year and I could move forward. I also did not realize that purging has punitive connotations.

I decided to finish sorting out her possessions. I could not bring myself to part with them, and so I put them into boxes, at first in her old bedroom and then in the outbuilding. I was saddened to find that in every single drawer and every shelf she had secreted away a small memento of her own mother, who had died in 1980. I had not known she had kept those old plastic curlers, nylon-bristled hairbrushes, embroidered handkerchiefs, and silk pincushions. It did not seem to bode well for my own bereavement. I couldn't help recall that my maternal grandmother herself had wept every anniversary of her own father's death. He died in 1946. I was born in 1969, and I could remember her grief clearly. At the time my mother died, she had hung my great-grandparents' photographs up at her bedroom door so she could see them every night before she went to bed. I took them down and hung them in the passage where I could see them all the time, especially my great-grandfather. I had never met the man, but he had been so much part of my life that I could not bear to part with him.

I wrote a story about my mother's death and what I hoped for my new life without her. I found it very cathartic. It was meant to set me free.

2000 to 2007: *The Years That Followed*

I started a new job at a university, and it kept me very busy. I scarcely had time to sort through my mother's clothing and other belongings, let alone inhabit my inner life. Every 18 months or so, I would sort out the spare room (where some of her things had mysteriously returned) and unpack the boxes in the outbuilding, in the hope of finally finishing what I had started in 1998. All this rearranging took a lot of time and energy. I didn't feel I achieved much, but I would congratulate myself on my small successes on letting go of an old garment or keepsake.

Then I discovered the wonderfulness of donating to charities. That made my actions feel less like throwing my mother in the dustbin. A whole lot of her peach and ivory striped towels went to Animal Welfare. I took boxes of old clothing and her beautiful shoes to the Hospice shop and Bargain Box charity shop. As much as it ripped at my heart, I felt I was making progress at last.

February 6, 2008: *The 10th Anniversary of My Mother's Death*

I scattered my mother's ashes today. It has taken me 10 years to reach this point, where I could take the ashes out of the bottom left drawer of my desk (where I hid them years ago so I didn't have to be confronted with them constantly) and go out to a point along the Cape coast to scatter them in the sea. I never wanted to keep them, and Mom never wanted them kept either. She told me when discussing how she wanted her funeral to be, that she did not want to be "trapped in a box in the ground forever." That's why she wanted to be cremated. She wanted to be free. And so I kept her in a small box in the bottom of my desk for a decade. The irony of this struck me only a couple of weeks ago.

You see, I was too busy caretaking everyone else in the family to do what she wanted with her remains, or to do what I wanted. Instead, I allowed myself to be browbeaten into keeping her ashes to keep relatives happy. One wanted them kept. He even decided that he wanted them kept in a hand-made earthenware lidded vase that Mom's artist friend (who later committed suicide) had made years before. Not only that, but I was to keep the ashes, because he didn't want to have them in his house.

But my decision to scatter her ashes now was not about times past. It started out as an angry reaction to some rude communications from the relative who accused me of letting Mom die. I suddenly decided that I was going to scatter the ashes because I'd had enough. He's never asked after them in 10 years, and I am heartily sick of being his skivvy. But the scattering became something else.

The moment I made that decision, something changed for me. I realized that I had spent 10 years of my life living in fear that I would hurt the feelings of a selfish bully. I had spent 10 years doing something I didn't want to do that had caused me distress and grief. Knowing her ashes were in my desk in my study made it difficult to work there. Maybe this was why I had never really sorted out my study and seldom worked in it.

It's high summer here now, and the days are hot and windy. I bought four helium-filled party balloons and hoped like crazy I wouldn't lose them when I took them out of the car. Everywhere I drove seemed to be chock-a-block with people sunbathing, sightseeing, or working on the roads, but at last I found a quiet place to pull over on the shoulder of the winding mountain road. It offered a short climb to a tiny, rocky bay. I took the balloons out of the trunk and the little box of ashes and scrambled down to the rocks. The sea was a deep blue with lacy edges; the sky was bright and cloudless.

I wondered what to say. How do you capture a lifelong relationship—one of the most complicated and important that you will ever have—in a few words? It came to me that this was not about words or saying the right thing, like a spell or incantation. It was about what the act symbolized. Eventually, all I said was, "I loved you very much, and I know you loved me. I am sorry that I didn't always behave as the daughter you wanted, but I know that you loved me more than anything anyway, and I never wanted another mother. I'm setting you free now, like you wanted, and I'm setting myself free too." Then I poured the ashes out into the waves and watched them dissolve in the foam.

My mother had had a hip replacement at 39, so her metal hip was in the box too. I had asked the funeral parlor to return it to me with her ashes—I cannot think why—but it seemed important at the time. Now I wondered what to do with it. As I stood there, holding it, I looked closely at its scratched surface and remembered its story, how sick she'd been, how she'd almost died, and how scared I was at nine, seeing her suffer so. How my father had left her to suffer, while he'd bought himself a sports car and palmed my brother and me off on my mother's parents for six months. How maimed she'd felt when she got out of hospital with a limp that she worked very hard to eradicate and a long, angry, ugly scar up her leg. How her marriage had failed anyway. How the wounds of those years were so bad that they had never really healed for any of us.

Then I looked at the blackened metal object in my hand and said, "You were not your wounds." And I threw it as hard as I could into the sea, where it disappeared without a splash. Then I let the balloons go. They tugged at my hand on their pretty ribbons; when I knew they wanted to break free, I let them slip out of my fingers. They hovered above me for a moment and then suddenly shot out across False Bay, tumbling higher and higher in the wind, turning against the blue sky. Smaller and smaller, they shrank until I could no longer see them.

June 2010: *I Return to Cleaning My Closet*

I finally managed to give away my mother's two best overcoats, my younger uncle's brown leather jacket, and my grandmother's multicolored tweed coat. I kept them in the spare room closet for years. I have accepted that I can never wear any of them and that it's time to move on.

June 17, 2011: *The Present Day—The Story Continues...*

My abstract has been accepted for the book on complicated grief! Now I can finally tell the whole story and put it all behind me. Maybe this will do the trick.

June 27, 2011: *The Present Day*

But perhaps it was wishful thinking. If I am over this story as I have been trying to be for so many years, why does retelling it now make me weep? Why do I still dream of my mother, and why is she always alive in my dreams? Why does this never cause me any perturbation until I wake up and remember she is not?

I admit that my feelings are not the same as they were in 1998; they are by no means as intense or all-consuming. I do not fall to pieces this evening. Instead, I dry my eyes, make a left turn into my street, and go inside to get changed for yoga. I tell myself that you cannot expect to get over a parent's death or the loss of a person you have loved very deeply. You can't forget them. Instead you learn to live with the pain, the anger, the guilt. The ghosts continue to haunt you, but you become used to them and learn to ignore them.

Have I finished my grieving process? I doubt it. I still live in the house I lived in with my mother all those years ago. I am not married. I have still not tidied out my study and do not work in it nearly as often as I should, even though her ashes are gone. I am still struggling to make ends meet. In some strange way—perhaps it's only my perception—I never quite seem to have got on my feet financially, even though I am conservative with money and have a much better job than I did in 1998.

I still don't know why my mother didn't tell me she was dying. I used to believe it was spite, but a friend suggested it was maybe a misplaced desire to protect both me and herself from something she could not bear to talk about. This seems more reasonable now. I am only sorry she did not feel she could discuss it with me. I would have done everything in my power to help and support her in her last days, instead of trying to escape from her.

I have, however, hung new pictures: framed Indian cushion covers in bright reds, purples, and pinks, covered with gold sequins. Somehow I doubt my mother would have approved, even though her grandparents' pictures now hang in the bathroom.

Discussion
The Problem of Creating a Pathology

The idea of creating a mental disorder, such as complicated grief, and identifying people as suffering from it is problematic (Parkes, 2006; Saleebey, 2000, 2009a). Parkes maintains that understanding a situation can make it easier to relieve people's suffering and might even help us understand that we are all vulnerable to these conditions; Saleebey's approach is more ambivalent. He is concerned that creating a disorder can lead to stigmatization and to people being pathologized, even being labeled as inferior or abnormal. I feel the same sense of ambivalence about saying that what I have experienced is complicated grief. Whereas Parkes chooses to identify complicated grief as a disorder and treat it, I am not so sure. The more I contemplate my own experience, the less certain I feel about whether to identify my own grief as complicated or not.

My chief concern about being labeled as suffering from complicated grief is that I do not wish it to become my "master status," my defining quality (Becker, 1963; Saleebey, 2009a). I am not only a complicated griever; I am a person who, among other things, has experienced an extended grieving period. There is a qualitative nature to the experience of grief that cannot be quantified or pathologized. The experience is not a set of criteria in a manual; it is instead a mental, physical, and spiritual event: Someone grieves, someone who lives in a specific context, with particular relationships and certain types of support.

The Recognition of Context

There are many causes for unresolved grief (Gunzburg, 1993). The context in which someone grieves can affect how their grief unfolds. In my case, context may have complicated my grief. I was isolated in my new environment, far from old friends. The key members of my family were all dead, and as a result, my family had ceased to exist as an entity. I no longer belonged anywhere. I had learned to grieve from a family that was terrified of grief and struggled unsuccessfully to work through it; I had not realized this until writing this chapter.

I had a great deal of unfinished business with my mother: I felt guilty about wanting to leave *her* and enraged that she had left *me* by dying; I felt angry that she had uprooted me and marooned me far from home with financial problems; I felt responsible for her death, although I knew I was not; I have always felt terrified of dying unexpectedly, and her death cemented that vulnerability; I felt utterly isolated. The vulnerability I already experienced as a result of the incurable illness that necessitated my transplant and the pessimism I felt regarding relationships after watching the two older generations of my family live together so unhappily for so long discouraged me from making any serious efforts to find a partner and have a family of my own. And so, emotionally, I persisted in living in limbo for years after her death.

I allowed this to persist by remaining in poorly paying jobs that prevented me from making substantial changes in my life and, more significantly, kept me in the same financial limbo we had existed in after my parents' divorce. Somehow we could never move past that either, and I relive the losses and deprivations of my adolescence every day. That limbo wasn't entirely my mother's fault. Although she remained emotionally and financially dependent on my father, believing his roaring tirades that she was worthless and incompetent, his constant legal battles to take alimony from her impoverished her further, and my illness effectively prevented her from working, because she was the only one left to look after me.

As much as I resented her succumbing to him, I too believe that I am not worthy of having proper financial support, so I choose work that doesn't pay properly and leaves me having to battle for survival. I always feel a need to prove that I deserve to have my job, over and over, because the one person I cannot convince is me. I seem to have gotten stuck in this emotionally and financially impoverished place when my mother died. I wanted to escape, but she got away, and I remained behind to deal with the family dramas and endless money issues. And I feel responsible for it.

The Recognition of Shame

Identifying shame as one of the most powerful emotions I felt after my mother's death and finally being able to see the depth of it allowed me to recognize the role shame played in my extended grieving and, to some extent, to exorcise it. The role of shame in grief was possibly the biggest discovery I made while researching for and writing this chapter. Perhaps part of the complexity of grief lies in its being a composite of so many different feelings. In the face of grief, one's world and one's identity are blown apart (Dubose, 1997). The way one relates to oneself and to others is changed, sometimes permanently. In the face of such destruction, one has to try to rebuild a life or build a new one. In previous times, rituals and societal norms that we no longer have would help protect us from some of the emotions, such as shame (Kauffman, 2010).

Whereas guilt can cloud one's perception of how loss has affected one, more pernicious than this and less visible is shame. Shame—covert, but omnipresent in death and grief—can disconnect one from oneself and one's context (Kauffman, 2010), leaving one feeling diminished. Likewise loss and deprivation are shameful too—they can seem to be a moral judgment (Kauffman, 2010). Growing up, when we had things taken away from us after my parents' divorce, my father told us repeatedly over many years that it was because we were bad. Why should other losses be any different? I recognize this now, but I could not see it then. Shame pervades my story on almost every level, from realizing that people might think I actually could kill my mother to feeling inadequate because I was not able to save her. The relief I felt when the doctor told me no one could save her is indescribable. Knowing you are not to blame and feeling you are not to blame are two different matters. Not being able to afford a coffin for your own mother at the age of nearly 30 is pretty shameful too. Not being able to be normal or to return to normality is a dark secret. You learn how to fake normality so others won't see the truth. You want to cover your dead mother's face, but no one will let you. Perhaps you accept suffering and deprivation because you feel it is all you deserve. After all, that is what you have been taught growing up.

The Recognition of Strengths

In considering the strengths-perspective approach to complicated grief, I find that I tend to focus more on deficit than on strength. I am so wrapped up in my sorrow that I can barely see anything else. And yet, I am resilient. I have survived (so far) an incurable chronic illness, the loss of my family, financial insecurity, loneliness, isolation, and despair. I do not think succumbing to complicated grief is about a lack of resilience; instead, it could be about a surfeit of shame, of losses, of problems, of unhelpful habits learned from one's family.

I could not have managed to carry this set of burdens had I not had certain qualities. These can be both strengths and weaknesses. I am used to surviving. I have had to do so much of it. But I do not know how to thrive.

I spend a lot of time on introspective tasks. This can give me insight, but can also cause me to brood. I use writing as a way of processing things. Sometimes this is easier than taking action. And I am stubborn. I don't let go of anything easily, especially not ideas. I realized in making this list that instead of seeing my life as half empty I could see it as half full. One's strengths can be surprising (Saleebey, 2009b). Once I saw that some of my supposed impediments could be reframed as empowering, I saw my complicated grief in a different way.

For example, considering my challenges and the background from which I come, it could be more empowering for me to remain without a family. Honoring and experiencing my grief and mourning the lost lives has taken a long time, but doing so gave me back my dignity. Allowing myself time to grieve so many things and to not adhere to a schedule has allowed me to be true to myself and to heal to some extent. The shame I felt after losing my mother was possibly a partial result of our Western culture losing its mourning norms (Kauffman, 2010) and the rituals that mark its passage. Instead of norms we have normative theories and diagnostic criteria (Kauffman, 2010). Perhaps we need more rituals for coping with grief, complicated or otherwise.

Writing as a Healing Ritual, Writing as a Mourning Ritual

A ritual of erasing an old identity and replacing it with a new identity (Turner, 1969; Van Gennep, 1960) might have gone some of the way to resolving the liminality of my complicated grief. I had left an identity—being the adult child of a living mother—and needed to understand and embrace my new identity. I find it significant that English has no word for adult orphan. I think this is what my writing was meant to have achieved over the years. It was supposed to be a way of containing the chaos and allowing my new status to form. At this stage, I feel more at peace about the experience because I understand more about it. For me, writing may have helped me to make this crossing more easily. Writing has always been a strength for me because I find it a useful way of clarifying my ideas; however, I also find it extremely difficult to express ideas that are fearful or in some way unacceptable. I know now that for any future progress, I would need to take this into account and perhaps even seek help writing. Writing for an audience can help if the audience is prepared to hear.

I can see that writing my early story (Richards, 1999) was merely a stage in my journey. I was "writing forward" toward hope. Hope is something we need to be able to feel in order to be resilient (Saleebey, 2009b). In some way, although I could not feel the hope in 1998, I knew it existed and that I needed to move toward it. I underestimated how long it would take me to heal. The losses had been multiple and complex and had occurred over a lifetime. They could not be dealt with in a year or two, but instead had to be worked on incrementally, as they had originally occurred.

I think I was on the right track when I wrote my first story of the loss of my mother. However, one might need to tell the story more than once (Wyatt, 2008). Grief changes you, and so does writing. Both are slow processes that take as long as they take. Healing cannot bypass mourning.

Hearing cannot bypass mourning either. In order to understand someone's story, one has to be able to hear the story. Strengths-based social work emphasizes this (Anderson, Cowger, & Snively, 2009; Saleebey, 2009a). You have to hear the story as it is, shame, guilt, anger, and all. This is not easy and may take time, even if it is your own story.

To avoid a normative framework, it is important to listen carefully to people's stories, including our own. Stories can repair a damaged identity (Bury, 1982; Frank, 1995) and empower one, but they can just as easily entrap one. One's own story might be disempowering, or one might unconsciously have adopted the stories among which one grew up, as I found I had done.

In writing this version of my story from beginning to end, I noticed some things I had not seen before. My family's pattern for mourning was one of silence, denial, and unending trauma, laced with dread. For us it was not the grief that lingered so much as the shame and an inability to deal with it. I can see this now, and I can see it doesn't serve me. As a child, I had secretly started telling myself counter-narratives (Nelson, 2001) in which I would escape my mother's and grandmothers' fates and be free to make my own life. Instead of feeling ashamed of my strange existence, perhaps I should embrace it, because I achieved what I always wanted to as a child: Unlike almost everyone else in my family, I escaped.

Conclusion

I started this chapter by reinterpreting part of the end of the story I had previously written. I was still striving toward closure. I have not found it, but I have found something better: the recognition that I do not need it. In 1999, I saw my story only as cathartic, because that is what I wanted it to be, but many years later I see there is much more ambivalence in it that I had imagined:

> The sun is rising on the morning after the purging of my heart. Sacred ibises will fly above the arum lily vlei. The Helderberg's scars will be greened with ashes and syringa blossoms will fall like stars. The radio tells me I am a Missing Person too. I switch it off. I want to hear the guinea fowl chuckle and the rain fall. I shake the cardboard box out on the stoep and watch the ashes melt into the rain. (Richards, 1999, p. 35)

The sun is beginning to rise, but it has not risen yet. The scars are not yet covered. The blossoms are falling, not blooming. I want to hear peaceful things, but I don't hear them. I do, however, scatter her ashes. In reality that took me another 10 years. And in all of this I am "missing." As for my heart, is it purged of something? And, if so, what is it? Or is it my heart that has been purged from me? I think the latter. A certain numbness that began growing in me after my younger uncle's early death in 1991 overtook me when my mother died a few years later. In some sense I removed myself from my life, because it hurt less that way. I taught myself not to feel strongly about things or to become too deeply involved in relationships. I did not know this in 1999.

When I first told my story, I was unconsciously trying to rewrite the family tale of mourning by ending it. But I had to rewrite at least two generations of family narratives around grieving. This cannot happen overnight or even over a decade. I also had to accept that one cannot prevent bereavement. It will happen as long as you have people you love. However, at this point in my narrative, I feel I have made significant progress by merely recognizing the nature of my grief, even though I still live in my mother's house and sleep in her bed. I was a missing person for a long time. In 2012, I feel that I might finally be found.

References

Anderson, K. M., Cowger, C. D., & Snively, C. A. (2009). Assessing strengths: Identifying acts of resistance to violence and oppression. In D. Saleebey (Ed.), *The strengths perspective in social work practice* (5th ed., pp. 181–200). Boston/New York: Pearson Education.

Becker, H. S. (1963). *Outsiders: Studies in the sociology of deviance*. New York: Free Press

Bury, M. (1982). Chronic illness as biographical disruption. *Sociology of Health and Illness, 4,* 167–182.

Dubose, J. T. (1997). The phenomenology of bereavement, grief, and mourning. *Journal of Religion and Health, 36,* 367–374.

Frank, A. W. (1995). *The wounded storyteller: Body, illness and ethics*. London: University of Chicago Press.

Gunzburg, J. C. (1993). *Unresolved grief: A practical, multicultural approach for health professionals*. London: Chapman & Hall.

Kauffman, J. (2010). On the primacy of shame. In J. Kauffman (Ed.), *The shame of death, grief and trauma* (pp. 3–22). New York: Routledge.

Nelson, H. L. (2001). *Damaged identities, narrative repair*. New York: Cornell University Press.

Parkes, C. M. (2006). *Love and loss: The roots of grief and its complications*. London/New York: Routledge.

Richards, R. (1999). "Luvandwar." *New Contrast, 27,* 27–35.

Saleebey, D. (2000). Power in the people: Strengths and hope. *Advances in Social Work, 1,* 127–136.

Saleebey, D. (2009a). Introduction: Power in the people. In D. Saleebey (Ed.), *The strengths perspective in social work practice* (5th ed., pp. 1–23). Boston/New York: Pearson Education.

Saleebey, D. (2009b). The strengths approach to practice: Beginnings. In D. Saleebey (Ed.), *The strengths perspective in social work* (5th ed., pp. 93–107). Boston/New York: Pearson Education.

Turner, V. (1969). *The ritual process: Structure and anti-structure*. London: Routledge and Kegan Paul.

Van Gennep, A. (1960). *The rites of passage*. London: Routledge.

Wyatt, J. (2008). No longer loss: Autoethnographic stammering. *Qualitative Inquiry, 14,* 955–967.

Chapter Seven

Complicating Grief with Violence

Vanessa Russell

In November 2006, I was awarded a six-month research grant to travel from Melbourne, Australia to University College Dublin. When I arrived in Dublin, the whole city seemed constantly wet, like the dribbling chin of a teething baby, so I hired a car for a week and went in search of the real Ireland. That is, the Ireland of the picture I'd torn from *Lonely Planet* that showed a stone cottage buried deep in vibrant green fields with sheep dotting the foreground.

Scouring the car's touring guide, I headed towards County Kerry, which looked idyllic. There I found Baile an Ollphéist. According to the travel guide, the vibrant town was full of writers, artists, and generally crafty sorts. It sounded perfect. I would settle there and travel up to Dublin for my university exchange. I settled in and extended my trip for another six months.

Eight months after I first arrived, I met Declan Ó Dochartaigh at a beach cleanup. His tawny-colored hair was pulled back into a ponytail, and his long, strong nose was beautifully shaped over his slightly oversized bottom lip. As we talked and laughed, I found out that he and the rest of the small group were members of the Green Party.

"Come on and join," Declan said, "it's only a fiver."

A bargain if it meant spending time with this happy, active community.

From there it all moved very quickly, and we soon had a baby, little Milo. But two years and three months after I'd met Declan, he had told me I was crazy, bad, dozy, provoking, controlling, codependent enough times that I no longer had time for beach cleanups or happiness. Instead, I spent my entire time trying to protect Milo and trying not to do anything that Declan could claim had provoked him into violence.

During the time Declan and I were together, his behavior escalated from an occasional outburst to a three-day rage every two months. During these, he spat on me, kicked me, punched me, then pulled hardback books from the bookcase and flicked them into my legs like ninja stars. He tried to choke me, then dragged me down the hallway by my hair. And more, and more, and worse.

His last sustained rage attack began on my birthday, two days before Christmas. During those last days I was with him, he was demented; there's no other way of putting it. He was driven mad with sickness and guilt and the knowledge that he'd destroyed everything, and he would only blame and hate me for it.

"You're dirt!" he screamed at me on that last night, after he'd broken through the door lock and shouldered the wardrobe out of the way. Milo, feeding on me, froze. He was only 14 months old, poor baby. He didn't deserve it, even if I couldn't see a way out, yet.

"You dozy bitch! Where are my keys? I've been standing outside asking you to tell me where my keys are. Where are my keys?"

I buried myself under the bed covers with Milo. For the five months since the physical violence had escalated, I had been constantly trembling with a hand held over my mouth. This was not happening to me. Another part of me acknowledged that it was, and I waited for a safe time to drive an hour and a half to the women's refuge. The calm, patient refuge workers had told me, more than once, that the most dangerous point was when the woman left. But I kept going back, delusional with hope that Declan would change.

"Shush," I murmured to Milo, trying to block out Declan's shouting. "Shush."

That last night began the year-and-a-half-long ordeal that complicated an already complicated grief. The new year saw me escape with Milo to Australia with our lives, six odd socks, and undiagnosed posttraumatic stress disorder (PTSD). Once I got to Australia, it would take Declan two hours to brand me a kidnapper and threaten to use the Hague Convention (a convention that aims to bring internationally abducted children back to their homes) to get me back to Ireland. Although the convention itself is outdated and does not acknowledge that over two thirds of all international child abductions are done by women escaping the violent fathers of their children, it worked. After six months I had to go back to Ireland. Once there, I was eventually awarded the right to permanently live with Milo in Australia. I arrived back in Australia in November 2010, shaken but determined to get myself into recovery and finally deal with my PTSD and complicated grief.

In the end, it seemed as if my grief was the least complicated part.

Complicated Grief in the Crucible

When I escaped from Ireland with my baby Milo, I believe I was already suffering from complicated grief. I was dealing with (or rather, not dealing with) the death of my father two years previously. He had died while I was living in Ireland, and I had buried my guilt and grief in the maelstrom of my relationship with Declan. Then I suffered two miscarriages, one before Milo, and one after. I barely acknowledged the second miscarriage, feeling monstrous at my exhalation of relief. While enduring Declan's increasingly violent and inexplicable behavior, I never acknowledged—let alone tried to resolve—my grief. I was being smothered under a grief that grew and festered, pulling down more loss upon me until I could barely breathe.

I can only write that *I believe* I was suffering from complicated grief, because I was never diagnosed. I was diagnosed with PTSD when I escaped to Australia, but not with complicated grief. So how can I credibly write about my experiences of complicated grief? Simply because no one, really, can be diagnosed with complicated grief, because it doesn't officially exist yet.

Clinicians have offered suggested diagnostic criteria for complicated grief. Horowitz et al. (2003) have proposed criteria that divide seven symptoms into three categories: (1) intrusive symptoms (unbidden memories or intrusive fantasies, severe emotion, and strong yearnings for the deceased); (2) signs of avoidance (feeling alone and empty and staying away from people, places, and activities); and (3) failure to adapt (sleep interference and loss of interest in activities).

Horowitz's criteria are widely accepted, but, officially, the diagnosis remains a hypothesis. This doesn't mean that complicated grief doesn't exist. It simply means that the medical establishment hasn't yet gathered enough case studies and debated the symptoms and diagnostic criteria for it to be included in the fifth edition of the *Diagnostic and Statistical Manual of Mental Disorders* (DSM-5), published by the American Psychiatric Association in 2013.

As I write this chapter, complicated grief is in the crucible, and clinicians believe they know how the smelting will result, but there is always the possibility that something completely different will be thrown up. As it stands, theories of complicated grief create questions and answers. For example, can unacknowledged grief become complicated grief when compounded by events other than deaths? And can complicated grief be caused by losses that are not physical, human deaths? Events like the loss of a serious relationship, violence, moving house—or countries—or losing your freedom to choose where you can live?

After leaving Declan and returning to Australia to confront the absence of my father, and to begin to accept my multiple losses, Horowitz's symptoms felt like a game of bingo:

- Intense intrusive thoughts;
- Pangs of severe emotion;
- Distressing yearnings;
- Feeling excessively alone and empty;
- Excessively avoiding tasks reminiscent of the deceased;
- Unusual sleep disturbances;
- Maladaptive levels of loss of interest in personal activities.

BINGO! What do I win? My prize was a diagnosis of PTSD, which gave me a way out, an explanation, and a strategy of recovery that I—in all my panic and fear, grieving and loss, escape and guilt—could not see for myself.

I can only wonder what would have happened if complicated grief had been medically recognized and was already included in the DSM-IV. Then my doctors and psychologist may have recognized my symptoms and seen them, not only as the symptoms of a woman who was subjected to violence, but also as the symptoms of an unaddressed and complicated grief. I may have received specific help to get over my losses and to resolve my complicated grief much more thoroughly and, more important to me, much more quickly.

Experts agree. Katherine Shear, who headed the first controlled trials of the treatment of complicated grief in 2005, firmly believes that complicated grief is a "specific condition in need of a specific treatment" (Shear, Frank, Houck, & Reynolds, 2005, p. 2608). Shear's study recruited 95 participants suffering from complicated grief and randomly split them into two groups (Shear et al., 2005). Both groups received two different treatments. The first group of 46 people was treated with traditional psychotherapy, usually used for sufferers of depression. The therapy focused on finding insights to the person's problems with the people and situations around them, with some focus on grief. The other group of 49 was treated with complicated grief therapy, which focused on the person's reaction to the death and involved the person telling the story of the death; having a guided, imagined conversation with the deceased; facing the issues that had been avoided; and working on life goals.

Shear's study found that 51 percent of patients who were treated with the specific complicated grief therapy said they were very much improved, compared with 28 percent of those treated with the more traditional form of psychotherapy. More studies are needed, but it seems clear that specifically treating complicated grief will let people deal more quickly and effectively with the losses in their lives. Maybe others will benefit, as I did not.

Avoidant Coping

My avoidant way of coping was well established by the time I left to go to Ireland on my research exchange. I'd originally decided to go to Ireland because I'd been reeling from an awful breakup of a four-year relationship. So I applied for an overseas scholarship to finish off my PhD. Like many people before me, I believed that getting away would magically give me new scenery, culture, people, and sights to focus on and make everything better. In Ireland, I wouldn't be able to see my ex-boyfriend, and I'd begin to heal, or so I reasoned.

Complicating everything, the week before I was due to leave, my father told me he was waiting on results to tests that would confirm he had a rare form of leukemia.

"I won't go," I said immediately.

"Go," he replied. "You'll be back in six months, in time for the stem cell transplant."

Instead of weighing up the rights and wrongs, the ethics and the plain decent behavior, I flew to Ireland. Avoidant coping has at its core dramatic solutions to difficult situations: deny, deny, avoid, minimize and—best of all—run away.

Every time I called home from Ireland, Dad told me his platelet counts were improving, but he was uncomfortable because of a bladder infection from a catheter or a stomach infection. He said that apart from that, the chemotherapy was going well, and it looked like the stem cell transplant would be a success. I swallowed it all down and made plans to go back after I'd been in Ireland a year. I ignored Mum's calls saying that Dad wasn't as well as he claimed, believing she was being overly pessimistic. As far as I was concerned, Dad was doing well, and I was going back soon, so my guilt over not being there for him would soon lift.

And then I met Declan.

Not long after Declan and I got involved, I got a call from home that even I couldn't ignore. Dad wasn't expected to live much longer. I got on the first available plane and arrived back in Australia. My father was in an induced coma, racked with staph infections from the hospital, pneumonia, and on dialysis for his failed kidneys. On the 11th day, he woke up.

"How's Ireland?" he rasped.

It was the first time any member of my seething family had asked me anything about my new Irish life. Theirs was full of gowning up for bedside visits, sending updates via group texts, meeting with gloomy doctors, waiting in rooms with televisions screwed onto walls, scrabbling to pay hospital car parking, watching the infected hole in my father's stomach grow to the size of a dinner plate, listening to him wheezing through a tracheal tube, and celebrating his hair growing back millimeter by millimeter. I can only guess the rest. I was there for only 11 days. Confronted with the reality of Dad's illness, and the fury of those there caring for him, I chose to run again and returned to Ireland.

Complicated grief seems to depend on how a person copes with loss. If, for example, a person suffering from previous trauma experiences a major loss, then they are much more likely to suffer complicated grief if their style of coping is to deny or distract themselves from the reality of the loss. This is what was happening to me. When Dad became ill, I was still raw, but slowly recovering from the breakup with my ex-boyfriend. I then distracted myself by moving overseas and getting into a relationship with a disturbed, abusive man. Researchers have found that if the avoidant way of coping continues for a period of time, then mental health issues begin to appear (Schneider, Elhai, & Gray, 2007). Sure enough, my brief period of feeling reborn when I first arrived in Ireland was soon subsumed by the murky sludge of undiagnosed, untreated depression.

After this point, events began to escalate. Looking back, it's easy to see when I started making bad decisions, but I knew nothing of avoidant coping strategies or complicated grief, or even how to know when you're in an abusive relationship. All I knew was that Declan treated me as badly as I felt I ought to be treated.

Miscarriage and Complicated Grief

When I got back to Ireland after my 11 days in Australia, I went to the doctors, who confirmed that I was five weeks pregnant by a man I barely knew.

"Is it mine?" Declan asked, "I've always wanted to say that. This isn't the first time this has happened." I buried that too, his history of getting women pregnant, of denying it and not being there.

A week later, I started bleeding and miscarried. I was devastated over the loss of my baby, which wasn't helped when Declan immediately packed up and went away, partying at summer music festivals. For him, I was only another woman he'd gotten pregnant who had miscarried or aborted—or not—no big deal. My fragile self-esteem collapsed, and all I wanted was a baby to hold and someone who loved me, even if only intermittently.

Three months after my miscarriage, Dad rang and told me he was stopping his treatment. He would turn off the dialysis machine, stop the antibiotics and the feeding tubes, and just go.

"I've had enough," he said.

That was it. I agonized over whether to return, but I felt I didn't have the resilience to cope. My friends in Ireland thought I would probably regret it, and Declan railed at me and would not understand that I felt too fragile to go back home. I couldn't deal with so many bad things happening, including Declan's behavior, so I pushed it all back and away.

By the time I could eventually accept the reality, Dad was dead, I'd missed his funeral, and I couldn't even imagine the vitriol that would be flung at me if I went home. So, I went deeper into denial. The denial encompassed everything: from wanting to get pregnant by a lying, absent man I didn't know; to ignoring his emotional jibes, putdowns, roughness, and slaps; to blaming Dad because he had said he was getting better.

Clearly I wasn't coping. I couldn't grieve with Declan watching me, blaming me, telling me I was angry at him because I'd done the wrong thing and hadn't gone home for my father's funeral.

"What kind of person doesn't go home for their father's funeral?" he kept repeating every time he got angry, which was increasingly often.

"I know," I kept saying, "it sounds bad, but I just couldn't. I just couldn't."

Then, a month later, I was pregnant again. Declan was furious. He said he was *glad* I'd lost the other baby, and I should have gone home to my father's funeral. What am I doing with this man, I asked myself from the bottom of a well.

His rages worsened. But I was five months pregnant; I had hope. I didn't realize that this was him: the rage, the irrationality, the blaming. I thought if we could sit down and talk about it I could make him see he was acting badly and that I only had his best interests at heart. So I agreed with him: I was taking out my grief on him. I took the blame if it would calm him down, but I didn't believe a word of it.

It didn't take long for Declan's violence to escalate. By the time Milo was 10 months old, it had got to the point where I never knew what was going to set him off. My focus was on looking after Milo and doing whatever it was that Declan wanted. Everything I did enraged Declan. He'd worked himself up to having three rage attacks a day, all in front of baby Milo.

I was completely unaware of the irony that I was alienating my family in Australia because I was fearful of their anger for not being there for Dad, when I was living with someone who would daily blow up and justify his behavior as simply a reaction to the kind of person who wouldn't go home to their father's funeral. There was nowhere I could go. No safe place. And worst of all, I felt I deserved it.

PTSD

In the end, it was my mother who helped me get out. The morning after that last night when Declan broke through the bedroom door, I was on Skype to her, showing her Milo. Declan sat out of eyes reach, listening, making sure I was playing happy families.

Then he left the house. I couldn't help it; I blurted out to my mother a little of the violence of the night before.

"Get out," she said. "Tell me where you're going so I know you're safe, but just go."

I packed a suitcase, milling in the dry clothes from a pile in the bedroom, and fled, leaving the computer and lights on. Declan had made me take out Milo's car seat from my car the night before, believing that would stop me from leaving. I hooked the seatbelt over and around Milo and drove to friends, two hours away.

Then I was on a plane, and then I was back in Australia at my mother's house in the pristine housing estate where, on the surface, it looked as if nothing had changed. In the house were the same La-Z-Boys, the same sterile cleanness, the same unused cream-colored living room. Except it had all changed. I went in and searched all the rooms for Dad.

"He's not here," I ventured to Mum.

"I know," she said. "I keep expecting him to walk out but he never does." He had been dead two years.

It didn't take her long to book me in to the doctors.

"They want to speak to you," my mother said, and thrust the phone at me.

The medical receptionist wanted to know how long I'd been back, how long I'd been in Ireland, and how old Milo was. In reply I jabbered and stuttered; I could barely speak. I didn't understand what she was asking. In tears, I handed the phone back and went to my room.

At the appointment, the doctor listened to me shudder, stutter, and shake and diagnosed me with PTSD. I barely blinked at that. It was as if I'd survived a war, which I suppose I had.

I was on a crazy ride that had abruptly stopped, and I was dizzy from being whipped out of everything I knew. I texted Declan and told him we were in Australia, and it took him two hours to call me an evil harridan kidnapper and threaten to invoke the Hague Convention. In his eyes, I had not escaped from him, I had internationally abducted Milo.

That began six months of even more tenuous uncertainty, during which we all waited for the Australian court's judgment on whether Declan's violence was enough of a reason for me not to return to Ireland and establish child custody. It turned out that it wasn't. It meant that even halfway around the world, Declan could reach out and crush us.

Interventionalist Counseling

While in Australia, waiting for the results of the court case to determine whether I had to return to Ireland, I spent 12 one-hour sessions with a clinical psychologist at the local doctors' surgery. Doctor Bob was perky, but sunken, like one of those kids who had been thrown into the rubbish bins at school, and who'd never quite shaken off the bullying, but was proud of what he'd achieved since. He wore a variety of checked shirts that matched his teeth.

For once, I told a psychologist everything. I didn't pretend he'd cured me and I'd made a miraculous recovery. I was too far down for that. I told him all my crazed thoughts and actions. I told him about my obsession to make Declan see why we had left, to prevent him from moving on to someone else, the spying, the breaking into his Facebook account, the dozens and dozens of phone calls.

Forgive me, was their basic plea.

I still desperately wanted Declan to apologize, to get well, to want us back. That was my main concern. I wanted him to say he understood why we left, that it was his fault, that he was going to go into treatment and get better. I thought my drastic move of running to Australia would prompt his realization. I didn't understand then that he would use it, that he would twist it, to say he was the victim of an international child abduction.

My other experiences of psychologists and counselors had generally fallen into the "I don't know, what do you think" category. My point had always been that I didn't know what I thought and I really needed some direction. So Doctor Bob's intervention style of straight-talking counseling was precisely the jolt I needed to finally accept the reality of my situation and begin to recover.

Every time he gave me a bit of truth, I began to feel lighter. I realized how much of a burden I was carrying by working so hard to deny reality. For example, when I told Doctor Bob that I wanted the real Declan, the good part of him, he smiled sympathetically.

"The part of him that never will exist," he said.

He continued, explaining into my blinking look of shock.

He said of all the thousands of people he'd counseled, he had only seen two abusive men change. "And they really wanted to change," he said, "and really worked at it, and even then, they have times when they go back." Then he apologized for the metaphor he was going to use—and it was horrible—but he said that violence was like a woman's hymen: Once it's broken, you can't put it back.

"How long would you want him to change before you took him back?" he asked.

"How long?" I repeated, still reeling from the hymen analogy.

"What kind of time frame?"

"Oh, ah, three months?"

"Try three years," he said.

I laughed bitterly. "He can't even be nice to me for twenty-four hours."

"Well, there's your answer," he said and sat back on his chair.

I often felt ruefully ashamed at the insights he gave me, simply because they seemed so obvious to him.

Trauma and Recovery

Judith Herman, in her landmark work, *Trauma and Recovery*, stated that there are three general stages to recovery from violence against women but acknowledged that these are not hard and fast and may include more or fewer stages. She wrote that safety is the first stage; after that is established, there is remembrance and mourning, followed by social reconnection (Herman, 1992). What she terms a successful recovery occurs when someone acknowledges they have been through a trauma, and builds a safe new life by using psychotherapy, support groups, medication, or perhaps cognitive–behavioral therapy.

What I liked about Herman's book is her open statement that there is recovery, that a person doesn't have to be scarred for life by their experiences. Herman said that to name the disorder and explain the symptoms can reassure the sufferer they have not lost their minds or their identity and can help them begin the process of recovery. This tallied up with what Doctor Bob was telling me: to acknowledge that my situation wasn't fair but was only an obstacle to my long-term plans.

It was reassuring to be told that I would feel better, that the pain would end, and that I would set in place skills and ways of living that would mean that I was not defined by my grief or losses. And, most important, that I would have the skills to negotiate abusive situations when they arose again.

Yet I wasn't able to fully begin recovering until almost a year later, after I'd been given permission by the Irish judge to relocate to Australia. Back home again, I was able to rent a house, get work, put Milo into occasional care, and write about what had happened. Before I knew it, I had a full book-length draft. I titled it *Loosestrife: Love and Losing It*. The writing left me exhausted and shaky, but I felt that it was a way for me to tell everyone exactly what had happened, and to prevent it from happening to other women.

Unfortunately, Declan seemed hell-bent on making me pay for getting away from him. When he threatened to come to Australia and take Milo away for three weeks, I got myself into a support group for women who had been subjected to violence. There I learned new concepts, such as a boundary is just a statement until you put a consequence on it; and, it's not about the child, it's about getting back at you. Every time I set and stick to a boundary with Declan's continuing bad behavior on Skype, I went to the support group and let them congratulate me. My self-esteem continued to build as they told me, over and over again, that I was strong with boundaries.

At the same time, I became involved in a 12-step program and really worked on making amends to all the broken relationships around me. As I apologized to people I'd long held grudges against, I felt like I could begin again, and live in a different way. I felt like I was starting again from a ground zero with a clear conscience, with a new way of actively dealing with people and situations without the need for shame.

Six months after Milo and I settled back in Australia, I took a free family violence course run by the local council. At the beginning of the eight-week course, I was so brittle I nearly broke. Why, I thought, do I have to spend more time thinking about Declan? At the beginning of the course, the facilitators asked what we all wanted to get out of it. I immediately said that I needed to know why he did it. The facilitators told me something that hadn't occurred to me: He has made a clear and conscious choice to use power and violence to manipulate and control.

"Oh," I said. "So it's nothing I did?"

"He has made a clear and conscious choice to use power and violence to manipulate and control," the facilitator reiterated.

The statement opened up something else in me. It didn't matter what I did, what I didn't do; it didn't matter what he said, that he maintained that I'd provoked him, that he was acting in self-defense, and even—most astounding—that we were in a sadomasochistic relationship. It didn't matter that I'd gone into a relationship with him instead of grieving for my father. He'd chosen to act abusively. It was not my fault.

By the end of the course, the facilitators asked us what we had gotten out of it. Strength, and a sense of inner peace, I said this time. When they read out the outcomes we'd wanted at the beginning, I immediately recognized the longing to know why as being mine.

"I don't need to know why anymore," I said. "That's not relevant. He's not going to apologize, he's not going to acknowledge what he's done, he's never going to be a good person." I shrugged. "That's the way it is."

I felt such relief that I'd seen myself progress, even within eight short weeks, and that I was finally acknowledging the reality of Declan's behavior.

Tackling Complicated Grief

Once my anger and hurt about my experience of violence were alleviated, I felt I had to tackle my grief. To find answers, I trawled through the idiocies and contradictions of the Internet, then decided to see what I could find in the generalist collection at my local library.

There, between the rigid stages of Kübler-Ross and the self-excoriation of codependency, I stumbled onto *The Grief Recovery Handbook* (James & Friedman, 2009). It immediately took my fancy because it promised to resolve my grief once and for all, just as long as I exactly followed their instructions. Best of all, the book was thin.

The authors believe that if you have suffered a loss, any kind of loss, from the death of a pet, to the loss of aspirations or ideals, then you have unresolved grief. Their definition is wide—maybe too wide—and implies that if every single person in the world looked hard enough, they would find that they too had unresolved grief.

But I dutifully did the exercises and wrote my father a Grief Recovery Completion Letter, in which I acknowledged all the things I could have done and said to my father and hadn't, all the resentments from the things he'd said and done and hadn't, and then made some "significant emotional statements" (James & Friedman, 2009).

The amazing thing was, it worked. I had said goodbye to my father; I had let go. I was no longer running from my feelings; I was no longer using avoidant techniques of coping. The grief from my father's death was resolved.

Was it really that simple?

With the help of Doctor Bob, getting stronger with the support group and the family violence course, and working through the 12 steps, I was able to face the grief I'd been avoiding. I'd inadvertently, and through so many channels, been given complicated grief therapy. It had taken three and a half years.

Finally, I felt like my life was opening up again, instead of shutting down. My complicated grief was resolved, my PTSD was recovered from (apart from the odd flashback), my avoidant ways of coping were examined and replaced with active coping. I had goals, I had pleasure, I had safety, and I was ready to live awarely with my son with all my new skills.

My life, for the first time, perhaps ever, had become blessedly simple.

References

Herman, J. (1992). *Trauma and recovery: The aftermath of violence—From domestic violence to political terror.* New York: Basic Books.

Horowitz, M. J., Siegel, B., Holen, A., Bonanno, G. A., Milbrath, C., & Stinson, C. H. (2003). Diagnostic criteria for complicated grief disorder. *Focus, 1,* 290–298.

James, J. W., & Friedman, R. (2009). *The grief recovery handbook: The action program for moving beyond death, divorce, and other losses including health, career, and faith* (20th anniversary ed.). New York: Harper Paperbacks.

Schneider, K. R., Elhai, J. D., & Gray, M. J. (2007). Coping style use predicts posttraumatic stress and complicated grief symptom severity among college students reporting a traumatic loss. *Journal of Counseling Psychology, 54,* 344–350.

Shear, K., Frank, E., Houck, P. R., & Reynolds, C. F. (2005). Treatment of complicated grief: A randomized controlled trial. *JAMA, 293,* 2601–2608.

Chapter Eight

Complicated Grief Endures

Elisabeth Hanscombe

Twenty years ago, when I was still young, I stood under the shower one morning and found a pea-sized lump in my left breast. I had soaped myself down as usual, and with my right hand I pressed the skin against my rib cage to feel the texture of my otherwise smooth breast. I was in search of imperfections.

A friend had not long before been diagnosed with breast cancer, and I was more diligent in my search than usual. Only that night I had dreamed of my friend's gaping breast cut open by a surgeon's knife. I took it as an omen.

"It's probably nothing, but it feels a bit fibrous." I imagine the doctor did not want to alarm me. "Best to get it looked at." It took a few anxious days before my next appointment.

"This won't hurt a bit," the specialist said, "just like a mosquito bite." He pushed a long, silver needle into my breast above the lump.

A mosquito bite? Clearly no mosquito had ever bitten this surgeon before, otherwise he would have known not to lie to me. On a scale of one to 10—toothache being one, childbirth 10—I rate this pain, from my memory today, at seven. But it was gone in a flash. The surgeon peeled off a pink bandage to cover the drip of blood from the pin-prick hole he left behind.

The results came back negative, but still, "to be certain we should take that lump out," the surgeon said. "I might have missed the growth itself."

The night before the day of the knife, I looked at my breasts in the mirror. I had a mixed relationship with them. They were the love of my babies' lives, but they stirred up unfathomable and ambivalent feelings in me. They were not, however, available for serious wounding. I woke from the anaesthetic without pain, still groggy from the drugs. The surgeon visited before my discharge.

"All fine," he said, and used an unintelligible word, which when translated into layman's terms means a benign fatty deposit. The white bandage held both breasts firm and hugged my ribcage. I was mummified. "Keep the bandage on for a week. Cover it with plastic in the shower. I'll be able to take the stitches out then."

In 20 years, the scar has faded, but it remains for me to see, a tiny junction on the left side of my left breast. "There is something peculiarly distressing about the first wound on new skin," wrote Byatt (1985) in her book *Still Life* (p. 157). And so it was for me—this scar, this wound, this mark on my breast. But as they say, I should be grateful, it could have been far worse.

I have other scars that are not so visible. They exist beneath the line of my skin, etched into my mind. These are the scars of trauma and grief, the complicated difficulties that have beset me from my earliest days. These are also the childhood scars that steered my vocation and later joined to form other scars through further traumatic experience. That is the way with grief; it becomes a scar, a hard inflexible stretch of skin that takes the place of healthy tissue, the body's attempt at healing itself. But scar tissue looks different; it is paler and denser. There is a limited blood supply available and therefore less movement and circulation, and in cases where there is too much scarring, it can block otherwise healthy functioning. So, too, when grief appears to have sealed over, when the initial trauma is past, the area of the wound or loss becomes less flexible. If we are to avoid such hardening, our grief must be worked through over time.

Francine du Plessix Gray (2001) developed Freud's thoughts about "The Work of Mourning." She wrote about the need for "time out ... the hard, slow, patient work, a meticulous process that must be carried out bit by bit" (p. 62). Along with this need to take sufficient time, du Plessix Gray emphasizes the importance of ritual, "the funeral, memorials, visits to the grave—draw them out, take your time ... Mourning rites serve in great part to protect survivors from the excesses of their pain" (p. 62). Has the business of skipping over ritual—a carnation thrown onto the coffin, which is then withdrawn behind curtains, to avoid the reality of death—made us less able to deal with our losses? The body is later cremated in the furnace room, and no one need see. In some ways, we treat the aftermath of trauma similarly. We try to sterilize the experience; it is simply too awful to know. Yet in other instances, we might try to find more helpful ways of dealing with life's losses, as I did through my career and later through my writing.

Suzette Henke (2000) wrote of the notion of "scriptotherapy" as "the process of writing out and writing through traumatic experience in the mode of therapeutic enactment" (p. xii). But for me, the serious writing came only years after I had attempted more traditional forms of healing, both in becoming a therapist and also in trying to help others deal with their own grief and trauma.

My decision as a 14-year-old school girl to dedicate my life to helping other people seems an obvious one to me now. Every family tends to have its internal therapist, a child dedicated to the role of trying to make things better. In those days in Melbourne, Australia, the profession of social work was in its infancy. There was only one university offering a course in social work, and even then it still held only diploma status. You needed to combine a social work diploma with an arts or other degree to be qualified to work in the field. I chose the arts and majored in psychology and English literature.

Until I arrived at my decision to help people from families like mine, I had wanted to be a poet. Once the idea of becoming a social worker took hold, I came to forget my literary ambitions and concentrated instead on getting into the social work course at Melbourne University, entrance to which required a high qualifying score. For the last three years of my schooling, every Christmas holiday, I wrote a series of letters to various institutions asking what I would need to do to become a social worker as my first preference. If I did not get a high enough grade, my second preference was to become a welfare officer or youth worker. I was determined to get into a career that involved helping people in trouble.

I was especially interested in helping the families of alcoholics. In those days, in my mind alcoholics were fathers, and their families suffered. My mother showed me so. She took us off to Alateen (an offshoot of Alcoholics Anonymous) as a way of helping us to cope, while she took herself off to Al-Anon, the group established to help wives, adult relatives, and friends to live with an alcoholic. Thus she began to cultivate her serenity. My mother's serenity became a burden for me, and to some extent for my siblings, though I cannot speak for them. It furthered my mother's tendency to opt out, emotionally speaking. She used her bid for serenity as justification for her emotional absence. Perhaps it was also her way of coping with the loss of her beloved homeland, Holland, after migrating to Australia with my father and four of my siblings in 1951. I was born the following year.

In retrospect, I suspect my mother was trying to do as the Al-Anon folks had urged her. "Do not let your husband's drinking affect you," they told her. "Do not buy into it." But how could we not buy into it? My father's drinking grew worse from the time of my early school days until well after I had left home as a 19-year-old. My entire remembered childhood is pockmarked by memories of my father's violent outbursts and unpredictable behavior, usually brought on by his drinking.

There have been many books written about the consequences of growing up in an alcoholic household. My mother's mantra became: Sons of alcoholics become alcoholics, and daughters of alcoholics marry them. We were doomed from the start. There was no way of escaping its grip. I took the Pioneer temperance pledge when I had my Confirmation as a 13-year-old—determined to set myself an example—but by age 18 and my first boyfriend I, too, had tasted of alcohol's forbidden fruit, and I had enjoyed it. I broke my pledge for the pleasure of alcohol. But my father's drinking always seemed to be driven more by desperation than by pleasure. He did not drink for taste or companionship, the loose easy way that moderate drinking can draw us out and disinhibit us. He drank for escape, from bottles of St. Agnes brandy covered in brown paper bags, which he kept hidden beside his chair. (The Pioneer Total Abstinence association of the Sacred Heart is an Irish organization established in 1898 that encourages its members to abstain from all alcohol and honor the sacred Heart of Jesus in an effort to curb alcoholism in Ireland. The practice of encouraging Catholic children when they make their Confirmation—a ritual of the church—around the age of 11 years to take the pledge and wear the Pioneer pin has spread to other countries, including Australia.)

At the time, there was no help available, as initially we could not even speak about our father's drinking. Zerubavel (2006) talked about conspiracies of silence and the ways we learn to keep silent about certain matters, for a variety of reasons, mostly to do with sparing ourselves and others embarrassment or other unpleasant emotions. Zerubavel offered the example of the alcoholic family, in which the alcoholism/alcoholic sits in the center of the living room like a huge boulder that everyone in the family, including those who visit, learn to skirt around. Not only do we learn not to notice the fact that there is a boulder in our midst and that we must skirt around it, we also learn that we must not talk about the boulder, nor must we talk about the fact that we cannot talk about it (p. 53).

Nor could we talk about my father's sexual abuse of my older sister, not at that time and not even now, without great discomfort, even after my father's death nearly 30 years ago. The sexualization of my experience as a child, through my father's behavior, alongside my mother's Catholic prudishness, turned our household into a hothouse of conflicting emotions.

In 1974, Drew, Moon, and Buchanan wrote a handbook on alcoholism, to my knowledge the first text of its kind in Australia. At the time, this book offered me some perspective on my father's drinking. For once, it seemed not so much a failure of his personality as an illness, though I have long considered my father's alcoholism as a symptom more than an entity in itself, one that was rooted in a history of family trauma and abuse. It is only recently, through painstaking research, that I have learned my paternal grandfather was imprisoned in Haarlem, Holland, in 1943 on charges of *ontucht*, which is old Dutch for "vice, lewdness, pornography, and prostitution." In his case, it could well have meant incest given that the charges were brought forward by his then 19-year-old daughter. My own father never spoke about this to any of us, and my mother is cagey when I ask her what happened. From the moment my father arrived in Australia, he stopped all contact with his parents and siblings, apart from an occasional letter to the sister who had brought the charges against their father.

As I came to understand later, the life my father led—his earlier experience as a child in a troubled family rife with sexual and other abuses, his many years fighting in both World War II and against Indonesia's fight for independence, the effects of migration, and the burden of raising a large family in a new country—contributed to the man he became. Despite his difficulties, my father was a proud, intelligent man who was also ambitious. He was ambitious for his children, too. He valued education above everything. Like many a migrant, he saw it as a means of getting a toehold in this adopted country, and he studied at night school to complete his accountancy qualifications. He inculcated a spirit of learning in all his children, though his drinking made it impossible for him to follow through with what he had begun with each one of us.

My father's many losses over time—of his homeland, his family of origin, and his self-esteem through alcoholism and financial failure—as well as the disappointment he felt in not succeeding in his ambitions, may have all contributed to the grief-stricken man he became in his later years. Even earlier, grief permeated his daily life, a grief that took the form of rage and discontent. My father took up many projects throughout my childhood. The first, he completed. He built our first real Australian home in Greensborough on weekends with little outside help, but thereafter his later projects stalled. He converted the pantry in the kitchen of our later home in Camberwell to a dark room for his photography. He drew up plans to build a yacht. He bought a business in rural Healesville that he imagined he might turn into a famous tourist destination. None of these later ventures succeeded, and as the years moved on, my father's energy and enthusiasm palled. His grief became his children's; we were the carriers of his memory. Marianne Hirsch (2001) wrote about postmemory, the process whereby the experiences of a previous generation or generations are carried on into the next generation and lodge there as unexpressed grief that can take the form of symptoms and difficulties that are otherwise hard to recognize.

I once had a bubble of Lourdes water in the crucifix of the plastic rosary beads an aunt had given me for my First Holy Communion. When I was 11 years old, I broke open the crucifix and poured the bubble of water into my father's cup of tea while he was not looking. I wanted to cure him of his drinking; that is, after I realized he was drinking. Before then, I had thought he was sick. Our mother always said as much. "Your father is sick." A strange sickness I thought even then, but I believed her until I was 11.

In those days, on Saturday nights, my father roamed the house naked. He walked into the kitchen intermittently to scream obscenities at my mother. He lunged at her and pulled her hair, or tried to rip off her clothes. One such night my father had bailed us up in the kitchen when, after one of his many visits to taunt us, my brother yelled across at my mother that our father was "a drunk." The word hit me with force. I began to imagine my father as a derelict abandoned in the gutter, covered in sores and dirt. The bubble of Lourdes water had no effect, though for a couple of weeks after I had put it into his tea, my father stopped drinking and I began to think a miracle had indeed occurred. It did not last, but my mother continued to look for miracles as the doctors searched for a cure.

Now I run the risk of shifting from grief to trauma. The two are intertwined. A traumatic memory is one that has not been properly grieved, perhaps. It runs parallel to Freud's idea of *pathological mourning*, or melancholia, the state that arises if the grieving process does not follow a certain course (du Plessix Gray, 2001). Freud's theory on trauma has been extended and developed. But essentially, as Caroline Garland (1998) wrote, "Trauma is a kind of wound" (p. 9). It pierces the psychic skin and breaks through the normal filtering process begun at birth with the aid of the mother/caretaker. The person's mind is flooded with more than it can manage as the trauma overrides all usual defenses, leading to a breakdown in functioning. The traumatized individual can no longer go about the business of everyday life in the usual way. There is a loss of any sense of predictability. The traumatized individual is increasingly vulnerable to overwhelming anxiety that emerges in the first instance from the external trauma but eventually coincides with anxiety arising from internal sources. Primitive anxieties from infancy are stirred up, including paranoia and the terror of annihilation (pp. 9–11).

More than 50 years ago, Bowlby (1961) began to explore the links between an infant's attachment to its mother and the ways a rupture of these links, as in early separation, sets in place the process of mourning. To the baby, the mother's prolonged absence can be felt as a threat of annihilation. A short absence might give rise to anxiety, but any sense of a permanent absence gives rise to pain and mourning. All later experiences of loss set in chain a similar process of mourning that features grief, the subjective state of mind and body that in Bowlby's words, accompanies "the persistent and insatiable yearning for the lost object" (p. 320).

Therefore, as I understand it, grief follows loss, and the experience of loss can be traumatic. Not only do we grieve for those we love who die or otherwise leave us, but also we grieve the loss of our hopes and expectations. We grieve when our world is thrown into chaos through war or political turmoil. Migrants grieve for their homelands. Those who are retrenched (laid off work) might grieve for their lost status and productivity. To some extent, we all grieve over time for the loss of our body's functional capacity as we age. Grieving is as much a part of life as is digestion, and in Freud's (1926) terms it goes back to that initial experience of separation when a baby recognizes her mother's separateness and absences, for example, when a toddler recognizes that his mother has left him at kindergarten and he must learn to cope in her absence until she returns. Grief can be acute, intense, and painful, or it can be prolonged and move into a chronic state of loss. Complicated grief relates to the experience of multiple losses over time, or a continual state of loss that becomes so entrenched it almost cannot be grieved. It becomes part of a person's landscape.

Most grief is complicated insofar as it derives from complex sources and arouses complex emotions. Even the seemingly straightforward death of a loved one can arouse intense but conflicting feelings. Even loving feelings toward a particular person, a parent, a partner, are never pure or straightforward. We have complex relationships with one another, as we do with ourselves, so to lose a loved one can be devastating and at the same time pose a strange sort of relief.

Recently, on the radio, I heard a program about the bush fires endured here in Melbourne two years ago. Many lives were lost. People are still recovering, still grieving. The local policeman on duty on the most intense day of fire activity has written a book about the story. It occurs to me that for this man there is a secondary gain out of a disaster, however much he might wish the fires had never happened. It has led him on to a level of fame, a recognition he might never experience in day-to-day life, and he thrives on it, however traumatic the original events may have been. It becomes a source of comfort, perhaps. This is not to say that were he given the chance to go back and undo the damage that is not his to undo he might not do so instantly—and thus go back to his former simpler life—but rather, that our losses can become triumphs, even as we continue to grieve what once was or what might have been. Writing about our trauma and complicated grief can transform such experience from one that feels unbearable into one that seems more under our control. Therefore, I write into my grief and trauma.

The difficulties of my formative years have fueled both my determination to help others and also to be helped through my profession. Through working with others, I sensed I might help myself, and make some progress toward addressing my rage toward my father and my grief at the vagaries of my childhood.

Even in adulthood, the scars of my early experience have affected certain choices I have made and the responses from others, especially certain of my psychoanalytic colleagues, regarding my writing. This has caused me further grief. In my mid-twenties I moved from social work into psychoanalytic therapy. I wanted to work in greater depth, and a few years later, this desire took me into psychoanalytic training, the most intensive form of training available in my hometown, Melbourne. But my involvement was short lived.

Twenty years ago, in September 1991, the year I developed the lump in my breast described earlier, I was dismissed from the psychoanalytic training with little explanation as to why. This is not an uncommon experience within psychoanalytic circles, but it is an experience that is not discussed openly, given the levels of shame induced in those who are dismissed. This experience and its aftermath, traumatic as it proved for me—given that I had invested several years in first applying for and then undertaking this work—became the impetus for me to complete a doctorate on the topic of life writing and the desire for revenge. I argue that this desire, as it is evoked by traumatic experience and shame, if it can be worked through and understood rather than enacted, can lead to creativity in the act of life writing. For me, the loss of the psychoanalytic training felt like a death, the stillbirth of my dreams. My experience of being dismissed from the training alerted me to certain feelings of shame and rage including my desire for revenge. As I have written elsewhere: On the day of the sacking I lost my bearings. I hid away from my colleagues. I felt soaked in my shame and could not speak about it. As time passed I became aware of an increasing sense of outrage with those who had dismissed me. I fantasized planeloads of analysts falling from the sky on their way to conferences I could no longer attend. The desire for revenge welled up inside of me and spread like an oil slick on an otherwise blue ocean.

In writing about the notion of complicated grief in the face of loss, not only through death of a loved one, but through other losses, Kauffman (2010) observed that "grief can arouse anger and rage, about which one may feel ashamed … Traumatic grief in particular is soaked in shame" (p. 4). In this same series of essays on the links between the shame of death, grief, and trauma, Costa (2010) wrote about the shame she experienced when her first child was stillborn. It was not so much the loss itself or her own grief that brought her shame, but the way people judged her for how she dealt with her grief, namely, her desire to keep her son's memory alive for years after his death. She felt the first inklings of this on the night before she was due to deliver her already-dead baby. The midwife had suggested she might want to bring her camera. The idea of taking photographs in the circumstances might seem "incomprehensible, perhaps even shocking to the world at large" (p. 26). Costa imagined public condemnation and experienced it later when she celebrated her dead son's first birthday. Her accusers, she writes, "wounded me unknowingly. What they had in common were remarks, gestures, or responses that in some way confirmed my fear— or knowledge—that there was little room in the world for my child" (p. 29). Costa has since given birth to a daughter, but she remembers her son who "occupies a quiet place in our immediate family" (p. 29). By inviting others to share her perspective on the need to remember this son, she recognizes a countervailing pressure not to grieve, to stop her grief, to forget. For "what is it to grieve," Costa asks, "if one cannot speak of the dead?" (p. 29).

The pressure to give up on our separate experiences of grief as though they are bits of paper to be filed away is to me inherent in the term complicated grief. There is a danger in pathologizing our experience should the notion of complicated grief be deemed another medical phenomenon, in the same way the experience of trauma has been turned into posttraumatic stress disorder (PTSD), with a subsequent devaluation of the experience (Young, 1995). Young wrote about the way our notions of trauma, redefined as PTSD, have changed over the past century, particularly in the wake of the two world wars and that of Vietnam. In his view,

> traumatic memory [and I would argue the stuff of complicated grief] is a man-made object originating in the scientific and clinical discourses of the nineteenth century; before that time there is unhappiness, despair and disturbing recollections, but no traumatic memory, in the sense that we know it today. (p. 141)

The same could apply to notions of complicated grief. Reflecting on the experience of Vietnam veterans, Young wrote, tongue in cheek, "How much simpler everything would be if researchers and diagnosticians had some way to bypass the things that men say about themselves and their pasts" (p. 175). Complicated grief and the processing of trauma can be seen as an attempt to deal with what life throws up, part of the rich tapestry of who we become, but the stories need to be told rather than simply labeled with an overarching diagnostic term that spares us the need to look more closely at the nature of human experience in grief and trauma. Similarly, Ogden (2001) described mourning as

> not simply a form of psychological work; it is a process centrally involving the experience of *making* something, creating something adequate to the experience of loss. What is "made" and the experience of making it—which together might be thought of as "the art of mourning"—represent the individual's effort to meet, to be equal to, to do justice to, the fullness and complexity of his or her relationship to what has been lost, and to the experience of loss itself. (p. 117)

At the end of her series of essays, *A Plea for Eros*, Hustvedt (2006) asked:

> Is the wounded self the writing self? Is the writing self an answer to the wounded self? Perhaps that is more accurate. The wound is static, a given. The writing self is multiple and elastic, and it circles the wound … I have to write the fear. (p. 277)

Hustvedt's fear, as she discovers in exploring her life, is one of the violence within her. Likewise, the violence within us all, that which others have perpetrated on us, becomes our wish to lash out. In my view, the desire for revenge as a response to pain and hurt inspires the writing, and thereby transforms the rage, the helplessness, and shame into a creative gesture. Hustvedt also calls this *sublimation*, the term coined by Freud to delineate "the transformation of inner dramas, fears and wounds into something else: a work of art outside the body of the artist" (p. 171).

The difficult experiences from my childhood follow me around, year after year, and invariably creep into my writing as if they insist on being heard. Do not forget us, they seem to say, these spectres from my childhood, these memories of a little girl overwhelmed in a world in which the people near me I now recognize were themselves overwrought with grief. My parents' migration into a new country, the legacy of my father's participation in two wars, my mother's loss of her parents left behind, and my father's shame at his disturbed and incestuous family all conspired with present difficulties—the burden of raising nine children, the weight of religion, my mother's Catholicism and my father's religious confusion (an agnostic, but five times baptized as a child), to cover our family life with a grief so powerful it is difficult to tease apart. In some ways the grief refuses to go away, even after I write about it year after year, even as I try to process through 12 years of analysis. It endures through my extended training as a psychoanalytic psychotherapist, through my failure to complete my training to become a psychoanalyst, and through the joys and hardships of raising my own family of four daughters with a loving and supportive husband.

Complicated grief earns its name through the notion that some grief does not come to a clear-cut resolvable conclusion, some sense of acceptance of the loss, generally of a loved one. Some occasions of grief insinuate their ways into our lives into the substrate of our personalities, and will not let us alone, even as we might manage otherwise satisfying lives. Complicated grief can mute our successes at best; at worst, it can turn a person into a sad shadow of their potential self. Complicated grief is more pervasive than we let ourselves know. It lies in our communal histories, lies in our memories as whole societies of war, of trauma, of genocide and starvation, even if we are but witnesses to these atrocities.

If we cannot consider our histories, reflect on past experiences, we run the risk of encapsulating our grief and passing it on in neat packages, like unexploded bombs, to the next generation. So my father did to his children, and so we children run the risk of doing to our children and through them to future generations.

My father's grief etched its way into my memory on Sunday mornings when he would reappear—hung over and without any more alcohol to keep up the rage of his drunken state—broken and apologetic. My mother once planned to put a tape recorder into the dining room wardrobe and keep it running during my father's drunken rambles so that he could hear himself the next day. My father drank so heavily he lost all memory of the things he said and did while drunk. He relied on my mother to tell him on his next sober day, at which he would suffer lashings of remorse. Grief, guilt, and shame are all closely related, one feeds the other.

This lump must be a sign of some inner badness, I thought at the time, and I remembered a fellow analytic trainee who had given up her training for a period because of cancer, one of those strange pervasive cancers, like leukemia. And yet she survived and came back.

I hear again the words: "A lump or thickening in the breast or else-where may be a sign," the announcer's warning on the television. "Many early cancers can be cured." I have cancer. I know I have cancer. Cancer like a crab crawling through my insides, digging in its claws, tearing at my flesh.

My mother's belly is big. She wears a loose dress with spots all over and a frilly apron to protect the front. I know I have cancer because the prickles of skin on my arm are like lots of little lumps that have erupted from the big one in the middle, the one in my stomach, and I cannot tell anyone. If I tell they will take me up the road to Dr. Shub's house, the one with the black-framed windows and the knocker at the door.

I go to see Dr. Shub with my mother. He takes her into his room and tells me to sit on a chair by the door. I watch as she climbs onto his high wooden bed. My mother tells me to wait. Dr. Shub pulls a curtain round my mother; I peek around and see the white mountain of my mother's belly. Her navel sticks out in the middle, and a dark line runs all the way down to the hairy part of her underpants.

Dr Shub leans down and puts his ear to her belly,

"All's good in there, all's well."

But it's not well with me tonight. I am going to die. The cancer will eat me up from inside and I will disappear. All that will be left will be a lumpy sheet of skin with holes where my eyes and mouth once were. And teeth and hair.

When I told my analyst about this memory, she suggested I may have been identifying with my mother's latest pregnancy because without knowing it, I hated my mother's unborn babies, the ones that had pushed me out. Especially as there was another one inside then: my soon-to-be-born baby brother.

More than anything else from the day of my dismissal from the psycho-analytic training, I remember the tissue box. It was yellow. A box of yellow tissues covered in yellow roses. My mentor handed it to me the moment I needed a tissue, the moment I started to cry. After I had yanked out the tissue, I let the box drop onto the floor beside my chair.

I could not stop myself from crying. The shock of her words: "The Prog-ress Committee have decided not to invite you to continue your training." I needed to twist the words around in my head to get at their meaning. They did not want me anymore. I was 36 years old, the mother of three. Not that this should have counted for much. Motherhood was not a prerequisite for the psychoanalytic training, but it gave me a sense of maturity then, to have survived the birth and early life of three daughters.

It was then three years since I had received my letter of acceptance into the analytic training, three years since the day I had danced for joy around the kitchen, hugging each of my daughters in turn. I was going to be a psychoanalyst. I had entered the training. I would now have the chance to be among the most highly qualified therapists in the world. Like Freud, who started it all, I had come home—I belonged; I was a place that was familiar and safe.

Or so I had thought, until home became a difficult and trying place, not at all as I had imagined. Sure, I knew it would be rarefied. I knew it had the other worldly feel of a religious institution. Hadn't my mother told me I had given up my religion for psychoanalysis? But I had never imagined the secrecy of the experience, the sense that I must not tell anyone about the training. It was okay to say I was in the training, but that was all. A bit like the way I did not tell many people I was in psychoanalysis itself. They might think I was mad. They might have all these fantasies concocted from stories in New York magazines about the likes of Woody Allen lying on the analytic couch, day after day, year after year, for 20 years, complaining to his invisible and unseen analyst, notebook in hand. The culture of complaint. They could not imagine what I might have to talk about. For this reason, I did not bother trying to explain the fact of my psychoanalysis, except to my closest friends. Certainly I found it almost impossible to explain the nature of the training.

The training prospectus read clearly enough. The tripartite division of the training into seminars that covered theory, Freud, Klein and the rest, including an infant observation and a psychiatric placement, if you lacked experience of working with psychosis; the personal supervision on at least two cases, each seen five times weekly over a period of at least a year, one a female, the other a male; and then, finally the personal psychoanalysis. For me, that third part was the most important and the best.

I had already been in analysis for three years by the time I started my training. My analyst, Mrs. Milanova, considered it not long enough. She had warned me, I give her that. She had warned me it was premature.

"It's the timing," she said when I first expressed an interest in doing the training, but once I was accepted, she cooperated. She even went through a process of being accepted herself.

When I started to see her for analysis, Mrs. Milanova was not a training analyst. If she were not a training analyst by the time I began the analytic training I would have needed to change analysts. I did not want to do this. Nor, I imagine, did she, though she never told me as much.

Behind the scenes, her own and mine, there followed a process of secrecy whereby the higher authorities sent messages to one another and made inquiries of other analytic colleagues about Mrs. Milanova's suitability to be elevated to the position of training analyst. After some months, she made the grade. That was when she agreed to increase the frequency of my sessions from four times a week to five.

When I first began analysis, Mrs. Milanova told me she did not work on Fridays. I hated the long analytic weekends followed by the long gap between Thursday and Monday, and I pleaded with her many times to make an exception and see me on Fridays, but she refused. My husband joked she needed her Fridays to shop at Safeway.

I knew Mrs. Milanova had been accepted as a training analyst after I had received my letter of acceptance into the training program, when she told me she could see me on Fridays, after all. So being accepted into the training gave me the added bonus of being able to see my analyst every day of the week, except on the weekends. Nirvana.

It might seem strange to a reader that someone could be so keen to undergo such a long, committed process, but in those days I believed in the value of psychoanalysis as the only means by which I might finally get some relief from my incessant insecurities, my relentless fears, and my sense that I was not very intelligent.

Analysis with a nonmedical analyst costs money, but I saw people myself for therapy and their fees to me, though considerably less than those I paid my analyst, helped cover some of her costs. The rest took the form of a debt to the bank, which my husband and I are still paying back.

My complaint was not about the analysis itself. I have no major regrets about my analytic experience. It has helped me to grow and to develop in ways I did not believe I could without that help. But somewhere deep inside, I harbored a grudge against my analyst. She has interpreted this to me many times: that I still blamed her for not protecting me from the consequences of the analytic training.

"You thought it was a kindergarten," she told me in the weeks following my dismissal. "It's not. It's a gruelling, sometimes mad-making experience that must be endured."

When my mentor told me that Monday that I could not continue, I wanted to make a fuss. I wanted to complain, to scream and shout. But I knew that, were I to make any fuss, it would be further confirmation of my unsatisfactory status. The Progress Committee believed, it seems, that I lacked the constitution to be a psychoanalyst. No one ever said as much directly; I guessed.

Although the breast lump proved to be benign, my dismissal from the psychoanalytic training became a traumatic event that has reverberated with earlier traumas from within my childhood. My decision some 20 years after the event to write about this, particularly within the context of my doctorate on the subject of life writing and the desire for revenge, has evoked a polarized response within my professional community, between those who believe I have violated professional boundaries in speaking out and those who believe I have written courageously about a topic that needs to be opened for discussion. The fury of this response complicates my grief further, along with my rage and desire for revenge (Hanscombe, 2010).

The child from my memory looks for ways to represent her experience for some future time, as if by putting the words down she can deal with the burden of her parents' strife. In this way, autobiography bears witness. The witness carries the weight of memory. To remember and to share is to find words for traumatic experience, beyond behavioral and bodily manifestations. Trauma in its essence, the unbearable, the unspeakable, is difficult to put into words. It is silencing and yet, as Gilmore (2001) argued, those who survive trauma are often required to voice their experience "in an effort to create the language that will manifest and contain trauma as well as the witness who will recognize it … to tell … what can't be spoken" (p. 7).

When I map the contours of my life, I can see a pattern: a series of rejections that become turning points, beginning with my experience of an alcoholic father. My dismissal from the psychoanalytic training took place in the fifth year of my analysis, an analysis I undertook to help me come to some better understanding of my childhood and subsequent life difficulties, my complicated grief. For several years, the rage and the shame I felt about this experience stayed with me, though I had no choice but to live with it and to begin to process it, initially through my analysis. In time, I came to write into my rage, shame, and desire for revenge, and thereby the experience began to take on a different shape. It became more bearable. The more I wrote, the more I was able to explore its meaning and to develop new perspectives.

This chapter reflects that journey, through all its winding tributaries, and now in conclusion, I suspect that any grief I experienced over the loss of my dreams, particularly in my dismissal from the psychoanalytic training, is complicated, not only by the fact that to some degree it persists, but also in the complexity of my response to it. So it is for all our grief. We can try to bury it, over time, sometimes prematurely, or we can linger over it, but we can also learn from it, such that our grief becomes a significant part of our selves and our story.

References

Bowlby, J. (1961). Processes of mourning. *International Journal of Psychoanalysis, 42,* 317–340.

Byatt, A. S. (1985). *Still life.* New York: Simon & Schuster.

Costa, S. (2010). Side by side. In J. Kauffman (Ed.), *The shame of death, grief and trauma: A book on the psychology of shame* (pp. 25–33). New York: Routledge.

Drew, L., Moon, J., & Buchanan, F. (1974). *Alcoholism: A handbook.* Melbourne, Australia: William Heinemann.

du Plessix Gray, F. (2001). The work of mourning. In K. Norris (Ed.), *The best American essays* 2001 (pp. 60–72). Boston: Houghton Mifflin.

Freud, S. (1926). Inhibitions, symptoms and anxiety. In J. Strachey (Ed. & Trans.), *Standard edition of the complete psychological works of Freud* (pp. 77–185). London: Hogarth Press.

Garland, C. (Ed.). (1998). *Understanding trauma: A psychoanalytical approach.* New York: Routledge.

Gilmore, L. (2001). *The limits of autobiography: Trauma and testimony,* Ithaca, NY: Cornell University Press.

Hanscombe, E. (2010, Winter). Straddling two worlds. *Island, 121,* 421–436.

Henke, S. (2000). *Shattered subjects: Trauma and testimony in women's life writing.* New York: St. Martin's Press.

Hirsch, M. (2001). Surviving images: Holocaust photographs and the work of postmemory. *Yale Journal of Criticism, 14*(1), 5–37.

Hustvedt, S. (2006). *A plea for eros.* London: Hodder Headline.

Kauffman, J. (2010). On the primacy of shame. In J. Kauffman (Ed.), *The shame of death, grief, and trauma* (pp. 3–8). New York: Routledge.

Ogden, T. (2001). *Conversations at the frontier of dreaming.* London: Karnac Books.

Young, A. (1995). *The harmony of illusions: Inventing post-traumatic stress disorder.* Princeton, NJ: Princeton University Press.

Zerubavel, E. (2006). *The elephant in the room: Silence and denial in everyday life* New York: Oxford University Press.

Part 3

The Death or Physical Loss of One's Child: Everlasting or Pathological Grief?

The previous section explored the thesis that one's grief and loss are often long lasting and unresolved. Many times, this is due to mitigating circumstances with respect to either one's loss or one's life. If ever there was a form of loss that could most profoundly represent a form of long-lasting and unresolved grief, it arguably would be the death or physical loss of one's child. This loss is often emphasized as perhaps the single most painful loss that one can endure.

Donna McDonald (chapter 9) begins this section by reflecting on the death of her infant son (at five and a half months of age) a quarter century ago. Much of her chapter discusses how writing about her son's death was healing. And yet, she also noted how she did not want her writings to "bury" herself into a constant state of grief. Indeed, much of McDonald's paper involves an appreciation for a sort of balancing for proper coping. For instance, though she says that support from others was critical, she did not want to become "crippled with grief" by constantly talking about her loss with others. McDonald discusses how she refused to be defined by her loss—even though others often queried her about whether she was a mother. She reflects that her loss may be as much about recalling the death of a precious newborn son as it is about the loss of what could have been had he not died. Indeed, McDonald reminds us that grief, particularly when it involves the death of one's child, rarely is not complicated.

Lynne Webb and Paige Toller (chapter 10) offer a very powerful account and academic analysis regarding the sudden death of the lead author's teenage son while at a summer camp. Much of Webb and Toller's piece examines not only the incredible pain associated with the death of Webb's child, but also how that pain is intensified by the fact that his death had no clear medical explanation at all. Webb and Toller further discuss how the presence of several other mitigating factors (for example, poor weather conditions that may have hampered the ability of medical staff to get proper care) further exacerbated this grief. Webb and Toller add that, particularly given these circumstances, feelings of complicated grief continue to persist. And, to label such grief as "pathological," in the view of Webb and Toller, "only serves to further stigmatize and disenfranchise her as well as her experiences." Webb and Toller's paper offers some very clear challenges to the notion that complicated grief is a condition that is inherently in need of psychological or psychiatric treatment—or, even if such treatment is offered, that it can fully eradicate such feelings of grief. Indeed, these feelings often define us as individuals.

Christina Houen (chapter 11) ends this section with an important consideration that the loss of one's child need not necessarily be due to physical death. Houen recounts the abduction of her three young daughters by their father in the 1970s. Houen suggests that a critical difference between child abduction and the death of one's child is that, with respect to the former, there is at least the hope of seeing one's child again. Like many other chapters in this volume, Houen considers how her writings allowed her to recover from this traumatic event. And, like many of these chapters, Houen suggests that a label of complicated grief tends to emphasize illness and psychopathology rather than personal strengths and resilience. She further adds that it is impossible to ever remove the reality of these traumatic events from her sense of self and life experience. Houen's chapter offers unique insight into the experience of losing a child other than to death (that is, abduction) and how difficult (if not impossible) it can be to ever remove the impact of such experiences from one's sense of self.

Chapter Nine

When Time Stops
The Courage for Joy

Donna M. McDonald

Prologue

I was shocked on reading the words *complicated grief* for the first time. As an Australian woman in her late fifties who lost her five-month-old son to sudden infant death syndrome (cot death) 25 years ago, I reacted hostilely to the prospects of my grief being defined as a mental disorder, and I fired off a sharp e-mail to Dr. Miller, the editor of this book, to tell him so. I told him grief should be respected for what it is: a rite of sorrow and an honoring of the person you have loved and lost, whereupon he invited me—or was it a challenge?—to write a more complete response for this book.

I had lived so long with my fixed understanding of my grief in all its moods that I had to unpack that understanding assumption by assumption. While I was reflecting on the intensity of my anger about "pathology creep" whereby every knock, blow, injury, or unwanted life event will, one day, be classified as a precursor to a mental health disorder, I remembered something my 85-year-old mother had recently said to me. I had telephoned her with the news that I would be graduating with my PhD at the end of the month. She said, "I'm very proud of you." I was about to thank her, but she rushed on ahead, speaking over my intake of breath and said, "You've had a remarkable life."

We were both silent for a moment. I knew she was not referring to my academic achievements. In that pause, I contemplated the essence of my mother's words. I *have* had a remarkable life. In writing this chapter, I have discovered something else. When time stops, it can be the portal to a new life, one in which you can find the courage for joy.

Who Am I?

Like all of us, I am many people. To my mother, I am her youngest daughter; I am also a sister. To the elderly couple who live in the apartment underneath mine, I am the friendly "young" woman who pops in occasionally, at the end of a day's work, for a chat and a glass of dry sherry. To my friends, I am someone they turn to for a lively conversation; a dinner out; a movie and, from time to time, words of wisdom. I am also someone they have, in turn, comforted and sheltered over the years. To my university students, I am their lecturer in disability studies. To all those people who do not know me well or who meet me for the first time, I am a woman with a speech impediment—or is it a European accent of sorts? I can see them wondering—who seems aloof, even going so far as to ignore what they say. I am not aloof; I am deaf and just haven't heard what they said. I am all of these people and more. And yet, rising over and above all these people, the person I most know myself to be is the mother who still misses her infant son, Jack, after his sudden death nearly 25 years ago.

From Then to Now

All these years later, I still find it difficult to describe in short, simple words the terribleness of Jack's death and the strenuousness of my struggle to survive. My tone variously swings from detachment (prompted in part by the self-enforced urge to rise to societal expectations of rectitude, to avoid the appearance of being clinging) to an almost poetic description of my time with Jack, thus giving rise to the suspicion that perhaps I have never separated from him after all, despite his long-ago death.

Jack was just short of 23 weeks old when he died. He had been my solemn-faced baby boy; my chest ached each rare time he smiled at me. At the back of his head, a tuft of hair stuck up, which I slicked with a lick to make it stick up even more. He liked to lean forward so that he could see his world open up before him; he would never sit back. I was 32 years old at the time, but still unprepared for the flurry and spin of my days and nights as my life expanded with the fullness of this baby of mine. And then grief came through my door, became my twin; my son hummed his last breath into the winter sky above his cot, and ghosted into my shadow child. I was unprepared, then, for the stillness, the silence, and the airlessness that seeped into my bones, into my heart.

For many years, my sorrow was a heavy weight on my heart and in my body, but I was reluctant to relieve myself of this pain. To do so seemed like an act of disloyalty to my son, and I preferred instead to adjust to its bulk somehow. I lived my life cautiously, as if that might make a difference. I worked hard; kept up my friendships; and was moderate in my diet, drink, and fitness schedules. Jack's father was long gone. After we buried our son at the Pinaroo Lawn Cemetery, we were unable to console each other. Instead, I fought with him, not out of blame, but in an unceasing and desperate urge to kick my pain away, to give it another reason to exist. Our struggle was terrible. He left me, unable to bear the gap in my arms, the tearing away of the flesh and blood that formed our son. I loved him and hoped his flight was temporary, but his absence stretched into years. He made a new life for himself, remarried, and had a new child, a daughter this time. My love for him drained away until there was nothing left at all. I was afraid that this made me a shallow woman and fretted about my apparent incapacity to keep love alive; indeed, this fear of my apparent lovelessness preoccupied me for as many years as my sorrow for Jack resided in me.

After such awfulness, how then do I come to be here today? How am I still standing, still living, working, writing, and (wondrously) enjoying the companionable love of all my friends, and my family of nieces and nephews. Who could ask for more?

When I first asked myself this question of survivorship in preparation for this chapter, I wrote a list of things I did immediately upon Jack's death and in the many years after. I thought these actions might provide a clue that might identify the necessary qualities that separate grief that is survived from grief that is buried. I thought, in fact, that there might be such a distinction between the two realms. This is the list that I compiled:

I resisted being defined as a bereaved mother. I went along to self-help support groups a few times but found the experience too oppressive. I was suspicious of being drawn into a coven (it was always women) of sorrow; what if I couldn't get out? I asserted my desire—and even my right—to be known as a mother certainly, but I equally asserted my desire to be known as a woman who was striving to rise above the images that the word *bereaved* conjures up: dressed in black, downturned mouth, pale cheeks, eyes lost in dark shadows, listless, tearful, obsessively reciting all the cherished details of the lost child. I resisted all this because these details too closely described my reality. I saw myself in the mirror each day, and saw all these grim images glowering back at me. They frightened me, and I worked hard to create other images. Bright clothes; glossy hair; red lipstick; animated conversations about work, movies, books, gossip, anything at all—but inevitably, my conversations turned back to my lost son, Jack.

I read a lot. I had always relied on books as a turning away from the humdrum of daily realities, but now I relied on my reading as means of turning inward for consolation. No, not merely consolation: Perhaps a miracle might occur, the sort of outrageously improbable miracle that would restore my son. I read Vicktor Frankl's *Man's Search for Meaning*, his 1946 chronicle of his experiences in a Nazi concentration camp. Other books followed. C. S. Lewis's *A Grief Observed,* in which he noted that his grief after the death of his wife in 1961 sometimes felt "like being mildly drunk or concussed." Ian McEwan's strange but teasingly compelling 1987 novel, *A Child in Time,* in which he described the scent of a baby's head as being just like that of a freshly baked bun, still warm from the oven; oh, how I ached when I read that! Keri Hulme's 1986 novel of inarticulate love, wordless isolation, and savage grief, *The Bone People.* Everything I read took on a special significance. Everything seemed to have been written just for me and imbued my grief with the possibility of meaning. Still, all this reading did not return Jack to me. Each time I resurfaced to the world from the book I had been immersed in, I experienced a chest-splitting, hiccoughing sensation—brief, but no less painful for its brevity—on realizing that no amount of clever, wise, or comforting words would bring back to me the body and life of my son, Jack. I felt hurt, surprised and saddened in equal measure every time.

I wrote a memoir and called it *Jack's Story* (McDonald, 1991). It did not start out as a book; it started as a journal. I cannot now remember the first day I sat down to write my journal, but my book records that when I wrote the words "Jack is dead" six weeks after his death, I shook uncontrollably and felt chilled. In my journal, I kept a record of all that I was experiencing; I used the writing process as a way of both describing and resisting the strong undertow of my grief. On looking quickly through my memoir just now (I have not read it in its entirety since it was first published in 1991), I see it is full of resolutions, one of which is my resolve not to die. I wrote,

> I fantasize about this [my wish to die]. What stops me is my ingrained sense of responsibility. I know the pain it would cause my family ... I worry too that they would see my suicide as an act of anger, rather than simply wanting to let go of life. ... From now on, I will affirm life because I have loved Jack and because Jack once lived. This is not a simple one-off decision. I have to invoke this over and over and over again. (p. 29)

I stopped writing my journal two years after my first entry, when I woke up one morning and caught myself in the act of sizing up the day ahead of me without Jack's presence. I lay in bed and thought for a long time about this. By the time I pressed myself up and off the bed at last to ready myself for work, I had made a new resolution: It was time for me to break the habit of grief. These are the exact words I used: "the habit of grief." I saw that the act of writing my journal had been a healing process but that it was now sliding into a new dimension: a cementing process. The combination of words and paper were acting like bricks and mortar: I did not want to bury myself into a fixed posture of grief, terrible and intractable though my sorrow felt. I suspected that I would miss the companionability of my hard-edged grief. At least it was constant; I could rely on it. If I wished, it would always be with me, a proxy for Jack. Still, I went ahead and tidied up my journal notes, recomposed them as a memoir of my love for Jack and sorrow for his death, and sent it off to a publisher. I hoped that my memoir would help others understand the confusions of love and grief, but mostly I saw it as an act of honoring and memorializing my son.

I talked a lot; my talking was compulsive and tiring. It must have been tiring for my friends too because when the flood of words eventually slowed down and ceased altogether, one of my friends said, "I'm glad you've stopped talking so much about Jack." I was shocked then; I confess to still being shocked now as I write these words in recollection. Although much of my talking about Jack was compulsive and out of my control, I was also deliberate in my talking. I regarded it as a way of honoring my son. I knew that my readiness to talk about him discomfited some people, and I cared about this. I was troubled by their unease. Despite this, I remained hypervigilant: I saw it as one of my mothering responsibilities to say Jack's name, to keep his reality alive, to fan the memories of him.

However, with the passing of time, my oratorical vigilance sounded shrill even to me. I softened my words and increasingly let opportunities to acknowledge Jack's existence pass me by (while keeping a weather-eye on Jack's shadowy presence in my orbit and *his* reactions to my silence). When even more time passed, I developed stock responses, shortcuts, so that I could fend off questions more easily (it is never *absolutely* easy). It has been 25 years since Jack's birth and death, but I am still asked if I have children. I continue to feel a pang on being asked (and I never ask others this question, not wanting to pass on the bruises). My stock answer is, "No, I wasn't blessed that way." It's a coy answer because I can hear it in my mind's ear in two ways: "No, I never had any children" or "Well, actually, I am the mother of a son, but he died at 22 weeks—sudden infant death syndrome, cot-death." I do not know how the listeners interpret my answer: Am I perhaps infertile? What happened? But my response is satisfactory for me because it forestalls further questions, and it reminds the questioner that perhaps *they* have been blessed. (Even if they only experience that realization for a second, that would please me.) At the same time, and confusingly, in the early days of my grief, I set boundaries about who could and could not talk about my son: I would be cool toward those I did not deem to have the "right" to talk about him. Such deeming was obviously irrational and cruel.

In between the talking, I listened a lot. Some of my friends' observations bothered me. In my memoir, I recorded how one friend described a visit to me:

> I walked into your house and even though you were there, and your parents too, it felt as though I was coming into an empty house. I felt as though no-one was at home ... it was almost as though I could put my hand right through your body, just like a ghost. (McDonald, 1991, p. 37)

I had been aware of this vacating of my body but did not realize until then that it was so apparent to my friends. I did not know what to do about this: How could I fill my own body when my son was gone?

I got angry; I lashed out at people. I spoke sharply to my mother, to my friends, to strangers. I hauled out some old crockery and smashed the already-chipped plates onto the concrete courtyard behind my kitchen. I rang Jack's father at work and berated him: Why was he traveling for work so much? Why was he coming home late every night? Where was he now? Didn't he know that I loved him, needed him, right now, this very instant? My anger rained down on him. I rang his boss and railed at him too: Why wasn't he sending Jack's father home earlier every night? Why wasn't he being more supportive? Couldn't he see how much I was hurting? My anger must have seemed like madness to him. God knows, it certainly felt like madness to me.

I worked hard, staying late at work and chasing new challenges. I climbed the career ladder (even though I found it a dry occupation: I worked in the public sector for too many years) and pushed my team; thankfully, they were tolerant. Work became my defining characteristic. Whereas others are known for their gregariousness, generosity of spirit, or hedonism, I was known for my apparently insatiable appetite for work. It was my source of forgetting. I could lose myself in work in the same way other people lose themselves in drink, drugs, sex, or any combination of those seductions. Work was my relief even while I resented it. It took my friends a long time to recognize this: I saw it before they did, but I pressed on with my compulsion anyway. I finally hesitated when a very good friend rang me in my office in the city late one night and said, after the merest hint of a preamble, "I think you might be a work addict." Her accusation acted as a lance, and I felt immense relief. Of course, the gift of insight does not necessarily bring about the reward of instant reform. However, that night I went home knowing that I would act in some way to bring about a change in my work habits: I did not know how or what it would look like, but I knew it would happen soon. In reality—as with any compulsion, habit, or addiction—I continue, even now, to find the pull of work as a distraction difficult to resist, but the difference now is that I practice daily mindfulness about this.

Swimming taught me mindfulness. I did not start swimming for this reason: My first morning swim at the local pool 22 years ago took place because my sister suggested it. She thought it would be good for me. "You can go with the kids before school," she said (she has four children). I was deeply reluctant as I am not a morning person, but I thought it was worth a try; swimming might prick my dulled senses back into at least a tingle of livingness. It took me a while (a couple of years, actually) to get into any real routine, and persevering with developing that routine was a struggle. But eventually, I got it. I came to understand the beauty of the meditative pull of the arm-over-arm, gentle kicking of feet, and the turn of my body through the water. Whereas other people moan about the boredom of swimming up and down that black line or thrash about with the efforts of breathing in and out in a synchronized rhythm, I find the water the best place in the world to establish mindfulness. When I am swimming, nothing else matters; I am awash with stillness. (Paradoxically, it is also a time of creativity. It is not unusual for me to spring out of the pool rejuvenated with ideas for improving this and resolving that.)

This, then, is my list for surviving grief: refusing to be defined by it; getting angry; reading, writing, talking, and listening a lot; working hard; and swimming. Reviewing this list set me back on my heels. It did not seem much of a list; something must be missing. How would these activities clarify the question of complicated grief and guide others? Surely my throw-away references to feeling mad occasionally and acting crazy at times were unhelpful? And what in God's name did *swimming* have to do with anything? Nor did my list shine much light on the nature of grief itself. What separates someone who survives grief from someone who becomes buried by it? Who comes to be accused of suffering complicated grief? And why does that term sound like an accusation anyway? Why do I rage at it?

Checking Assumptions

I renewed my reflections on the words, *complicated grief,* with a view to checking my assumptions. The first and most self-evident assumption is that I believe I have the right to grieve for my son until the end of my own days and in any way I choose.

On the 20th anniversary of Jack's death—and even I concede that this is rather a long time later—I organized a small ceremony to commemorate his life and to speak of his death. It took place one Sunday evening after Mass. I saw this as an opportunity for healing. I wanted to acknowledge not just my loss, but also the loss to my extended family—especially my nieces and nephews who, as my photographs show, had cradled Jack in their arms when they were only little children themselves. As we stood around the altar, the local priest read out some prayers and gave a blessing. I gave them each a polished marble egg with the word *love* or *joy* etched into it, and I thanked them for their support over all the years. Organizing such a ceremony outside the standard Catholic rites was unusual in my family; it was a one-time event. We blushed, muttered, and shuffled our feet. My mother looked stern in her effort to hold in her emotions. My sister chewed the inside of her cheek. My youngest nephew grinned helplessly. My eldest nephew raised his eyes heavenwards and examined the church ceiling as if assessing its sturdiness. My niece searched for a place to rest her gaze. After it was all over, my brother-in-law thumped me on the shoulder and said, "That was bloody terrific." None of us have referred to this event again, but all the same, I sense a relaxation of sorts within me. It is as if I released a long-held breath that night and breathed in anew.

Some people might question the wisdom of my act of commemorating my son in such a ritual (blessed by the Catholic church though it was), but surely no one would seriously argue against my right as a mother to memorialize my son in the private grieving spaces of my heart and soul. Such a prolonged expression of my grief might complicate the lives of other people because it interferes with their expectations of timeliness and restraint, but does that mean that my private but enduring sorrow is complicated?

But there! Look! I have changed the words. I have substituted the word *sorrow* for the word *grief.* This is worth drawing attention to. Sometimes, I use the word *melancholy.* At other times, I say *sad,* or *down-hearted,* or *teary.* (*Mourning* is another possibility, but this word seems to be rarely used these days outside formal discourse or to identify a widow's dress as her mourning clothes.) I reserve the word *grief* for those awful ripping, rupturing, exploding, imploding, catastrophic moments that can stretch into hours and even whole days and nights. For those times when the tears will not stop, or when a spasm of intense remembering gives rise to nausea, or flattens me to the floor with arms splayed, stretched to the fingertips to release the pain. Such times are extremely rare now, but they were frequent in my life once. Spying a baby with a green beanie in a stroller, or seeing a poster about sudden infant death syndrome, or catching the tail end of a radio show about the perils of leaving the heater on in the baby's room—all these and more once had the power to destroy my day, to undercut my imperceptible but gradual rise to wellness and wholeness. Nowadays, such events are just as likely to induce a wistful desire to feel the baby weight of Jack in my arms again or a fresh tug of anxious guilt ("Perhaps it *was* my fault?"), but I am able now to readily move on. I do not hang onto that wistful desire or that guilt with the same attachment that I once did.

My choice of words goes to the heart of my own understanding of complicated or prolonged grief. There are several models or frameworks available for understanding grief. While there has been "a change in thinking about models of loss and grief [which] has seen contemporary researchers moving away from the earlier stage/phase models of psychodynamic, social learning and cognitive–behavioural theorists" (Clark, 2006, p. 43), most discussions continue to fix on the word *grief*. Very few discussions, if any, seem to engage with the richness of nuances available in the English language. This feels important to me. When I look back over my own 24-year grief history, I recall that time as a cyclical process involving "themes of shock, protest/demand, defiance, despair/resignation and movement towards integration … with recurring feelings of fear, anxiety, searching and yearning … [in] varying levels of intensity" (Clark, 2006, p. 43).

This is the staged or thematic structure of grief that is most familiar to us, and it is certainly consistent with my own experiences. However, I also recall my grief history by different words; it was a time in which my feelings transitioned from *numbness* (mercilessly truncated) to raw, hard-edged *grief* to the erratic riptides of *self-pity* and *melancholy*. My feelings then moved on to the washing tides of *sorrow*, their rhythms slowing down and lengthening as the years rode on, before settling into a gentle but ever-present awareness— sometimes in my peripheral vision, sometimes nestling beneath my skin—of an absence, a *missingness*, whose name is Jack.

Lately, I have come to understand that my nostalgia for Jack is born of an idealized son. I miss Jack in two ways: as the solemn but playful baby boy who left me too soon, and as the perfect, loving 25-year-old son he might have been today. When my friends reach their maturing parenthood mile-stones and chat with me about their adult sons and daughters, I catch new glimpses of Jack. He might have been engaged to be married; he might have had children by now; I might have been a grandmother! How wonderful that might have been! These glimpses of Jack dart about like butterflies: I have to be quick to see them, and I know, by now, not to drag myself down into pointless reveries. And besides (I tell myself), what if Jack had grown into someone else, unrecognizable even to me, his own mother? What if my son had filled himself with resentments, anger, and hate-filled emotions I could not bear to think about? There are, after all, other kinds of deaths: Mothers lose their sons to mental illness, to personality-disordered anger, to delu-sional revisions of family history and finely honed resentments of injuries done to them as boys—whether imagined or real, the pain is the same for everyone. I have witnessed the grief of such mothers and felt simultaneously ashamed and relieved, relieved that my sorrow is simpler, more consolable, more *respectable*, yet ashamed to have these feelings. I have a son who is not with me, but I know where he is and how he died: I know this because I found him in his cot and buried him seven days later. I know too that his life, though as brief as a telegram, was filled to bursting with shy love. Jack teased me with his restlessness, and I loved him with the coltishness of a first-time mother. Other mothers have sons who are missing, lost in the thrall of their self-fueling anger and delusions. The grief for this rarely acknowledged type of loss must surely be unbearable. What words could possibly assuage it? As my local Iranian fish and chips shopkeeper said to me one evening, "When you have no children, you have one problem. When you have many children, you have many problems," and she looked at me in a knowing way as she shared her wisdom with me.

The Habits of Resilience

So, I have looked now at some of my grief-survivorship activities following Jack's death, and I have examined my assumed right to grieve for my son in the manner of my choosing, and reflected on the language of grieving. I have also owned up to the possibility that the son I grieve for is an idealized son. I am sorrowing now as much for what might have been possible as for what actually happened: the swift fall of death's sword on my infant son. In covering such territory, I am mindful that I have still not directly addressed the question of complicated grief and my hostility toward the pathology implied in that term.

On pausing now, I think my hostility is embedded in fear. I fear being robbed of the infinite prospects of honoring my son. I fear having my memorializing activities being named in any number of ways—mad, inappropriate, unhealthy, unwise, unseemly, *complicated*—and having them either therapy-talked or medicated out of existence. I also fear for the prospects of a healthy life being oversimplified. Life is hard; surely we all understand that by now? And surely we also understand that the difficulties of our lives are also what enrich our lives? The grain in the oyster shell leading to the pearl and so forth?

I don't want to stand accused of trivializing grief. Why would I do that? And nor do I want to stand accused of masochism, of relishing grief. That would be equally cruel. But I do want to point to other possibilities of understanding how to survive loss, sorrow, and enduring grief.

I point now to the importance of prehistory; I will focus on my own personal prehistory. Long before my son died, I had endured other grief, hardships, and difficulties. It does not take any great leap of imagination to understand that the life of a little deaf girl born into a hearing family, maturing into adolescence in a mainstream school, and then finding her way through tertiary education and eventually into a professional life would inevitably have been accompanied by many jumps over hurdles, turning aside of hurts, and gritting of teeth. It also requires little imagination to intuit that this daughter of an alcoholic father might also have wrought small miracles of coping with angry drink-sodden nights and sullen mornings after; adapting to my father's late-in-life embrace of sobriety required fresh skills of orientation to, and accommodation of, his new persona. Add to all this the commonplace blows to our psyches that life pounds into us from time to time: disappointments in love, job interviews gone humiliatingly awry, the day-to-day frustrations of not getting what we want. In other words, long before my son died, I had learned that life was an unreliable trajectory that required constant negotiating. What I had not realized but came to understand later—very much later—was that the difficulties I met, faced up to, and resolved (along with the ones that I did not resolve) all added up to an arsenal of tools called *coping strategies*, or *resilience*. I realize I am wandering into treacherous territory here because I am swapping one assumption-heavy concept, complicated grief, for another, resilience. While owning up to this, I will press on, but I will confine my remarks to my own experiences and let others draw any generalizable findings from my observations.

The advent of terrible grief such as the sudden death of your infant son is not the best time to learn new skills of coping or resilience. It is the time for putting into place—even if subconsciously, as if sleepwalking—the lessons of coping and resilience that have already been learned. We might add to that arsenal of tools, but to stare grief in the face for the very first time devoid of any knowledge or skills of coping defies my comprehension; it would be too terrible to endure; how would you start?

All those activities that I have written about were driven by my habits of resilience, by my values of hope and perseverance. Hope was not a word that sprang to my mind in the early years after Jack's death, but in hindsight, I believe it was hope that pulled me along, hour by hour, day by day. I have come to believe that, for hope to do its work, it is not necessary to name it or even to acknowledge its presence. In fact, I recently stumbled across a study that argues it may be possible for hope to do its work even while it exists alongside hopelessness: The two emotions swing to and fro in a rhythm of sorts, with hope winning out in the end (Thornburg, 1993). This duality of hope–hopelessness makes sense to me.

In contrast, I suspect that perseverance *is* a quality that has to be named and known before it can be acted upon. This is the lesson I draw from my swimming routines. I was dogged in my efforts. Not only did I learn how to show up to the pool regularly, I also learned how to show up to my life each day. Not only did I discover the joy of sustained effort by attending the pool every day for a week, then for a month, and then watching the months grow into years—a satisfyingly big number of years—but I also came to discover the joys (admittedly, sometimes they are unsatisfactorily small, but you take your joys where you can) that can only come when you stick around in your own life: the joy of long-term friendships; the contentment of completing a task of several years duration; the warmth of reunions with long-ago friends, colleagues, companions; the pleasure of learning new things (riding a bicycle, painting, using an iPad). These moments of joy resided, at first, in those tiny in-between times of relief from my grief, and then they seemed to exert an expansionary push–pull effect by which they pressed apart the walls of my grief so that my times of relief grew wide and then wider still.

Thus, my life eventually expanded to be filled with more than all those grief-survivorship activities I have listed. The pace of my life has picked up its speed, at first in incremental fits and starts, and then in a steady momentum since that instant when time stopped at 7:30 A.M., June 4, 1987. People scoff at clichés such as "when time stopped," but I remember the days after Jack's death as a time-emptied expanse. I felt only the stillness of that moment when his death rode through me, while everyone around me glided forward as if on roller skates. All these years later, I am reminded of this fracture in time when I read in the newspapers and witness on television fresh disasters, tragedies, and catastrophes and know that time has stopped, at least temporarily, for other people. My own daily rhythms are now once more in tune with the movements of the sun and the moon. My days move with the ebb and tide of new feelings of delight, contentment, laughter, and—of course—fresh sorrows and challenges because life does move on once more.

Having described my grief-survivorship activities and identified some of the values that shaped my responses to my son's death, I want now to make a further point: All this took courage. This point might seem lame and self-evident, but the sort of courage I am particularly thinking about as I write these words is more unlikely and perhaps difficult to understand if you have never experienced the plummeting falls of grief. I write now about the courage to be happy. Happiness is a sort of forgetting. It is the emotion—sometimes mercurial, sometimes steady—that springs forth when we forget our gripes and discontents; forget ourselves; and, more dangerously, forget our grief. Forgetting our grief is dangerous because we might also allow ourselves to forget momentarily who we loved and still love. And wouldn't this be disloyal? Wouldn't even the briefest moment of joy prove our deepest suspicions about ourselves—that we had not deserved such love in the first place? I confess to enduring this struggle over many years, in which I vacillated between striking out for healthy joy on the one hand and conserving my sorrow in the name of my son on the other hand. I never spoke of this because surely everyone wants to be happy? Who would understand my dilemma? That long-ago morning when I lay in my bed contemplating the habit of grief was when I first sowed the seeds of courage to hold two forces at once: the force of happiness and the force of sorrowing remembrance. I swapped the habit of grief for the habit of resilience, somehow intuiting that I could have both, side by side; one does not have to rule out the other. If anything, each enriches the other.

Of course, I did not immediately comprehend this in one blitzkrieg of insight; this understanding has evolved over time and still evolves. Perhaps if I had been less circumspect in what I chose to reveal to my friends and family—after all, the quality they most wanted for me was happiness (if only to lessen their own distress)—or perhaps if I had been more open with the occasional counselor I visited, I might have sped through my confusion about choosing sorrow or choosing happiness. I muddled along and saw myself as being stoic. But while writing this chapter, I understood that the grim word *stoic* does not do either me or my efforts justice. I chose courage.

The Importance of Other People

No one survives anything alone; it is simply not possible. We might feel alone in our efforts to cope. Sometimes—or even very often—we might feel horribly alone. Our lives might, in fact, look alone and lonely to people watching us from the safety of their outsider perspective. However, I am sure that I would not have survived my own grief without the intrusions, invasions, and insistence of other people into my sorrow. Some were friends who telephoned me, took me out, or cooked me a meal; some were strangers who offered unwanted but canny wisdom; some were people who did not even know they had entered into my life—people I read about, people whose stories I heard, people I observed. I collected advice and hoarded tips, and I drew from this pool of wisdom as and when I felt appropriate. I still do.

My gratitude for the presence of others in my life is utterly heartfelt. So much so that I insist on naming their presence as the single element that is critical to surviving grief. Curiously, however, my experiences of attending self-help support groups were discouraging. I tried several times, but I always left those sad meetings even more saddened. I had hoped the older women in the meetings might be a particular source of consolation or wisdom, but whenever I sat with them, I saw the prospect of my being like them in 20 years—sitting in a musty, floral-curtained room dotted with butterfly motifs (the symbol for compassion), talking about my baby and my sorrow. I was young and impatient; this was not how I saw my future. Instead, I saw my future in the lively face and warm home of one of my mother's old friends, whose daughter had died not long after her birth. I saw my future in the homes of my own friends, with their partners and children (even though this did not come to pass for me; I never did re-partner or have more children). I saw my future in the mess and tumble of the lives happening all around me: I wanted to be part of *that*, not sitting in a room crippled with grief, talking about death.

Conclusion

Because this chapter is about grief—my grief—its narrow scope inevitably masks the breadth of my life since Jack's death 25 years ago. I have achieved much: I have studied hard, worked well, traveled widely, and taken up new interests. But best of all, I have sustained my friendships and made new friends. With my mother, sister, and nieces and nephews, they make up my family and my joy.

So I come now, full circle, back to my mother's comment about my "remarkable life," in which she took in the sweep of who I am and what I have done, and implicitly acknowledged the trail of my sorrow which, like Ariadne's thread, has weaved its way through all my accomplishments. I have described myself as having many roles in my life: daughter, sister, friend, lecturer, neighbor, passing acquaintance, and stranger, but most insistently, as a mother saddened by the death of my infant son. Is this complicated grief? I think not. Do I admit to an enduring nostalgia that reminds me of who I once held in my arms and loved with awe? Yes. The insistence of my sorrow does not, these days, intrude into my relationships, and nor does it fracture my days into chasms of hollowness and crashes of chaos. Instead, my life is routinely and manageably full as I juggle the demands, irritations, and joys of my various roles. Sometimes, it's even complicated!

References

Clark, J. M. (2006). *Wanting to hope: The experience of adult siblings of long-term missing people* (Doctoral dissertation, University of Queensland, Brisbane, Australia).

Frankl, V. E. (1946/1984). *Man's search for meaning.* New York: Simon & Schuster.

Hulme, K. (1986). *The bone people.* Auckland, Australia: Spiral/Hodder & Stoughton.

Lewis, C. S. (1973). *A grief observed.* London: Faber.

McDonald, D. (1991). *Jack's story.* Sydney, Australia: Allen & Unwin.

McEwan, I. (1987). *A child in time.* London: Picador.

Thornburg, P. D. (1993). *The meaning of hope in parents whose infants died from sudden infant death syndrome* (Doctoral dissertation, University of Cincinnati, Ohio) (Publication No. AAT 9329939). Retrieved from ProQuest Nursing & Allied Health Source.

Chapter Ten

Communicative Coping with Ambiguous Death
The Search for Answers and Acceptance after the Death of a Child[1]

Lynne M. Webb and Paige W. Toller

The first few weeks after my son's death, my emotional experience was one of standing on the edge of a very tall cliff. Whenever I closed my eyes, I felt dizzy, as if I could topple over very easily, and it would be a very long way down. I came to believe that I could simply take a few steps forward and free-fall into permanent madness. I knew I could lose myself in my grief, abandon rationality, and the whole world would understand. I lost my child to unknown causes. No one could provide me with a medical explanation as to why my child died unexpectedly at age 13. In my culture, with advanced, lifesaving medical technology, experiencing the unexplained death of your child is perhaps the only acceptable excuse for madness, because such a death is a kind of psychological torture. And it was torture. I had to clean out Reed's room and dispose of his possessions, knowing as I did so that I was literally disposing of the last definitive evidence of his place in our family and of his very existence on earth. But as his mother, it fell to me to complete this and so many other torturous tasks.

For parents, the death of a child is profoundly painful and devastating, as a child's death defies the natural order of life (Becvar, 2001; Gamino, Sewell, & Easterling, 1998; Klass, 1997; Rando, 1991). When the anomaly of a child's death is further complicated by the lack of a definitive cause of death, the loss moves from tragic to incomprehensible. Because a child's death is catastrophic (Oliver, 1999) and life shattering (Janoff-Bulman, 1992), bereaved parents may be particularly vulnerable to complicated grief

---

[1] The authors gratefully acknowledge the editorial assistance of Randi R. Cruz-Green (BA, 2011, University of Arkansas) and Robert B. Moberly (JD, 1966, University of Wisconsin) in preparing this manuscript.

(Dyregrov, Nordanger, & Dyregrov, 2003; Rando, 1993). Conceptualized as a maladaptive pattern of mourning, complicated grief is often characterized by obsession with the deceased, feelings of disbelief, avoidance of reminders of the deceased, hallucinations of the deceased, and survivor's guilt (Prigerson, Maciejewski et al., 1995). Research has linked complicated grief to severe physical and mental health issues, including suicidal ideation, heart problems, high blood pressure, and cancer (Chen et al., 1999, Prigerson, Bierhals et al., 1997; Prigerson, Silverman et al., 2001).

The purpose of our chapter is to share one mother's story of loss and complicated grief after the sudden, unexpected, and unexplained death of her 13-year-old-son, Reed. Her story is a vivid, painful, and heart-wrenching narrative that goes beyond scholars' definitional and diagnostic debates about complicated grief (see Breen & O'Connor, 2007, for a review of this debate). Rather, her story is an evocative narrative (Ellis & Bochner, 2000) that communicates the depth of her suffering as well as the complicated nature of her grief and ultimate recovery. Ellis and Bochner (2000) described evocative narratives as stories that

> activate subjectivity and compel emotional response. They long to be used rather than analyzed; to be told and retold rather than theorized and settled; to offer lessons for further conversation rather than undebatable conclusions; and to substitute the companionship of intimate detail for the loneliness of abstracted facts (p. 744).

We invite readers to deeply engage in this story and to experience its narrative truth (Ellis & Bochner, 2000). Throughout this chapter, we interweave the first author's story with scholarly literature to present a multidimensional portrayal of complicated grief.

The Dream of the Perfect Family

By age 34, I had earned tenure and promotion at a Research One university and was happily married to the handsome man of my dreams, a fellow scholar who understood my work and personal issues. My dream man came with two wonderful children from his first marriage. I took to motherhood like a fish to water. They were the most wonderful children on earth. I bragged about them constantly, attended their sporting events, and assisted them during their adolescent and young-adult emergencies. I loved them utterly.

However, adding the next two children we had planned proved problematic. I was unable to become pregnant. Fertility drugs, exploratory surgery, and trips to multiple clinics all yielded the same results: I suffered from "undiagnosed infertility." In other words, no one knew what was wrong, only that I failed to maintain a pregnancy. In many ways, undiagnosed infertility was my first taste of complicated grief and ambiguous loss, as I had no medical explanation or rationale as to why I could not conceive. For a time, I mourned the biological children I would never birth. I was deeply disappointed in myself and entered a period of depression.

Then, one night, I had a dream that changed my life. In my dream, I was in a large, dimly lit room with bare walls painted beige. Other people I did not know were there milling about. It seemed to be a waiting room. I heard a baby cry, and so I looked around for the child. Seeing none, I listened more intently and began to follow the direction of the cry. It was coming from a room just beyond the one in which I stood. I methodically began searching the building for the child. As my search continued, I came to realize that I was searching for my child. I woke with a start and a realization. My child was already in the world. I merely needed to find the baby. I woke my husband at 4 A.M. with the good news: Our baby was alive. We just needed to find him or her and adopt this special little person. I was so happy, so very happy.

Fourteen months later, I held him in my arms. He arrived from Seoul, Korea at age 17.5 months. He smiled the first time he saw me with an ear-to-ear grin. He climbed into my arms with no hesitation and rested there, relaxed and utterly at ease, as if he'd always been there. From that moment, I believed he was meant to be with me, that destiny brought us together. We named him Reed. He was my baby boy, the light of my life, and my most precious one.

He brought me the greatest joy I have ever known. He turned my life upside down and remade me. He rounded all the edges by making me as happy, crazy, and angry as I have ever been—forcing me to rethink my whole life, to reprioritize. But primarily, he made me feel so very happy, very complete, and very loved. With him I experienced emotions I had never even imagined possible. He was, is, and always will be the defining and decisive influence on who I ultimately became.

This narrative is about Reed. I am telling it to you because I can no longer tell it to Reed. He died unexpectedly at age 13, leaving behind a shattered dream. His death was senseless, without reason, and literally has medical no explanation whatsoever.

Reed was and remains the most beautiful child I have ever seen. He was a handsome boy, even though he had Marfan syndrome, a serious connective tissue disorder (for more information, see www.marfan.com). We lived in a university town with a medical school hospital. We had excellent insurance. It was a perfect adoption placement. When his condition worsened with age and the university doctors recommended heart surgery, we shifted into high gear and did our research. We discovered the three top surgeons in the country who performed this kind of operation. We choose the Johns Hopkins Medical School team because they were the very best. We started flying to Baltimore every six months; at each visit, Reed saw seven doctors in 48 hours—a complete workup each time. He saw his medical team 10 days before he left for camp that fateful summer. They told me, "Send him to camp. He's going to have a great summer. He will need back surgery in the next six to eight months, but his heart is sound and he is doing well." They were perhaps the only people on the planet more shocked than his parents when Reed died.

The Death

At 12:20 A.M. on a warm June night, Reed awoke in his tent with chest pains. He woke his camp counselor who had Reed in an ambulance within 10 minutes—no small feat. The person who rode in the ambulance with him was the camp codirector, a Duke University–trained pediatric trauma nurse. She held his hand the entire way and later told me that she had never seen a child look that bad and survive. His fate was sealed even then.

It was raining hard that evening. If it had been a clear night, Reed would have been air-evacuated to Duke Medical. The rain killed my boy—or at least that's one explanation I've toyed with over the years.

Reed was taken directly to the nearest hospital, a small county hospital in rural North Carolina. When the emergency room physician attempted to intubate him to regulate his breathing, he went into cardiac arrest. They never got his heart restarted, despite 45 minutes of extreme measures, including open-heart massage. When they came to the waiting room to tell the camp codirector that Reed was dead, she apparently ordered them to continue cardiopulmonary resuscitation or "I will do it myself, and don't think I won't." She then called her sons' pediatrician and persuaded him to come to the hospital at 1:30 A.M. in his pajamas to assure her that nothing more could be done for Reed.

That poor pediatrician, whose name I do not recall, called us at 1:45 A.M. to say, basically, you don't know me, but I'm here with the camp director and your son is dead. Of course, we told him he was wrong; our son would never die in a hospital. I remember saying, calmly, please put him on a portable heart–lung machine and take him by helicopter or ambulance to a large hospital. I repeated what his doctors had always told me: If anything goes wrong, just get him to a hospital. He'll never die in a hospital. Apparently, they were wrong.

When we realized our son was actually dead, we called the hospital back and asked that his organs be harvested for donation. A doctor came on the telephone very quickly to tell us that none of his organs were usable because he had Marfan syndrome. We were even denied this, an opportunity for some good to come immediately from his death.

The two camp directors and Reed's camp counselor, who had placed him in the ambulance, were in my living room the next afternoon to tell me all the details surrounding Reed's death. Even though I know what happened to my son, I have no idea why he died. I wanted a cause of death. I think any parent would want to know what caused their precious child to die unexpectedly. I was a ferocious mother of a special needs child, and a trained social scientist. I needed a cause of death. I mean, kids don't just die. Even sick kids don't just die for no reason, or so I thought.

The Search for a Cause of Death

Marfan syndrome is an insidious condition that affects all the connective tissue in the body: heart valves, joints, connective tissue holding up the lenses in the eyes, and so on. Reed had a medium-to-severe case. He also had asthma. Because he awoke with chest pains and trouble breathing, I first thought the cause was asthma. But when I called the Johns Hopkins Clinic at 8 A.M. the morning he died, they did not. They thought he suffered from heart issues and immediately called the North Carolina Coroner's Office to acquire x-rays, tissue samples, slides—the whole shebang. Reed's Hopkins case manager, an eminent pediatric geneticist who was following over 500 cases of pediatric Marfan syndrome worldwide, cried on the phone. The man graduated from Harvard Medical School, held multimillion-dollar grants, and authored more than 100 articles in medical journals—but he cried openly on the telephone as he spoke with me. He vividly remembered Reed and mourned the loss of this very special patient.

The night we received the news of Reed's death, the hospital telephoned us three times asking what to do with Reed's body. We'd never had the responsibility of a death before, let alone a child's death. We had no idea what to request. On the third call, we asked them to send his body to the only funeral home in that small town. Regrettably, they embalmed Reed's body—thus destroying the possibility of conclusive autopsy results. In North Carolina, the death of anyone under 18 triggers an automatic autopsy, so the funeral home worker violated state law by embalming the body. That error caused physicians at the North Carolina Coroner's Office and the Johns Hopkins Medical School to talk back and forth for weeks and to call me—ulti-mately—to report that we will never know how or why Reed died.

So my simple question is this: How am I supposed to live with that ambiguity? How can I accept the fact that my 13-year-old son, the only child I was privileged to call my own, died, and I will never know why? How am I to mourn a loss that I cannot explain or fully understand? At least parents who lose a child to cancer or a school shooting have some sort of answer or explanation. They have a villain to blame and a cause to adopt. "Donations can be sent to the American Cancer Society." How could I ever accept that my son was taken from me for no reason?

Boss (1999, 2004) coined the phrase *ambiguous loss* to describe grief and losses that leave survivors without closure or explanation. She argued that ambiguous loss occurs when a loved one is physically absent but psychologically present (that is, an abducted family member) or when a loved one is physically present but psychologically absent (that is, a loved one with dementia). This mother's story reflects a third kind of ambiguous loss, never before considered (to our knowledge) in the social scientific literature. No rationale or explanation exists for her son's death. She was never given a reason as to why her son suddenly went into cardiac arrest and died. Ambiguous loss strongly affects grief, taking a tremendous physical, mental, and emotional toll on survivors (Betz & Thorngren, 2006; Boss, 1999, Weiner, 1999).

When Reed was only four years old, he had his first medical procedure. A cardiologist injected dye in his veins so that the team could videotape his heart pumping blood and ascertain the extent of the damage to his heart valves. I stayed overnight in the hospital with him, of course. Then there were the overnight visits to Johns Hopkins and the many, many visits to see various doctors at the university hospital (pediatrics, genetics, cardiology, orthopedics). When I became frightened during a medical procedure, I always had the same two thoughts: First, he cannot die, because I could not endure it if he died. Second, God never would have brought him halfway around the world and chosen parents for him with the skills and means to seek the best medical care in the world for him, only to let him die young. These two thoughts comforted me innumerable times. Of course, when he actually died, they brought no comfort whatsoever. In fact, they led me to conclude that this death was a terrible mistake and that I needed to discover exactly what had happened so I could ensure that the mistake did not happen again to another family.

Losing a child creates a crisis of meaning (Braun & Berg, 1994; Wheeler, 1993–1994), as a child's death challenges parents' prior meaning systems and value structures (Attig, 1996; de Vries, Dalla Lana, & Falck, 1994; Rando, 1986) and shatters their assumptions about the world (Attig, 1996) and about the fairness of life (Janoff-Bulman, 1992). Consequently, developing any coherent sense of what happened and why is difficult for parents as their child's death appears to have no purpose or reason (Gamino, Hogan, & Sewell, 2002).

For months after Reed's death, I woke up every morning listening for him. It would take me two or three minutes to remember that there was no need to lie still and listen to the house to see if I could discover what he was doing. I was still driving a mini-van that smelled like him inside. Should I sell a vehicle he had loved? Was I to keep it forever? At meal times, I set the table for the wrong number of people and kept making too much food. As the months continued to pass, I hated doing laundry; it was so obvious he was gone. There was literally nothing more I could do for him. Or was there? Didn't I owe it to him to discover why he died? But how do I proceed? How could I achieve that end when there appeared to be no answers?

I filed for a copy of the official autopsy report. I knew the coroner was required to list a cause of death. I had to see what the report said. They sent me an autopsy report for a 74-year-old man who died in a house fire. They sent the wrong autopsy report. That was when I knew the agonizing truth: I'll never know what happened to my boy. I'll just never know. My husband telephoned the coroner's office; they apologized for the "clerical error," but it did not matter. Of course, when the report on Reed's death finally arrived, the cause of death was listed as inconclusive.

Then we thought of the medical records. We wrote to the hospital requesting the medical records from the emergency room where Reed spent his last minutes on earth. We received illegible copies. So we hired a lawyer to obtain legible copies. The hospital apologized for sending smeared copies, but the records they sent also were unreadable, given the illegible hand writing. Another court order for a typed transcription yielded incomprehensible medical jargon. Our attorney sent the documents to two physicians who rendered opinions on the efficacy of our son's treatment: No errors were made; he simply died. Once again, our search for answers was futile.

So I called the coroner's office and spoke to the physician who conducted Reed's autopsy: "Now, you cannot tell me he is gone and you don't know why. You are the coroner. Tell me why my son died. Tell me what I did or failed to do. How can my son be dead at age 13? How is that even possible?" Her answer: "Nothing points to a death from complications from Marfan syndrome or asthma. I checked the body carefully and found no evidence of an insect bite. I cannot do blood work on an embalmed body. We will never really know how or why he died." In other words, I would never truly know what caused my precious son to be taken from me so quickly and suddenly.

The Person He Was

Of course, as his mother, I think Reed was so very special. However, the documented facts support my evaluation. He was attending a magnet middle-school for students gifted in math and science. He was a "geek" who could get the picture-in-picture on our new television set to work at age four when two parents with doctorates could not. He was doing household repairs at age seven. He created his first Web site at age eight in 1992, when most Americans did not have an e-mail account. He played in national chess tournaments beginning at age nine. At age 11, in the fifth grade, he tested out with an 11th-grade vocabulary and 11th-grade math skills. He sang in church choir and volunteered at his middle school helping severely handicapped students learn to use technology. I can only imagine what an amazing young man he would have become had he lived.

Although all the intellectual achievements are impressive, the most impressive thing about Reed was his personality. He was one of those people who radiated life. He had a smile that wouldn't quit, and he loved games of all kinds, but especially cards. I used to say he could always deal cards in Vegas if college did not work out! He had a wonderful, dry sense of humor, a way with words that entertained and comforted everyone. He was always drawn to helping others. He talked with children with severe mental disabilities at church when the other children ignored them. He defended classmates when bullies picked on them, and readily defused tense situations. He made friends with everyone he met. At the reception after his memorial service, no fewer than four children privately told me that Reed was their best friend. Reed always told me he did not have a best friend because all his friends were important to him. How could a life force, a spirit of that strength and magnitude, simply die?

Writing about the Death

It's been 12 years since Reed's death, and I think I can finally write about it. I begin writing today, in part, because yesterday the Casey Anthony verdict was handed down. How could a mother not report her child missing? I freaked out if my child was missing for two seconds. I lost him once in a shopping mall. He was three years old and thought it would be fun to hide from me in one of those round carousels of clothing. I think it was the terror in my voice as I screamed his name that made him meekly reappear with an apology on his lips.

By now, Reed's been gone longer than he was with me. That's a strange thought because he's still with me every single day, or at least I think about him every day—often multiple times a day. Yet so much still remains unknown. Will my life ever resemble anything like normal again? Is my grief longer and more difficult because of the many unknowns in the equation? Did my son die in vain because we've learned basically nothing from his death that will help others? Maybe that's why I am writing this—to provide meaning to the death and to give his life meaning. How can a child just die? I mean, who just dies? And how can a mother learn to cope with that? How can any parent cope with the inexplicable death of a child? I've gone from undiagnosed infertility to the unexplained death of my child. Neither left me feeling well settled in grief or in life.

For many mourners, talking about their grief and loss is fundamental to the grieving process (DeGroot & Carmack, 2012). In particular, the act of writing can be therapeutic for the bereaved (DeGroot & Carmack, 2012), providing catharsis (Sofka, 1997) and preserving memories, thus eliminating the need to ruminate on them continually (Pennebaker, 1997). Furthermore, disclosure about loss and grief has been associated with health improvements (Pennebaker, 1997).

Is my grief worse or more complicated because I have no cause of death? How could it not be? If Reed had died on the operating table while doctors attempted to cope with his Marfan syndrome, at least I would know that he died trying to prolong and perhaps improve his life. Of course, I would have mourned the loss of my precious son. To die nobly trying to live on, to die raging against the night—as Dylan Thomas describes it—is one thing. But to be snatched in the night by the angel of death for no apparent reason conjures images of a mother who failed to maintain the watchful vigilance that was her duty. Without a cause of death, how could I not forever believe that I somehow failed my child?

About three months after Reed's death, I began attending a self-help group at my local hospice center. A social worker helped about a dozen of us think through and reframe our losses. My fellow mourners disclosed lost spouses and siblings, parents and grandparents. Although the social worker advised us that all loss is profound and that it was inappropriate to compare our grief and losses, every single person in that group told me, "Your loss is so much greater than mine." Yes, to lose a child, they all agreed, was the worst loss a person can know in our culture. However, when it was my turn to share my story in detail and I told them that I had no cause of death, their faces crumpled into tears. Even the social worker cried. "How can you go on?" they asked. Indeed, that was the million-dollar question.

Missing Reed

While I have never before written professionally about the loss, I've written privately to Reed many times. When I am overwhelmed or just confused by the grief, I find comfort in explaining my thoughts or my behavior to Reed.

Reed, I'm mailing your watch to your cousin Philip. The fact that I believe you would approve of the recipient does not change how painful it is to give away so personal a piece of your property. The things you wore everyday are so valued—those are the hardest items to give away. Why must I give these things away at all? Why is it so hard to keep them and so hard to give them away? Each time I give something of yours away, I feel like I part with a piece of you. I know your things are not you, but they are all that I have left of you. When they are all gone from my possession, will I finally have to admit you are completely and utterly gone too? Will it continue to feel as if I am giving you away when I want to keep you in my heart forever?

Many bereaved parents struggle to stay emotionally connected with a physically absent child (Toller, 2005). Mourners often vacillate between wanting to retain reminders of the loved one and wanting to avoid reminders to diminish the intensity of the grief (Bowlby, 1980). Not surprisingly, keeping a deceased loved one's personal belongings is an indication of the bereaved individual's desire and longing to be with the deceased (DeGroot & Cammack, 2012).

When my longing to see my son overwhelms me, I write to my favorite angel, and he seems to banish the demons for a while. Obviously, the act of writing is likely the balm that heals, but the "Missing Reed" file on my hard drive continues to fill with documents.

Challenging the notion that "healthy" grieving must involve complete detachment or decathexis from the deceased (for example, Freud, 1917/1993), bereaved parents may cope with their loss by continuing some form of a relationship with the deceased child (Attig, 1996; Klass, 1993; Toller, 2005). Referring to this relationship as a "continuing bond," Klass (1993, 1997) argued that bereaved parents form such bonds with their deceased children by creating and interacting with an inner representation of their deceased child, sometimes feeling that the child somehow continues to influence their everyday thoughts and actions. Through such communicative activities as rituals, telling stories, and holding memorials for the deceased child (Grout & Romanoff, 2000; Toller, 2005), parents work to maintain these continuing bonds.

Dear Reed, I confess that one of the hardest parts of missing you is not knowing if this profound grief comes from missing you or because of what I am missing. Is it a selfish desire to still have you, or is it honestly missing the real you? Is it possible to separate those things?

I have this sense that everyone else has accepted that you are gone and it is only me who cannot let go. Does this make me weak? Does this make me mentally ill, or just unable to imagine me not your mother? Or is it simply how completely convinced I am that I will see you again in Heaven and that you can see me even now, tune in at will, see me missing you, and perhaps read my thoughts? I don't want you to think no one remembers you or misses you, my sweet. Because I still do. And I will as long as I walk the planet. I miss tucking you in at night. I miss reading you to sleep. I miss washing your clothes. I miss playing with you and Dad. I miss you beating me at cards. I miss seeing you run in the surf at the beach. I miss hearing your voice call to me as you walk in the door after school. I miss watching you gobble down food. I miss you complaining about chores. I miss seeing you and your Dad in those silly matching shirts on your way to play golf. I cannot remember a thing about you that I don't long to experience again. I know you don't want me to be sad. It is just so very hard to let go. I still miss you more that I can say. I wish I knew why you had to go.

Bereaved parents may experience the dialectic of presence–absence (Toller, 2005), a "desire to hold on to the deceased while simultaneously letting go" (DeGroot & Carmack, 2012, p. 162). Despite the healing and comfort of the continuing bonds, this relationship is inherently paradoxical, as parents somehow must let go of the past and move forward in their own lives while simultaneously needing to stay connected with the past and their child (Silverman & Nickman, 1996). This paradox places bereaved parents in two different, yet simultaneous, worlds as they somehow must exist in the world of the living and concurrently maintain ties with nonliving children who exist in a spiritual world (Becvar, 2001).

The Ongoing Grieving Process

Nothing prepared me for the death of my child. Ironically, I studied death and dying as a college student. I knew what to expect when I grieved. I knew I'd go through the stages: denial, anger, grief, bargaining, and acceptance (Kübler-Ross & Kessler, 2005). However, no one told me that the stages cycle back on themselves. I'm still in denial. I hope against hope that the doorbell will ring and he will be there. For years, I thought if only I had a cause of death, maybe I could know, really know, the truth of it all and accept what must be the reality. The bleak reality is this: I haven't seen my son in 12 years. He must have died. Right?

I still feel guilt. I was his mother, and it was my job to keep him alive. That was job one. But he died, so it has to be my fault. I must have done something wrong. With no cause of death, the list of my possible screw-ups is virtually endless: Did I fail to pack something for camp that he needed and that would have saved him? Had his inhaler expired without my realizing it? And then there are the actual pictures in my head of him dying in that emergency room surrounded by health care workers that he did not know. Was he afraid? Did he cry out for me when I was not there? Did he wonder why his father and I sent him to camp? Did he think, even for a second, that we did not love him?

A child's death can call into question parents' abilities to protect and provide for their children (Klass & Marwit, 1988). Further, a grieving parent may experience multiple overlapping phases of grief simultaneously (Parkes, 1972).

I still grieve. If I think about him for more than three or four minutes, I begin to cry. I cry right in public and cannot stop. My husband and I can no longer attend church because I always cry uncontrollably at some point. I miss having Reed sitting between us and it hurts when they play a hymn he particularly liked or sang in youth choir. Grim, that's how I experience the reality of grief. It's grim to contemplate a future without my little boy, a world in which he never moves again, a life without his warmth, laughter, and charm. Yes, he charmed me, made me love him, love him until he became the light of my life, and then in the blink of an eye, the light vanished. Grim. Like an old black and white film shot in half-darkness in which the characters discuss the plot in black-and-white terms. A grim existence with a few shades of gray; there is no color to illuminate the vibrancy of life itself. Grim. As if the rest of my life is simply a waiting room for death—a time when I might finally be reunited with my son in Heaven.

Bereaved parents wrestle with the identity of still being a parent to a nonliving child (Rando, 1986, 1991; Toller, 2008). To relinquish that parental role and identity symbolizes a letting go of the child and all that he or she represents (Silverman & Nickman, 1996). The death of a child creates a liminal identity for parents, as they struggle with feelings of being both a parent and not a parent to an emotionally present yet physically absent child (Toller, 2008).

I still bargain. If only I had taken maternity leave, maybe I would have gotten to know him better, earlier, such that I would have known what would happen if he went to camp. Maybe if I hadn't gone to that conference with my husband the week before Reed went to camp. Maybe if we hadn't been in the process of moving, he would have been less stressed, and then, whatever it was that happened would not have happened to him. And of course, the big one: If I'd been a better mother in some amorphous way, perhaps he'd still be alive.

Acceptance is an ongoing challenge. Reed was the center of my life. When I drove him places in the car, we'd play rock-and-roll songs and sing to each other. When Sister Hazel first released "I Do It All for You," I sang that to him all the time. I saw my life literally as an example that I provided for him, so that he could witness how responsible adults behave. Am I really expected to continue living my life when there is no child to bear witness?

On the other hand, I accept the death on a certain level. In my class lectures, I talk about him, his death, and the way it reconfigured our family dynamics. My husband and I endowed a scholarship in his honor. I've asked everyone I know to never send me presents on any occasion again and instead to make a donation to what we call "Reed's scholarship fund."

Neimeyer and Levitt (2000) framed grief as a disrupted narrative in which the death of a loved one fragments the mourner's life story. Using the term chaos, Neimeyer and Levitt argued that loss leaves humans scrambling to make sense of their once-coherent story. To restore a degree of coherence to their fractured lives (Neimeyer, Prigerson, & Davies, 2002), bereaved parents may engage in meaning-making practices to cope with and adapt to such a profound loss (Wheeler, 2001). Talking about who their child was, making accounts, and telling stories about their child's death are often ways parents attempt to find meaning in their loss (Bosticco & Thompson, 2005; Harvey, 2000; Sedney, Baker, & Gross, 1994; Toller, 2005).

Angels Who Reveal Divine Destinies

During that first dark, dark night, my husband and I slept very little. We mourned, we wailed, we held on to each other, and we cried until we literally passed out from exhaustion. I awoke at dawn to see my husband's face twisted in grief as he slept. I knew then that it could have been worse. Yes, what if both my son and husband had died together in a car accident? Then no one who loved Reed as I had, as only a parent can, would be left to hold my hand through this impossible nightmare. Because I am a family communication scholar, my mind immediately went to the research, and suddenly I recognized the first great hazard I would face: losing my husband. I knew that some marriages do not survive the death of a child (Schwab, 1998). In that moment, I used my anger at the death in a constructive way by vowing to stay with this man no matter what followed, to do whatever I had to do to survive this nightmare with my marriage intact. I was determined to deny the angel of death, who had so successfully snatched my son in the night, the taking of my marriage as well. "You won't get this one too!" I said out loud. It was the first time in my life I had spoken directly and overtly to an angel, but it would not be my last. Later that week, I talked to my angel son for the first time. I looked to Heaven and promised Reed that I would somehow survive this grief, even if it was only sleep walking, to take care of his father for him.

The core conditions for change and recovery after trauma include the individual's personal and social resources (Saleebey, 2000). This mother's resources included knowledge of the interworkings of the grief and family processes. Almost immediately, she began tapping those resources. According to Saleebey (2000), "[t]he character and tenor of the helping relationship" also represent a second powerful component of change and recovery (p. 131). As described below, this mother's friends helped her with frank talk that facilitated the reframing of extreme grief to a maternal mission. It is noteworthy that these friends expected the mother to rebound and simply invited her to join their certainty, granting her what Saleebey described as the two key ideas for change and recovery: hope and possibility.

The first week after the death, more than 100 people stopped by our house to offer condolences. A few people said very hurtful things: "You knew he was very sick when you adopted him, right?" Were they saying I brought this on myself? "He's in a better place." As if a child could be any place better than in his mother's loving arms! "He was always a child of God; he was yours for just a few years." Were they saying that I never should have grown so attached to my son? My belief that these people did not mean to hurt me intentionally detracted not one iota from the pain they inflicted. Only later did I realize that their remarks hurt so much because I so desperately desired help, support, and understanding.

In contrast, two people spoke truth that resonated at the time and stayed with me for years afterward. One friend, Jim, saw my pain and quite spontaneously said, "Time. Time is the great healer." Those simple words held such hope. They allowed for the possibility that there might come a moment when I was not in excruciating pain all the time. I asked another friend, Linda, "How will I survive this?" She looked me right in the eye and said, "Oh, you'll survive. You're strong. You're a survivor. And you'll do it because you have no other choice. Reed's life will have meant nothing unless you live to do something important in his name. Oh, you'll live. You'll figure out that it's the very last thing you can do for him. And you'll do it. You'll do it for him." Armed with the belief that I needed to move forward to save my marriage, to take care of Reed's father, and to do something important in Reed's name, I entered week two of life on the far side of happiness. At least I saw a future and had goals. They were my proverbial "rod and staff" that comforted me in my darkest hours.

In the coming months, I developed a series of mantras that I told myself and others who asked how I was doing: "I wish it had been me and not him. If I could switch places, I'd do it in a heartbeat, but I can't, so on I go, putting one foot in front of the other." That grim thought morphed into the next mantra: "I'm moving forward. I can't go back. If I could, I would, but life doesn't let you go back, so I am going forward." During the fifth month, an incident occurred at work that prompted me to engage in a political battle. I led the charge that saved a colleague's career. In the process, I discovered I had no fear—literally none—of what could happen to me. I had my final mantra: "Only one good thing came from my son's death. I now know that the worst thing that is ever going to happen to me has happened. I have nothing more to fear from life. That was my son's last gift to me: courage, undaunted courage."

About nine months after the death, I had a dream that enabled me to abandon my quest for a cause of death. Like the first dream in which I heard Reed crying for me, it was in color, vivid, and very real. It began with the sound of his laughter and then the image of him alive and running down a hill of green grass with his Bible in his hand. He ran to a group of boys his age who were playing soccer in the flat space at the bottom of the hill. Instead of joining the game, he called the boys over to him. As I drew closer to watch, I realized I was witnessing an amazing scene. The boys were of different races and cultures. Reed was speaking multiple languages and the boys began sitting in a circle. Reed opened his Bible and read a brief passage, then he began explaining its meaning to the boys in terms they could understand. Suddenly, Reed's death made sense for the first time. Reed was in Heaven converting boys who, like him, had died before their time. Reed was the perfect choice for the job. He was so gregarious that his laughter and beliefs were infectious. Reed looked so happy, like he was living his destiny. Then I knew why God took my boy. Reed was needed to be an angel in Heaven. For the first time, I was able to let go, to begin my path to acceptance. Reed was living his destiny. It was time I began to live mine.

"There is no change without the dream, as there is no dream without hope" (Freire, 1996, p. 61). Mourners must manage their sorrow by discovering how the world—their world—will change and ultimately function again, without the deceased (Attig, 2001). Such metamorphic change is a gradual process that occurs over time.

I awoke feeling calm and peaceful. A few months later, I came across Reed's Bible and placed it on my nightstand, where it remains to this day. It's my daily reminder that my son is living his destiny. He's doing fine without me. I would do best to move forward and embrace my destiny, whatever that might be. I still miss Reed every single day. Now I accept that I will always miss him. That, too, is part of my destiny, along with my wonderful marriage, taking care of my husband, and donating to Reed's scholarship fund. But that is not my entire destiny. There will be more to come. It will slowly but surely be revealed to me.

Conclusion

We hope that you have found this narrative compelling and thought provoking. Our goal was to provide an intimate, detailed look at complicated grief as experienced by a mother whose life was forever changed by the ambiguous death of her son. Her story reflects a preoccupation with her son's death, profound sadness, and survivor's guilt—all symptoms of complicated grief (Prigerson, Maciejewski, et al., 1995). Nonetheless, like Walter (2000), we believe that grief is often "policed," and to label this mother's grief as pathological or abnormal only serves to further stigmatize and disenfranchise her and her experiences.

We urge readers to view her story from a strengths perspective (Saleebey, 2000), whereby her ongoing struggle to come to terms with her son's ambiguous death reflected resilience, not pathology. As Saleebey so eloquently stated, "the strengths perspective and the resilience literature obligate us to understand that however downtrodden, beaten up, sick, or disheartened and demoralized, individuals have survived, and in some cases even flourished" (p. 135). This narrative reveals a mourner who "summoned up resources, coped" (p. 135), and survived to tell the tale.

Despite not knowing why or how her son died, this mother continues to move forward in the world, guided in part by the precious memories of her son and her promises to him. Her life as a mother, her grief for the loss of her son, and her dreams of him appear to have become an ongoing part of the fabric of a new life—a life in which she is mindful of mourning without being centered on her mourning, a life in which she, as do so many others, searches for her destiny in the real world of the living.

References

Attig, T. (1996). *How we grieve: Relearning the world*. New York: Oxford University Press.

Attig, T. (2001). Relearning the world: Making and finding meanings. In R. A. Neimeyer (Ed.), *Meaning reconstruction and the experience of loss* (pp. 33–53). Washington, DC: American Psychological Association.

Becvar, D. S. (2001). *In the presence of grief*. New York: Guilford Press.

Betz, G., & Thorngren, J. M. (2006). Ambiguous loss and the family grieving process. *Family Journal, 14,* 359–365.

Boss, P. (1999). *Ambiguous loss: Learning to live with unresolved grief*. Cambridge, MA: Harvard University Press.

Boss, P. (2004). Ambiguous loss. In F. Walsh & M. McGoldrick (Eds.), *Living beyond loss: Death in the family* (2nd ed., pp. 237–246). New York: W. W. Norton.

Bosticco, C., & Thompson, T. L. (2005). Narratives and storytelling in coping with grief and bereavement. *Omega: Journal of Death and Dying, 51,* 1–16.

Bowlby, J. (1980). *Attachment and loss: Vol. 3. Loss, sadness, and depression*. New York: Basic Books.

Braun, M. J., & Berg, D. H. (1994). Meaning reconstruction in the experience of parental bereavement. *Death Studies, 18,* 105–129.

Breen, L. J., & O'Connor, M. (2007). The fundamental paradox in the grief literature: A critical reflection. *Omega: Journal of Death and Dying, 55,* 199–218.

Chen, J. H., Bierhals, A. J., Prigerson, H. G., Kasl, S. V., Mazure, C. M., & Jacobs, S. (1999). Gender differences in the effects of bereavement-related psychological distress in health outcomes. *Psychological Medicine, 29,* 367–380.

DeGroot, J. M., & Carmack, H. J. (2012). Blogging as a means of grieving. In T. Dumova & R. Fiordo (Eds.), *Blogging in the global society: Cultural, political and geographical aspects* (pp. 161–177). Hershey, PA: IGI Global.

de Vries, B., Dalla Lana, R., & Falck, V. T. (1994). Parental bereavement over the life course: A theoretical intersection and empirical review. *Omega: Journal of Death and Dying, 29,* 47–69.

Dyregrov, K., Nordanger, D., & Dyregrov, A. (2003). Predictors of psychosocial distress after suicide, SIDS, and accidents. *Death Studies, 27,* 143–165.

Ellis, C., & Bochner, A. P. (2000). Autoethnography, personal narrative, reflexivity; Researcher as subject. In N. K. Denzin & Y. S. Lincoln (Eds.), *Handbook of qualitative research* (2nd ed., pp. 733–768). Thousand Oaks, CA: Sage Publications.

Freire, P. (1996). *The pedagogy of hope: Reliving pedagogy of the oppressed.* New York: Continuum.

Freud, S. (1993). Mourning and melancholia. In G. H. Pollock (Ed.), *Pivotal papers on identification* (pp. 21–39). Madison, CT: International Universities Press. (Original work published 1917)

Gamino, L. A., Hogan, N. S., & Sewell, K. W. (2002). Feeling the absence: A content analysis from the Scott and White Grief Study. *Death Studies, 26,* 793–813.

Gamino, L. A, Sewell, K. W., & Easterling, L. W. (1998). Scott & White Grief Study: An empirical test of predictors of intensified mourning. *Death Studies, 22,* 333–355.

Grout, L. A., & Romanoff, B. D. (2000). The myth of the replacement child: Parents' stories and practices after perinatal death. *Death Studies, 24,* 93–113.

Harvey, J. H. (2000). *Give sorrow words: Perspectives on loss and trauma.* Philadelphia: Brunner-Mazel.

Janoff-Bulman, R. (1992). *Shattered assumptions.* New York: Free Press.

Klass, D. (1993). Solace and immortality: Bereaved parents' continuing bond with their children. *Death Studies, 17,* 343–368.

Klass, D. (1997). The deceased child in the psychic and social worlds of bereaved parents during the resolution of grief. *Death Studies, 21,* 147–175.

Klass, D., & Marwit, S. (1988). Toward a model of parental grief. *Omega: Journal of Death and Dying, 19,* 31–50.

Kübler-Ross, E., & Kessler, D. (2005). *On grief and grieving: Finding the meaning of grief through the five stages of loss.* New York: Scribner.

Neimeyer, R. A., & Levitt, H. M. (2000). What's narrative got to do with it? Construction and coherence in accounts of loss. In J. H. Harvey & E. D. Miller (Eds.), *Loss and trauma: General and close relationship perspectives* (pp. 401–412). Philadelphia: Brunner-Routledge.

Neimeyer, R. A., Prigerson, H. G., & Davies, B. (2002). Mourning and meaning. *American Behavioral Scientist, 46,* 235–251.

Oliver, L. E. (1999). Effects of a child's death on the marital relationship: A review. *Omega: Journal of Death and Dying, 39,* 197–227.

Parkes, C. M. (1972). *Bereavement: Studies of grief in adult life.* New York: International Universities Press.

Pennebaker, J. W. (1997). Writing about emotional experiences as a therapeutic process. *Psychological Science, 8,* 162–166.

Prigerson, H.G., Bierhals, A. J., Kasl, S.V., Reynolds, C. F. III, Shear, M. K., Day, N., et al. (1997). Traumatic grief as a risk factor for mental and physical morbidity. *American Journal of Psychiatry, 154,* 616–623.

Prigerson, H. G., Maciejewski, P. K., Reynolds, C. F. III, Bierhals, A. J., Newsom, J.T., Fasiczka, A., et al. (1995). Inventory of Complicated Grief: A scale to measure maladaptive symptoms of loss. *Psychiatry Research, 59,* 65–79.

Prigerson, H. G., Silverman, G. K., Jacobs, S. C., Maciejewski, P. K., Kasl, S.V., & Rosenheck, R. A. (2001). Traumatic grief, disability, and the underutilization of health services: A preliminary investigation. *Primary Psychiatry, 8,* 61–66.

Rando, T. A. (1986). The unique issues and impact of the death of a child. In T. A. Rando (Ed.), *Parental loss of a child* (pp. 5–43). Champaign, IL: Research Press.

Rando, T. A. (1991). Parental adjustment to the loss of a child. In D. Papadatou & C. Papadatos (Eds.), *Children and death* (pp. 233–253). New York: Hemisphere.

Rando, T. A. (1993). *Treatment of complicated mourning.* Champaign, IL: Research Press.

Saleebey, D. (2000). Power in the people: Strengths and hope. *Advances in Social Work, 1,* 127–136.

Schwab, R. (1998). A child's death and divorce: Dispelling the myth. *Death Studies, 22,* 445–468.

Sedney, M. A., Baker, J. E., & Gross, E. (1994). "The story" of a death: Therapeutic considerations with bereaved families. *Journal of Marital and Family Therapy, 20,* 287–296.

Silverman, P. R., & Nickman, S. L. (1996). Introduction: What's the problem? In D. Klass, P. R. Silverman, & S. L. Nickman (Eds.), *Continuing bonds: New understandings of grief* (pp. 3–27). Washington, DC: Taylor & Francis.

Sofka, C. J. (1997). Social support internetworks, caskets for sale, and more: Thanatology and the information superhighway. *Death Studies, 21,* 553–574.

Toller, P. W. (2005). Negotiation of dialectical contradictions by parents who have experienced the death of a child. *Journal of Applied Communication Research, 33,* 44–66.

Toller, P. W. (2008). Bereaved parents' negotiation of identity following the death of a child. *Communication Studies, 59,* 306–321.

Walter, T. (2000). Grief narratives: The role of medicine in the policing of grief. *Anthropology & Medicine, 7,* 97–114.

Weiner, I. (1999). *Coping with loss.* Mahwah, NJ: Lawrence Erlbaum.

Wheeler, I. (1993–1994). The role of meaning and purpose in life in bereaved parents associated with a self-help group: Compassionate Friends. *Omega: Journal of Death and Dying, 28,* 261–271.

Wheeler, I. (2001). Parental bereavement: The crisis of meaning. *Death Studies, 25,* 51–66.

Chapter Eleven

The Lost Mother
A Refracted Memoir

Christina Houen

Introduction

The memoir extract included in this chapter revisits a time in the 1970s when I was separated from my three young daughters as a result of their father's abduction of them to the United States. After 18 months of legal negotiations, I had my first access visit to them, and a second one a year later, before their father brought them and his new stepfamily back to Australia to live.

My overwhelming experience of loss was not relieved by the visits; I felt like a missing person, and I was lost—not only to my children as mother—but to myself. In the memoir, I search back through memories for my lost mother-self and reconstruct the sense of being absent, not real, on those visits. Fragments of memory are assembled in a collage that has many gaps.

The second part of the memoir reflects on my journey and the resources I have found to help me live with grief. I argue that complicated grief need not be pathologized as a neurotic disorder, but can be understood and treated in many ways, depending on the circumstances, culture, and resources of the subject. My work as a mental health nurse made me realize that binary divisions between the sane and insane, pathological and healthy are not necessarily the most productive ways of responding to the phenomenon. My studies of poststructuralist philosophy and trauma theory have given me understanding of the social forces that create such divisions and of the psychodynamics of trauma. My creative writing has brought release from the worst of the effects, and a measure of acceptance and healing through the empathic response of readers. I fold and unfold the origami of the self through the agency of memory, which manipulates time, revisiting the past to recreate former selves and enable new patterns to emerge in the future.

It was such a short interlude in my life. When I look back at it, searching for human figures in the picture, it is like looking into a broken mirror. There are bits missing, large bits, and the images I see are distorted by fracture lines. There is no order to the pictures; they are all jumbled up. How can I arrange them so that they make sense? How can I see myself?[1]

The cab stops outside a gabled house in a street below the wall of mountains. The light stabs my eyes as it reflects off powdery snow covering the sidewalk and gardens. There they are, three small figures standing awkwardly in a row on the front doorstep. Sophia's long hair, parted in the middle, shows her pale, broad forehead; her hands pick at each other. Penelope, in the middle, clutches her white cardigan; her white blonde hair sticks out like a bush around her round face. Caitlin's hands are clasped, her knees turned in, her feet splayed, her mouth tucked into a half-smile.

They all look anxious and uncertain as they watch me open the cab door and climb out. I run up the path, leaving Mum to pay the cab and watch the driver unload our bags. I drop my handbag as I kneel down and reach out my arms to hug all three of them. We cling together, our foreheads touching.

Do not speak, because if you do, you will scream or cry. What are they thinking, my little girls?

"But Mother, where have you been?" Penelope pulls back. I meet her eyes, seaweed green.

I have no answer. I hug her closer to my breast.

Caitlin burrows her head into my neck, and makes a noise, something between a sob and a cry of joy.

Sophia strokes my face, and her tears spring onto my cheek.

My knees are turned to ice; I cannot move. We will become a statue, frozen at the threshold of his house, together but not living, because we cannot live together.

I make myself come back to life. I kiss each child on the eyes and cheeks to melt the frozen tears, loving, present, but inside, the mother that was me is shrunken, small like them, unsure of anything except this crushing pain of loss and longing. And to numb it, I must act, I must pretend that everything is all right, that we are a normal family, that I have never left them, that they are not lost to me.

---

[1] Parts of this memoir appear in my unpublished doctoral dissertation, 2009, and are being reworked in a book-length memoir. Names have been changed to protect privacy. Scenes have been reconstructed from fragments of memory. Inevitably the memoir is a subjective account of a painful time and does not pretend to be accurate or to tell how it was for any other person in the story. It is my truth, no one else's. My daughters have given their permission for me to publish this story.

Sophia and Caitlin want to ride on the merry-go-round. They climb onto brightly painted ponies, with long manes and tails that swing out as they sweep round on movable poles. I want to sit with Penelope in a little carriage on the fixed platform, but they are all full, so I hold her in front of me, with the pole between us, on one of the bigger ponies. The music starts, and we begin to move. We are going faster and faster, the ponies swing out higher and higher. The faces in the crowd become blurred. The centrifugal force of the racing ponies is so strong, I can barely hold onto Penelope. I cling to her, my arms aching. I can feel her body being pulled away. I open my mouth to scream, to call for help, for the merry-go-round to stop, but no sound comes out. I can hold on no longer—she flies from my arms, up into the air, across the heads of the crowd. (Houen, 2002, p. 79)

I started to dream this dream when I was in Sydney, Australia, pretending to live a life without my children. I would wake at two or three every morning screaming inside, my throat closed. I would get up and sit on the balcony, watching the lights across Iron Cove, from my balcony on the third floor of a block of flats on the border of Balmain and Birchgrove.

The glassy black of the harbor sparkled and danced with lights of moored ships and factories on the shores of Drummoyne. Large red letters, "DUNLOP," reflected as spilt scarlet flame on black satin, were a landmark by which I navigated as I let my consciousness float and bob on the water's oily surface. There was no wind; the only sounds were the dull hum of traffic across Iron Cove Bridge and the occasional squeal of tires in a nearby street, as some night reveler blundered home. The dying light of the old moon was reflected from the roofs of office buildings, factories, flats, and tenement houses. I seemed to be the only one in the neighborhood awake, apart from a stray black cat that prowled across the rooftops and dropped down into the weed-choked backyard of the next-door delicatessen, looking for the little rodents that work the night shift.

I was the night watcher on the balcony, waiting for the dawn, for it to be light, so that my demons could sleep and I could return to unconsciousness for a while. I drank red wine to numb my brain and stop my thoughts so I could rest, but I could not sleep. I drank Cinzano, so much it made me vomit, but still I could not sleep.

Gradually the sky grew paler. The shapes of houses and factories became more distinct. A cold dawn breeze rustled the leaves of elm trees down in the car park, carrying a drift of sweetness from the night-scented jasmine that clung to the brick wall of the building. The breeze chilled my face as I sat huddled in my mohair rug. The city was waking, and at last my thoughts were starting to slow down. If I tried to remember what I was thinking even a minute before, I could not. (Houen, 2002, p. 74)

On that mad roundabout, it was me that was thrown off, me, not my baby daughter. She is real, warm flesh, rosebud soft; it is I who am dying, cut off from the stem.

During the hours the girls are awake, I act like a normal mother, and keep busy when I'm not cooking or looking after them by doing crochet and embroidery. I am making a shawl for Mum, in creamy wool, with an elaborate border of flowers in purples, dark reds, and pinks. The pattern is wrong, and as I sit unraveling and reworking sections, I think of all the steps that have brought me to this place, all the choices I made without realizing the consequences. I drop the crochet sometimes—will I ever finish it?—and creep into their bedrooms. I bend over them as they sleep, watching their faces, creaseless and innocent, and inhale their sweet breath.

But when they are asleep and Mum has gone to bed, the numbness returns. I drink red wine and sit listening to music until at last sleep seems possible. In the morning, I look in the mirror and see a face, the face of a woman older than me, with sharp lines under her eyes and around her mouth, etched by the dry mountain air, cold winds, and lack of sleep.

I can't stay here. I will dry up and wither away before I grow old.

I feel invisible, moving through their daily lives like a ghost that materializes at times but keeps fading. I have to force myself to enter their world, where I feel excluded; no matter how they cling to me, wanting me to stay, I know I have to leave again and cannot return except under the temporary license of the one who keeps me away from them. I struggle to love them, to let my flesh meet theirs, because I know I will have to tear it apart again.

The last day comes. We have an hour to be together. Penelope sits on my knee, holding Happy Face, the cloth doll I gave her in Australia before we were separated. Caitlin leans against me, my arm round her. Sophia does headstands, her tight-clad winter legs poised trembling above her slender body, her skirt half veiling her long fair hair and tear-wet face.

"It helps stop the tears," she says in an upside-down voice.

Afterthoughts of a Lost Mother

> *To become worthy of what happens to us, and thus to*
> *will and to release the event, to become the offspring of*
> *one's own events, and thereby to be reborn, to have one*
> *more birth, and to break with one's carnal birth. ...*

Deleuze, 1990, p. 150

How could I become worthy of what had happened to me? How could I live with this loss, and live with my self, who had allowed that man to take them from me and remove from me any control over how they were brought up, how they were loved or not loved, how they were educated, how they grew into the world? How could I reclaim my past, connect with that woman who made those choices, who abandoned her children? How could I go on living? How could I still be their mother, still have a part in their lives, still be there, when I had failed so terribly to protect them and myself from the hand that separated us?

When I saw my children again for the first time, I had fought a legal battle for a year and a half to get access to them; I was very afraid of seeing them again on their father's territory. I was afraid of loving them too much, of them loving me too much, of inevitably having to separate from them again, of our time together being spied on by their father, his girlfriend, and her children. I was in enemy territory, and had little say in how I could behave while I was there. All these conditions subjectified me as failed wife and mother, and came between me and the immediacy of my self as mother, the exchange of love, our reunion. As Henri Bergson puts it, I was a ghost, a colourless shadow, acted rather than acting:

> The greater part of the time we live outside ourselves, hardly perceiving anything of ourselves but our own ghost, a colourless shadow which pure duration projects into homogeneous space. Hence our life unfolds in space rather than in time, we live for the external world rather than for ourselves; we speak rather than think; we 'are acted' rather than act ourselves. To act freely is to recover possession of oneself, and get back into pure duration. (Bergson, 1960, pp. 231–232)

My children had conditions that limited their experience too, but the innocence of childhood, the lack of awareness of time and its inevitable processes of regulation and measurement may have protected them from some of the fear and pain that I felt. But their pain of having been separated and having to separate again without understanding why would have been difficult or impossible for them to overcome at the time.

Because it was such a painful experience for me to see them again, I numbed myself a second time. This had happened before, when I separated from them, leaving them with their father in his home state.

We had returned from England to Australia, our marriage very shaky after I had had an affair with a man who lived in the same village as us, in the same street. My husband and I had been married for 13 years. Although I knew not long after we married that I had walked into a trap at 20 years old, I was not strong enough to leave him, to make a life for myself. After five years of marriage, faced with an ultimatum from him, I agreed to have children. Our first daughter was born in Australia, the second two in England, where we went so he could pursue his career. I loved being a mother and threw myself into that. The marriage was tolerable to me because he was away a lot at work, at conferences, on short-term academic visiting fellowships. He had two affairs during this time that I knew of, and as I found out later, many more. But he declared he would not do anything to endanger our family life, that his family was all-important, and he would not leave me. I was technically faithful but had several crushes on other men and flirted with a few. Until, one day, a man knocked on our door and announced that he was our neighbor and thought it was time to get to know us. It was that knock that shattered our bourgeois marriage. The man who lived across the road and I fell in love and had a brief, furtive affair; we agreed to tell our partners. The result was, he stayed with his wife, who fell apart when he told her, and I stayed with my husband, who declared we must return to Australia so he could be near his family.

I felt more trapped than ever, as he, fired by jealousy, demanded sex with me whenever he felt like it. Seeking escape, I succumbed to the advances of a man I met at a party, and this time I told my husband straight away. He suggested that I spend a weekend with this man in the state capital, so I could decide whether I wanted to be with him. I returned, and told my husband I didn't know whether I wanted to be with the other man, but I didn't love *him* and couldn't be his wife. I suggested we live as coparents, either together or separately. He told me he would kill me, the children, and himself if I tried to take them from him. He said I had disgraced myself and humiliated him in his hometown, and he demanded that I go and stay with my mother in Sydney, leaving the children with him. So I did, and two or three months later, while my lawyer and his lawyer were negotiating some sort of agreement on joint custody and access, I received a phone call. He told me he was in the United States and had our children with him, and that I'd never see them again.

How did he manage to take the children out of the country without my knowledge or consent? Over the years, when I have wondered about this, or people have asked me, I've pieced together an understanding. Before we left England, he persuaded me to let the children have individual passports. He said it wasn't fair that they should be on my passport and not on his. I agreed. When he took them out of Australia, it was 1972, before the Family Law was changed to allow no-fault divorce. To divorce me in Australia, under the current law, he would have had to wait five years, as well as prove my adultery. This would appear to have been easy, as I'd had two affairs in quick succession, but he was complicit in the one that caused the separation by suggesting my visit to the city with my lover, and even paying my expenses. He had also confessed to two affairs, one of which I had witnessed. He no doubt knew these faults on his part would be argued in a court case. Moreover, he had been pretty much an absentee father throughout our life in England, and the children's bond with me was very strong; they were very young: seven, five, and less than three years old. And of course, I had fallen into his trap by agreeing for them to be on separate passports. I now think he expected, maybe even hoped for, this second affair and had made plans accordingly. I discovered later many devious things he had done without my knowledge, which suggested that he calculated for the worst that could happen and protected himself in any way he could.

His righteous stand was more precarious than I realized, and his awareness of that would have dictated his aggressive action of taking them out of the country. He did not allow me to see them again until he had shored up his possession of them; first, by removing them from the jurisdiction of Australian courts; second, by securing custody of them and legal separation from me in an American court. I felt even more powerless when I saw them again than I had felt when I left them the first time. Then, I had allowed myself to believe I could somehow return to being their mother, if not his wife, and that he might agree to some form of joint custody. The second time I left them, I knew there was no hope of seeing them except on his terms until they had grown up. I would always be in the background, unable to protect them.

When I returned to university study at the age of 59, I did so because I wanted to tell my story, to make sense of it. I found a supervisor who asked me about my life, and when I told her how my life was torn apart, she suggested that I could interpret what had happened in terms of the bourgeois family, using Freudian theory and poststructuralist feminist theory to deconstruct the narrative of the deserting wife and abandoning mother. These last words were burnt into my soul, when my ex-husband phoned me on a public holiday, in the spring of 1972: "I'm ringing from Los Angeles, on my way to Boulder, Colorado. The girls are with me. You're a deserting wife and abandoning mother, and you'll never see them again!"

Part of my master's degree was a creative work, which I wrote as an autobiographical novel. A strange thing happened when I came to write the episode of the phone call that shattered my life. I felt numb and empty, and no words came. I sat for a while, then put my fingers to the keys.

When I did so, a figure that I came to call the Crone appeared unbidden.[2] She simply popped up in the midst of an unfillable void, and once there, although the narrative of my descent into physical and emotional breakdown continued, she reappeared at certain moments of intense awareness of loss and unfulfillable desire in the story. The Crone's appearance becomes a refrain in the narrative that creates a place of regrowth in the soil of the plains that surrounded my childhood home, and in my psyche.

Enter the Crone

If you were to visit the Hay plains at night, when people and the animals they tend are asleep, you would, if you walked far enough, come across a curious sight. An old woman, wrinkled and skinny, sits on a patch of red earth, her head bent, intent on a patient and silent task. Her fingers, though knotted and twisted, move nimbly back and forth. It is not wool she is shaping into a simple chained fabric that gleams silvery-grey in the moonlight, but vegetable matter that she unwinds from a large irregular ball lying on the bare earth beside her. Her fingers twist in and out, and the soft, earthy smelling fabric falls on the red soil, spreading over it, cloaking it with a damp, springy, resilient cover. Soon the bare patch is clothed, and she winds up the ball and pokes it into a string bag she slings over her shoulder. She scrambles up and walks with the help of a knotted stick to another bare patch, and squats, muttering a few sounds in a guttural tongue and laying her stick and

---

[2] The Crone appears in my master's dissertation, creative component. My reflections on the Crone are drawn in part from my article, 'The Crone: A figure of Desire for Revenge and Healing in the Writing of a Life', published in 2008 in *Lifewriting Annual: Biographical and Autobiographical Studies*, *2*, 194–212, and further developed in my 2009 doctoral dissertation.

bag beside her. She begins again her endless task of restoring a moist, living cover to the plains ravaged by harsh sun and wind and many cloven hooves.

At the time I wrote this passage, I did not understand why the Crone suddenly appeared, though I was happy to allow her to do so and to disturb the flow of the narrative. When I reflected on her, I saw her as a mythological dream figure. The Crone is allied with the figure of the sorcerer, described by Gilles Deleuze and Félix Guattari, the radical French poststructural philosophers, as an agent of change, a reterritorializing force (Deleuze & Guattari, 1987). In Deleuzian terms, a territory is more than a space; it is an expression of the self that occupies it. Territories are constantly "being made and remade, reterritorializ[ed] and deterritorializ[ed]" (Macgregor Wise, 2005, p. 79). Thus, in the case of the Crone, the Hay plains is a territory that has been deterritorialized from a liveable place for animals, plants, and people by the ravages of clearing, erosion, and grazing. In psychic terms, the territory of my childhood had been destroyed by my father's actions. He left the family when I was in my eighth year, and did not return until I was a 14-year-old away at boarding school. When he returned, he took possession of the farm, to which he had kept the title, and forced my mother to leave, carrying only a suitcase. So I lost my father in early childhood—he did not answer my letters, and I didn't see him again for 40 years—and when he returned, I lost my childhood home. The second major loss in my life was the abduction of my children after the marriage failed. This was a second deterritorialization of my psychic space, which had been folded in the shape of a mother and a wife. In deterritorializing my wifehood, I inadvertently destroyed the possibility of having a space, a territory, in which I could be a mother. And my children's territory of childhood was split apart by my actions and the reactions of my husband, so that they lost their mother and were subjected to a territory created by their father, one that became occupied by a stepmother and stepsiblings. Ironically, I (and my ex-husband) did to my children what had been done to me as a child.

The Crone is working, in my story, to re-cover the barren earth, to make it habitable once more for the animals that graze off it and the people that tend and make their living from them. She works as a refrain. For Deleuze and Guattari, the refrain is not just a musical device, it is the song of the earth, the sea and the wind, the Cosmos (Deleuze & Guattari 1987). The child in the dark sings under her breath to comfort her fear; she seeks to create a calm center at the heart of chaos (Deleuze & Guattari, 1987). Elizabeth Grosz, a feminist poststructuralist philosopher and critic, explains the refrain as "a kind of rhythmic regularity that brings a minimum of livable order to a situation in which chaos beckons" (Grosz, 2008, p. 52). The Crone makes the soil livable again, organizing a limited space by drawing a circle around a fragile patch of bare earth and covering it with her woven salt-bush, then moving on to another bare patch. She reconstructs from wasted ground a home, a safe space for insects, plants, and animals.

In the Deleuzian understanding of life, desire is a primary, impersonal connective force that flows through all life in a Spinozan universe that is composed of one substance, distributed on the intersecting yet distinct planes of the virtual or invisible (where chaos reigns) and the material or visible. Desire is immanent creative energy that produces, on the material plane, folds of time, memory, material forms, and subjectivity, that, "like origami, can be unfolded and refolded into different shapes" (Deleuze & Parnet, 1987, p. 65).

In writing the Crone, I draw a circle on the page, the visible plane, in the effort to bring calm and safety out of chaos. The Hay plains are a metaphor for my shattered, deterritorialized psyche (a shattering that began in childhood, and was repeated when I lost my children), and the Crone is an aesthetic figure or persona for the writer, who seeks to heal the self through writing. I am thus allied with the Crone in my unfolding of the terrain of the bourgeois family, and my creation of a safe, regenerating space through writing, using fabulation and aesthetic figures. The persona of the Crone works in my psyche and my writing in transformative and healing ways.

The Crone's refrain helped me to refold my life after the lines of flight I took from my marriage had plunged me into a black hole. Black holes are Deleuze and Guattari's metaphor for the catastrophic outcomes that can result from too violent a change or line of flight from the organized forms we have become folded into (Deleuze & Guattari, 1987). They counsel that, if we want to live more creatively, "[y]ou don't do it with a sledgehammer, you use a very fine file" (p. 160). I had become stratified in a bourgeois marriage to a man I didn't love. I had three children whom I loved, but I felt trapped living with a man who expected me to have sex with him and be faithful to him although I did not desire him, and he had been opportunistically promiscuous himself. I tried to break free by allowing my desire for love to lead me on a line of flight, and I plunged into a black hole that all but destroyed my relationship with my children. I loved my children and wanted to be with them, but I felt unable to fight him for them and had no money to do so. I was intimidated by my husband's threats, and I felt guilty that I had broken our family apart. His action in taking them out of the country took them beyond my reach, emotionally, geographically, legally, and financially.

The first stage of my recovery from the shattering of my life was a career in mental health nursing. Adrift and broke, unable to continue with my second attempt at a higher degree, I applied for a job as a psychiatric nurse, where I could train while I worked. I learned from my encounters with patients that my reality was not the only way of seeing. I learned to walk in the shoes of the insane, and I saw that there but for the grace of God, went I. To put it in Deleuzian terms, we—the sane and insane—are not divided by a binary line, we inhabit the environment we call life, and within it, our consciousness is formed by the experiences we have, the forces we encounter. Medical discourse classifies symptoms, divides behavior into categories that are distinguished as ordered or disordered, and produces "research, treatments and interventions that produce more symptom clusters, etc" (Skott-Myhre & Taylor, 2011, p. 41). After 12 years, I left mental health nursing, partly for personal reasons, but also because, although I saw my work as meaningful, I felt limited and frustrated by the system within which I worked, which had created a revolving door that functioned on short-term treatment and the suppression of symptoms, mainly through drug therapy, which produced damaging side effects. I had, in a sense, used my work as my therapy. I was a wounded healer. For 12 years, my work with the insane kept me from falling apart, through the long separation from my children, through the torment of glimpsing but not fully knowing their lives, through the discovery that they were being damaged by the family that should have kept them safe.

About a year after my second visit to the States, my children's father brought them back to Australia, but to a city in another state. For the rest of their childhood, I saw them twice a year, until my youngest daughter decided to come and live with me after she turned 14, and changes to the Family Law Act of Australia meant that she could make this choice without having to go to court. They are all grown up now, with children of their own. Each of them has had to face and fight their demons, and each has survived and found love and happiness. But that's another story, not mine to tell here.

My work in mental health, my writing, the encounter with the Crone, and my studies have not taken away the wound to my psyche. At times, when I revisit the memories, or when I write them or read what I have written, I feel waves of grief and regret, I want to go back, to turn back time and live it again. But I want to live it without the loss, the bar that was set on me by that man, who had been my husband, who was my children's father, and his pre-emptive actions in taking the children from me.

My children. I want the unquestioning bond that I had with them before they were taken from me, the certainty of knowing that we were a circle of love, unbroken. I want to relive their childhood with them, to have a second chance to give them the unconditional love that I had lost in my childhood.

I want the impossible.

Nothing can make up for what they and I lost, yet we have learned so much, suffered so much. All that we are now, the love that we share, is given by life, mixed up with the pain and the grief we lived through, bittersweet.

The hardest thing to accept is that one cannot change the past. I push back the screen to revisit the long separation we endured in their childhood, and the screen behind it, to revisit the first loss of the children, and I get stuck. All the words I have written become mere words, saying over and over again in different ways that it is too late, I can never change what happened to them, I can never repair the damage done by their father's and my actions, and by their stepfamily. Nor can I see how I, as I was then, *could have* changed what happened to them. I inherit the events that I both made and did not make, and I must submit to the necessity of them (Grosz, 2004). More than that, I must affirm the past, my children's past and mine; I must become worthy of it, as Gilles Deleuze counsels, so that I can will and release it and thereby be reborn. I return again and again to these words, because they give me comfort and hope and the courage to go on. Worthiness is not a constant state, a stable position, it is a becoming. And in that becoming, the circle forms again, unbroken.

Return from the Void

Complicated grief has been a major theme in my life, like the theme that runs through a symphony, changing as it is reprised and reworked in different movements. It is, in terms of trauma theory, a wound to the psyche, one that is inflicted unexpectedly and is repeated in nightmares and other unwanted psychic experiences (Caruth, 1996). It is not simply a pathology or disorder that needs to be diagnosed and treated. It is a complex and multifaceted psychic phenomenon that can be interpreted and responded to in different ways, depending on the circumstances, culture, beliefs, and resources of the subject, as well as how she or he chooses to deal with the wound. The psychiatric model may be appropriate in some cases, especially when there is an inability to cope with the demands of daily life. However, as Saleebey (2000) argued, not "all people who have been traumatized become damaged goods" (p. 129), and the paradigm of psychopathology and illness—in its focus on the problematic rather than the possible—needs to be balanced by practices based on the strengths and resilience of people.

Traumatic returns of the original wounding event, in forms that may be seen as pathological, are stories that need to be heard, witnessed, and understood. Dori Laub tells us that

> Trauma survivors live not with memories of the past, but with an event that could not and did not proceed through to its completion, has no ending, attained no closure, and therefore, as far as its survivors are concerned, continues into the present and is current in every respect. (Felman & Laub, 1992, p. 69)

To "undo this entrapment," he said,

> A process of constructing a narrative, or reconstructing a history and essentially, of *re-externalizating* [sic] *the event*—has to be set in motion. This re-externalization of the event can occur and take effect only when one can articulate and *transmit* the story, literally transfer it to another outside oneself and take it back again, inside. (p. 69)

Laub's preferred way of reconstructing the history of trauma is through psychoanalysis, and his practice has centered on survivors of the Holocaust. I have had several encounters with psychoanalytic psychotherapy and counseling, and all have helped me in some degree, but I can say without reservation that writing and theorizing my life has brought a degree of self-awareness and creative release that no external therapeutic intervention has.

Through all these years, though I have gone on living and recreating myself, I have carried my secret wound, which I have treated, in the last 12 years, by telling my secrets, writing my story. The wound is still there, it is part of me. But it has been the source of compassion and has taught me the meaning of unconditional love, and it has connected me with others who have suffered. Narrating my story has allowed me to understand better why my life went wrong, why I failed my children, why they and I have had to suffer so much. Writing my life has given me strength and resilience, and expressed my desire for wholeness. The other psychic force that has healed my life is the desire for atonement. At times I have lost courage, but always I am brought back to my strength when something goes wrong for one of my children, when they are having difficulties, and I am able to support and help them to recover their center and their strength. The third force that helped me through the dark days after the loss was my work as a mental health nurse; I was a wounded healer, who treated my own wound by helping others. The people who worked with me were themselves flawed and damaged beings, but most of them were good-hearted and wanted to make a difference. Many of us wanted to change the system, to improve the conditions in which our patients lived, and to help them to get strong enough to return to their outside lives, if they had one. Some of our patients were long-term, and the hospital was the only home they knew. It was a very imperfect, topsy-turvy world, a looking-glass word where much was recognizable but much more was strange, ugly, disturbing, and confronting. My wound protected me from despair and resignation, and the desire to soothe it—perhaps to heal it—kept me alive and was the source of my compassion and my desire to help. I knew what it was like to face madness, destruction, loss of all that I loved, even death, and I wanted to help others to step back from the brink, to live again and enjoy life. After a time, however, I saw that my ability to help them was limited by the system I was part of, and I left that work because I could not change the system.

Before I made the decision to study for a master's degree, I had some psychotherapy sessions. My therapist told me that the things that had gone wrong in my life were not my fault, that I had done the best I could in difficult circumstances, and that my choices were shaped by the system I was born into. I didn't fully understand him at the time. I thought that I had made wrong choices that had caused the loss of my children. When I discovered the writings of Michel Foucault, I saw the pattern of the bourgeois family in which my life had become trapped, and the power structures that cast me in the role of the deserting wife and abandoning mother. Had I understood these forces better, I might have chosen differently. After I completed my master's degree and had a break for a year or two, I returned to study and did a PhD in life writing. From Freud, Foucault, and Irigaray, who had helped me deconstruct the bourgeois family, I moved on to Deleuze and Guattari, who showed me a way out of the maze. Foucault and the other theorists I read for my master's degree had not shown me how I, or anyone, could live a desiring life without being trapped. Deleuze and Guattari introduced me to a universe in which desire is not framed in loss and lack; it is a primary, impersonal, connective force that flows through all created beings and creates life in all its forms. The self is not fixed and determined by the stratum it is born into; we can use our powers of thought and expression to connect with other strata, to live more creatively and joyfully. In particular, writing is a tool for creating alternative worlds, for revisiting the past and unfolding and refolding the self differently. Deleuze and Guattari have taught me that it is possible to create a space in which one can be a desiring woman, one who is positive, nonhierarchical, and inclusive; I have written about this elsewhere.

I recognize that if a person can no longer function in the real world, cannot sustain relationships, work, or manage the daily tasks of living, then there is a place for professional intervention. Counseling has helped me, from time to time, to bridge that chasm that opened up in my life. Mostly, I was fortunate that, apart from an illness that took a physical form and prevented me from working for a month or two, I was able to keep working and surviving my days.

I have been asked what is the difference between abduction of one's child, and the death of one's child. I cannot answer this, as I have not lost a child through death. When I try to imagine what that would be like, I feel as though I would not want to go on living. It would only be the thought of my other living children, and their children, that would keep me alive. When I lost my children, at least I had the hope of seeing them again, and I wanted to be there for them in any way I could, albeit at a distance and occasionally in person, on holidays. I had access to them. To have no access, except in dreams and visions, to know one's child will never grow up, never complete their journey in life, is unimaginable, and stops my thoughts.

Concluding Thoughts

My grief has become, for me, like the grain of sand in the oyster. I did not choose to incorporate it into my self, but once it was there, I could not remove it. I had no choice but to live with it, to grow protective skins around it, between it and my self, like a child in the womb, an implanted life, separate yet connected. This child is alive yet unborn; it will never separate for me, and when I die, it will be released from my spirit and I will be free of it. I did not seek to close it off or expel it, for I knew I could not, short of dying. I had to grow around it, and in doing so, I created a pearl of great luster, which I am not ashamed of nor try to keep secret. It is the pearl of loss and grief, of remorse and regret, transformed into creativity, compassion, and unconditional love through a lifetime of atonement and creative expression. Through it all, the theme that has accompanied loss has been hope, which has kept me alive and inspired me to keep re-creating my self, my life, my love for my children and for my self.

References

Bergson, H. (1960). *Time and free will: An essay on the immediate data of consciousness* (F. L. Pogson, Trans.). New York: Harper.

Caruth, C. (1996). *Unclaimed experience: Trauma, narrative and history.* Baltimore: Johns Hopkins University Press.

Deleuze, G. (1990). *The logic of sense* (M. Lester & C. Stivale, Trans.). New York: Columbia University Press.

Deleuze, G., & Guattari, F. (1987). *A thousand plateaus: Capitalism and schizophrenia* (B. Massumi, Trans.). Minneapolis: University of Minnesota Press.

Deleuze, G., & Parnet, C. (1987). *Dialogues* (H. Tomlinson & B. Habberjam, Trans.). London: Athlone Press.

Felman, S., & Laub, D. (1992). *Testimony: Crises of witnessing in literature, psychoanalysis and history.* New York: Routledge.

Grosz, E. (2004). *The nick of time: Politics, evolution and the untimely.* Crows Nest, Australia: Allen & Unwin.

Grosz, E. (2008). *Chaos, territory, art: Deleuze and the framing of the earth.* New York: Columbia University Press.

Houen, C. (2002). The smell of rain: An autobiographical novel (Unpublished master's thesis, creative component). Curtin University, Perth, Australia.

Houen, C. (2008). The crone: A figure of desire for revenge and healing in the writing of a life. *Lifewriting Annual: Biographical and Autobiographical Studies, 2,* 194–201.

Macgregor Wise, J. (2005). Assemblages. In C. J. Stivale (Ed.), *Gilles Deleuze: Key concepts* (pp. 77–87). Montreal: McGill-Queen's University Press.

Saleebey, D. (2000). Power in the people: Strengths and hope. *Advances in Social Work, 1*(2), 127–136.

Skott-Myhre, H. A., & Taylor, C. (2011). Autism: Schizo of postmodern capital. *Deleuze Studies, 5*(1), 35–48.

Part 4

The Effects of
Intergenerational Grief

T his section advances the idea that complicated grief often cuts across several generations. As such, complicated grief may not necessarily be due to a singular traumatic event experienced by a given individual, but rather to a lifetime of loss during which trauma is sometimes "passed down" (usually inadvertently) to other family members.

In chapter 12, Mildred Antonelli offers an especially strong example of how complicated grief and trauma can be passed down through generations, thereby producing an intergenerational effect. Antonelli first discusses the traumatic experiences that her mother and family endured after the Bolshevik revolution of 1917 as a result of religious persecution and pogroms. Antonelli considers how she felt much angst because of the ongoing trauma her mother experienced and how this, in turn, may have fueled broader anxieties within Antonelli herself. She writes of the irony that years of psychoanalysis never really allowed her to appreciate the nature of her mother's trauma, and how this affected both her and her mother. Antonelli concludes that though "[w]e cannot take away the emotional impact of horrific events, [w]e can help the traumatized person feel less alone." Antonelli stresses that many of her therapists never considered how her mother's trauma may have affected her life; this point underscores the need to understand the complex and often intergenerational nature of complicated grief.

Chapter 13 by Rae Luckie is a reminder that intergenerational themes of complicated grief often have a way of affecting our life perspectives and how we attend to subsequent trauma. Consistent with many other chapters in this volume, Luckie notes how autobiographical writing can allow one to find meaning and resilience after grief—perhaps more so than any possible biomedical treatment. Much of Luckie's story details her struggle to write about her mother's death, in large part as a result of a pact with her sisters to not have a funeral. Luckie also discusses her attempts to come to terms with her adult son's diagnosis of advanced cancer. Even though Luckie emphasizes the importance of writing in coping, she also notes how family members can cause, exacerbate, or mitigate grief experiences within the family unit.

In chapter 14, James Wren offers a fascinating consideration of how certain themes of complicated grief may affect members of different generations, even if there is not a singular event per se driving this grief. In particular, Wren highlights experiences from the lives of his grandmother, mother, and his own experiences. In doing so, he notes how issues of abuse (for example, verbal, physical, and emotional) often appear throughout all of his accounts, as do challenges associated with personal and cultural identity (for example, gender, race, ethnicity, and sexual orientation). Taken together, Wren makes a compelling case for how certain themes of complicated grief may reoccur across different generations.

Olivia Sagan in chapter 15 completes this section with a narrative of the consequences of her father's death as a result of complications from Alzheimer's disease. Sagan stresses that her father's death was incredibly painful for her mother; and yet, allowing her grief to run its course was critical to her adjustment. Beyond the question of whether it is best to encourage one to freely experience one's grief, Sagan's piece also considers how the bereaved often struggle to understand both words spoken and never spoken prior to a loved one's death, and how this can remain with individuals for a lifetime.

Chapter Twelve

Transgenerational Transmission of the Trauma of a Pogrom

Mildred Antonelli

To understand the trauma of those who have been victimized and rendered helpless and hopeless by political and social forces over which they have no control, we need to know the context in which the violence occurred. My mother survived a pogrom, the context of which was anti-Semitism in Europe and Russia, pogroms in Russia, the Russian Revolution, and the civil war following the revolution. After describing this context, I discuss my mother's experience and some of its intergenerational effects—their transmission to my brother and, especially, to me and my children. I also share some thoughts on therapy with survivors and their descendants.

The Context

Stereotyped perceptions targeting specific groups are the fertile soil from which those who want to enhance their power can reap the harvest of explosive violence and repressive legislation, providing pseudosatisfaction to those who feel frustrated and powerless. For centuries, stereotypes about Jews and organized and unorganized action against them were part of European and Russian society. In Russia, this was expressed in pogroms and repressive legislation. *Pogrom* in Russian means to break up, destroy, lay waste, or demolish violently. Before the Russian revolution that led to the transformation of tsarist Russia to the Soviet Union, pogroms were usually conducted by disorganized bands. After the revolution, armies often conducted the massacres (Russian Civil War Pogroms, 2005).

The Russian revolution was actually a series of revolutions, movements, and stirrings that grew over many years. Beginning to be visible and effective in the 1880s, it included many groups, movements, parties, and actions that were assuaged by concessions on the part of the tsars. The revolution finally centered on two main events: the February revolution and the October revolution, both in 1917.

The February revolution, which established a provisional government led by Alexander Kerensky, developed spontaneously in Petrograd while the tsar was away visiting troops on the World War I front. The war was going badly for Russia, and it was becoming increasingly unpopular. Because heavy military setbacks had brought much of the army to a state of mutiny, the army leadership felt they could not suppress this uprising. The tsar abdicated ("Russian Revolution [1917]," 2011).

Centered in Petrograd, the provisional government, which chose to continue fighting the war, did not have the support of the majority of Russians. The more radical network of Soviets—the Bolsheviks—led by Socialists with the allegiance of the lower classes and political left, who wanted Russia to withdraw from the war, insisted on influence in the government and control of various militias ("Russian Revolution of 1917," 2011). A chaotic period followed, with frequent mutinies and many strikes. In October 1917, the Bolsheviks, supported by the workers and Soviets, overturned the interim government, established the Soviet Union, and ended the war with Germany. This revolution was followed by a civil war—a confusing sequence of shifting alliances; coups and countercoups; and invasion of foreign countries, including the Allied powers and those fighting for national independence and identity, nations absorbed by Russia during a period of territorial aggrandizement and political eexploitation beginning with Peter the Great (1682 to 1725) and ending with the abdication of Czar Nicholas II (March 15, 1997). After Russia withdrew from the war, German forces that had occupied the Ukraine during the war and managed to maintain some order withdrew, adding to the chaos in the Ukraine, where my mother lived.

My Mother's Story

Education was the primary integrating focus of my mother's striving upper-middle-class Jewish family. Her father, a successful businessman, was determined that my mother and her two younger siblings would have the best education available. When the revolution came, the Bolsheviks confiscated the family's shoe factory. The family fled the chaos and fighting in the region in which they had been living to settle in Proskurov, in the Ukraine, which until 1919 was a calm and secure place where my mother and her siblings could continue their education.

In 1919, everything changed suddenly. The local revolutionaries decided to combat Petlura, who headed a nationalist government in the Ukraine. This rebellion was suppressed. In celebration of this victory, one of the victorious regiments decided to take revenge on their enemies, declaring that the main enemies of the Ukraine were the Jews (Shvidler, 1926).

A month short of her 18th birthday, my mother was awakened one night by soldiers breaking into the house. She grabbed her seven-year-old sister and ran out of the house. From items in the house, the soldiers realized there were five people in the family and tried unsuccessfully to find the missing two. Apparently resigned to not finding them, the soldiers brought my mother's parents and brother out of the house. From where they were hiding, my mother and her sister watched as the soldiers shot them. My mother and her sister joined some other Jews who were lying down, pretending to be dead, in the basement of the house of a neighbor who was sheltering them. My aunt was crying. My mother was told that if my aunt did not stop crying they would have to kill her, because her crying would betray them to soldiers who might enter the house looking for Jews to kill.

My aunt went to live with an aunt and uncle who had no children. My mother, who was attending school, lived in another part of the city. In spite of the danger of civil war raging in the streets, because my aunt was so traumatized, my mother visited her every day.

This pogrom, which an article in the *New York Times* described as going beyond "the scope of ordinary pogroms," to assume "the character of slaughter" ("Jews slain in Ukraine," 1919), received enough publicity to come to the attention of my mother's maternal uncle, a pharmacist living in Bayonne, New Jersey. Reading a Jewish newspaper that listed the names of all the people murdered in that pogrom, and knowing there were two other children in the family, he arranged for my mother and her sister to immigrate to the United States. They lived with him and his family until my mother married my father. My parents moved to Brooklyn, where my brother and I were born and grew up, and where my mother continued to live until she was too old to live by herself.

My Mother's Posttraumatic Stress Disorder

There are three major aspects of the trauma my mother experienced. First was the trauma of being hunted and targeted for murder; second was the loss of her parents and brother—her family; third was the loss of the future they had worked for.

Targeted for Murder

In my decades of psychoanalysis, my mother's traumatic experience was never noted. After having seen several analysts, only one remarked on how frightened my mother's family must have been as they fled the violence in the area controlled by the Bolsheviks. Even after that, the impact of this experience on our relationship was never examined until I was in therapy with someone who did not demonize mothers and had worked for a number of years with patients with posttraumatic stress disorder.

Seemingly out of nowhere, these patients would become uncontrollably angry for inconsequential reasons, and they would lash out, usually at close family members. One day, as I listened to a patient describe one of her episodes, the image of my mother in one of those states came to my mind. My patient was describing what I experienced with my mother. I thought, "That was my mother. She had posttraumatic stress disorder." It was so obvious.

When I was a child, my mother would suddenly turn on me or my father or brother as if she had been attacked, her life threatened. She would become physically violent with me and verbally abusive toward my father. Her emotional state was such that I was sure I might be killed.

Goleman (1995) said, "Horror is frozen in memory." Traumatic memories, mental hair-triggers, evoke emotions associated with the original attack. Dissociated vulnerabilities surface in response to anything the traumatized person sees as a threat to survival or as an attack on the integrity of the self. This provokes an automatic counterattack that to the targeted person seems unprovoked and unexplainable. The traumatized person experiences life's ordinary occurrences as potential catastrophes, a pattern more deadly for victims of violence who have been intentionally targeted than for victims of natural catastrophes.

To a lesser degree, I have struggled with the same problem. I always knew that I wanted children very much, but working as a psychologist, I became frightened as I listened to mothers telling me how, after not wanting to be like their mothers, they found themselves acting just like them. I waited until my late thirties to start trying to have children. My first few years with my first child were very encouraging. I was not like my mother. Then one day I found myself in a state of rage with my son. Though I was not nearly as violent and out of control as my mother, she came vividly to my mind. Most frightening was my feeling that there was no alternative to the way I reacted. This happened more than once. Whatever self-esteem and self-confidence I had developed in years of psychoanalysis crumbled. My analyst and colleagues confirmed my worst fear: I was being just like my mother.

It also happened with others. When in the best possible mood, suddenly a barely noticed inconsequential remark or question could send me into a rage, and I would verbally attack. After years of psychoanalysis, this happens to me very rarely, and I can recognize the feeling and refrain from retaliating with sarcasm or a cutting remark, but the impulse to self-defense is still there. In an intense conversation, a comment or question reflecting a different frame of reference from mine makes me feel empathically disconnected, betrayed, and annihilated. That is probably what was happening between my mother and me. Something I said or did felt to her like an assault and revived the trauma that accompanied the destruction of her world, and she attacked in self-defense.

As an adult, my brother, too—basically a warm, caring person—could become emotionally and verbally violent in response to an error or presumed attack. It interfered with his vocational life and made life difficult for his family.

I hypothesize that this stress reaction is what happened with my mother and me. Children do not think or perceive things as adults do; they can do or say surprising things. Something I said or did assaulted my mother's organization of her experience of her world. The emotional experience that destroyed her world was revived, as it is in trauma victims, and she attacked me in perceived self-defense.

Another consequence of being targeted for murder was extreme anxiety, a chronic subliminal state, probably mostly dissociated, that was easily triggered by the most minor mishap. Anything could feel like the beginning of the end of the world. I have a vivid memory of my parents arguing about who was to blame that my father missed a turn in the road as we were driving somewhere in an area familiar to us. Sitting in the back of the car with my younger brother, listening to them, I felt as if my father had made a fatal mistake.

I was allowed to take the subway on my own at age 14 without being given a detailed, practiced route. I remember getting lost, panicking, asking someone for help, getting it, and realizing that getting lost was not fatal. At that time, one could always find help in the city. I remembered my parents' panic in the car that day and realized that it was unnecessary, a terrified response to a situation that was not dangerous.

Mirroring my mother, anxiety has been a chronic continuous subliminal state in my life, mostly dissociated, and easily triggered by any uncertainty, setback or loss. After decades of analysis, I reached the point where I could realize that although I might feel that way, each problem was not the end of the world. After more years of analysis and experiencing the deaths of several people close to me—something that happens after one has put middle age behind—I no longer need to resort to denial and dissociation to manage these feelings. I usually do not panic and often feel no distress at setbacks that are not serious, as I used to. Still, feelings of calm and well-being are for me islands in a sea of low-level anxiety, islands that are becoming bigger but continue to feel exceptional—strange, to be honest.

My younger son, who in daily life is calm, competent, and confident and relates easily to people, struggles with anxiety and worry and works hard to manage these emotions, especially for the sake of his family.

The Loss

My mother sometimes spoke about her parents and her brother, but never of how they died. She kept a small photographic portrait of her mother on her dresser. I knew this was my grandmother after whom I was named.

My parents were secular. My mother followed some customs on her own terms, not as prescribed. The only aspect of Judaism to which she adhered as prescribed involved memorializing one's deceased parents. On the Day of Atonement, one of the high holy days, she always attended the service for parents who had died. On the anniversary of their deaths, she lit the prescribed special candles, called Yizkor candles, that Jewish people light on this occasion. *Yizkor* is the Hebrew word for remembrance. She never said a word about her parents on these occasions, but there was always an air of reverence. I noted that the two candles meant that they died on the same day, but I never allowed myself to even wonder about it. When the parent's level of anxiety about something is extreme, children do not need to be told what not to do, or think, or feel. They know without knowing that they know.

I learned about my grandparents' fate one day, visiting my father's sister and her family in Bayonne, New Jersey. My father was the fifth of six children. This sister was the fourth, and she had been like a mother surrogate to him, so we were very close to this family, even though we lived in Brooklyn and could not see them more than a few times a year. My aunt had married and started a family in her middle teens, and my father did not marry until he was 30. So her oldest children were more peers of my parents and my aunt than of me. The youngest was a year older than me, and we were very close.

When our families met, my mother (who normally kept too close an eye on me) would be so absorbed in conversation with my older cousins and my aunt that she barely noticed me, even though my cousin and I were playing in the same room, so we in turn felt completely private. On one of these visits, when I was about nine, my cousin suddenly started telling me my mother's story. Immediately the two candles came to my mind. I had the answer to the question I had never been able to formulate. I never spoke about it until I was an adult.

Besides the loss itself, my mother went from being the oldest child in a stable family—with a father who made all the important decisions and a mother who was always there—to being on her own as a late teenager, responsible for herself and a very traumatized younger sister. From what I know of my mother's personality, what I observed and experienced, and what I was told, I think she must have managed this devastating loss by dissociation of her own feelings and by concentrating on what needed to be done in the present. She had to finish secondary school, and she had to be the one on whom my aunt could rely. But she had an inordinate fear of loss, with no awareness of the disconnection between the intensity of her fears and the actual situation.

If someone arrived home more than a few minutes late, or if when I was away I did not write as often as she expected, she was obsessed with fantasies of disaster. My whole family would pressure me to comply with my mother's demand. My mother would even enlist the help of anyone I was with to demand that I keep in much more frequent contact, even though without pressure I was in touch with her more than any of my friends were with their parents. My younger brother could not go to sleep until everyone in the family was home.

My father's business involved selling what was then called general merchandise: clothes, furniture, linens, jewelry on the installment plan. His customers were immigrants—first Italian, then Puerto Rican. They usually did not speak English well enough to navigate the world of shopping on their own, and they did not have the money to pay cash for what they needed. My father taught himself Italian, and then Spanish. He took his newly immigrated customers shopping or brought them samples. He paid for what they bought, and they repaid him in small installments over time, which he would collect by visiting their homes. He spent a lot of time in the car.

If there was a snowstorm, he would get home very late. Even though he was clearly delayed because of the snow, my mother would be consumed with worry, and no one in the house could think of anything else. And as always, instead of being happy and relieved when he arrived, she would be angry that he hadn't called to reassure her.

Years later, living in the suburbs and commuting to work, I would sometimes be caught in a blizzard coming home, not on a highway, but on one of the smaller roads where traffic barely moved. It was clear that the worst thing that could happen would be minor damage to the car. I would think of my father driving the dark, clogged, snowbound Brooklyn streets. There was no way he could park the car, get out, and make a phone call; and the danger was minimal.

I envision these moments opening up for my mother what George Atwood and his imaginary friend Dr. E. refer to as the abyss of madness (Atwood, 2010). I envision the earth opening, spewing forth raging turmoil, endless in time and space. Though for my mother, her reactions were emotionally compelling and impossible to disconnect from in such moments, to the object of these anxieties her behavior seemed impossibly demanding and controlling, bizarre and inexplicable. And I believe that to my mother, too, having had no therapy, and probably no one with whom to share the experience in depth, her subjective experience must have confused and frightened her.

Another one of these episodes that I could not understand until recently happened when I was five years old. I attended kindergarten in the morning. One day my mother was not there to pick me up when the session ended. I must have expressed apprehension (insecure attachment) to a classmate, who came to my rescue. Her older brother always walked her home from school, passing the building in which I lived. They would take me home. Relieved, I went with them, feeling proud when I arrived at home that I had solved my own problem.

What must it have been like for my mother to arrive and be unable to find me? When she came home and saw me she became extremely enraged and physically violent—out of control. I was terrified and confused. Would I survive? Why did my resourcefulness make her so angry? As a mother of young children, I too was inordinately anxious, but in moments that evoked that level of anxiety I thought of my mother, and I was able to manage better than she did. And I would be thrilled and happy when these moments were relieved by a benign outcome. But even today as a grandparent, I have many moments seeing my sons and their wives having no anxiety if their children are delayed returning home, or when they are swimming while their parents are on the shore, or bicycling on their own and out of sight. The parents are confident and assured that all will go well, while I can imagine only disaster. All I can do is distance myself, bury my head in a book, or go to another room and get involved in something on my own, because I am so afraid my anxiety might be communicated and contaminate their experience. As a parent, I tried to have others—their father, friends, reliable babysitters—take over in situations in which I felt I could not trust myself to manage my anxiety.

Attending a workshop run by a therapist who worked on the high-risk maternity unit of a hospital, I had another moment of instant enlightenment. She described a woman who at age seven had lost her mother, panicked when she became engaged to be married, and panicked when she delivered a healthy baby after a previous unsuccessful pregnancy. I understood her. She was afraid of falling in love, becoming attached, and risking another loss. I saw my mother and her profound difficulty being a parent.

Another residue in me of the insecure attachment with my mother resulting from her fear of loss is an inordinate anxiety when I need to depend on someone for something very important to me. I become obsessively focused on what is negative in the situation and am convinced I will be betrayed and sabotaged.

The closest my mother came to experiencing understanding, connectedness, security, and joy in a relationship was with my aunt. Having shared the most horrible experience of their lives, they had an unbreakable bond.

As to my mother and my father, I remember most vividly when they fought, sometimes heatedly. After one of these fights, my mother suggested I go to a movie with my father. We went, and on the way home, passing my aunt's apartment, my father stopped to see if my mother was visiting and needed a ride home. I asked, "How can you do that when she was so mean?" My father said, "Oh, she's crazy."

My mother and father were introduced by my father's sister, who met my mother in school studying English. My father's nieces and nephews loved my mother. She was a very good listener, sympathetic, empathic, interested, and supportive, with helpful suggestions when they had problems. Aware of aspects of her personality they thought were strange—maybe cold at times—they did not fault her. Attributing these aspects to her trauma, they made allowances.

The Loss of Her Anticipated Future

The loss of her future took the most devastating toll on my mother and her relationship with my brother and me, especially me. She could not bear our individuation because it reminded her of her lost future. Her determination and dissociation failed when I reached the age when my need for autonomy was most urgent, and as my brother's was surfacing. My mother, overcome by buried or denied emotions of the past, which she attributed to the present, "lost it." She became aggressively negative and discouraging when we needed encouragement. Always a strong supporter of perseverance in the face of discouraging circumstances, she now found a caveat in every situation to bring down the mood and make us feel confused. A family psychologist told me that he found that the age at which the child experienced a crisis was the same age at which the parent had experienced a similar crisis. I thought of myself. In spite of the problems in my relationship with my mother, I had, to a point, gone through my life doing what I needed and wanted to do with confidence and enjoyment. When I began graduate school, I fell apart internally. Although pursuing my plan to become a psychologist and psychoanalyst, as well as building my social life, I did not feel as I had expected I would. Though I maintained a façade of confidence, I felt confused.

I now realize that my mother's attitude toward me changed at the stage in my life that corresponded to the point at which her life fell apart. Her support for my determination to be economically independent and have a career about which I was passionate had become ambivalent, and she aggressively opposed and undermined any dating relationship in which I felt intense and enthusiastic.

I think that when I reached the stage of life in which she lost everything, the "abyss of madness" (Atwood, 2010) overwhelmed her. Unable to keep me from experiencing the freedom and mobility that would inevitably bring what she had lost to the forefront of consciousness, she felt my whole being as an attack on her sanity. Her reaction was to fight. Seeing me becoming independent and autonomous was not an affirmation of her success as a mother. Our relationship changing appropriately was experienced as another loss, evoking the emotional memory of the trauma in which she lost so much. What I did not notice was that she was changing profoundly, and that the change in her was undermining me. This happened partly because without being aware of it, I was empathically experiencing her fragmentation and was myself then feeling fragmented, and partly because seeing me as the cause of her own feelings of overwhelming, unbearable anxiety and emotional pain, she was disconnecting and attacking me.

My brother was targeted differently. More comfortable in the world than I was, he wanted to go to college away from home. She opposed this, and he could not function in her presence. He started at Brooklyn College, but he was oppositional and defiant, could not concentrate on the work, and fought with my mother constantly. The only alternate life plan of his that she could not disparage, because she was a Zionist, was his decision to become part of a Zionist labor group with high universalist humanitarian ideals. Although loyal to my mother, he moved to Israel, out of her reach, to live on a kibbutz. She ultimately retired there years after my father died, when she could no longer live alone.

As our children grow and mature, our input into their decisions and our control over them diminishes, yet our sense of well-being continues to be determined by how their lives are progressing. My mother managed her anxiety and feelings of annihilation by being inordinately controlling of us; and she could not empathize, never having gone through the stage with her parents that my brother and I were struggling with. To her, we were failures, and she—who had always strived to be a good mother—was a failure as a mother.

Not long after my brother emigrated, I realized that no matter how much I struggled, in years of psychoanalysis, I could not keep from fragmenting if I had any contact with my mother. I had to decide to have no contact, even though it meant giving up my entire family, who were loyal to her and could not understand my need. Confirmation as to why I could not maintain a positive image of myself in her presence came after she died and I reconnected with my family. My cousin's wife, who had become very good friends with my mother, told me that my mother talked about me all the time, but she would never have recognized me from the way my mother talked about me. I think my disconnection and my brother's emigrating were the major tragedies of my mother's life.

Another aspect of my relationship with my mother that I believe developed out of her loss of her future and not being able to mourn this loss involves anticipation and promises, which were a very murky experience between us. Much of the satisfaction in life involves anticipation—looking forward, an important component of hope.

My aunt's wedding was emblematic of this difficulty. There were many weddings of the children of my father's older sister, and I wanted to attend them. My mother would say no children were invited, and then I would hear that there had been children at the wedding—probably nieces and nephews of the bride and groom—and I would feel lied to. My aunt would then assure me that I would be at her wedding. But I wasn't.

One day I accidentally overheard the mother of the family with whom we were sharing a bungalow in the country say to my mother, "You can go to the wedding. You can leave your children with me." "What wedding?" I asked. My mother said, "Ann is getting married." I said, "I'm supposed to go to her wedding." I don't remember her answer, but my mother did go, and I did not. Years later I reminded my aunt of this broken promise. She told me that my mother would not tell her whether or not she was coming, and she did not know whether or not she would be there until my mother arrived at the ceremony.

As a child, especially in my relationship with my mother, I never felt certain a promise would be kept. Sometimes it was, and sometimes it wasn't. Often I could not get a commitment for a long time, until what seemed like the last minute, while I endured the anxiety of not knowing. Often when a promise was broken there was no acknowledgement of it, and when I objected my feelings were dismissed. So I grew up never feeling I could confidently look forward to anything I planned. This is still a problem, though less intense. There is always an unreal element in my experience of anything I plan.

In more recent years, I learned from others who sustained unexpected unusual losses—one of a teenaged child, the other of his wife of a few years just at the time that should have been their most joyous, when they had a six-month-old baby and a newly purchased house—that since these deaths, they could not assume that anything they planned would happen, and they would not make firm commitments, even while making plans. So it was with my mother. Having written off her need to anticipate and look forward with hope, she could not empathize with this need in others.

After years of psychoanalysis I have improved, but the problem persists. I often worry about potential catastrophes or difficulties that could interfere either with the fulfillment or the quality of the anticipated experience. Assuming others have the same anxiety, I try to be meticulous in letting people know when I am going to or might be late for any appointment, to keep them from worrying.

And to this day, if I have anything, I don't believe it will last. In my mind I may be happy with what I have, but the least untoward event can make me fear I will lose everything I cherish. As mentioned earlier, when I had my first child, and I was relieved to realize I was not being like my mother, on a deeper level, it felt unreal. If a babysitter was late, I was afraid she would not come, and that if I did not have a babysitter, I could not work and could not keep the baby, even though his father could take care of him without my income. If I fell into a depressed or other troubled mood, I was afraid the baby would lose his happy, enthusiastic, outgoing disposition. As an adult, my older son has told me that he feels his life has always felt like a crisis, where everything could suddenly fall apart. It reminded me of my fears when he was a baby.

What to Do

There is no one approach to the treatment of trauma; there is no recipe, but there are guidelines. All traumas are different depending on the cause, the context, and the individual's response, which depends on many factors. And as in all therapy, what is needed or optimal varies with the individual patient and therapist. I will speak from my experience and will emphasize what I think might have helped my mother and our family.

Trauma upends the victim's entire experience and view of himself and his relationship to the world. The first challenge to the therapist is to accept the seemingly unbearable experience of not being able to fix it. We cannot fix disability from physical injury. We cannot take away serious illness. We cannot bring back the dead. By our empathic, caring presence and attitude we can help the patient be more aware of his limitations, the emotions evoked by this awareness, and the impact on his life—what has been lost and its ramifications, and how to manage. We cannot take away the emotional impact of horrific events, but we can help the traumatized person feel less alone. From his experience with grief, Stolorow (2007) believes that what is most disturbing in trauma is the feeling that no one can understand. Empathically listening to them describing their experience with this feeling, we can help people feel less alone with the experience of feeling alone.

These patients urgently need help in not upending their interpersonal worlds. In some cases, the patient's uncontrollable, unpredictable explosions of rage erode his most important relationships. In some cases, his despair and other changes in personality and life circumstances become unbearable to whomever he most depends on. In some cases, patterns of difficulty long overlooked or accepted as unimportant no longer feel bearable. Unmet needs force their way into awareness and cannot be managed. Validating this experience and helping address these difficulties is important, even though we cannot take away the physical, emotional, and interpersonal effects of the traumatic reality. Having someone who can listen as no one else in their lives can, who can bear the pain with them, even though feeling it only in a limited way, makes an enormous difference.

The tragedy of my mother's disconnection from her children as we became adults could have been at least somewhat averted if she had had therapy focused on how she experienced her current life. I believe this would have led her to address what had happened to her, and perhaps also preexisting personality patterns.

In people who have experienced trauma, the dissociation, though a destructive force in their lives, also enables them to live. In therapy, as their frightened selves begin to come together, their interpersonal lives improve, and they become more hopeful; they return gradually to the trauma itself. Sometimes it might take two years for someone to remember the pivotal moment that was most disturbing.

I wish my mother had had someone to talk to immediately after her trauma, just to say what happened. Immediate, routine, empathic (but not necessarily verbalized) response to her experience of the event and to her plight in the moment might have mitigated the need to dissociate and muted its destructive and self-destructive power. I see my mother as someone who needed to be approached immediately in this way. It might have in some way weakened her conviction that she had to live her life needing nothing from anyone, and that she had to control everything and everyone around her.

The International Trauma Treatment Program, founded and directed by John R. van Eenwyk, PhD, in Olympia, Washington, works with victims of catastrophic events. He and his team work with populations affected by torture and other war trauma. They train professionals in areas suffering catastrophic events, who in turn train other professionals to work with the victims. The training is a collaborative effort that integrates the particular culture's way of working with trauma with the understanding the team has developed. The team communicates with other human rights groups so that their work can include understanding the culture and the political context in which the trauma occurred. Programs of this nature are needed to help victims of catastrophic events.

When an epidemic strikes, we know there will be many people who fall ill and need treatment. We need to make the same assumptions with regard to the victims of catastrophic events. We need to approach people, not wait for them to come to us. Mohammed Majid (1981) has developed a questionnaire that helps people realize that they have been emotionally wounded and need treatment.

Writing this chapter, I was appalled by the fact that I was in analysis so many years, with several analysts, and this important aspect of my life was never even noticed. As psychoanalysts and psychotherapists, I think we need to be alert to when there has been trauma in the lives of our patients, and when trauma in the lives of their parents, grandparents, and even more remote ancestors is a factor in the difficulties in the lives of our patients.

I began therapy in an era when analysts had only just begun to treat relationships with parents as centrally significant. Then, I believe we went through an era of demonizing parents, especially mothers. Even though we looked into the lives of the parents of our patients, there was concern that understanding the parents might shift the balance away from the patient's need to appreciate his own experience toward downplaying the damage to the patient resulting from the relationship with the parents.

I think we need to learn ways to help our patients appreciate how their parents got to be who they are, while appreciating the problematic aspects of their parents' impact on their own lives. With regard to trauma in the lives of previous generations, patients will often present the information but gloss over it, so that we don't focus on it. Anyone who has experienced a loss of a parent at an early age, or when he or she was at the threshold of adulthood, has almost always been seriously traumatized, and the effect will be felt or transmitted to the offspring and descendants. War, natural disasters, ethnic violence of one sort or another, loss of a child—after or before birth—make people vulnerable to the effects of trauma in their lives and the lives of anyone in a significant relationship with them. As therapists and psychoanalysts, we must be alert to note or find out when this has occurred in the life of a patient or the patient's family. We need to keep it in mind and address it as soon as it is relevant.

I also think the work needs to be conducted with an understanding of the context in which the catastrophic event occurred. Someone working with my mother would have needed to understand the context of the assault that devastated her life and her world. I believe that in working with all victims of traumatic events, we are more effective to the degree that we appreciate the political, economic, social, and cultural context in which the events occurred, as much as we must know the previous experience of the individual patient.

References

Atwood, G. (2010). The abyss of madness—An interview. *International Journal of Psychoanalytic Self Psychology, 5,* 344–356.

Goleman, D. (1995) *Emotional intelligence.* New York: Bantam Books.

Jews slain in Ukraine: Their former minister in that country sends a review of the pogroms. (1919, September 19). *New York Times.*

Majid, M. (1981). *Personality stress analysis* (Unpublished; on file at the World Health Organization, Reference No. M4/180/1).

Russian Civil War Pogroms. (2005). *Zionism and Israel—Encyclopedic dictionary.* Retrieved from http://www.zionism-israel.com/dic/Russsian_Civil_War_pogroms.htm

Russian Revolution of 1917. (2011). *Wikipedia.* Retrieved from http://en.wikipedia.org/wiki/Russian_Revolution_(1917)

Shvidler, M. (1926). The Proskurov massacre (excerpt from *Jewish Pogroms 1918–1921*; M. Werbach, Trans.). Retrieved from http://www.felshtin.org/resources/proskurovmassacre.pdf

Stolorow, R. (2007, June 27). *Trauma and human existence: Autobiographical, psychoanalytic and philosophical reflections.* New York: Analytic Press.

Chapter Thirteen

Writing through Grief

Rae Luckie

People who write about their loved one's deaths are paradoxically engaged in a search for the meaning of their loved one's lives. They want to make a record: they want to describe their loss and their grief. But they want to discover, too, an overarching meaning for this death so that it will not have been for naught.

—Louise DeSalvo, *Writing as a Way of Healing*

*I*t appears we are in an era of what Thomas Szasz referred to as "the medicalization of everyday life" (2007), in which antidepressants are prescribed for sadness, loneliness and grief; amphetamines are prescribed to manage behavior; and surgery and drugs are prescribed for obesity. Though Szasz doesn't explicitly talk about resiliency, he is an advocate for personal responsibility (Szasz, 1960). He argues that we cannot live without meaning and that we are mistaken [in psychology] by

> looking to the individual rather than to the world in which he lives. …We must look instead at the conditions under which people govern, give help, teach, and arrange incentive systems in particular ways. In other words, we must look to the culture as a social environment. (Szasz, 1974, pp. 3–4)

This chapter represents an autoethnographic approach to explore the nature of resilience in personal grief—perhaps best described as "cumulative grief." Though grief of this nature does not accord with the proposed *Diagnostic and Statistical Manual of Mental Disorders—Fifth Edition* revision in that it is not focused on a single person, it is still outside cultural norms and as such could be misconstrued as complicated grief (Frances, Pies,

& Zisook, 2010). Autoethnography is described by Smith and Watson as a subgenre of life writing where "the writer-observer is self-reflexive and critical of the discursive practices and history of the field" (2010, p. 259). By combining elements of autobiography and ethnography, autoethnography "seeks to describe and systematically analyze personal experience in order to understand cultural experience … thus, as a method, autoethnography is both process and product" (Ellis, Adams, & Bochner, 2011). It is intended that this product will allow the reader to experience an individual's processing of personal grief, and demonstrate that resilience is a key factor in that process.

Various studies have defined resilience as an aspect of personality, a series of psychological traits linked to positive emotions that play a pivotal role in adaptation to stressful events (Ong, Bergeman, Bisconti, & Wallace, 2006). Bonanno suggested that the major response to trauma is resilience, and also explored an individual differences or personality traits model but suggested that rather than a resilient type, "there appear to be multiple and sometimes unexpected ways to be resilient, and sometimes resilience is achieved by means that are not fully adaptive under normal circumstances" (2005, p. 135). Miller linked resilience to the individual's search for meaning and the strengths-based approach of the positive psychology movement, and argued that although an ultimate definition of resilience is difficult, resilient behavior is easily recognizable (Miller, 2003).

May 2, 2011

We're at Royal Prince Alfred Hospital in Sydney, Australia, watching the plastic-encased chemotherapy cocktail drip into our son's arm. It has been a month since Shane was diagnosed with advanced cancer of the esophagus. Surgery was out of the question—the tumor was too near the aorta and had already spread to the lymph nodes. My husband Barry and I put on a mask of hope in front of Shane, but I've been researching, and it seems there is none (Cunningham et al., 2008; Herskovic et al., 1992).

Shane was born on September 23, 1967. It was halftime at the Victorian Football League Grand Final—Richmond versus Geelong—and the midwife seemed more excited about the score than what was happening down below. That was also the date set for our wedding in 1961, but we changed it to the week before because my mother rang my father and threatened to shoot him if he went. He then declined the invitation, but I changed the date to the 16th just in case.

We sit quietly for five days at the end of his bed—Shane comatose but showing pain despite the oxycontin, endone, endep, and other concoctions. When he was a little boy, he'd wake up with sunshine in his eyes and a smile on his face—every morning—as if each day was a magic gift just for him.

Each day they take him for radiation. His skin is gray. Each day Barry and I surf the waves of anticipatory grief. Each night I surf the Internet, searching for understanding. I revisit memories of past deaths and loss, and begin writing again. My journal keeping has always been erratic—driven by illness and death. I haven't needed to write since Barry was diagnosed with leiomyosarcoma.

Friday, January 18, 2002

Can it be only six days? I was calmer this afternoon, but on ABC radio talkback around 2 A.M., Trevor Chappel's topic was "what is happiness." The last caller said good health and began to weep as her husband is dying. I am so conscious of every mention of death. I think I have faced the worst; or have I? I start to panic then try to stop my brain racing forward. I can't bear the thought of anything happening to him.

Hopefully I'll look back and see my worries are unfounded. I can't think how many times I've said please please God, but I have no religion to comfort me. Late last Saturday the general practitioner rang. I knew straight away. Barry just kept saying yep yep yep, and a couple of times he glanced at me and rolled his eyes. The doctor said he'd made a mistake. It wasn't a cyst he'd partially removed. It was a rare cancer, but Barry couldn't remember the name other than it started with lyo.

Now on the ABC it's about what scares you or what gives you the creeps in movies, and I remember when I was a kid holding my fingers in my ears and closing my eyes to make scary things go away at the Saturday afternoon matinees. I want to do it now.

As soon as Barry went to bed that night, I started the Internet search. Narrowed it down to liposarcoma or leiomyosarcoma. I wrote the two on a bright pink Post-It note and thought, "please let it be the first one." The next morning when Barry said the second one, I tried not to let him see my terror. Monday the general practitioner rang Dr. Clingan, the oncologist at Wollongong. I fluctuated between anger with the general practitioner and myself for not nagging enough to go sooner, but I realize we can't change what has been done and have to move forward.

The blessing is that Barry can sleep as normal. He said I'm doing enough worrying for the both of us. We make "Star Trek" jokes, and I suggest that he wear a set of pointy ears; he said not on the first appointment. Dr. Clingan has midlife graying hair and crumpled trousers. He doesn't beat around the bush. It's potentially fatal. I just want to grab Barry and take off somewhere. Maybe the south island of New Zealand. I forget now if it was Thursday or Friday, and Barry said I want you to promise me just one thing: that you'll finish the PhD.

> *Writing is desire, pleasure, the return to the self and its loss, the construction and hence the deconstruction of identity, it is the memory work and the talking cure; the autobiographical is everywhere.*
>
> —Anne Freadman, *Feminist Literary Theory*
> *(A Question [or two] about Genre)*

I had been procrastinating with the PhD since 1993. It consisted of a body of autobiographical writing and an accompanying exegesis. The problem was I kept digressing with the research for the latter and found it difficult to be objective, as the task was to theoretically critique one's own life writing. Rosamund Dalziell (1999) contended that the process of grieving and the autobiographical process are closely connected; memories are reinterpreted as one revisits experiences of loss and reviews and evaluates the past. But now I am writing against a future loss, with a feeling described as "anticipatory grief" (Reynolds & Botha, 2006).

When my father, Ken Kelly, died of lung cancer in 1987, I felt no grief. He had been mourned throughout the first 16 years of my life. Barry and I had just started going out together when I first met him at my grandparents' 50th wedding anniversary in 1957. After that, time remembered with my father could be counted in days, but he telephoned me when he knew he was dying. He asked me to visit him at St. Vincent's Hospital. He said he had loved my mother and had wanted to see me when I was growing up, but he was happily remarried with two sons. He didn't want to rock the boat. We had perhaps half an hour together before his wife arrived. He phoned and said not to come again, as me being there had upset her.

In March 1989, my cousin Ted died of a brain tumor in the same hospital where Shane lay in 2011. I held Ted's hand and stroked his forehead. He wept about his mother Madge, who also raised me. We talked about her and about my mother Nell, who had been dead for many years, and their sister Kit who lives in Canberra—these three sisters who never hugged or said "I love you." Later, I took a message to his mother in the nursing home in Canberra and told her he loved her. She wept and said she should have died in his place. They would not see each other again.

I was the only one from our side of the family at Ted's funeral. Madge died later that year and left written instructions for her daughter Jan to obey the pact she, Nell, and Kit had made years earlier.

The pact was made in the spring of 1977. Nell came to Bega for a holiday early in September. Barry was in the police, and we had been transferred there. Like Auntie Mame, Nell adored and enchanted the kids. She had a rich throaty laugh, a wacky sense of humor, and even though she was 60, she was fit and trim and could do the splits. She always brought the latest Dr. Seuss books and 12-inch LPs. This trip she brought Meco's "Star Wars," Queen's "A Day at the Races," and "The Best of the Doobie Brothers." Trish, Tracy, and Shane made up dances and belted out "Tie Your Mother Down" along with Freddy Mercury.

Kit rang; her husband Arthur was dying of lung cancer. Nell went to Canberra to be with her.

September 27, 1977

I ring Nell and ask, How was the funeral service?

"There wasn't one; Kit and I are sitting in the lounge [living room] having a couple of beers."

"Don't joke, you mean after . . .?"

"Nope. Kit said everyone who mattered had said goodbye to Arthur, and she doesn't believe in all that false hand wringing. He's probably being cremated right now. There's just the undertaker there, and his ashes will be sprinkled on the rose garden."

"I think that's awful, how can she . . ."

"We had a talk with Madge this morning, and it's what we all want. We've made a pact—just a cremation. We don't want anybody there."

"Don't be stupid, anyway you're not going to die."

"I swear to God it's what I want. What we all want. If you give me a funeral I'll come back and bloody haunt you. I mean it. Just you remember."

I swallowed the lump in my throat as she made me promise, cross my heart, and spit my death. I didn't know what else to say; we'd never talked about death or love. Nell stayed with Kit for a couple more weeks, then returned to Manly.

It's Thursday night, November 10, 1977, and I'm listening to the late news in bed. Freak storms have unroofed houses at Canberra and Manly. I ring Nell, but there's no answer. I ring my cousin Jan. Madge lives in a flat attached to their house.

"Glad you're okay. I've been trying to ring Nell for a week. She's mad being out on a night like this—how's Kit doing?"

"You know what she's like, she just gets on with life."

"Give my love to Madge."

I keep trying to ring Nell. There's no answer.

November 11, 1977

It's Friday. I'm getting dressed and listening to 2BA. The announcer says on this day in 1880, they hanged Ned Kelly. I remember asking my Grandpa Kelly if we were related and his stony silence. It wasn't fashionable to be related to bushrangers in those days. Then the announcer brings me back. "It's Remembrance Day, the eleventh day of the eleventh month." I'm now at work, and it's almost the eleventh hour.

I have my two minutes' silence alone in the photocopy room at Bega High School, where I'm a teachers' aide. I'm walking back to the office along the wide corridor. Barry is in uniform walking toward me. Momentarily, I think something must be wrong with one of the kids. There's a strange look on his face, the worn floorboards seem to ripple in the gap between us, and everything seems to be in slow motion. "I know why you haven't been able to get Nell. The police phoned and told me she was found dead." He holds me close and contains my sobs. I don't remember telling the kids. Edna from next door says she and her husband Herb will look after them. Herb had been the news correspondent at the local ABC radio station for 40 years. He can turn a handkerchief into a mouse and make it run up his arm.

We drive to Sydney to Manly Police Station. I sign for a manila envelope. It contains my mother's watch; the band is encrusted with maggots. A detective says there'll be an inquest and hands me a small bottle of *Nil Odor*. "They use it at the morgue," he said. He hands me the business card of an undertaker and says they will give me a good deal on the funeral. "She doesn't want a funeral," I say.

My mother has been dead for nine, hot November days. We scrub and spray—Pine-o-Clean, Flash, Glen 20. Her flat had been a sanctuary the year before when Barry's father was transported to Royal North Shore Hospital, after a car accident that left him a quadriplegic. His eyes pleaded, and tears dripped; we took turns at wiping them away. We sat with him, crooning and telling him not to worry. We rubbed his forehead and told him we loved him. Nell would have oysters, prawns, and a cold beer for Barry and make us laugh. "Life goes on," she said. He died seven months before Nell. My grandmother Kelly died a few weeks before him.

I'm on my hands and knees. Scrubbing. "Come on, we're getting out for a while," Barry says.

It's nearly lunchtime on a sunny Saturday. There's a tangy salt breeze. Along Little Manly past the pie shop, curry is on special. Across the road, the carnival has come to life; shrieks from the octopus echo across the water. Around the corner onto the Corso, past the barbecue chicken and deli opposite the junk shop where Nell buys her Chinese ornaments and brush-stroked bamboo wall hangings. Kids are running and jumping, dragging beach towels, plastic buckets and spades, urging parents to hurry.

Halfway along the block, the Pearl King is just below footpath level in the shopping center. He stands next to his portrait. His long, bushy beard attracts kids who beg for a 20-cent piece to toss over the edge. If it lands square on a brown cardboard box, they get the contents—hoping to find a pearl instead of colored glass. Nell says no—it's a waste of money, just like the bubble-gum machines.

Toward the beachfront, past the queues at the fish and chip shop, the Norfolk pines stand guard over little kids building sandcastles and swimmers spearing foam-tipped waves. Seagulls are swirling, lifeguards are drilling, and coconut-oiled bodies are roasting in the sun. I can't bear life as usual going on around me; I want to scream. Nell is dead. My mother is dead. I want the world to stop; I feel unbearably alone.

I ring Kit. She's still grieving. Arthur's been dead five weeks, and now I have to tell her that her favorite sister is dead. I ask her what to do.

"You know damn well what she wanted, just have the guts to bloody well go ahead and do it."

We finish the cleanup. We can only take what will fit in the second-hand orange Peugeot. We are on the road as Nell is being cremated.

In August 1989, Madge dies, and I spend a week in Canberra with my cousin Jan. Kit is appalled because Jan is going to have a funeral. Barry and I are sitting in the chapel. Jan walks beside the lily-draped coffin in time with the Royal Scots Dragoon Guards' version of "Amazing Grace." Madge left a letter: "Private cremation, no flowers, no casket, please adhere to my wishes." I don't know whether to laugh or cry. I keep looking at the ceiling, terrified that Nell and Madge will come swooping down, banshee-like. As the coffin slowly glides back and the curtains close, I have a flash of an old Vincent Price movie where the body is being cremated—alive.

Kit died two years later. No funeral, no obituary, no flowers, no chance to grieve.

I think that not to be present at the funeral of someone we love can leave an unassuageable sense of unfinished business.

—Inga Clendinnen, *About Bones*

I don't want you to think I go about wallowing in grief—if it's here on the computer, I can get on with life. I scan and store the tangible fragments of lives, evidence that these women have lived—letters, photographs, recipes, newspaper clippings, postcards, receipts, birth certificates, death certificates, marriage certificates, divorce papers, court reports, obituaries. I write the memories—the stories they told, the ditties they sang. I research the eras of their upbringing and their parents before them. I ache with the desire to fill in the gaps—to glean what I can from public and private records—to discover why the three sisters would demand "no funeral."

I discover that when he was 10, my mother's brother died of meningitis. He was refused a Catholic funeral because his mother had married a divorcee. I try to imagine her grief and the grief of her mother when four of her children died of diphtheria during one week in May of 1885. My great-grandmother was an illiterate Irishwoman who struggled to survive, following her husband around the goldfields of central west New South Wales. She had 11 children at the time and my grandmother, her youngest child, was five years old.

> No public funeral should be held at a house in which there is a case of diphtheria, nor in which a death from diphtheria has recently occurred. Except under extraordinary precautions, there should be no public funeral of a person who has died from diphtheria. No child should attend, and it would be better in most cases that few adults should attend a funeral of a person dead of diphtheria. ("Destriction and Prevention of Diptheria," 1885, p. 79)

Perhaps these experiences led to the passing down of the no–funerals edict. I write their lives, and in so doing I fashion my own memorials. Their presence continues in their absence.

> Eventually the culturally shaped cognitive and linguistic processes that guide the self-telling of life narratives achieve the power to structure perceptual experience, to organize memory, to segment and purpose-build the very

"events" of a life. In the end, we *become* the autobiographical narratives by which we "tell about" our lives. (Bruner, 2004, p. 694)

I finish the PhD—I finish the business.

Doris Brett is an Australian writer and clinical psychologist who has worked with oncology patients. In her memoir, *Eating the Underworld* (Brett, 2001), which documents her own cancer, Brett was able to write in the voice of the therapist, knowing that when cancer is diagnosed, it prompts a review of life that she documented. As such, her memoir could be categorized as autoethnography. My own writings forced a state of continual life review, a traumatic revisiting and rewriting as each member of the previous generation who had influenced my life died. At times I wished I was writing fantasy, creating a place like the science-fiction world of Dr. Who, where one could overcome death through time travel or the attainment of immortality. I recall a passage in David McCooey's *Artful Histories*, in which he wrote that it is death that symbolizes the difference between autobiography and fiction.

> Fiction is not written in the face of death. The autobiographer writes not only to relive, but to confront death: his own and other people's. This is what makes autobiography interested not only in representation, but also in interpretation. Fictional characters die fictionally, people die in actual fact. (McCooey, 1996, p. 190)

I came to the conclusion that writing the death of others was also a way to rehearse my own. In his essay "Being and Nothingness" in *The Penguin Book of Death*, Phillip Adams—who dresses in constant mourning—says he doesn't fear death so much as resent life's brevity. He described death as, "The verbal counterpart to a full stop. Which, of course, is exactly what it is. A full stop to the life sentence" (Adams, 1997, p. 42). He jokes about the names of funeral parlors that parody life. I'm sure he would be amused to know that residents of Kiama are dispatched by *Crapp Funerals*. Adams said death is what gives life meaning—I think all of us reach a moment when we realize that life is a death sentence. I had occasionally contemplated mine and Barry's but not that of our son. I am in uncharted territory. Barry and I comfort each other. We talk. We try to envisage the future.

John Archer (1999) wrote,

> The bereavement felt by parents who lose an adult offspring has been relatively little studied, although ... some studies of "death of a child" have

included adult offspring. In one of the earlier accounts of bereavement, Gorer (1965) suggested that death of an adult offspring is a particularly traumatic form of grief. He referred to it as "the most distressing and long-lasting of all griefs." (p. 200)

Archer (1999) found that while some studies were "complicated by involving a traumatic source of bereavement, notably, war," the overall evidence indicated there was an "intense grief reaction among parents who have lost an adult son or daughter" (p. 202). As parents, we were spectators in a different war—the war on cancer. Sontag (1978) documented the military metaphors used: cancer cells invade and attack the body's defenses; they colonize other sites in the body; patients are bombarded with radiotherapy; chemotherapy is chemical warfare; the treatment aims to kill or destroy cancer cells; new drugs are described as "magic bullets"; victims fight for their lives; and we ultimately hope for a victory over the disease (pp. 68–69). She stated, "It is thought that nearly any damage to the body is justified if it saves the patient's life" (p. 69). Sontag was diagnosed with breast cancer in 1976.

> Ignoring the advice of oncologists, she had radically high doses of chemotherapy for 2½ years; the odds were against her living. "I was terrified," she said, "Horrible grief. Above all, to leave my son. And I loved life so much. I was never tempted to say 'that's it'. I love it when people fight for their lives." (Sydney Morning Herald, 2004, p. 24)

Shane is fighting for his life. But as the year passes and I observe a body ravaged by aggressive radiation and chemotherapy with no cure possible, I search for meaning in Shane's intense suffering and remember how his grandfather begged Barry and I to kill him during his.

> The list of horrors is endless and crushing if we do not creatively oppose it. Which means writing as cure. Not completely, of course … I won't use the word *therapy*; it's too clean, too sterile. I only say when death slows others, you must leap to set up your diving board and dive head first into your typewriter.
>
> —Ray Bradbury, *Zen in the Art of Writing*

Writing is my therapy. I wake in the early hours of the morning and place words on the computer screen. I am researching grief. Sometimes it's hard to see for tears. Each Monday morning I take a fragrant bunch of flowers to work: purple and mauve lavenders, dianthus and geraniums, and green fronds of fishbone fern. I put on a lipstick smile. I leave my grief on the hard drive. Our preservice teachers are on their professional experience. I sit quietly in the corner of classrooms and delight in watching children experiencing, discovering, experimenting, learning. I walk across playgrounds where children are hopping, jumping, laughing, and bouncing balls. I once overheard Madge talking to Kit when I was a child. "No matter what happens to Rae, she always bounces back."

> **resile**: draw back, shrink, recoil—F. *resilir* or L. *resilire* leap back, recoil f. re- + *salir* leap (see SALIENT). So **resilient** returning to the original position. **salient**: leaping, jetting forward, pointing outward.
>
> —C. T. Onions, *The Oxford Dictionary of English Etymology*

A number of the participants in a study into individual resilience in a rural community in Queensland "used the analogy of a rubber ball and its ability to 'bounce back' as a way to describe resilience" (Hegney et al., 2007, p. 6). David Spiegel wrote that resilience to stress relates to how people "handle their emotions" and that "finding meaning in the midst of a distressing situation has been linked with a positive psychological state" (Spiegel, 1999, p. 1328).

Through writing, I search for meaning. Jeffrey Berman suggests that the "talking cure and the writing cure are parallel efforts towards self-discovery and self-healing" (2010, p. 256). Barry and I talk through our tears. We try to cure each other.

Inspired by the works of Peter Elbow (1981, 1986, 2000), I've taught creative writing in the community and at university for 14 years, using techniques such as free writing and encouraging what Elbow describes as private writing. Private writing gives students "a chance to work out and put down their thoughts, feelings, and opinions without the need to share or defend them, they can more easily reflect on the various sources of these feelings and views" (1999, p. 154). The technique is also valuable for essay writing; I encourage our preservice teachers to get their thoughts and ideas on paper rather than staring at a blank page waiting for inspiration.

According to Janet Emig, writing is a multirepresentational activity that requires the engagement of hand, eye, and active participation of both hemispheres of the brain. Citing the work of Jerome Bruner, Jean Piaget, Lev Vygotsky, and George Kelly, she argued that writing plays a unique role in learning, in that the writer must engage in a "deliberate structuring of the web of meaning" (Vygotsky, cited in Emig, 1977, p. 125). I am trying to weave a new web of meaning.

Should this writing be kept private?

Today is November 1, 2011—Melbourne Cup Day—the day a horse race stops a nation. Barry is flying to Broken Hill to spend time with Shane. I gaze out the window at the beauty of a stray gray cloud in the shape of a whale—swimming in the pale blue sky—its underbelly brushed with pink from the rays of the rising sun. Soon it will be November 11—Remembrance Day. I want to stop time.

April 17, 2012

The bitumen road stretches straight ahead. Instead of kicking up red dust, the emus are stalking around newly sprouted green scrub. New lakes have appeared on either side of the road, ancient waterways filled for the first time in centuries. It seems strange to see pelicans soaring with eagles. A scatter of crows joins them, reluctantly leaving the rotting kangaroo carcasses as our car approaches. We stop every so often to clean the dead bodies of insects off the windshield. Barry is speeding as I count down mileposts; I hold my breath each time we overtake a thundering road train. It's 1,400 kilometres from where we live at Batemans Bay to Shane's at Broken Hill. We don't know it yet, but Shane had refused the medication that would ease his pain but take away his consciousness until we arrive. He knows we are there. We talk inanely about the trip, and share memories across the bed with other family members. We sit with him for three and a half hours, his hand gripping mine. As he slowly slips into unconsciousness, the labored breaths gradually subside. The palliative care nurse who has guided him through this year moistens his eyes and whispers to him—it's nearly time. One by one, she unhooks our fingers.

The real grieving begins. I am counting on resilience.

References

Adams, P. (1997). Being and nothingness. In G. Carey & R. Sorensen (Eds.), *The Penguin book of death* (pp. 42–52). Ringwood, Australia: Penguin Books.

Archer, J. (1999). *Nature of grief: The evolution and psychology of reactions to loss.* New York: Brunner-Routledge.

Berman, J. (2010). The talking cure and the writing cure. *Philosophy, Psychiatry, & Psychology, 17,* 255–257.

Bonanno, G. A. (2005). Resilience in the face of potential trauma. *Current Directions in Psychological Science, 14,* 135–138.

Bradbury, R. (1992). *Zen in the art of writing.* New York: Bantam.

Brett, D. (2001). *Eating the underworld: A memoir in three voices.* Sydney: Vintage.

Bruner, J. (2004). Life as narrative. *Social Research, 71,* 691–710.

Clendinnen, I. (1997). About bones. In G. Carey & R. Sorensen (Eds.), *The Penguin book of death.* Ringwood, Australia: Penguin Books.

Cunningham, D., Starling, N., Rao, S., Iveson, T., Nicolson, M., Coxon, F., et al. (2008). Capecitabine and oxaliplatin for advanced esophagogastric cancer. *New England Journal of Medicine, 358,* 36–46.

Dalziell, R. (1999). *Shameful autobiographies: Shame in contemporary Australian autobiographies and culture.* Carlton South, Australia: Melbourne University Press.

DeSalvo, L. (1999). *Writing as a way of healing: How telling our stories transforms our lives.* San Francisco: Harper.

Destriction and Prevention of Diptheria. (1885, March 10). *Burra Record,* p. 79. Retrieved from http://trove.nla.gov.au/ndp/del/article/36017928?searchTerm="destriction and prevention of diphtheria"&searchLimits=

Elbow, P. (1981). *Writing with power: Techniques for mastering the writing process.* New York: Oxford University Press.

Elbow, P. (1986). *Embracing contraries: Explorations in learning and teaching.* New York: Oxford University Press.

Elbow, P. (1999). In defense of private writing: Consequences for theory and research. *Written Communication, 16,* 139–170.

Elbow, P. (2000). *Everyone can write: Essays toward a hopeful theory of writing and teaching writing.* New York: Oxford University Press.

Ellis, C., Adams, T. E., & Bochner, A. P. (2011). Autoethnography: An overview. *Forum: Qualitative Social Research, 12.* Retrieved from http://www.qualitative-research.net/

Emig, J. (1977). Writing as a mode of learning. *College Composition and Communication, 28,* 122–128.

Frances, A., Pies, R., & Zisook, S. (2010). DSM5 and the medicalization of grief: Two perspectives. *Psychiatric Times, 27*(5).

Freadman, A. (1993, June 11–13). *Feminist literary theory (A question [or two] about genre).* Paper presented at the Jane Gallop Conference, Australian National University Canberra.

Hegney, D. G., Buikstra, E., Baker, P., Rogers-Clark, C., Pearce, S., Ross, H., et al. (2007). Individual resilience in rural people: A Queensland study, Australia. *Rural and Remote Health, 7,* 1–13.

Herskovic, A., Martz, K., Al-Sarraf, M., Leichman, L., Brindle, J., Vaitkevicius, V., et al. (1992). Combined chemotherapy and radiotherapy compared with radiotherapy alone in patients with cancer of the esophagus. *New England Journal of Medicine, 326,* 1593–1598.

McCooey, D. (1996). *Artful histories: Modern Australian autobiography.* Cambridge, England: Cambridge University Press.

Miller, E. D. (2003). Reconceptualizing the role of resiliency in coping and therapy. *Journal of Loss and Trauma, 8,* 239–246.

Obituary: Mother of Invention—Susan Sontag. (2004, December 30). *The Sydney Morning Herald: Summer Spectrum,* p. 24.

Ong, A. D., Bergeman, C. S., Bisconti, T. L., & Wallace, K. A. (2006). Psychological resilience, positive emotions, and successful adaptation to stress in later life. *Journal of Personality and Social Psychology, 91,* 730–749.

Onions, C. T. (Ed.). (1966). *The Oxford dictionary of English etymology.* Oxford, England: Clarendon Press.

Reynolds, L., & Botha, D. (2006). Anticipatory grief: Its nature, impact, and reasons for contradictory findings. *Counselling, Psychotherapy, and Health, 2,* 15–26.

Smith, S., & Watson, J. (2010). *Reading autobiography: A guide for interpreting life narratives* (2nd ed.). Minneapolis: University of Minnesota Press.

Sontag, S. (1978). *Illness as metaphor.* London: Penguin Books.

Spiegel, D. (1999). Healing words: Emotional expression and disease outcome. *JAMA, 281,* 1328–1329.

Szasz, T. (1960). The myth of mental illness. *American Psychologist, 15,* 113–118.

Szasz, T. (1974, December). Against behaviourism. *Libertarian Review, 111,* 1–4.

Szasz, T. (2007, December). The medicalization of everyday life. *Freeman, 57,* 18–19.

Chapter Fourteen

Prolonged Grief Disorder in 3-D
An Emerging Portrait across Time and Space

James A. Wren

The reexperience of traumatic loss mentally and physically becomes itself a permanent condition or state of being. Such a complication, for example, arises when grief is prolonged, and this situation clearly can have negative results. In extreme instances, the prolongation is so overwhelming that avoiding any reminders of trauma—so-called triggers, which can be uncomfortable and even painful—becomes symptomatic of and suggests a larger disorder, what may be termed prolonged grief disorder (PGD). It can be anticipated that those who go through extremely traumatic experiences often have certain symptoms and problems afterward. But as the matter takes on larger significance, it becomes necessary to differentiate between the normal expression of grief and its abnormal complications. Just how long, for example, is too long?

The answer by and large has been arbitrary. Although not a formal medical diagnosis, PGD refers to a reaction to loss that lasts more than one year, but such an arbitrary limit seems disingenuous, especially in light of the effects: PGD is characterized by the grief reaction intensifying and thereby affecting all of the sufferer's close relationships, disrupting his or her beliefs, and—in the case of the death of a loved one—it tends to result in the bereaved experiencing ongoing longing for the deceased. But is prolonging of the expression the only complication? What other elements may be discernible?

To answer these questions, it is perhaps beneficial to examine grief as experienced within the context of a personal narrative involving the reaction to loss, or to discern its iconographic nature by looking at multiple generations and their shared responses. Consider for the moment the personal narratives from three generations in which each person who has experienced loss seems either not to have learned to grieve, has not completely completed the various stages of grief, or has not yet fully comprehended the depths that grief might take. Examining in some detail how a particular life relationship was brought to an end with the death of a loved one, how the grief built and was manifested over a period of some 30 years, and how it ended without consolation or resolution might expose other characteristics commonly seen as contributing to the disorder. When viewed as part of an extended narration across time and space, such an examination might suggest a discernible pattern of experiences. This intertext, composed of the particular shared responses, as the enumeration and delineation the elements of an iconography in the larger portrait, can provide the framework upon which a far less arbitrary and much more satisfying definition of prolonged grief rests.

Personal Narratives across Three Generations

Tsuji, My Grandmother

Tsuji was born in September 1910, in a small village outside of Kumamoto, Japan (on the southern island of Kyushu). She was the eldest among nine children in what was an oddly "blended" sort of family for the time, in that at that time in Japan young women were married away to other families once they reached "adulthood" (menses presented itself). (Tsuji was 25 when she married, some 12-plus years beyond a "normal" time frame for marriage.)

When she was 25 years old, she was seen in a marketplace, unaccompanied, by Wilhelm Alan, a German scholar who was traveling through Asia. Three days later, when Wilhelm departed the city, Tsuji was in his company. They returned to Germany, where he took up a university post. They had been married about six weeks before she learned the intimate details of his earlier life, including that he was previously married and widowed and that he had three surviving children (ages 14, 7, and 4).

In late September of 1947, with the first ice already accumulating along the mountain ridges, Wilhelm lost control of his bus, drove off a bridge, and plunged down a 40-foot ravine into the icy river below. Nine days later, he died. His death was labeled the result of a "coronary event," in other words, a stroke, likely resulting from complications of high blood pressure.

After Wilhelm's death, his employer arranged for a lawyer to visit Tsuji, ostensibly to discuss the nature of the payout of an accidental-death policy he held. He entered her apartment, documents already in hand, and aggressively cajoled her into signing them. He then made clear just how he intended to handle matters from that point on.

Later that afternoon, Tsuji's daughter Mari returned home to find her mother prostrate, helpless, and speechless on the floor. Her clothing had been ripped, and she was still bleeding from cuts over several parts of her body. Mari remembered the moment, however, for another reason entirely: It was, to her recollection, the only time she ever witnessed her mother in tears. That same evening, the women in the room across the hall came in to help Tsuji "pull herself together." Mari remembered hearing among their hushed tones a new word, one that until that moment was completely foreign to her: rape.

Many years later, sometime after 2:30 A.M. on an autumn morning in 1999, Tsuji's daughter Mari and her grandson Alani helped her into bed. Keeping with their nightly ritual, both took turns giving her a hug and a kiss, followed by pulling her blankets up to her shoulders and remembering to pull them away from her feet. They followed up by placing atop her head a small white handkerchief, meant to ward off any draft. Wishing her pleasant dreams, they retired for the night. By six that same morning, Tsuji had passed on, without even the slightest of sounds, the white handkerchief still exactly as it had been placed only hours earlier.

Mari, My Mother

In the midst of an increasingly dangerous undercurrent of ethnic hatred across Europe, Mari was born in Germany to Wilhelm and Tsuji in 1939, less than a year after the notorious *Kristallnacht* (the "Night of Broken Glass," a wave of vicious pogroms—state sanctioned, anti-Jewish riots—in communities across Germany). By late 1940, Tsuji and Wilhelm had taken Mari and managed to leave Germany, eventually finding themselves in the mountains of Tennessee. In spite of the hardships imposed by leaving one country for another, she remembers her childhood as being quite happy, and she holds the fondest of memories of her father.

Every Sunday afternoon, or so it seemed, an elderly preacher from nearby would pay the extended family a visit. And every time, he insisted that Mari settle herself upon his lap, as he taught her to count on her fingers. Only later as an adolescent would she come to realize that as she proudly sat before a captive audience, held forth her hands for all to see, and struggled with increasing difficulty to count each finger, her teacher would slip his hand beneath her Sunday dress and, in time with each of her words, slide a finger into her genitalia. She knew that everyone was watching her every move, and yet no one noticed such a heinous action, committed before their very eyes. They did express some general concern, however, after weeks of the same routine: "Tsuji, why, she can't even count to ten!"

For Mari's 15th birthday, a young man from a neighboring school asked whether he might escort her to the local skating rink. He was from a well-known political family, a family of sufficient means and standing in the community, so her mother had, after some pleading on Mari's part, acquiesced, provided of course that she be home no later than nine.

The clock struck nine, then 10, and just after midnight Mari pushed the door open. In doing so, she headed into a battlefield of admonitions, squarely in front of her mother. It took several minutes, but Tsuji then noticed that Mari's dress was torn and soiled. Blood stains could be seen between the lower pleats, but her daughter's unsightly appearance only brought forth further rage from Tsuji. Throughout this time, Mari was trying to offer an explanation, how she and her date were returning home at about nine o'clock, when he suggested that they take a shortcut home through a small cemetery in the center of town. How once among the shadows and the scattered headstones, he had hit her, almost simultaneously forcing himself on her. Though Mari had not fully comprehended the severity of the matter, her mother did.

As a woman from across the hall was attempting to help Mari undress and wash away the blood as best she could, Tsuji calmed herself just enough to summon the police. There was an eventual trial, at which Mari attempted to explain what had happened, and there was an almost immediate consensus in the verdict: statutory rape, with the father of the young man being "requested" to pay Tsuji no more than $250 to cover any potential damage. Case dismissed.

Years later, Mari would wed W.G., but she was oblivious to her husband's penchant for macabre activities. She remained, in fact, "safe" and as always at a distance. W.G. directed the sexual abuse to his oldest child, his son, and in time he began "sharing," then "renting out" this particular child to any number of older individuals. Excruciating sexual abuse became the norm, initially under a veil of secrecy and then in what became increasingly blatant public displays. He seemingly found gratification of a sort by flaunting his ability to wreak havoc and destroy lives.

As Mari was delivering her second child, a daughter, W.G. returned home, alone, with his infant son. When Mari followed from hospital later in the week, she found Alani, burned from the waist down and passing blood into his diaper. The explanation: Children are children, and thus, it was completely within the realm of believability that he might have crawled into the kitchen, pulled himself from the floor up to the top of the refrigerator, and somehow managed to entangle himself with the cord to the coffee pot (placed out of reach, W.G. explained matter-of-factly, just so this sort of thing could not happen). Yet, somehow, this particular child had managed to do the impossible, by dragging a pot of boiling coffee onto himself. "But that was almost a week ago," W.G. was quick to explain, "so I see no need for medical attention."

Mari quickly conceded to his way of viewing events, and the matter became nothing more than one more story to entertain neighbors with over Sunday coffee and danish. Thus, this sort of sinister behavior—in particular the abuse of the elder son—became a matter *de jour*.

Mari remained committed to her marriage, however much over the years she had been confronted with blatantly public displays of infidelity or the irrational bursts of rage that always ended with an act of child abuse, sexual or otherwise. But even she had her limits, which were reached when, after 27 years of marriage, her husband began to take week-long vacations with a female business partner of easy reputation and an arrest sheet long enough to address any questions heretofore left unanswered.

With time, the other children had grown up and away, having already completed any preparations necessary to begin promising careers. They had dated frequently since their mid-teens, had met several potential partners, and eventually settled into a routine of marriage. In doing so, both made a conscious decision to have no more than a single child each. Contented in their new lives, they also put into place a deliberate distance between themselves and their mother, the source, as they had come to believe, of much of their negative childhood memories. So remarkable was that distance that they actually severed any contact with her, ostensibly forbidding any contact by telephone or by mail—a communicative "disconnect," ongoing since they had finished high school.

However much she had been reticent to "let go" and accept the end of her relationship and however much she could not bring herself to forget her "love," her unquestioning devotion to him, with one well-baked turkey left in the oven, Mari announced her intention to divorce her husband in November 1985.

Alani, Myself

I was born in late autumn, 1959, the first child of Mari and W. G., 11 months after they were married. And perhaps because I came into their relationship at such a premature time, when they were very much only beginning to know each other, because I was the firstborn grandchild to Tsuji, or for whatever reason, I became an immediate source of tension in their relationship.

Bolstering my earliest memories is my father's repeated insistence, monotonous and unchanging as I grew older, that he never be seen in public with me. I endured a series of hurtful remarks and ethnic slurs on a daily basis, cast either toward me or my mother and me. Alongside these memories is that of another somewhat shocking notion on my part, namely that I was not with my "real" parents. Of course, many children likely express similar concerns, especially when they learn that it elicits particular responses time and again from the parents. From quite an early age, in fact, I had questioned whether I might have been adopted. It was only when I was approaching the age of four, just after my brother was born, that my father began to make the question a matter of seriousness. He would suddenly become angry and refuse to speak; my mother would disappear momentarily, always to the bedroom to sit before a large mirror and brush her hair over and over. I began school sometime later that year, and it was at about that time—I was four years old and trying to duplicate particular letters from the alphabet in crayon—when my mother and grandmother explained that there was a possibility. With that, they would go no further.

Over the next few years, the story came to light: When I was born, a couple from Puerto Rico shared the same recovery room, after having also given birth to a male child. They quickly identified the dark-haired child in the nursery as theirs, and name tags only confirmed as much. My parents immediately recognized the blonde child as theirs—and the nurses would bring these children in to the respective mothers. Several days later, however, the positions changed. Within the week, the nuns at the hospital had begun to question the procedures in place for identification, and at some point, my parents returned home with a dark-haired child. The blonde, similarly, went with the other couple. In truth, the very issue of my identity remains a subject of discussion even today.

Beyond these immediate issues of physical and psychological/verbal abuse, and however much photographs of me from this period might indicate otherwise, my childhood remained relatively peaceful, at least on the surface. The absence of a smile—or more likely, the inability to smile—was not meant to indicate that I was either unhappy or maladjusted in some way. I simply was—and that in itself was enough.

Of equal importance, from my earliest sense of myself, I understood much about individual sexual orientation. I was always in some way attracted to other boys. It had nothing to do with finding a suitable playmate or anything like that; there was something stronger at play. Called to mind is my memory of being seven years old, of watching my male friends tease and chase the little girls around the classroom or across the playground. It was apparent to me that these boys and I might have shared many things, but we seemed to have different interest, different responses. I also quickly understood that others might perceive this difference in a negative light, so I remained content to distance myself from any settings in which tensions might arise.

To be completely clear, I delayed any sort of personal relationship until I was 24 and well into graduate studies. I also happened to be abroad, so I found myself in a particularly safe environment, far removed from any possibility of familiar abuse. It was at that time that I had what might be termed my first date. Thereafter, I found myself making time on weekends to go out and meet other people. Being comfortable with my sexual orientation had never been an issue. Feeling safe from the long reach of abuse, however, was quite a different matter. And within that mindset, though I dated from time to time, I rarely felt any serious emotional attraction to anyone I met. But that would eventually change.

I was 26 and still absorbed in graduate studies when I happened upon someone of interest. As I stood in a department store, looking at a particular shirt in my size and in a color that might somehow make me look "more alive," I looked up and noticed a young man about my age standing across from me. I continued to search for my size, and at some point it became obvious that he was no longer interested in finding a shirt for himself.

I looked up and smiled, quite expecting to be greeted with a barrage of derogatory terms. I fully expected that I was about to be taken down a notch or two—and worst of all, in public view.

Instead, he smiled and introduced himself as Kim. We shook hands, laughed somewhat naively at how easily we had seemed to cross so many bridges all at once, and headed out for coffee.

A few years later, late into the night, the hall phone of my residence began to ring. I grabbed my robe and headed down the hall, not wanting any of the other residents to complain about such unholy hours or the like. I picked up the phone and began speaking without hesitation, "Kim? Kim?" but was met with silence.

Only after a lengthy pause, the voice on the other end responded, somewhat hesitantly. "Jim? Jim, this is Pinpin." Pinpin was a very dear friend of Kim's and mine, but despite that fact, I was a bit surprised to be hearing from her. "Jim, has anyone spoken with you yet?" The remainder of the conversation was hopelessly one-sided, or perhaps there had been some words exchanged. Nothing was making any sense, and yet I understood her words well enough.

I did not have time enough to return to Seattle before the services were held, before his parents arranged for him to be returned to Korea. And in the blink of an eye, in a single moment I lost any sense of well-being, any sense of the contentment or security that I had earlier so enjoyed.

In 2000, I left my university post for an early retirement on disability. The diagnosis of Parkinson's, following years of fighting the ravages of lupus, proved more than enough bad news for any of the few friends left around me. And then there was only one left to loiter.

No longer in a position to go out to meet other people, or even communicate with anyone beyond the all-embracing arms of my chair, I found myself again living with my mother and grandmother. Then, Tsuji passed, leaving my mother and me alone, without relationships and with no expectations on the horizon. And that pretty much accounts for my where-abouts to date.

Reading the Narration

The importance of narratives to understanding on a deeper level the emotional responses to death and dying has only recently attracted much critical attention, with the exception of a faith-based collection of tales of women who have lost their husbands (Francis, 2011).

But several caveats need be acknowledged. First, and perhaps peculiar to this set of narratives, is the presence of concomitant issues that present themselves. These include the presence of pre-existing trauma: In each instance, the narrators return time and again to issues of verbal, physical, and emotional abuse. Tsuji relates an incident of rape (albeit this occurred post-loss). Mari acknowledges having been raped on her first date and reflects something of the trauma of a trial and the testimony. As well, her narrative suggests some emotional abuse within her relationship with her mother, as well as makes explicit the obvious verbal and emotional abuse she endured from her spouse. And Alani recognizes his own abuse on all levels (including issues of neglect and abandonment by his father) and suggests a problem on Mari's part with being able to separate her self-identity from that of her first child (in fact, her younger children were neither viewed nor used as a "replacement" for her in terms of sacrifice or actually taking her place sexually). That said, these issues very well meet the definition of a deep psychological trauma; we are then unable to rule out with any certainty the issue of posttraumatic stress disorder (PTSD). More to the point, this link to a traumatic event is what makes PGD—like PTSD—problematic, for the tie is really to the memory of an event.

The other concern is much more general and involves the very nature of personal narratives as a whole. It has been a half century since Wayne Booth (1961) alerted the literary world to the inherent issues with the profound relativity of understanding inherent to point of view, in particular with first-person narrators and the rejection of any absolute authority or standard for judgment. He opened the door to an understanding built upon the reflexive relationship between the structuring of ideas and those narrative strategies elected by any narrator to present these ideas to an audience. His is the beginning of poststructuralist insistence that texts are self-enclosed verbal constructs not necessarily directly related to an outside reality, what would later be termed a "fiction of the referential" (Miller, 1976) or a "referential fallacy" (Eco, 1976).

A barrage of questions necessarily follows. What expressive techniques are used to translate, and thereby mediate, personal experience? How do we establish and interpret an interview (or a written first-person narrative) as a piece of evidence? Does this evidence suggest that a particular argument be made based solely on itself? As we address these questions (significant philosophical questions underpinning the concepts of being and knowing—well beyond the scope of this chapter), we reposition ourselves in such a way as to discuss both the specific problems faced in constructing an evidence-based story and the solutions we then wrangle from these problems.

Admitting as much, we can now focus on identity and subjectivity in connection with issues of prolonged grief. To do so necessarily means that we address matters of gender and sexual orientation, of race and ethnicity, as well as of nationality and culture.

Of immediate importance to our reading of these narratives is the issue of gender. Although we have three generations represented, we have the potential for difference, between two female narrators (Tsuji and Mari) and a single male (Alani). This is important because gender differences in coping strategies may suggest ways in which men and women differ in managing the stress of psychologically traumatic events.

Equally important to any discussion of self-narration is the matter of culture in general and performance of self in particular; clearly, liminal and dialogic identities change from day to day across a variety of cultures, disciplines, and social realities. This is likely to represent a point of difference with our three narrators: Tsuji spent her formative years in Japan within a Buddhist value system. Mari, while born in Germany, was reared in the United States, within a loosely defined Judaic tradition. And Alani spent his formative years in Japan and the United States, noticeably identified as a minority in both cultures.

Obvious from the outset with these narratives, complicated grief can have a generational dimension. This suggests the possibility of a potential genetic link (which portends the possible detection via analysis of individual genetic makeup, something well beyond our purview at present), even as it reinforces what we already know, namely that expressions of grief can have a learned component.

Specifically, when society sees no reason to grieve—whether with the death of a spouse for Tsuji, the permanent breaking of a commitment to remain together inherent in Mari's divorce, or lack of acceptance of same-sex orientation and the lack of information available to Alani before the funeral of his partner—then there is no allowance for a change in demeanor, behavior, or outlook as might ordinarily accompany bereavement. Most pointedly, the unending grief accompanies—even as it highlights for us—the sense of disenfranchisement.

By association, each narrative shares a lack of opportunity whereby each person is allowed to experience the pain of loss, in large part because of the "forbidden" nature of the relationship in the first place. Certainly, Tsuji's family immediately grew angry when she left Japan for Germany. Likewise, Tsuji expressed displeasure in the immediacy with which her daughter located a spouse and was married. And Mari expressed her pent-up disregard and loathing of her son's partnership, made obvious only when she forbade him to visit to her home. In each instance, particular situations give rise to a heightened sense of discomfort and an accompanying atmosphere so uncomfortable that none can express grief aloud.

Complicating matters further, perhaps we need to question whether prolonged grief is in and of itself the greater "unspoken secret." Clearly, these narrators survive in situations where they generally have little opportunity to express themselves, and as a consequence, any emotion is itself left unnoticed or misunderstood as grief by those around them (Oesterreich, 2004; Pettit, 2000; Sheppard & Steele, 2003). And whereas traditional forms of grief are more widely recognized even in nontraditional living situations, few support systems (traditions or institutionalized laws putting into place bereavement leave, for example) are actually made available to those whose grief is in part the result of having experienced disenfranchisement within their groups, be they family, peers, or colleagues (Doka, 1989). For when grief is not openly acknowledged, socially accepted, or publicly mourned, as with these situations, it is in fact the alienation itself that results in prolonged grief. That is to say, prolonged grief is not a matter of an individual's being unable to accept the reality of grief; it is, instead, the result of events whereby there has been no external concrete focus on it. We see as much with these specific narrators, each of whom holds on to grief all the more tenaciously, precisely because no one else will recognize it.

But most obvious when the narratives are compared, as disenfranchisement is experienced, an expression of anxious avoidance—the period of grief that in these cases is prolonged—results not only in the inability to reconnect with other individuals or to allow someone new into their lives, but also in a complicated series of machinations, the purpose of which is to prevent the recurrence of the possibility for relationships to thrive. Or perhaps more accurately, there can be no reinvestment of emotional energy in *another* relationship if only because this one still exists, if only in the mind.

Such an observation necessarily requires that we look further at the details that compose memory, because it is memory and not the loss itself that results in the prolongation of grief. Again, taking our cue from poststructuralist readings, we already should hold suspect what enters the narrative and, by association, when precisely it is so spoken. As these narratives suggest, expressions of depression, anxiety, or other subtle psychological disorders arise, in and of themselves, not from the static moment in death and loss; their origins more likely lie in a memory that has been elaborated, given new significance, or perhaps even unconsciously fabricated. In short, each attempt to give voice to grief suggests that what constitutes memory does in fact grow in complexity over time as new information is learned, added, or, just as likely, manufactured. Since at least the emergence of self-consciously fictional forms in the late 17th century (in the Western tradition, at least), we have accepted on some level that the boundary between those techniques representing past history as a narration are both permeable and contested. Serious readers then place their focus on the persuasive usage of rhetoric inherent to the act of representation, of memories recalled and recounted. Currently, among social scientists—in particular those care workers who evaluate individuals for PGD—the agency inherent to memory in negotiating this borderland has been largely overlooked.

If we may reframe the discussion, recall that, when PTSD was first added to the American Psychiatric Association's *Diagnostic and Statistical Manual of Mental Disorders Third Edition* (DSM-III) in 1980, it came in response to the need for a diagnosis to recognize what many saw as the unique suffering of Vietnam veterans. At that time, traumatic memories were considered reasonably faithful recordings of actual events. But as research has since shown repeatedly, memory is spectacularly unreliable and malleable. That is to say, we routinely add or subtract people, details, settings, and actions to and from our memories. We conflate, invent, and edit in what becomes "false memories" (Loftus, 1997). This conclusion bolsters a study by the Veterans Administration from earlier in the decade, when Gulf War veterans ($n = 59$) were asked about their experiences a month after their return, and again two years later. The latter interview noted that 70 percent of the veterans ($n = 41$) reported at least one traumatic event they had not mentioned a month after returning, and 24 percent ($n = 14$) reported at least three such events for the first time. Those veterans who recounted the most "new memories" also reported the most PTSD symptoms. This suggests that for those experiencing PTSD were, in fact, dealing with an ever-changing and therefore ever-present amalgam of details they had recognized and mistaken for a single entity, memory itself (McNally, 2006).

When read together, then, the three self-narrations become in a sense my ongoing attempt to rectify memories. As such, the use of such narratives may potentially clue us into something of the iconography of the process in grief, and are of value in the particular instances, as well, because they demonstrate not necessarily *that* we are dealing with a form of emotional behavior but *how* we do so. However much grief may be viewed as a learned response and thereby dismissed, in truth these three individuals become the lone survivors of the extended process of grief.

And, although adaptive coping methods improve functioning, PGD arises from within a maladaptive coping technique that may temporarily reduce symptoms, while maintaining and strengthening the disorder. Perhaps because maladaptive techniques are more effective in the short-term rather than long-term coping process, the resulting PGD is overlooked or dismissed. Just as harmful, these coping strategies necessarily interfere with the ability of a person to unlearn, or break apart, the paired association between the situation and the associated symptoms of anxiety. At the risk of oversimplification, it is the cumulative effect of maladaptive strategies that serves to prolong expressions of grief and maintain the disorder. And while such observations have led to a discussion of an effective treatment for complicated grief, by treating the reactions in the same way as trauma reactions (Bonanno, 2006; Shear, Frank, Houck, & Reynolds, 2005), it seems premature to assume any long-term benefit from such an approach, in and of itself.

Up to this point, we may safely assume that any definition of what constitutes PGD remains the subject of much heated debate. But there does seem to be consensus that in such instances the disorder does not arise from the death per se. Nor is the harm necessarily immediate, but it is cumulative, and can be lifelong and debilitating. And just as certain, perhaps, distress of one sort or another is a response to pain and loss or a sign of a psychic wound that has failed to heal.

But distinguishing between whether PGD is a result of a natural process of adjustment or a much larger issue presents several problems. Most important among these is whether the diagnosis be incorrect, erring in being dismissive or being overly sensitive, thereby mistaking a natural process of adjustment for a dysfunctional state. Hence, the need for better elucidation, more carefully constructed definitions. In truth, we would anticipate that those who go through these types of extremely traumatic experiences often exhibit certain symptoms and undergo particular problems afterward. In fact, a frequently problematic issue is the danger of mistaking depression/grief for conversion disorder and, in doing so, erasing the importance of the issue and the diagnosis. If this is the case, then, the extended narrative of an individual's coping (following Snyder, 1999; Weiten & Lloyd, 2008; and Zeidner & Endler, 1996) might better help us to discern patterns of experiences characterizing these particular responses and, by enumeration and delineation, help us use these to arrive at a more efficacious definition for appraisal and diagnosis of issues associated with prolonged grief. For only by overhauling both the diagnosis and the treatment, as well as the system of care provided, can we ensure better care for patients with genuine PGD, as well as those who have been misdiagnosed.

References

Bonanno, G. A. (2006). Is complicated grief a valid construct? *Clinical Psychology: Science and Practice 13*(2), 129–134.

Booth, W. (1961). *The rhetoric of fiction.* Chicago: University of Chicago Press.

Doka, K. J. (Ed.). (1989). *Disenfranchised grief: Recognizing hidden sorrow.* Lanham, MD: Lexington Books.

Eco, U. (1976). *A theory of semiotics.* Bloomington: Indiana University Press.

Francis, M. (2011). *The sisterhood of widows: Sixteen true stories of grief, anger and healing.* New York: Morgan James.

Loftus, E. F. (1997). Creating false memories. *Scientific American, 277*(3), 70–75.

McNally, R. J. (2006). The expanding empire of posttraumatic stress disorder. *Medscape General Medicine, 8*(2), 9.

Miller, J. H. (1976). Stevens' rock and criticism as cure. *Georgia Review, 30,* 26.

Oesterreich, L. (2004). *Understanding children: Moving to a new home.* Des Moines: Iowa State University Extension Service.

Pettit, B. (2000). *Moving and children's social connections: The critical importance of context.* Princeton, NJ: Center for Research on Child Wellbeing.

Shear, K., Frank E., Houck, P. R., & Reynolds, C. F. III. (2005). Treatment of complicated grief: A randomized controlled trial. *JAMA, 293,* 2601–2608.

Sheppard, C. H., & Steele, W. (2003). Moving can become traumatic. *Trauma and Loss: Research and Interventions.* Retrieved from http://www.tlcinstitute.org/Moving.html

Snyder, C. R. (Ed.). (1999). *Coping: The psychology of what works.* New York: Oxford University Press.

Weiten, W., & Lloyd, M. A. (2008). *Psychology applied to modern life.* New York: Wadsworth Cengage Learning.

Zeidner, M., & Endler, N. S. (Eds.). (1996). *Handbook of coping: Theory, research, applications.* New York: John Wiley.

Chapter Fifteen

Stories My Father Never Told Me

Olivia Sagan

The Then: Illness and the Stealing of Narrative

When my father was diagnosed with Alzheimer's, it was in some ways a blessing. We, his beleaguered family, had struggled through decades of an undefined, shifting, and often cruel mental illness that had no name, or at least none we were allowed to speak. This illness had a number of cards up its sleeve—one of many was its ability to impersonate—appearing as mad one moment, bad the next, then sad later on. Each incarnation elicited a different response, and each riddled us with surprise, despair, and guilt at what was always, is always, the wrong response.

It is very different now, for although stigma remains and family secrets are still kept in locked cupboards and behind silenced lips, there are more words with which to say things, and perhaps more ways to hear these words spoken. There is also some understanding that in families outside of the mainstream culture (as mine was), for whatever reason, illness, madness, suffering and subservience to these take shapes different from those of the dominant culture. Different shapes need a different recognition, another way of decoding and of articulating. As Steedman (1986) noted, "The stories that people tell themselves in order to explain how they got to the place they currently inhabit are often in deep and ambiguous conflict with the official interpretative devices of a culture" (p. 6). At that time and place, for us—an immigrant woman and her two daughters—what was required was a gritted and knitted front; a shielding of the blows alone; a strict rule of not talking about them; and one of never, ever asking for help.

The ebb and flow of my father's pre-Alzheimer's illness, an illness in which he hated and hurt and blamed and feared by default, in which he twisted our words, policed our thoughts, and criticized and belittled, was the tide by which we lived our lives. At high, rough tide, we ran for cover. At low, calm tide, we surveyed the horizon and took small and cautious sails out to warm our faces in the sun, knowing at all times that a storm could well up at any moment and we'd need to batten down the hatches. We were never secure; seldom relaxed; and rarely, if ever, belly-laughed. This illness had eroded the love, nerves, and hope of us all by its wreaking havoc on narrative coherence, and its demands on empathetic capability.

In the swell of these emotional upheavals, memory was also a casualty. We misremembered; part of our survival depended on us repainting dark weather days as fair; on us pretending that, fine sailors that we were, we weathered and mended and made good as new. We also forgot: that which was too bald to be looked at in the face; that for which we had no words; and that which, unnarratable, could find no foothold in memory other than as fleeting sensations: shudders, aromas, shadows, and scenes glimpsed thinly. And, as inveterate storytellers (Ricoeur, 1990) we constructed entirely new memories that acted as fantasy safe spaces, right down the years, even now, even in bereavement.

In this dread of shipwreck, the narratives we built about ourselves with which our identity would be entwined and by which it would be configured were fidgety, slippery, and liquefied. Our stories floated lightly, the fetch of the waves wreaking havoc on their narrative coherence. The spitting, multi-lingual malapropisms with which my father struggled lent these weightless stories curious tics and spasms. A yearned-for narrative as "daddy's little girl" would survive momentarily, only to be dashed against the rocks. For my mother, a narrative of "good wife" would be invited, lured, scripted, then submerged. We gave obligatory laughs in response to his infrequent, lame, and repeated jokes. When I'd be dispatched to ask him if he would like a piece of cake, he often replied wryly "No, I'd like peace of mind." I would smile, feign a giggle—good little girl that I was—I knew what was required, on cue. Who were we to be in all this? How were we to chisel out words to tell a self story when, dull little vessels bobbing perilously about in his prevailing wake, our narratives were only ever permissible as the flotsam and jetsam of his?

Such tidal tremblings pushed and pulled our empathetic capability and left us hardened over time. This knitted and gritted front sculpted us into it, and we became wall-like, barnacled. Not able to take pleasures easily or feel we deserved the small rays of sun we stole, we felt hardened to him, to life, but mostly hardened to ourselves, unable to love until much, much later.

In that later, there were to be years that enmeshed me in a personal and professional absorption in the formidable strategies, sometimes unconscious, that are deployed as an individual attempts to make sense of the non-sensible, and follow an urge to "autopathograph" (Stone, 2004, p. 17). The stories my father told me, those he tried but failed to tell me, and those inscribed on me like cicatrixes through our joint being, crafted my adulthood and professional trajectory (Sagan, 2007). In becoming a narrative researcher, I finally found some tools—clumsy though they were at times—with which to explore dimensions of lost narrative, of narrative dispossession, and of narrative reclaimed.

The Alzheimer's

Alzheimer's was indeed a kind of gift, for unexpected reasons. First, relatives of those who succumb gradually to the disease have usually previously experienced that person as having a coherent narrative, with the characters, plots, and a linear trajectory that we generally recognize in a "sensible" story. My father, in contrast, had always struggled with language. It would not do as he wished, was simply not there when he summoned it. Idioms merged and then disintegrated all intended meaning. He would switch wildly from his mother tongue to English, to fragments of other languages learned, adopted, and often bastardized, sometimes in the same sentence. Each language was emotionally charged; he would demand sometimes that we speak one or the other, choosing and excluding depending on the current memory permeating his internal world. This linguistic miasma, however, lifted sometimes, albeit briefly. Then we would glimpse what could be: lucidity, purpose, and perhaps a happy ending.

Sometimes my father told stories, and these were as tantalizing as our rare family Saturday afternoons, coming back from Hornsey, apprehensively storm free in the Fiat 600, laden with rollmops, rye bread, and a treat or two. When they were magically enabled, these stories entranced me as a child. With their distance, their difference, their snowy forests, and wild protagonists they were to quilt a unique genre that nestled somewhere in me. This sedimented a seam rich enough to tap into in bleaker times of barren words, of which there would be many—rich enough too, to last me well into my present, a present indeed, from my father.

In small moments, it seemed that when my father was able to reconnect with a native land he had long since left and with which he had a troubled relationship, he would show a kinder, more wistful, and momentarily integrated side. This side and its rare appearance made me wonder about what manner of wrenching had taken place. For it seemed that a wrenching had occurred, between him and the very soil. There was now a disparity in his ideas of home and country for which we, his family, never could compensate. Speaking of the distance created between ourselves and the land itself, Macfarlane (2007, p. 203) warns that "new maladies of the soul have emerged, unhappinesses which are complicated products of the distances we have set between ourselves and the world."

And such was the texture of my father's unhappiness: complicated, about distance, disjuncture. Such was his battle with words. Often, what began as a story would splinter at the oncoming of a memory of his, one real or imagined. Then, a coldness would steal in, one that would take over and break up the storyline as frost crystals formed across the tundra of its telling. In this freeze, players would be chilled into silence, the stage rendered barren, and purpose and coherence would whither in the icy breath of recall. This echoed observations by the psychoanalyst Wilfred Bion: "The words that should have represented the meaning the man wanted to express were fragmented by the emotional forces to which he wished to give verbal expression; the verbal formulation could not 'contain' his emotions" (1970, p. 94).

This chaotic denouement would leave the listener scared sometimes, especially as children, but often also curiously depleted and wasted, as though an attack on thought and the goodness it might bring had been launched. It would take me unawares. I would not be able, as a result, to think, but be sunk instead into "fragmentation, amorphousness, entropy, chaos, silence, senselessness" (Stone, 2004, p. 18) through which, I was to surmise many years later, I entered his world entirely.

Bamberg (2004) urged us to appreciate the "small stories," those that privilege the fleeting and fragmented in order to understand narratives outside the mainstream. Baldwin (2006), in his study of patients with Alzheimer's disease, suggested that this is one way to enter into an understanding of the narratives of such sufferers. But with my father, we had always done this; we had long since stopped expecting extended, logical narrative, and we were content with scraps. Bizarrely, the scraps of narrative my father produced as a person with Alzheimer's disease were largely of the timbre that we knew, only, with an added and new gentleness. It seemed that he slowly became unable to remember the many crimes and horrors that bedeviled his memory in earlier years, and in the absence of these memories, his narrative fragments were denied their chill.

So splinters of narrative and the driftwood of memory didn't bother us. Neither did contradictory stories or disjointed speech; we had lived a lifetime with these. As children of the diaspora, whose very narratives in any case are made of fragments, of seeds dispersed to far flung corners, we were prepared. Gradually, as we sat with him in his nursing home, a new warmth spread through us, as it appeared that a space was also opening up for us to finally become daughters and wife. My father gradually became a different man, even gentle, uttering from time to time soft words we had never heard, from within his even more fragmented memory and plot. He had forgotten whatever crime it was that had formed the backdrop of his life, and in so doing, for the most time, he also forgot to blame, to hate, and to castigate. In her critique of interventions in the care of patients with Alzheimer's that she considers "coercive," Goyder (2009, p. 187) wisely cautions against an overzealous use of therapies such as reminiscence therapy, in which nurses are encouraged to use memory aids such as photographs with patients to help recall their pre-Alzheimer's lives. Though I have no doubt this kind of work has its merit, I'm in agreement with Goyder in asking, "But what if a memory aid triggers a disturbing memory and causes distress?" For my father, whose pre-Alzheimer's life was always a precarious process of keeping memories at bay, Alzheimer's actually seemed to afford a period of release, literally, the long-awaited peace of mind. And this was a sweet spot of his life, one during which he was still well enough to function within his shrunken and limited realm, but ill enough to forget to hate. It was a short time, but in it we loosened, paddled in rock pools, even perhaps loved.

In this loosening was my father's next story, and almost a final triumph over my mother's narrative. Despite the limited research on Alzheimer's and the marital relationship (Harris, 2009) the impact on the "one left behind," who is the holder of the memory of perhaps decades together, is tremendous. For my mother, the impact was complicated by the *way* that Alzheimer's changed my father—in becoming a gentler person she did not lose him to Alzheimer's as is commonly the case, but, cruelly, in it she was to find him.

The Dying

When my father died, suddenly, quietly, and privately, leaving a fragile, cold shell that surprised me with its delicacy, nothing prepared me for the grief my mother was to endure. This grief glared in the face of baffled bystanders who knew of the tyranny of my father and the pain he had chiseled into the very marrow of my mother's narrative. This bafflement added, no doubt, to her loneliness in this grief, reminding us of the very uniqueness of the bereavement process (Thompson, 2002), its chameleonic presentations and roots, its impenetrability as an experience. Few knew of the added twist of the gentleness of his last months, and how, in a way, she had lost him thrice when he died. She lost the person with whom she had had a deeply troubled and ambiguous relationship for decades; she lost the person he had become through the building of him as villain in a narrative that defended and protected her; and now, she lost the person he became: gentler, but all too little, too late.

Her task was to grieve each of these losses in a way that enabled her to survive intact. It is a testament to her strength that she did so. In this survival, ironically, but not coincidentally, it seemed it was her ability with narrative, despite her own complicated relationship with her mother tongue and adopted language, that enabled her to move on. It was narrative's positive force as a mechanism through which the choice for life is made and then lived (Bauer, McAdams, & Pals, 2008) that turned the tides.

But first, there was the grieving, and hers was a grief laid bare in its outpouring. My mother, refined and careful of outward appearance and well-heeled in keeping her pain to herself, now found license to howl and rage against the world for taking him away. It was unjust that now—when he had seemed so well, now, when he had spoken tenderly to her just the day before, now, when he had ceased to shout and scare us so—, now … he had died. I wondered whether added to that mix was the sheer fury that consciously or not, yet another narrative that my mother deserved and had carefully begun building piece by careful piece, one in which "my husband has Alzheimer's, he is in a home, I am at last an attentive and loved wife," had been yet again dashed upon the rocks.

A sense of injustice sprang from decades of crimes. Those of my father and those of a sociocultural order that had contributed to her isolation and failed her the very few times she had timidly asked for help. These crimes crystalized into a here and now encounter with this death that seemed so wrong. Wrong because it had no place, in its present form, in any of her narrative resolutions. The shock that my mother was encountering was horrible to watch because it was fathomless; multilayered and complexly intertwined with a severing, not only from the physical body of her husband, which had dominated and threatened but nevertheless accompanied her through so many years, but a severing from fantasies, hopes, longings. In speaking of human suffering and agency, Frost and Hogget (2008) noted that, "Some experiences threaten to go beyond our capacity to digest them because we lack the resources to symbolize and give meaning to them" (p. 449). Indeed, watching my mother grieve was to witness the body not being able to contain the hollow of its loss. In this she was floundering, drowning, wildly searching for a life raft of resources with which to face what had been lost, an irretrievable part of herself—one essential to her "sense of coherent identity" (Clewell, 2004). My mother's grief was so complete, so unshakeable, that it drew heavily on my resources as a daughter. My own grief, whatever shape it was to take, became submerged by her infinitely bigger pain; I will never again overlook how when someone dies, each person's bereavement is bound up tightly with the form and shape, the very weather—of the bereavements of others.

Watching my mother desperately trying to script some sense, trying to find a way through the weight of what seemed an attack, tested to the utmost whatever understanding I had of illness, melancholy, and the profound sadness of bereavement (Freud, 1925). There was some solace for me, as ever, in the words of those who had tried to understand some of these complicated processes. In *Mourning and Melancholia,* Freud (1925) spoke about mourning taking place in response to the death of a loved one, but also in response to "the loss of some abstraction … such as one's country, liberty, an ideal, and so on" (p. 243). And I wondered what abstraction had been given life-blood throughout our years of bobbing around in my father's seas; what my father had become for my mother; what fantasy had been nurtured, through necessity, living with all the painful unpredictability of his wild attempts at making sense of his own personal chaos. I feared too, the realization of Freud's observation (1925) that anger originally felt at the object would be internalized and reversed, berating the ego and thwarting attempts at health and a narrative of agency, for my mother was becoming frail. Anger and grief were taking a physical and mental toll that was known and indeed documented (Sanders, Ott, Kelber, & Noonan, 2008) but is crushingly difficult to observe firsthand,—especially when the person diminishing before you is your mother.

In my mother's speech, as in her sleepless nights, there was a reliving, in a process of "obsessive recollection" (Clewell, 2004) of memories both near and far in time. Maddeningly, my mother, a new widow, seemed to be deeply engrossed in rescripting what had happened and how, reinventing again who my father was, perhaps internally protecting good objects through fending off the bad (Klein, 1946). The revered ideal of not speaking ill of the dead was being laid down as law for my sister and I, who listened, cared, offered solace as we could, and attended to our own bereavement in snatches. I worried that this disavowal of anger at my father himself, an anger totally justifiable given our family history, may have driven it inwards "where berating the self takes the place of criticising the deceased" (Clewell, 2004, p. 54). It seemed wholly unfair that decades of being berated by my father during his lifetime were continuing in his death through an unremitting self-reproach (Bowlby, 1980), a twist in the story of a codependence in which an attachment to the pain itself is maintained.

I knew what was needed for the grief work was time, lots of it. Time to begin to revisit aspects of the lost object in a process Leader (2008) likened to that of producing a cubist image, reconstructing parts of the lost object until a new merging of those pieces creates a new totality. Yet I worried because my mother, into her 80s, didn't have this luxury and seemed in some way bound to a "bad faith" narrative (Craib, 2000), in which, denied agency, she was bound to a campaign of self-punishment. Going round and round in her memories now re-tinted, I feared my mother was becoming entrenched in a chronicity that situates "the individual in a wasteland," (Kleinman, 1988, p. 438). And all we could do was watch. Unable to restore whatever former order for which my mother was grieving, whatever we provided seemed to fall short and be felt, "almost as an insult" (Bowlby, 1980). In watching, caring, and holding, we hoped our daughtering was good enough.

Was this complicated grief best left to run its own course? Only each person bereaved in this way can determine this. In my mother's case, it was essential that the cryings and railings of pain be gathered and held by the cumulonimbus of family that gathered above her; essential that she be free to express the grief in whatever noisy, messy, and apparently inexplicable ways came to her, and that these expressions be contained and digested by us rather than negated or tidied away. Because she had this, because we were able to be this, and because her own working through was occurring, this seemed sufficient to get us to a place when we could rain down and cry together in our own personal ways. In the absence of this, or in a more utter desolation that can slip into deep depression—as often sadly is the case in late widowhood—then one would hope that treatment, primarily in the form of bereavement talking therapy, would be available and gently ushered in. Such bereavement therapy offers a space where, through tears, silence, and outpourings, meaning can be both constructed and discovered, and crucially, a narrative of self salvaged from the wreckage.

The Now

"It has often been said that one's past determines one's future. Let it be underlined that one's present and future—how one commits himself to existence at the moment—also determines his past" May (1958, p. 88)

This is the story of how my father, in dying, presented my mother with his tallest demand yet, to forge out of his death a new narrative, the story he never told us. It was a narrative that, like all stories, held out the promise and threat of going either way; crossing the thin line from one of bad faith (Craib, 2000) and entropy to one of reparation (Klein, 1998) and growth (Pals, 2006). All by the swift flick of a word, a substituted memory, a touch differently remembered.

Having worked with many sad, ill, and deprived people through my work as a narrative researcher and counselor, and having watched my father's battles over the years, I have been touched at times by the workings of Freud's death instinct (1920). Through this instinct, a continual battle is wrought with Eros (Federn, 1932), and anything seen to embody or enhance life. The death instinct attacks narrative; turns it in on itself; disperses meaning; shatters coherence; and scorns the potential of words to build, to soothe, and to provide dreams. But sometimes, there is a moment, as many counselors, therapists, health care workers, and friends or relatives of loved ones will testify, when an individual simply chooses life. I say simply though in actuality how this choice is made, and through what small glimpses of states of grace in our psychological makeup this choice is laid before us, seems to be a matter of profound complexity bordering on mystery.

I also do not know how these states get to be accessed by some and not by others, although the healing power of social and familial ties ought never be underestimated. But I do know that there is something in the power of words and narrative, be it in talking therapies, in writing, or even in a silent wording within, that may nurture a resolution with ourselves and bring about a more benign meeting with what Kristeva called "the foreigner within ourselves" (Kristeva, 1991).

Perhaps my mother, through a lifetime of being on the receiving end of hurtful words and having to rebuild that which was continually dashed, rallied her best talent and authored a second chance (Pals, 2006). Kristeva (1989) noted that triumph over sadness is possible, though "the ability of the self to identify no longer with the lost object but with a third party— father, form, schema" (p. 23) and narrative may perform such a function, of dislocating the "I" from "I was" and "I have been," and rescripting it into an "I am" and "I will be." Semantics perhaps, but the idea that we say, therefore we are is compelling. Indeed, the role of narrative in managing difficult life events has been long documented (Pennebaker, Mayne, & Francis, 1997), its meaning-making properties in bereavement noted (Lobb, Aoun, & Monterosso, 2006), and its direct relation to widowhood observed (Bennett

& Vidal-Hall, 2000). Narrative is a quiet tool of reparation, our narrative working ceaselessly on rebuilding our internal world and its damaged objects, forgiving, repairing, taking blame, responsibility, apportioning and reapportioning, reassessing, bringing black and white together into a hundred muted hues. And yet we are perhaps guilty of having performed less unpacking of precisely how narrative works to reintegrate the psyche and help to fashion a future worth living, and how sometimes narrative works so obstinately against life.

After many months of a circular, destructive narrative, in which my mother became weaker and we became more tired and despairing, like spring, something fresh and green broke through. Unlike spring, it did not follow a clear trajectory and go from bud to blossom, and there were times when that elusive suggestion of life and a new narrative buried itself underground again. But, perhaps through her own resilience, warmth, shelter, and the help of family, a phase was worked through. It seemed that finally a bereavement was managed, and rose-tinted memories were modified again, good and bad brought together in a more true and three-dimensional alliance. Gradually, the black and white of love/hate good/bad merged into the reality of gray, and a new sense of self was shakily reinstated. My mother, the widow, the new woman, rescripted, began once again choosing books in secondhand shops; crocheting doilies for us to "ahhh" at; and grabbing the iron from our incompetent (by comparison) hands to show us how to properly iron a collar, a cuff, a border.

And then came later. It is early autumn. Running in the park, I notice the first turning of the leaves and in the air, at dusk, inexplicably, the smell of wood smoke. Soon, I'll go and visit my mother. She'll be welcoming, warm, and the television or radio will be playing too loudly, as she is gradually becoming more deaf than anyone admits to. Indeed to admit this, or mention it, seems paltry, a small observation of an inconsequential element of a life now old. She will talk 19 to the dozen, her accent as thick and idiosyncratic as ever, riddled with entrenched, endearing, substituted pronunciations. These my daughter reproduces perfectly, having the distance of a generation to enable that particular type of gentle jibing. My mother will make sense, however—wonderful, simple, lucid sense—each little story clearly demarcated with chronology and a narrative flow. She'll also make me tea and repeatedly offer to feed me. Loving these thoughts, and feeling the anticipation and warmth of them spread through my body, I register all over again the grim learning that took me to a place, here, where I could love them.

Taking pleasure in life had seemed an ability that for a time had been robbed from me. Such a tranquil ability was part of me in my earliest years;

I remember the enthrallment of watching sycamore leaves spiraling down as they fell and the bosky smell of dug-up soil in the garden. But then that ability disappeared. It was taken, somehow, and always felt like a stealing rather than a losing. Regaining it took time, work, the help of friends, and the kindnesses of strangers. I had, as it is known, a corrective emotional experience. Without bitterness I can say that this human ability, to take pleasure in life, the simple gifts of it, was eroded by the presence—rather, the omnipresence—of my father. But, as May suggested in the quote at the start of this final section, the way we commit to our present, the way we script the narrative of now, determines our past. It determines what we tell; how we tell it; and, more fundamentally, what we remember and how. Something in the stories my father told, or tried to tell me, stayed with me, lingered in my thinking and brought me to a now in which I can rediscover a passion for snowy landscapes, tall with trees and long with howling. I can also, without rancor, look back and tell this short story of how one man's passing away was so complicated, when it should have been so easy. It is still complicated, implicated as it is in my own "I am."

References

Baldwin, C. (2006). The narrative dispossession of people living with dementia: Thinking about the theory and method of narrative. In K. Milnes, C. Horrocks, N. Kelly, B. Roberts, & D. Robinson (Eds.), *Narrative, memory & knowledge: Representations and aesthetics contexts* (pp. 101–109). Queensgate, England: University of Huddersfield.

Bamberg, M. (2004). Talk, small stories, and adolescent identities. *Human Development, 47,* 366–369.

Bauer, J. J., McAdams, D. P., & Pals, J. L. (2008). Narrative identity and Eudaimonic well-being. *Journal of Happiness Studies, 9,* 81–104.

Bennett, K. M., & Vidal-Hall, S. (2000). Narratives of death: A qualitative study of widowhood in later life. *Ageing and Society, 20,* 413–428.

Bion, W. R. (1970). *Attention and interpretation.* London: Karnac Books.

Bowlby, J. (1980). *Attachment and loss, volume 3: Sadness and depression.* London: Hogarth Press and the Institute of Psychoanalysis.

Clewell, T. (2004). Mourning beyond melancholia: Freud's psychoanalysis of loss. *Journal of American Psychoanalytic Association, 52*(1), 43–67.

Craib, I. (2000). Narratives as bad faith. In S. D. Sclater, C. Squire, & A. Treacher (Eds.), *Lines of narrative: Psychosocial perspectives* (pp. 64–75). London: Routledge.

Federn, P. (1932). The reality of the death instinct especially in melancholia. *Psychoanalytic Review, 19,* 129–151.

Freud, S. (1920). *Beyond the pleasure principle.* London: Hogarth Press and the Institute of Psychoanalysis.

Freud, S. (1925). Mourning and melancholia. In *The standard edition of the complete psychological works of Sigmund Freud* (Vol. 14, pp. 243–258). London: Hogarth Press and the Institute of Psychoanalysis.

Frost, L., & Hoggett, P. (2008). Human agency and social suffering. *Critical Social Policy, 28,* 438–460.

Goyder, J. (2009). Alzheimer's disease, personhood, and intervention: A perspective. *Alzheimer's Care Today, 10*(4), 183–188.

Harris, P. (2009). Intimacy, sexuality, and early-stage dementia. *Alzheimer's Care Today, 10*(2), 63–77.

Klein, M. (1946). Notes on some schizoid mechanisms. *International Journal of Psychoanalysis, 27*(2), 99–110.

Klein, M. (1998). *Love, guilt and reparation: And other works 1921–1945.* London: Vintage.

Kleinman, A. (1988). *The illness narratives: Suffering, healing & the human condition.* New York: Basic Books.

Kristeva, J. (1989). *Black sun: Depression and melancholia* (L. S. Roudiez, Trans.). New York: Columbia University Press.

Kristeva, J. (1991). *Strangers to ourselves* (L. S. Roudiez, Trans.). New York: Columbia University Press.

Leader, D. (2008). *The new black.* London: Hamish Hamilton.

Lobb, K. L., Aoun, E., & Monterosso, L. (2006). *A systematic review of the literature on complicated grief.* Australian Government Department of Health and Ageing. Retrieved from http://www.health.gov.au/internet/main/publishing.nsf/Content/palliativecare-pubs-rsch-grief

Macfarlane, R. (2007). *The wild places.* London: Granta.

May, R. (1958). *Contributions of existential psychotherapy.* In R. May (Ed.), *Existence: A new dimension in psychiatry and psychology* (pp. 37–91). New York: Simon & Schuster.

Pals, J. L. (2006). Authoring a second chance in life: Emotion and transformational processing within narrative identity. *Research in Human Development, 3,* 101–120.

Pennebaker, J. W., Mayne, T. J., & Francis, M. E. (1997). Linguistic predictors of adaptive bereavement. *Journal of Personality and Social Psychology, 72,* 863–871.

Ricoeur, P. (1990). *Time and narrative.* Chicago: University of Chicago Press.

Sagan, O. (2007). Research with rawness: The remembering and repeating of auto/biographical ethnographic research processes. *Ethnography and Education, 2*(3), 349–364.

Sanders, S., Ott, C., Kelber, S., & Noonan, P. (2008). The experience of high levels of grief in caregivers of persons with Alzheimer's disease and related dementia. *Death Studies, 32,* 495–523.

Steedman, C. (1986). *Landscape for a good woman: A story of two lives.* London: Virago Press.

Stone, B. (2004). Towards a writing without power: Notes on the narration of madness. *Auto/Biography, 12*(1), 16–33.

Thompson, N. (Ed.). (2002). *Loss and grief: A guide for human services practitioners.* London: Palgrave Macmillan.

Part 5

Cultural and Societal Constraints and Complications of Grief

This last major section of this volume considers some of the many cultural and societal constraints that can further complicate grief. Indeed, it is foolish to presume that cultural and societal factors cannot (or do not) influence how we understand, perceive, or experience complicated grief. These papers make a very convincing case that in order to understand one's personal experiences of grief, we must be mindful of these factors.

Kathleen Cassity (chapter 16) makes a very critical point that by viewing complicated grief as a mental disorder, we may be overlooking grief that is exacerbated by sociocultural factors rather than individual pathology. Much of Cassity's analysis considers how the grief associated with the loss of her parents was likely complicated by many cultural factors that prevented her from receiving appropriate social support.

Parag Sharma's chapter (chapter 17) is a unique contribution in that it considers the pervasive grief felt by the author caused by lifelong perceptions of feeling ugly and repulsive. This analysis considers some of the conflicting emotions the author felt upon the sudden death of a relative who was the source of constant ridicule. This chapter also considers these struggles in the cultural context of having moved from India to America. An important and fascinating question suggested by this chapter is whether bereavement must necessarily be a trigger for complicated grief. Clearly, from the words of the author, complicated grief was experienced for reasons other than the death of a loved one.

In chapter 18, David Purnell offers a compelling account about his brother's death due to complications from AIDS. Much of his chapter serves as a clear reminder that certain conditions often imply stigma and shame, which, in turn, can complicate grief reactions for the survivor. Though Purnell considers that societal attitudes toward AIDS and homosexuality may have shifted somewhat in recent years, he maintains that there still is a need for greater awareness and acceptance. Purnell adds that he could only experience his grief once he allowed himself to feel his loss. This point advances a theme addressed in earlier chapters, that is, sometimes a reevaluation of the self (which typically occurs with the passage of time) allows one to make sense of and cope more effectively with complicated grief.

Jason Barr's essay (chapter 19) is one of the few chapters in this volume that does not feature a personal account of loss per se. Even so, Barr makes many astute and sharp observations about how new technologies may be serving as a way to both alleviate and, in some cases, worsen one's grief. For instance, Barr discusses cases in which people have relied on voicemail messages from deceased loved ones as a way to remember them. Others have turned to Facebook and related Web sites to commemorate loved ones. Barr also notes how technology has helped to commemorate many prominent tragedies, such as 9/11. However, he notes that such technologies can foment trauma by diminishing the nature of the event. Barr highlights an issue that will have continued importance in understanding how people grieve and cope.

Annette Anderson-Engler (chapter 20) concludes this section with some important and new perspectives on how gender affects the grieving process. She notes that, clearly, there already exists a substantial literature documenting that both genders do grieve, though sometimes in different ways. Though society may encourage greater emotional expression in women, Anderson-Engler considers how women's grief can become so overwhelming that it becomes almost impossible to physically show—to the detriment of these women. Anderson-Engler offers a critical analysis of this thesis by drawing on both her experiences as a social worker and pertinent clinical and academic literature.

Chapter Sixteen

Scapegoating the Complicated Griever in a Toxic World

Kathleen J. Cassity

Before we can proceed," said the preacher, "I have to ask: Do you believe your father was really saved? Because if there's any question, it will be hard for me to preach a sermon that assures the congregation he's in heaven." My father's body had been cold for less than an hour, and cold is what I remember whenever I think about that January night; unusually for Seattle, snow covered the ground. In a moment of black humor I'd joked that this was why Dad had chosen tonight to leave: He *hated* snow, perhaps because he hadn't even seen it until, at age 20, he left his birthplace of India.

It was hard to know how to respond after having been asked whether I believed my father might be burning in eternal flames. The cruelty of that question—so obvious to anyone outside a faith community believing this—remains curiously oblique to those within communities who do ("You can't lie to people," a minister's wife once said to me when I suggested it might be unfeeling to tell survivors that their loved one is in hell).

I had officially left the family church 13 years before my father died, when I was 18; unofficially, I'd left long before. Sunday school teachers and youth group leaders had considered me especially vulnerable to the wiles of Satan because I asked complex questions rather than glibly accepting their prefabricated, decontextualized interpretations of Bible stories. In the end I was driven away by multiple factors; the most significant included my inability to accept that most people, past, present, and future, are going to hell; my failure to feel overjoyed at that prospect; and the anxiety generated by believing that even for the "most holy" within our sect, eternal salvation was tenuous. According to our church, you could be a perfect Christian all your life and lose your salvation in a flash, not only for bad behavior but for harboring a fleeting unorthodox thought—even if that thought took the form of a question, and even if that question remained unanswered. My father had, all his life, been a questioner.

He had also been an active member of his congregation—serving as deacon, attending services at least thrice weekly, trying to live his life in what he considered a Christ-like manner. As an adult, I realized that my father's questions demonstrated how seriously he took the implications of faith (as Tennyson put it, "There lives more faith in honest doubt, believe me, than in half the creeds"). But those ensconced within the church's power structure—including many family members—didn't see it that way. Many of them felt free, in the presence of my father's grieving family, to voice the possibility that even as we speak, my father might be writhing in the eternal flames.

Dad's questionable spiritual status stemmed from multiple factors ("overdetermined," a cultural critic might say). For one thing, his identity was shifting and not widely understood, making it hard for people to categorize him—especially those steeped in an ideology that insists on this or that, right or wrong, black or white. For another, like the poet Rilke, my father preferred questions to answers. His 30-year membership in a denomination emphasizing divine vengeance and doctrinal purity didn't stop him from speculating and contemplating—in a world where one of the worst epithets a person can hurl at a fellow believer is "intellectual."

Furthermore, when my father died he was wearing rosary beads. They weren't his; they had been draped around his neck on his deathbed by his youngest brother, who was visiting from England on behalf of their mother. My paternal grandmother and this visiting uncle were Catholic; my parents' church sent Christian missionaries to Rome in an attempt to convert "the papists." My father had immigrated to America in the 1950s, leaving most of his family behind in England. Because we weren't affluent and didn't travel internationally, I didn't meet most of my paternal relatives until I began visiting England in my twenties. I'd always known some of Dad's family were Catholic (and, therefore, hell-bound), but I had incorrectly believed my father to have been a lifelong Protestant, Anglican before meeting my mother, and I was 28 before I learned of his interim Catholic phase. Mom, her relatives, and her church family considered this too scandalous a revelation for children's ears.

It wasn't the first secret my parents had kept from me, and if Catholicism had been "all" that was "wrong" with Dad, that preacher might have kept his mouth shut. But Dad pushed the comfort zone of Mom's world in too many other ways. Most damning of all, he was *foreign*. In our sect, many believe that after the Hebrew people "broke" their covenant with God, God instituted a new covenant, this time with the early founders of America. I was taught that America has become the "new Israel," chosen by God to lead the world to righteousness; the cosmos is engaged in an ongoing metaphysical war between God and Satan, and we are all warriors whether we know it or not. In this conflict, there is no such thing as conscientious objection, no neutrality: *He who is not for us is against us.* Most people—even most who "mistakenly" think of themselves as Christian—serve as soldiers on the side of Satan, however unwittingly, so it is up to "us"—born-and-bred Americans, Caucasians, fundamentalist Christians—to take on the divine mission of saving the world.

Dad not only hailed not from "the World," he had been born and raised in one of its most heathen cultures: India. Our church taught us that literal demons exist and are responsible for the development of incorrect religions—that is, any belief other than ours, including other branches of Christianity. Thus, other belief systems or cultural practices are not just false, different or even merely wrong, but Satanic, sinister, evil, and anyone who interacts with those who believe incorrectly risks demon contagion, in the same way that the uninoculated risk infection by communicable disease. Thus, spending time in demon-plagued areas, especially in non-Christian cultures, poses a grave risk, and overseas travel is a venture best avoided by the "spiritually immature." (Soldiers and missionaries are considered somewhat safe, clad as they are in both literal and metaphorical armor.)

"So is your dad Indian?" people used to ask me when they learned of my father's birthplace. (They often didn't; Mom preferred that we tell people Dad was from England. For some people, the news failed to compute even when they were told the truth; 15 years after Dad died when I ordered my original birth certificate to prepare for an adoption, I learned that according to officials in Washington State, my father had been born in Indiana.) Some people would say, "Your dad kind of looks Indian, but he kind of doesn't."

"Kind of" was the best answer I could give. My father's ethnic identity isn't well known: He was Anglo-Indian, part of a mixed-race minority community that has existed in India since the initial days of European trade in the subcontinent. During the 19th century, this community was known as "Eurasian" and—in less complimentary terms—as "half-caste," "eight-anna," "blacky-white," and "chee-chee" (a term denoting contempt). Scholarship of the community has documented how imperial racism became more intense and more codified as Britain consolidated its rule in the subcontinent (Anthony, 1969; Gaikwad, 1967; Gist & Wright, 1973; Hawes, 1996;

Maher, 1962; Stark, 1926; Younger, 1987). British colonists directed their racism not only at those in Indian communities but at those of mixed race, whom they considered to be tainted by "a touch of the tar brush." Accordingly, Eurasians grew increasingly marginalized from their British colonial overlords during the eighteenth and nineteenth centuries, whereas their European paternity isolated them from their Indian cousins. As a result, the mixed-race community became insular; for two centuries Eurasians tended to marry others within the community, leading to great variety in physical appearance among Anglo-Indians and making it difficult for Anglo-Indians today to quantify their ethnic background in mathematical terms.

Numerically the Anglo-Indians have always been few, particularly in the context of India's massive population. In India today, they number less than 100,000, thanks to a global Anglo-Indian diaspora that followed India's Independence and Partition in 1947. Nevertheless, the Anglo-Indians played key roles in operating India's imperial infrastructure, especially during the period between the first Indian uprising of 1857 and Independence and Partition in 1947, when the colonial government reserved positions specifically for Anglo-Indians in the railways, telegraphs, schools, police, hospitals, and military. After 1947, Anglo-Indians composed a significant portion of the first wave of postcolonial emigration; they and their descendants are now scattered throughout the world, with concentrations in Britain and in Commonwealth nations. In the latter half of the 20th century, many diasporic Anglo-Indians married within their new host countries, whereas many who stayed in India married into Indian cultures. Thus, descendants of Anglo-Indians often do not identify themselves as such, and the distinctly Anglo-Indian identity is slowly vanishing.

External scholarship regarding Anglo-Indians is scarce. Typically, their existence is either brushed aside or altogether ignored in studies of postcolonial diaspora and hybridity, despite the fact that Anglo-Indians constitute one of the prototypical hybrid/diasporic postcolonial communities. When Anglo-Indians have been portrayed in artistic forms such as literature and film, both during and after the colonial period, such representations often draw on crudely stereotypic caricatures. Some of the most pervasive of these include the Anglo-Indian man as shiftless; the Anglo-Indian woman as brassy and promiscuous; Anglo-Indians of both genders as lacking work ethic, suffering from pervasive imperial nostalgia, and harboring a racially based "superiority complex" toward other Indians (Cassity, 2010). Finally, Anglo-Indians are often stereotyped as obsessed with passing as European, especially if they appear to be of European descent.

Whenever one critique prevailing stereotypes, it is not unusual for somebody to point out (or think, if one dare not say so) that certain stereotypes are true and thus assume their proliferation is not a problem. Yet it is important to remember even when a stereotype appears to have reference points in reality, this may not stem from an inherent character flaw but from the social marginalization to which a targeted group has been subjected. The Anglo-Indian phenomenon of passing is one example: Many European-appearing Anglo-Indians were discriminated against if they revealed their mixed ethnic background, begging the question of who should bear the blame when it comes to passing—the individual doing so, or the societal bigotry that makes passing advantageous.

I'm admittedly sensitive on this point because, for several years, my father tried to pass as English. I didn't learn the truth of his birthplace until I was in second grade, when I point-blanked Dad at dinner one evening in preparation for a class project. Some researchers (who never met my father) describe this as a "psychological distortion" (Gist & Wright, 1973). My father, who lived the reality of an Anglo-Indian life—first in a stratified colonial Indian society and later as an immigrant in England, Canada, and America—tells the story differently.

"I didn't tell your mother I was Anglo-Indian until after the wedding," he told me one afternoon shortly before he died, during a rare lucid moment when steroids had temporarily reduced the swelling in his brain. "I was taking her to meet my mother, and I thought it would be wise to explain." (My father had moved to Seattle for his career and married my mother, after a hasty courtship, before introducing her to his family—who didn't attend the wedding.) With his mellifluous BBC accent, my father, despite his dark hair and eyes, might have conceivably passed for English, provided one didn't ponder where he obtained his glowing suntan during a Seattle winter. But his mother was one of those who clearly *looked* Indian and sounded it too.

"You didn't think it would be wise to explain *before* the wedding?" I asked him.

"If I'd told your mother the truth," Dad sighed, "would there have *been* a wedding?"

I already knew the answer. When I was a teenager Mom had once told me, "If I'd known the truth about your father before I married him, I would have said no."

How do you maintain allegiance to abstract concepts like truth, when your existence depends on truth *not* having been told?

"Do you wish you hadn't married him?" I'd asked my mother back then.

"No, I'm glad I married him," she had said. "We've had some hard times, but he is a dear man, and anyway it was the Lord's will, not mine. The Lord wanted me to say yes."

Which means the Lord must also have wanted my father to—well, not exactly lie, but at least withhold key information. Convincing my father to conceal his birthplace and ethnic origins was no doubt an easier task for the omnipotent Lord than convincing my mother, raised in the bosom of evangelical American fundamentalist Christianity, to believe it might be okay to marry a not-entirely-white man born in "demon-infested" India. Nor was it easy for the Lord to convince some in my mother's circle that the offspring of this union—my brother and I—weren't fatally tainted. Though we both looked mostly white, we suntanned easily, and some relatives used to warn my mother, "You might want to keep them out of the sun; we wouldn't want people to think they were from Someplace Else."

"Don't talk about India," I overheard Mom telling Dad more than once, "you don't want people to know you've been exposed to demons."

My father did have his demons (as do we all), but more in the sense of the secondary dictionary definition—"an obsession thought of as torturing"—than that preferred by our church, "an evil spirit or devil." Three of my five paternal uncles told me that for two years after their father died amid the chaos of 1947, my father stopped speaking. Even when he resumed using his voice, his personality was permanently altered. As the eldest son, my father had found himself suddenly responsible, at age 17, for his grieving pregnant mother and six (soon to be seven) younger siblings. The family had no money. My grandmother and the younger children moved to Pakistan to live with an uncle, while an aunt (a teacher, whom everyone referred to as a "spinster") paid for one of my father's sisters to obtain teacher training in Bombay. That same aunt paid for the two eldest sons—my father and my uncle—to travel by ship to London, where they lived in a South London council house with 15 relatives who had emigrated a few months prior.[1] While in England, my father and uncle discovered that disclosing their background often raised hackles and closed doors, so they fell into the habit of not mentioning it. Eventually, the family pooled enough money to bring my grandmother and her five youngest children to England, where my father helped them obtain a terraced council house on Hampshire's largest housing estate. Once the

---

[1] Council housing was developed by the postwar British government to assist those who could not afford open-market housing.

whole family lived in England—with some members appearing more Indian than others—passing became more difficult, and immigrants, especially the visibly non-white, did not always feel welcome.

Despite their mixed reception, Dad always believed that emigrating had been the right thing to do. Government grants helped him fund his training in aerospace engineering at a North London polytechnic while he worked full-time to support the large family for whom he had, by default, become responsible. "I always wondered," Dad used to say, "what we would have done without our extended family, and without Britain's commitment to postwar housing and education for those who struggled." Yet my father's appreciation of Britain was always mixed with annoyance: The British government would never acknowledge my grandparents or their offspring as genuinely British, despite the fact that my grandfather had served the British Empire, first as a soldier in World War One and later as a police officer in colonial India. Because they were not quite white, for the colonial British, the Anglo-Indians did not quite count. On the passport my father used to travel from India to Britain, he is identified as a subject of the empire, not as a citizen.

On that same afternoon in the hospital, I asked Dad why he'd decided to leave England. He replied, "Well, there was Ma, of course." (That "of course" conveyed several decades' worth of anguish that we all implicitly understood.) "And I was tired of worrying about everything—who's English, who's Indian, who's Anglo-Indian, who's upper class, working class, from here, not from here, who belongs where. Finally I just said, enough of this. Enough." Dad sighed. "Besides, I'd dreamt of building airplanes in America ever since I was a small boy."

It must have been a farfetched dream for a young Anglo-Indian in Madras in the 1930s. Somehow, my father had achieved it.

"And I thought by coming to America, I could get away from it. But in the long run I couldn't get away from any of it. It's everywhere." I didn't ask him what "it" was. On this afternoon of rare and dwindling lucidity, he continued, "When will the world come to its senses? All people deserve decent treatment, end of discussion. I say, enough."

When I was a teenager, most of my friends found my father's background exotic and fascinating. I asked my mother once why she, her family, and her church were not more interested in it. Mom explained, "When you become American, it's just like becoming a born-again Christian. Whatever you were before, you leave behind. Old things are passed away, all things are become new." (That last sentence is a direct quote from 2 Corinthians. Mom quoted the Bible a lot.) In my mother's world, for my father to talk about his past would not be a mere nostalgic fallacy, but a sin.

Dad had tried to leave "it" behind, only to find he couldn't. When I look back, I believe the shift occurred shortly after Dad suffered his first heart attack, at age 39. After that health crisis, he started patronizing Indian restaurants (which, back then, were hard to find in Seattle). He bought cases of Patak's hot pickles at specialty stores, smearing them on whatever meals my mother cooked and Indian-izing everything from tater tots with green beans to tuna-and-noodle casserole. This happened around the same time that I learned the truth about our background, though I cannot remember how, where, or when that knowledge was revealed. One thing I do remember: In the last weeks of his life, while musing on how far he had traveled since his India boyhood, Dad said, "The one thing I learned is that you can never really run away."

Three Januarys after Dad left us, I found myself in England for the funeral of one of his younger brothers, a teacher of college literature who, at age 53, had dropped dead of a heart attack while browsing bookshelves at the local library. I'd always enjoyed this uncle's company—his erudition; his deep incredible knowledge of history, literature, and antiques; and his rollicking sense of humor—even though I'd not met him until I was 22 and had probably seen him only six or seven times in my life. Shortly before Dad's illness, my husband and I had lived in England for a little over a year, partly because I wanted to become better acquainted with my paternal relatives. But during that year, even with long-awaited geographical proximity, I hadn't seen that much of them. During childhood, I'd largely been denied access to half my family tree, while feeling misunderstood by the half to which I had access. When I first met my father's family, I discovered people who not only looked like me, but who (apparently) thought like me, acted like me, and preferred the same things I did. On our first visit to England, in 1984, I told my husband, "I've finally found a place where I belong." Belonging, it turned out, was as tenuous as our church's view of salvation.

The deceased uncle we now mourned was the family member I knew least well. Still, I'd wanted to be at his funeral, to represent Dad's side of the family and express my condolences to the others. This was my first visit to England since my mother's death six months earlier. Just two years after Dad died, Mom—still in her sixties—had died of an unexplained and devastating neurological illness. With a couple of exceptions, I hadn't received many condolences from my paternal relatives, neither after her death nor during the horrific two-year ordeal that preceded it.

After Dad's death, I'd received from one of his family members not a sympathy card but a scathing letter, blasting Americans and castigating my mother for "killing" my father by requiring him to "work excessively." I'd previously adored this relative, who is fiercely intelligent, creative, and resourceful, and who I resemble nearly to a tee. Family members had often warned me that she could, at times, be "difficult," in the same way our grandmother could be. When I opened that letter, anticipating condolence, I felt smacked in the stomach. This person had left England several years earlier and so wasn't present for this uncle's funeral. Yet even so, I sensed a dark cloud descending, as though my presence wasn't entirely appreciated. For several years, my recently deceased uncle had enjoyed the company of what everyone called a "lady friend." At the reception this lady friend told me, tight-lipped and steely-eyed, "Apparently your mother needed your father more than she thought." Unsure how to respond to a comment so untempered with sympathy, I simply nodded and asked for directions to the toilet.

Later that evening I asked my favorite uncle—the eldest, the one who had first lived with Dad in London—whether some in our family had been angry at my mother. "Ah, well," he stammered, "I didn't agree with all of her beliefs, but I always liked your mother."

"What about the others?" I persisted.

"Ah, well. They didn't really know her, though, did they?"

Sensing his discomfort, I dropped the subject. For the rest of that short visit, I flashed back to strange behaviors on the part of certain people and, slowly, came to realize that Dad's family had never forgiven him for leaving. Perhaps it was easier for them to blame my mother than to acknowledge that he had wanted to go.

At my mother's funeral, I mused, "I am too young to be an orphan." The downward spiral that began with losing both parents within such a short time span was further darkened by perpetual uncertainty: We never knew why our mother died, what illness caused her to flee into fast-moving dementia (too rapid for Alzheimer's) followed by aphasia, paralysis, and near catatonia. Even after autopsy, the nature of Mom's catastrophic neurological illness remained a mystery. I had not agreed with my mother's world view; I'd left her church at an early age, and we'd argued extensively about religion all my life. Still, she had been a nurturing mother, and despite our differing worldviews I'd always known she was devoted to us and truly believed she was doing the right thing.

For many in Dad's family, my mother had played the part of villain. With Mom gone, I felt as though I were the new target for the hostility once projected onto her. Those doing the scapegoating had accepted the "half of me" that reminded them of Dad; the other half, they could do without. This felt sadly familiar: For the first part of my life I'd felt that same sense of disapproval, emanating from my maternal side. Relatives from both sides have, at various points, told me my parents' marriage should "not have happened." Of course, each side had completely different reasons for thinking so—completely different reasons for wishing my brother and me away, one half-piece at a time.

Coping with my parents' earlier-than-expected deaths and the devastating illnesses that preceded them would have been challenging enough. Clearly, losing one's parents does not upset the natural order of things as does, say, losing a child, or even losing a sibling early. In terms of inevitability, a parent's death should be an easier grief to bear, if you're operating within the realm of logic. But human beings don't operate solely within the realm of logic, and as Nancy Miller (1996) pointed out, "The death of parents—dreaded or wished for—is a trauma that causes an invisible tear in our self-identity" (p. x). Adult orphanhood may be a rite of passage that most will undergo, but it's still fiery, especially when it's not yet expected.

Not that death is ever expected. When I was pregnant, a friend told me, "Nobody can prepare you for the reality of parenthood," which turned out to be resoundingly true. No one can prepare us for the reality of adult orphanhood either. There is no easy grief, no way to "fix" the sadness I felt (and still feel) while celebrating major milestones—my three college degrees, the birth and adoption of my children, our silver wedding anniversary—without my parents as witnesses. Still, I believe I might have spiraled out of the depths sooner had I not had to grieve, in addition to my parents' deaths, the loss and lack of extended family. My husband remained my bulwark, but he had to perform singlehandedly the work meant for an entire family system, which at times became overwhelming for both of us.

Even so, I caught occasional glimpses of what familial support might feel like. In the first few hours after Dad died, his rogue younger brother—the Catholic uncle who had, against Mom's objections, draped the rosary beads around Dad's neck—sat with me, allowing me to ventilate my outrage at the nefarious speculations of the preacher. When the other uncle died three years later, the family followed Anglican funeral protocol by seating "immediate next of kin" in the lead processional car—my grandmother, an aunt and four uncles, and—as the oldest living member of my father's family—me. "Next of kin car?" one of my uncles quipped, "I'd call this 'next to die' car." Black humor is an aspect of British culture that the

Anglo-Indians have embraced, and on that day I remember teasing and laughter that felt both relieving and slightly wicked. At such moments I felt connected to my father's family and, by extension, to him. It's just that there weren't enough such moments.

"Next to die" turned out to be my grandmother, nearly five years later, and in another five years, my oldest uncle. Having just given birth, I couldn't fly from Honolulu to London for my grandmother's funeral, but I did attend my uncle's. That was when I realized my discomfort at the prior funeral hadn't stemmed from paranoia. While poring through my recently deceased uncle's photographs and correspondence, I learned that after my father's death, some of my relatives had written to the courthouse in Seattle requesting details regarding Dad's estate. The courts had nothing to tell them since my parents had avoided probate with a simple will. I then learned that my grandmother—and several others—believed that my father had squirreled away a fortune intended for them. They also believed my mother had stolen it by changing Dad's will while he was on his deathbed—and that when my mother died, the fortune accrued to me. This "fortune," however, exists only in certain family members' imaginations.

By this time, 12 years after Dad's death and 10 years after Mom's, my "complicated grief process" had for two years been deemed resolved by my therapists. But resolution is always relative. I sat through the latest family funeral feeling like I'd been pummeled by an explosion of falling meteors, mourning too many losses: not just another uncle, but my naïve belief that I had ever belonged with Dad's family; my sense of trust; my sense of connection to those who loved, missed, and remembered the same people as I did. Once again, uncertainty reigned: I didn't know the origins of the tall tale. Had my father stoked the flames by originating the story? If so, had he done so deliberately, while still healthy? Or did it happen after his illness so that we should blame it on the tumor? Or did he never say anything—was it my grandmother who fabricated the story, from the residue of her own wrenching disappointment? With none of the tale's potential originators still alive to interrogate, I will never know—though perhaps I wouldn't have been able to discern who was telling the truth anyway.

I find already problematic the label I was slapped with three years after my mother's death—"complicated grief"—as though any grief is meant to be simple. I acknowledge that my grief wedged in more stubbornly than most. Yet I believe my difficulty stemmed not so much from individual psychopathology as from the profound sense of isolation that compounded my already wrenching losses.

"Do not be sad, dear," says a sympathy card I received from one of Mom's church friends. I vaguely recognize the name of the friend but can't summon her face—which may be just as well. "We know your mother is in heaven with Our Lord, and perhaps your father is there also."

Perhaps.

Today I feel no anger toward the woman who wrote that card—nor at the preacher who suggested my father may be writhing in hellfire, nor at my mother, nor at the maternal relatives who suggested we should stay out of the sun, nor at Dad, nor at the paternal relatives who scapegoated Mom and imagined her (and me) as thieves of their imaginary fortune. I remember it all, of course, but with a sense of sad resignation to people's imperfections rather than with anger. For if I'm hesitant to identify individual pathology as the cause of my own complicated grieving, I have to allow that the shortcomings of others may not stem primarily from individual pathology either. As Watson (2010) pointed out:

> Only in modern times do we prioritize the individual above the family or community, and believe that the individual must be cured first. But through the healing of the family and the community, individuals will heal.... As long as families and communities remain dysfunctional, individuals will not be healthy. (p. 131)

"To understand one life," says the fictional narrator Saleem Sanai in *Midnight's Children,* "you have to swallow the world" (Rushdie 1982, p. 109). If my parents' lives, and mine, can't be understood apart from the complex cultural, historical, and social web that produced and shaped them, then neither can the lives of those who, perhaps without realizing, said and did things that exacerbated and prolonged my grief. I don't intend for anyone in this story to emerge as a villain. Everybody is tangled in a messy web of potentially toxic discourses that have disabled our collective ability to feel and express compassion, celebrate and mourn with genuine feeling, and live in community—something that thinkers throughout the centuries have pointed out is vital for human well-being. To understand the lives of these people, including the behaviors that caused me pain, it is necessary to understand more than just the individuals involved, for none of us exist in isolation.

Accordingly—despite the proscriptions of my childhood church against "intellectualism"—I sought some resolution through intellectual explanations. In the work of social psychologist De Zavala regarding collective narcissism (De Zavala, Cichoka, Eidelson, & Jayawickreme, 2009),

I recognize the dynamics of our religious group: "Collective narcissism is seen as an extension of individual narcissism to the social aspects of self. It is an ingroup, rather than an individual self, that is idealized" (p. 1075). (Notably, one can be a member of a collectively narcissistic group without being individually narcissistic.) The research of De Zavala et al. confirms correlations between collective narcissism and social dominance orientation, right-wing authoritarianism, and intergroup aggressiveness. Collective narcissism also fosters "outgroup enmity," with members often excessively sensitive to real or perceived slights by outsiders and easily threatened by perceived dissent within.

De Zavala et al.'s (2009) findings resonate whenever I recall my childhood—the collective belief that God has commanded a strict hierarchical code which humans are now violating, the preference for authoritarian social structures (arguably, in direct contradiction to the Sermon on the Mount), and the belief in a collective divine mission as warriors in the cosmic battle. Church members often expressed a fierce persecution complex that, even when I was young, I thought sounded like collective paranoia. The mechanism for this I find in De Zavala et al.

> Collective narcissism is a form of high but unstable collective self-esteem that needs constant external validation but accepts no validation as sufficient. We found that collective narcissism is highest among people who hold their ingroup in high regard but believe that others do not recognize its value properly. (p. 1091)

Of further interest are the potential consequences to insiders: "The perceived threat to the assumed greatness of the ingroup may be chronic because ... the unacknowledged doubts about the ingroup's greatness may motivate collective narcissists constantly to seek signs of criticism or disrespect of the ingroup" (De Zavala et al., 2009, p. 1091). Unacknowledged doubts by insiders, in other words, are often projected onto outsiders.

Here the work of Rene Girard (1996b) regarding the scapegoat mechanism becomes pertinent: "The signs that indicate a [scapegoating] victim's selection result not from the difference within the system but from the difference outside the system" (p. 116). In other words, the ingroup member most vulnerable to scapegoating will be someone who maintains friendships outside the group, or who somehow gives voice to supposedly settled questions. The dual status of this "borderline crosser" suggests to insiders that outsiders may perhaps be less different from them than they imagined, instigating another spiral of protective behaviors designed to defend the ingroup from perceived outside threats.

The kind of religious group I was raised in—collectively narcissistic, exclusionary, authoritarian, and hierarchical—has always existed (and not just in Christianity), though the prevalence, visibility, and influence of such groups have waxed and waned with historical and social contingencies. During my childhood in the 1960s, this version of Christianity was every bit as alive and well in America as it is now, though in significantly smaller numbers, thriving at the margins rather than at the center, and largely devoid of political influence. Today in America, this strand of Christianity has gained cultural ascendancy, become intertwined with politics and power, and has influenced U.S. domestic and foreign policies. I am concerned that this type of belief may further erode America's already threatened sense of community. Human beings require a healthy sense of community for optimal health and functioning, but a ruthless capitalist ethic that prioritizes profit over the greater good, combined with a fear-mongering media, has wreaked havoc on America's social fabric. Against this backdrop, the conservative Christian church arguably offers the most resonant promise of belonging. Yet to belong often comes at the high cost: The enforced orthodoxy that all outsiders are going to hell effectively cuts off the possibility of community with anyone outside the fold. Thus, the proffered cure for social isolation—a microcosm that helps people to feel they belong—paradoxically inhibits a larger sense of belonging by isolating those within that microcosm from the macrocosm of wider society.

My life has been shaped by a similar paradox: The theology I was raised with had a psychological effect analogous to drinking poison. When it made me sick, I was told the cure lay in drinking more. Yet the belief that everyone outside our fold is toxic, perhaps even demonic, was itself the source of the harm. Drinking more of that would never cure me.

To understand my father's family, I turn to postcolonial theory. Here the work of Homi Bhabha (1994)—though he does not mention Anglo-Indians per se—resonates with the experience of my Anglo-Indian family, particularly Bhabha's evocation of the "un-homed" postcolonial subject who occupies both a figurative and psychological intermediate space between established boundaries. Exiled (whether literally or figuratively) from the culture of one's birth, the un-homed subject dwells in a border zone, "as though in parenthesis" (p. 9), "inhabit[ing] the rim of an 'in-between' reality" (p. 13). Often represented in literature through "twilight, a descent into night, an invasion of the shadow," postcolonial "unhomeliness" speaks of "the traumatic ambivalences of a personal, psychic history to the wider disjunctions of political existence" (p. 11). To be un-homed, Bhabha specified, is not to be literally homeless but reflects a psychological state produced by the traumas of the 20th century: upheaval, border crossing, and fluctuating sense of identity and belonging.

Reflecting on the stories told by my father, grandmother, uncles, aunts, and cousins, I recognize the dynamic described by Bhabha (1994) when he elucidated the perpetual nature of the "unhomely moment" and the role of art in providing momentary relief from perpetual ambiguity: "When historical visibility has faded, when the present tense of testimony loses its power to arrest, then the displacements of memory and the indirections of art offer us the image of our psychic survival" (p. 26). For Bhabha, the function of art is not merely the expression of an individual experience, but a gesture toward community:

> To live in the unhomely world, to find its ambivalences and ambiguities enacted in the house of fiction, and splitting performed in the work of art, is also to affirm a profound desire for social solidarity: "I am looking for the join ... I want to join ... I want to join." (p. 27)

Here again the work of Girard (1996b) becomes pertinent, as he describes the scapegoating process: First, a crisis occurs that may be "symbolic, real, or simultaneously symbolic" (p. 119). The crisis may be seen as a "consequence of the scapegoat's misdeed" (my mother's insistence on marrying my father) "rather than as a cause" (my father's original desire to leave England and his subsequent pursuit of my mother). Next, a particular individual "stands convicted" and is "seen as the cause of the crisis. This is scapegoat projection" (p. 119). The scapegoat usually bears "preferential signs of victimage" (p. 119)—my mother's status as foreign outsider in my father's family. The "culprit" is then "killed, expelled, or otherwise eliminated" (p. 119), thereby restoring order into the disrupted system. The only part of Girard's formula that fails to apply in this context is his claim that once order is restored, its resolution is projected onto the scapegoat, who then becomes idealized and serves ritually as a "founding ancestor or divinity" (p. 119). Rather than idealizing my mother after her death as Girard's theory posits, my paternal relatives continued to view my mother as the source of family disruption; after her death, the role of scapegoat shifted from her onto me. Eventually, thanks to extra-familial "personal, friendly, supportive, and dialogical relationship(s)" that Saleebey (2000) posited are essential for "healing, transformation, regeneration, and resilience" (p. 128), I could cease internalizing the projections of others, gain perspective, and come to understand that the mechanisms giving rise to my painful experiences were not "about me," but stemmed from a complex web of postcolonial traumas that still haunt my father's family today. That realization finally helped me to work toward healing from a grief process that, at times, I thought might never cease.

In the field of social work, a strengths approach empowers

> individuals, families, and communities [to] see and utilize their capacities; recognize the options open to them; understand the barriers and scarcities they may face; surface their hopes and aspirations; and align them with their inner and outer resources to improve the quality of their lives. (Saleebey 2000, p. 128)

For my own eventual emergence from a seemingly bottomless abyss, I credit my husband, my children, those biological relatives who did provide support, and a circle of close friends who constitute my "family of choice." Important to Saleebey's (2000) definition of the strengths perspective is the fact that resources exist not only within the individual, but also within the social environment as well: "Even in the most demanding, tough, lean, and mean environments, there are natural resources—individuals and families, churches, associations, groups—available to individuals, groups, and families. While some are clearly more bountiful than others, all environments have assets" (p. 129). Here it is important to note the potential harm that may occur when an environment or relationship that *should* be a "natural resource" becomes instead a source of further trauma (something that can be attested to by anyone who has been abused by a trusted adult). When someone who has suffered a major loss is doubly traumatized by lack of social support during a time of intense need, it feels triply cruel to pathologize that individual's grief. To do so is analogous to taking someone with a broken leg to visit an orthopedist each week, only to discover that, rather than setting and checking the limb, each week the orthopedist has been deliberately smashing another small nearby bone—and then, despite that culpability, blaming the person with the broken leg for failing to heal.

The truth of grief is that none of us will avoid it. Like Job, we howl into the whirlwind only to have the wind respond without directly answering, reminding us that are we puny and powerless—yet also reminding us that grief, which always feels so intensely personal, is broadly experienced.

However devastating our loss, we can always find someone with a more tragic story, which may trigger guilt for the depth of our own mourning. We can also find those whose lives seem "better" than our own; dwelling on this can cause bitterness. Yet neither bitterness nor guilt supports healing, and the process of grieving is not like writing a compare-and-contrast essay. There is no hierarchy, no cosmic "American Idol" where people can call in their votes to determine which of us is most entitled to mourn. At the heart of grief lies the paradox that amidst this most human experience of loss, each of our losses remains our own. Our task in the face of loss and grief is to work through our own pain. Though this is never easy, it becomes possible in the presence of supportive others, and nearly impossible to do alone.

Because there are no perfect individuals, there will never be any ideal social structures. The scholarship of Girard (1996a, 1996b), Bhabha (1994), and De Zavala et al. (2009) reminds us that the family and community on which we depend for our sense of belonging are often double-edged swords, with belonging depending as much on whom we shut out as whom we let in; thus, the promise of belonging always carries the inherent potential for cruelty. Still, I hold on to the belief—because I would not have survived my grief without it—that a more humane, connected, and caring world is possible. In such a world, as Watson states, it might be easier to develop healthier social structures that support, rather than hinder, the healing of individuals who are experiencing grief.

References

Anthony, F. (1969). *Britain's betrayal in India: The story of the Anglo-Indian Community.* Bombay, India: Allied Publishers.

Bhabha, H. (1994). *The location of culture.* New York: Routledge.

Cassity, K. (2010). 'There are no soldiers anymore': The persistence of Anglo-Indian stereotypes in *Bow barracks forever. International Journal of Anglo-Indian Studies, Vol. 10.* Retrieved from http://home.alphalink.com.au/~agilbert/covij17.html

De Zavala, G., Cichoka, A., Eidelson, R., & Jayawickreme, N. (2009). Collective narcissism and its social consequences. *Journal of Personality and Social Psychology, 97,* 1074–1096.

Gaikwad, V. R. (1967). *The Anglo-Indians: A study in the problems and processes involved in emotional and cultural integration.* London: Asia Publishing House.

Girard, R. (1996a). Python and his two wives: An exemplary scapegoat myth. In *The Girard reader* (pp. 118–141). New York: Crossroad Publishing,

Girard, R. (1996b). Stereotypes of persecution. In J. G. Williams (Ed.), *The Girard reader* (pp. 107–117). New York: Crossroad Publishing.

Gist, N., & Wright, R. D. (1973). *Marginality and identity: Anglo-Indians as a racially mixed minority in India*. Leiden, the Netherlands: J. Brill.

Hawes, C. (1996). *Poor relations: The making of a Eurasian community in British India, 1773–1833*. New York: Routledge.

Maher, R. (1962). *These are the Anglo-Indians*. Calcutta, India: Swallow Press.

Miller, N. (1996). *Bequest and betrayal: Memoirs of a parent's death*. Indianapolis: Indiana University Press.

Rushdie, S. (1982). *Midnight's children*. New York: Penguin Books.

Saleebey, D. (2000). Power in the people: Strengths and hope. *Advances in Social Work, 1,* 127–136.

Stark, H. (1926). *Hostages to India, or the life story of the Anglo-Indian race*. Calcutta, India: Fine Art Cottage.

Watson, T. (2010). Homelessness. In C. Howes & J. Osorio (Eds.), *The value of Hawaii: Understanding the past, shaping the future* (pp. 125–132). Honolulu: University of Hawaii Press.

Younger, C. (1987). *Anglo-Indians: Neglected children of the Raj*. Delhi, India: B.R. Publishing.

Chapter Seventeen

Just Don't Laugh

Parag Sharma

Physical perfection is an ideal pursued by every nation, culture, or tribe around the world, and arguably thousands of individuals have perished in the pursuit of this perfection. It is not so much the idea of looking good or ugly, but more importantly, it is about fitting into the prevalent culture's notion of physical perfection. As a migrant living in the United States for more than a decade, straddling the sociopersonal expectations of the popular cultures of two radically different cultures hasn't been easy. Living up to the ideals and expectations of family and friends while carving a niche for myself and keeping away the pain and indignation caused by relatives back home have been tough challenges for me. Hailing from an extended, middle class family has its own pitfalls, and the negatives of such a family assume greater magnitude when one permanently shifts base from one country to another because you have to deal not only with personal tribulations, but also the hidden demons from the past that haunt your present.

I am from a family of four—my parents, my elder brother, and myself, and we were once a part of an extended family consisting of 18 people. We are originally from Calcutta, India, and I moved to the United States in 2001 for higher studies. Because our family was (and is) very closely knit, getting oriented to the individualistic culture of the United States was very difficult. However, what made this struggle acutely disorienting was the lack of requisite social skills to befriend people. Though this inability could be attributed to the jitters of finding myself in new surroundings, at a deeper level, it stemmed from a perception of being a failure. As long as I can remember, I have always harbored a conviction that I am physically imperfect. This idea always colored my imagination, whether it be at the work place or my more immediate social circle. I brought this well-bred malaise over to the

United States, and this cognition was self-generated as well as impinged upon me by my relatives back home who constantly harassed me about my unconventional physiognomy. Consequently, when two of those relatives passed away in 2006, I felt a sense of relief. Unfortunate and inhumane as my reaction might be, these tragedies brought a sense of quietude and closure to my deep-seated angst that resulted from the memories of humiliation and self-loathing. Even though the incidents of harassment occurred a long time ago, the repercussions have stuck with me even today, and the resultant inferiority complex has dictated my moral and social discomfiture in the society; these relatives' deaths have yielded in me a complicated grief that is an admixture of the deepest sympathy and a deeper hatred. As pointed out by Lobb, Kristjanson, Aoun, and Monterosso (2006), though grief is a normal response to bereavement or unhappy incidents/occurrences in life, it can actually be "acutely distressing, persistent, and functionally impairing" (p. 93). Today, whenever I find myself floundering at a social gathering, unable to break the ice or initiate a conversation with an individual, regardless of his or her gender, I revert back to the memories of my childhood and see myself as a loathsome individual, who cannot and should not have the right to socialize. So, while these individuals' deaths have definitely brought about the usual grief and agony one associates with such an occasion, their demise also provided me with an opportunity to exorcize the wrongs I suffered at their hands and thence, the inability to accept myself as the person I am.

Body dysmorphic disorder, or dysmorphophobia, is a medical condition that is also termed *imagined ugliness*, in which the subject in question imagines that he or she is extremely ugly and obsesses with the body to the point of being a self-chosen social outcast. Though the degree and extent of such an ailment obviously varies, this type of ailment can be psychologically debilitating because it not only has its roots in structural brain differences or genetic factors, but also can be a product of the environment where negative experiences affect an individual's perception of self. At the age of eight, a freak accident left me with a permanent scar on my body (and my mind?): a crooked set of overlapping teeth that refused to naturally set themselves straight, and in the process, provided me with what I perceived to be a horrible smile. Coming from a culture where physical beauty or perfection makes or breaks how an individual is perceived and tolerated in the society, I was constantly reminded of my "handicap" right from that age, by both my family and friends. Interestingly, as I grew up, I realized that this drawback was as much psychological as social. I developed a mental block and a consequent apathy about people and the society in general, so much so that I refused to smile at friends and family and even harbored a mortal fear of facing the outside world. This apathy somehow transformed into the deepest and most stringent of cynicism toward life that has persisted until now. This physical drawback never failed to make me realize that I was not only undesirable and unworthy of consideration in the larger scheme of things, it also prevented me from participating in school debates, fancy dress competitions, or the like. My self-consciousness was heightened to an inordinate degree, so much so that anyone I had a conversation with seemed to me to be staring at my mouth and judging my physiognomy. Consequently, this condition channeled into a self-loathing and a pessimistic outlook on life; despite moments of clear-headed self-analysis of my physical condition, I refused to believe that it wasn't so bad. Since I was intermittently reminded of my drawback, either in a passing, jocular vein or in a cautionary, corrective tone by the people I encountered in my life, I had to cope with a peculiar grief that resulted from a demise of my sociability and interpersonal skills, a grief that I could not and have not shared with anybody until now.

As mentioned earlier, we had a joint family, and when 18 people from the same family live under the same roof, it is not a pleasant experience. Not only did I have to contend with sibling rivalry with my elder brother, I also had to contend with a rivalry that extended to my cousins and a cousin's cousin and so on. Owing to a difference of just couple of years, the sibling rivalry between my brother and us was quite healthy; at the same time, it never boiled over into a fierce competition for our parents' attention or the like. Because I was the second child, I always looked up to my elder brother for guidance and inspiration and always tried to follow in his footsteps. I tried to emulate his success at school, popularity among his friends, and affability in our extended family. Though all these dynamics of a family are commonplace, there was something that rendered our bond special. He had always been supportive of me in whatever I did, and he never made me feel inferior. My mother and father have also been the pillars of support in my life; however, they could never subconsciously stop comparing me with my brother. As a child, because I was compared with my brother at every step, the matter of physical appearance was frequently harped upon. Once we had a family gathering of my cousins and uncles and aunts. I was made the butt of ridicule—albeit in a lighthearted vein—in that gathering. Frequent allusions were made to how my teeth were horrible and beyond repair, how I should "always cover the mouth" while laughing and purse my lips while talking so that the deformity could be hidden. Though incidents like these were commonplace, it was also true that I did not bother to retaliate because

I was convinced I was ugly. It wasn't that the jokes came trickling in at a later stage. Grief has its foundations in a cogent basis of hurt and depression; for me, it was more a matter of unqualified anger at myself; at God; and eventually, at my parents as to why they did not take care to find braces for me, why I wasn't made aware of my ugliness earlier.

What makes our culture unique are the idiosyncrasies existing within the subcultures based on petty concerns. All of us cousins were frequently compared on the clothes we wore, the food we ate, how healthy or strong we appeared, how wealthy we appeared, and so on. Thus, an inferiority complex was instilled in me, not only because of my physical appearance, but also because of my family's social status. I wasn't immune to the idiosyncrasy existing within my culture, and an unspoken hatred built up within me toward some of my relatives on the basis of these little incidents. Now, death of a relative or family member is never easy to deal with, especially if that individual has lived with you under the same roof for your entire life. However, the phenomenon of death can sometimes become complicated because of the emotions involved. Whereas common reactions to death are one of grief and long periods of mourning, sometimes the death of a relative can also bring a sense of quietude, if not relief. Complicated grief involves experiencing certain grief-related symptoms at a time beyond which is considered adaptive, namely "feelings of disbelief, mistrust, anger, shock, and detachment from others" (Dodd et al., 2008, p. 415). My complicated grief, an amalgam of all the aforementioned symptoms, is related to two such individuals and how those experiences of death—the only ones I had closely witnessed—molded my entire perception of what I am emotionally capable of.

My dad and mom had numerous siblings, because of the pre-independence Indian mentality that a bigger family meant more happiness. My dad was the fifth of a family of 12; he also had a twin brother. This individual was a spoiled brat, and as he grew up, he turned into an autocrat, intolerant of anything or anybody within the family that did not adhere to his demands and whims. For instance, he coaxed some of his younger siblings into signing on blank stamp papers and took over their ancestral portions (whatever was assigned to them in his parents' will). When we were growing up, we would always hear stories about what type of personality he was, but in our later years, we witnessed firsthand evidence of his consummate evil nature. He would constantly harass our family and my dad in particular because he could not digest the fact that my grandfather bequeathed a plot of land to my father and not him. He was always seething with jealousy and often tried to oust us from our ancestral home in Calcutta.

He was an extremely fit and agile individual compared with my dad. He was in constant motion, an active socialite, and never lived a dull moment. So, it was a complete surprise when we heard about his sudden heart attack at the age of 53. While he lay in the hospital, all of us were pondering if and when should we visit him. He was suffering from a clogged artery and very high levels of blood sugar. Suddenly, I found tears rolling down my face. I was bewildered by my reaction because I obviously had no respect for him. He passed away within five hours of being admitted at the hospital. He did not die a painful death, as I had wished as a child. In hindsight, that was very inhumane and selfish of me, but I held him responsible for my deep-seated self-loathing. The interesting thing is how in my mind I had firmly established the connection between a perverse satisfaction from his death and some kind of vindication of the karmic belief system that I was brought up with. I soon began to develop a deep remorse about my hatred and wished I could undo my attitude or how I spoke to him. However, my anxiety and agonies did not end there. A few months after his death, when I left for the United States for my education, I had even deeper feelings of guilt because even as I was happy about my new opportunity for a better life, I could not help wishing he did not die so that he could see how successful I had become. I grieved over his death, and yet, I was feeling relieved. This relief was quite painful and went against my humanitarian sensibilities.

I tried to resist these feelings of anxiety and push them aside. However hard I tried, I could not dissociate myself from this feeling of ill-timed indignation toward this man, even during his funeral. My last encounter with him wasn't a pleasant one. In retrospect, one incident in particular haunts me every now and then. Because we lived together under the same roof (but on different floors), our families had open, free access to each other's room and corridors. On one occasion, he had inscribed something on the walls of our corridor to the effect of "return to where you guys came from" and "he is a failure." My dad held a job in another state, and every year we would come to Calcutta for a visit. So, though my dad had a perfectly legitimate claim over the ancestral property and resided there, he had to constantly justify how and why he should be allowed to live there, as if he did not "belong" to the family So, such inscriptions on the wall, in addition to being illogical and hard to justify, weren't easy to ignore. Those inscriptions still adorn our walls, even though my uncle has been dead nine years now. In addition, my uncle had an inexplicable grudge against my elder brother and me. He would never spare any opportunity to poke fun at my physical appearance or my brother's academic failures. Though his barbs were apparently innocuous, in hindsight, he wasn't mature enough to understand the indelible impression he was creating on tender minds by mocking their personal lives (my brother and I were 13 and 11, respectively). Needless to say, the emotional trauma that I suffered as a result of these incidents indirectly shaped my self-perception as well as the unnecessary cynicism that I exercise toward people around me. Though I accede that he wasn't entirely responsible for this personality trait of mine, I have come to relate these childhood incidents of attack on my personality and family as special catalysts that have affected my self-perception and self-confidence.

My first cousin came over to the United States in the early 1990s to pursue his higher education. When I was in India, I would periodically hear news of him and what he was up to, and we would be constantly compared to this cousin who did the family proud by traveling abroad for education. Some 10 years later, when I was preparing to leave for the United States, I received news of his being in India. What was surprising, however, is the way I heard about him. My mom walked up to our family and said to us, "Binoy has come back to the country and wants to see all his relatives." My first question was, "Why does he want to see us now? He never tried to contact us before and neither did he want to." My mother replied, "Well, he is back from the United States to spend the rest of his days. I have heard he was sent back." My mother's language immediately raised an alarm, and on further inquiry, it turned out that he was suffering from lung cancer and had only two and half months to live. My first reaction was of shock and disbelief. I had witnessed many deaths in my family, but no one had died of cancer, and I had never had to deal with a terminally ill patient. Being related by consanguinity, all of us were quite depressed and sad on hearing this new. He was just five years older than me and was leading a healthy lifestyle in the United States. He did not do drugs or drink alcohol. He was also a nonsmoker, which is why the incident was all the more baffling.

Having a joint family had its pros and cons. Though you were supposed to honor social mores and maintain ties with others from your clan, the reality of circumstances pointed toward something else. Bogged down by disputes over ancestral property and intrafamily bickering, we were left with little or no sympathy for each other. We did not have quarterly or yearly reunions, nor did we know the whereabouts of each other. Under these circumstances, the news of Binoy's cancer was something deeply disturbing, yet it presented me with a predicament. I say "me" and not "us" because my parents' and brother's reaction to this incident was quite different than mine. As Dodd et al. (2008) have pointed out, "It is generally agreed that the symptoms of separation distress are at the core of complicated grief, relating to the idea that complicated grief is a form of an attachment difficulty resulting from separation" (p. 416). Whereas my parents and brother were deeply moved and almost took their reaction to the point of bereavement (because of the impending tragedy), my reaction was more complicated because of how I had been treated by my extended family. I personally did not believe that I should go and visit my cousin because he did not try to keep contact with us when he was hale and hearty. Not only was he conceited and arrogant, but he never even tried to maintain contact with his roots when he left Calcutta. However, my parents' logic of forgiving everyone, especially one who won't be around for long, won me over and—albeit reluctantly—I agreed to pay him a visit.

Traumatic experiences change our perception of who we are as individuals because they test not only our fortitude, but also our capacity to transcend our personal sorrows and emerge a better individual. In addition, according to Bowlby (1969), grief can be an extension of a general response to separation where an attachment has been broken. Even though we weren't attached by geographic proximity, on meeting with Binoy for the first time in my life, I had a weird feeling of kinship running through my head. I was meeting him for the first time and yet could not help feeling that we were related to each other through an individual who I abhorred. On seeing Binoy for the first time, all feelings of vicarious animosity went away, and only the vestiges of kinship prevailed between us. His appearance was horrific to say the least. He had so many tumors on his head that it appeared as if each was trying to climb on top of the other for prominence. This grotesquerie was further accentuated by his inability to turn sideways while lying down because of his tumors. He could not go to the bathroom without suffering excruciating pain. He could not be lying down on one spot for a long time because the tumors would transform into pressure points, and pus would ooze out once they ruptured. I felt an intense sympathy for him because here was a young life wasting away in front of my eyes. But at the same time, I was curiously indifferent to his suffering. We got talking about his stay in the United States, his time at the IBM branch in Colorado, his cancer diagnosis, subsequent treatment, and so on. Throughout our conversation, I realized how lonely and isolated he was. He kept asking about my family, our past, things I have accomplished in life, and my future plans. It was as if, at least what I perceived, he vicariously desired to live his life through another individual about to embark on the same journey that he had undertaken 13 years before. It was a moment of epiphany for me. Here I was about to start a new life and couldn't care less for a dying individual. Ironically then, I was going to pursue a degree in the humanities without having the ethical and moral compass to act on my humanitarian impulses in a real-life scenario. When he passed away 41 days after our first conversation, I left for the United States. I did not bother to attend his funeral even though there was an opportunity to do so, perhaps out of deep-seated spite or sheer indifference to the circumstances surrounding his death. According to research, "involvement in post-bereavement rituals may prove to strengthen the separation distress type symptoms" (Dodd et al., 2008, p. 423). I feared that if I attended his funeral, I might become empathetic toward his family and by extension, forget the injustice meted out to my family through the years. I am basically a forgiving person, but my innate tit-for-tat nature got the better of me. In retrospect, perhaps, that could be the reason why his death still rankles in my mind. These two deaths, within the space of one year, left quite an indelible impression on my mind. But I could not fathom how or why I harbored an inexplicable hatred and indifference toward these individuals.

Traveling to another country for the purpose of education has had its pitfalls. While I have been away from my family for a long time, the idea of suffering alone and being away from them for long periods of time have played a crucial role in how I have come to perceive myself and my capabilities. Because of my negative self-perception, I tried to convince myself that if I took an abnormal satisfaction in someone's death and yet felt sad for it, I must be a sadomasochist. Once that feeling took over me, I began to be even more cynical about everything and everybody around me. The idea of dating never came to me because by the time I made the journey to the United States for higher education, I was very determined and focused to concentrate on that. Because I was convinced I was ugly and should be ashamed of being in the public spotlight, I tried to maintain a low profile as much as possible. There have been quite a few incidents that influenced my thought processes and almost drove me to the point of committing suicide. However, when I tried to analyze the main cause behind such atrocious thoughts, I figured out that my self-imposed isolation from companionship contributed greatly to the thoughts of suicide. I would talk everyday to my parents overseas, but I gradually started to withdraw more and more; consequently, the wretched feeling of worthlessness grew on me.

My grief has had origins in a lifelong struggle with identity crises. It has resulted not only from witnessing relatives' deaths and an abnormal reaction to the same, but also, and more important, from a lifelong inferiority complex instilled into me by my family and friends alike. My responses have varied from withdrawing myself for extended periods from any social gathering to criticizing myself at every possible opportunity for not being born with better physical features. Another way that I successfully exercised my frustration at the self was to deliberately reminisce about unpleasant incidents from the past and relive the horrid memories to remind myself how unsuccessful I have been. Though complicated grief is generally associated with the inability to cope with the loss of a near and dear one, my grief stems from the inability to forget how I look and am perceived by strangers, notwithstanding how much I have accomplished.

Until I came to the United States, my complexity did not fully rear its head. On arriving here, I became more conscious of myself and my ugliness. In a society driven by personal success and cutthroat competition to look and be the best, I found myself completely out of sorts. I came to this country for education, but I was fending myself against my psychological anxieties relating to personal appearance and social orientation. Dysmorphophobia is a medical condition whereby the subject has a strong belief that he has an abnormality or defect in his appearance and continually strives to improve upon the same. As mentioned before, my childhood experiences with my family, especially my uncle and cousin, largely contributed to the feeling of being unwanted and inferior to others around me. While I was in India, even though I suffered periodic bouts of depression or stress, I never could name them as such because in my culture, one does not frequently resort to medical terminology for what I then thought of as trivial cases of mood swings. In the United States, a country that worships über-commercialism, materialism, and the quest for the so-called perfect life, I found myself in a glaring spotlight of drawbacks and negativism. Even though I was mistreated by people back home, the feeling of worthlessness and self-loathing did not completely set in until I started going to school in Tennessee.

Until my first semester, I had some sort of control over my feelings pertaining to personal drawbacks. My recent separation from family, new surroundings, new collegiate atmosphere, and pressure of grad school, consumed most of my attention through the first semester. However, I gradually began to preoccupy myself with my appearance and frequently looked in the mirror to scrutinize my nose, eyes, ears, and particularly my teeth. Surrounded by physically attractive people both on and off campus, I would come home and compare myself with people I had seen or talked to, thinking about their beautiful smiles and amicable appearances. More acutely, I noticed that eight out of 10 individuals had a perfect set of teeth, at least on the surface. I would closely observe their smiles, their laughter, the delicate contours of their mouths, how they moved, and so on. When I turned around and was left to myself, I would hold my cheek bones, feel my jaw, and wonder what went wrong. Every day I would call home, talk to my parents, share new things, but weirdly, I would never mention anything about my new life or environment. They would ask questions about the same, and I would sidetrack the issue by segueing into some random topic. While I talked to them, I would pace back and forth in front of the wall-length mirror and glance at myself now and then. In hindsight, while it was an effort to perceive how I looked to others while I talked, I was simultaneously becoming more and more uncomfortable with how I looked. This was a very early stage of my perpetual state of depression that was about to follow.

One incident that heightened my insecurity happened at the university writing center. All the writing assistants were getting introduced to each other, and when my turn came, I hesitated for a second and introduced myself. However, I almost mumbled under my breath to hide my teeth, and it was embarrassing to be asked to repeat myself. When I looked around, I saw, or at least I thought so, that while I was talking, people on my either side were staring at my mouth and then at my eyes. It was very uncomfortable and nerve wracking; I knew I could speak with more clarity, and yet I did not choose to. From that day on, I began to convince myself that people around me look at me in a judgmental, negative manner, owing to my ugliness (notwithstanding my foreign accent). Even when I was invited to hang out with friends, I declined out of the fear that they would take special notice of my appearance in a negative light. Once my malaise degenerated into paranoia, it began to affect my sociopersonal interaction and reputation. I soon began to hear rumors that I was rude, unfriendly, proud, and full of myself. Though I knew I wasn't that and wanted to prove otherwise, I could not find an opportunity to do so because I chose to isolate myself. One particular aspect of my personality aided this process. I am a very nervous individual and get rattled easily if something is out of the order or does not proceed according to a set schema or pattern of things I am generally used to. In addition, I cannot take criticism easily. When occasions surface that bring forth these two facets of my personality, I get very defensive and retrogress further into my negative state of being. I began to associate my ill-favored physiognomy with such rumors, and I became extremely self-conscious about my appearance, to the extent of skipping some of my tutoring duties and even one or two classes. On one occasion, I refused to go the writing center and have a picture taken of myself (for university record) because I did not believe I looked decent.

Two early incidents of unsuccessful attempts at socializing further worsened this issue. One day, while I was walking through the corridors of my university, a girl came up to me and introduced herself. We shook hands and after a very nervous, initial introduction, I simply froze. I did not know how or where to take this conversation. She was in my field, junior to me by a couple of years. After a brief moment of awkward silence, she simply walked away. I felt mortified, angry, and dejected. The other incident involved a failed attempt at a blind date that went horribly wrong; the worse part is that I felt so lonely, depressed, and desperate that I tried to have a relationship with a married man, albeit unsuccessfully, because it was nipped in the bud before anything happened. Though these attempts were part of a normal drive to socialize and fend for myself, at a deeper level, it was an attempt to prove myself that I was not lacking in manhood. On each of these occasions, I backed off because I perceived that I did not have the requisite qualities to pull through. These initial incidents created a deeper self-hatred, to the point that I did not know whether to consult my folks back home or consult student services. Coming from a new culture and mindful of my current status (doctoral student), the latter option was out of the question. I thought about the former quite seriously, but I was reminded of my parents and family back home and how they'd feel about this. It was almost like a never-ending cycle because I considered my larger family and the incidents back home as responsible for my current predicament, and yet I had to resort to the same people for support.

I had roommates from my country, and I could have shared my feelings with them as well; yet I chose not to. It would appear that I was deliberately perpetuating my condition of self-pity and loathing, which was partially correct. However, on the other hand, when the support system you'd like to count on turns against you, there's nothing an individual cannot do. My body dysmorphic disorder became more acute in the United States because I was made more conscious of it by my new friends here. It is understandable that deep-seated angst toward home folks might be misplaced, but when new people in your life begin to poke fun at your physical aspects, you hate yourself; there's no respite from the inflicted damage. My new roommates gradually began to adopt the same jocular, mocking vein that my folks back home used while making fun of my dental setting. I was told that I should have them operated on, put on braces, cover them up with my upper lip, and so on. The pattern was incorrigibly similar; I became even more convinced that it was me, my teeth, that was the root cause of my social failure. I did not think of putting on braces or the like because I was (and am) defiant of about my appearance. However, in hindsight, I never thought of a medical diagnosis because it never occurred to me that I was suffering from a possibly treatable condition. Every other day or so, I would read articles about individuals similar to myself, read their cases on search engines like Wikipedia, and see how they coped with their problems. I did not like the suggestions of putting on your best smile, focusing on your personality, the positives of your personal appearance, and meeting new people. I even joined forums to exchange ideas with people with similar issues. However, I soon realized that the more I read up and tried to find a solution, the deeper I sank into self-pity. I soon started pondering karma, and a vindictive god paying back my dues for hating my cousin and uncle. I could not see any light at the end of the tunnel. I did not contemplate suicide. Not yet.

When I got a full-time job in Texas, I felt overjoyed because I thought this would be a new beginning—new place, new life, new surroundings, new people. I decided to put everything behind me and start afresh. I remembered my lessons from online perusal and decided to project my best personality at my new place because no one knew how I was in the past. Coincidentally, about the same time, I felt the urge to settle down in life because I was 29 and without a significant other for eight years, largely because of this one, single complication in my personality. Not too long after starting my full-time job, I met someone at my yoga class. We went out on a couple of dates and had a great time. However, again, the fatal pattern started to repeat itself. I acted strangely, tried to be what I wasn't, and did not know how to handle complicated situations. Once, while we were sitting in a car, she asked whether I knew the meaning of the word *foreplay*. I was taken aback by such forwardness and was left tongue-tied. Needless to say, the date went horribly wrong because I was self-conscious the whole time and noticed that she was staring at my mouth during our conversation. I obviously must have felt uneasy because soon after that, I was walked out on with these parting comments: "In this country, things are done faster and you have to learn that before dating someone." What I learned that day was that I was completely lacking in confidence in every sphere of my life and that resulted from a very low self-esteem, which, in turn, germinated from my acute self-consciousness and paranoia. This condition wasn't limited to a particular geographical setting; I could and would not leave behind this malaise and move on. I did not think that any therapy or personality check would be helpful. I was driven to the verge of committing suicide because I felt neglected and singled out for mistreatment. Though I might have known that all these things were untrue, I could not help myself rise against such misgivings. Even today from time to time, I feel paranoid, threatened, and lonely because of how I perceive myself and my appearance. Things have gotten much better because I am older, have a stable job, and decent lifestyle, but I think I will live with a perpetual state of self-loathing for the rest of my life.

References

Bowlby, J. (1969). *Attachment and loss Vol. 1: Attachment.* New York: Basic Books.

Dodd, P., Guerin, S., McEvoy, J., Buckley, S., Tyrrell, J., & Hillery, J. (2008). A study of complicated grief in people with intellectual disabilities. *Journal of Intellectual Disability Research, 52,* 415–425.

Lobb, E. A., Kristjanson, L. J., Aoun, S., & Monterosso, L. (2006). An overview of complicated grief terminology and diagnostic criteria. *Grief Matters: The Australian Journal of Grief and Bereavement, 9*(2), 28–32.

Chapter Eighteen

My Brother's Keeper

David F. Purnell

The fiction of Russell Banks emphasizes the human capacity for both causing and enduring pain. But it also has a redemptive quality. Many of his characters are storytellers. They seek relief from the pains of human experience through storytelling as if that is what retrieves a life from those painful experiences (Brown, 1989). By telling the story of my brother's death, I am able to revision my loss with a reflexivity that I did not possess at the time of his death. Revisioning (see Ellis, 2009) allows me to view my brother's death in a more positive way, which allows me to use my grief for my own personal growth, to reconnect with him and make him a part of my life now.

Telling the story of rejection juxtaposed with a story of grief and the loss of a terminally ill child, I hope to bring about a discussion of accepting our loved ones despite our personal opinions of how they live. Before forcing a family member out of your house or out of your life, try to understand who he or she is. I do not think that we need to find common ground as much as we need to try to understand each other. Perhaps understanding will bring us more comfort when we face death, instead of regret for not allowing ourselves to understand each other because we believe we have nothing in common.

Gelfand, Raspa, Briller, and Schim (2005) explained how "in a society in which so many different stories are told and heard about [the] end of life, it is especially critical to consider how the construct of culture permeates the discourse" (p. 210). It is also important to understand that we do not receive stories, but rather stories live within us and help shape social understandings (see Frank, 1997). Furthermore, the effect of storytelling "is not a way of declaring 'this is how it is' but a means of inviting others to consider what it (or they) could become" (Bochner & Ellis, 2003, p. 507). Through the examination of constructs that shape our understanding of grief, it is possible to start viewing the positive aspects of grief (see Stroebe, 2001).

An Unexpected Visit

It was strange to hear the doorbell ring. My friends always just walked in the house, as I never locked the front door until I went to bed. Not wanting to deal with any church invitation or school magazine subscriptions, I almost didn't answer. A second sounding of the annoying chime rang throughout my rented home in Long Beach, California. "All right, all right, I'm coming," I yelled. I swung the door open with more force than I intended, revealing my annoyance. The suitcase was the first thing I noticed, followed by the tall, lanky frame, face smiling at me from behind a pair of dark sunglasses. My older brother Harold—or H.P. as we called him—was standing there waiting for me to invite him into my home.

"Arntcha gonna ask me in?"

"What the hell are you doing here?"

"Let me in, and I'll tell you."

I stood at the door shaking my head. This was not the first time H.P. had shown up on my doorstep. As I stood there contemplating what to do, I thought about the last time he asked to stay with me. I had refused to provide a warm place for my own brother, despite the fact that he was standing in front of me at my home in Atlanta, Georgia, without a coat as snow fell to the ground. I had given him a firm "No" as a reply to his request for shelter, shut the door, and sat on the couch as I continued to watch television. After the second set of commercials began, I was overwhelmed by guilt. I can't even remember the program I was watching. Thoughts of my brother out in the cold kept me from enjoying my relaxing evening in front of the television. I got up, put on my coat, and opened the door to go find my brother. As I opened the door, I was considering which direction to start my search. Lost in concentration, I nearly plowed my way through my brother, who was still standing at the front stoop of my home as he said, "I knew you couldn't leave me out here." I smile at the memory.

"Come on in."

"Thanks. I knew I could count on you."

"What can I say? I'm a sucker. Let's start with the basics. Why are you here? How long are you planning on staying? And when do you plan on leaving?"

I look at him. Waiting to hear what fantastic tale he's going to spin to make me feel sorry for him and let him sponge off of me until I can't take any more of his irresponsible antics, I notice a tear trying to break free from his lower left lid. Other than during the beatings he received as a kid, I had never seen my brother cry. He is now aware that I'm aware of the tear trying to burst free, and he breaks down. He sobs uncontrollably for a good 20 minutes. I offer little in the way of comfort. I stare at my brother, still not sure if this crying fit is a new tool that he has crafted to perfection to gain the sympathy of the next poor victim of yet another con, or if his heaves and sighs are signs of genuine emotion—something that I never considered my brother to even be capable of showing. H.P. looks up at me, and I can see the fear in his eyes. For the first time, I believe his tears are real.

"I have AIDS," he mutters through the last remaining deep sighs caused by his crying.

I am not sure how to react.

"Shit," is the only word that I can muster at first. "Have you been seeing a doctor?" The tears are pooling in the corners of his eyes again. I finally hold him. "I will take care of you. Whatever you need."

"I knew I could count on you."

"You're my brother. Of course you can count on me."

Telling Mom

I sold my car in order to afford two tickets for H.P. and me to go back to Danville, Virginia, our hometown. The phone call to our mother was the hardest call I have ever made, but we had to prepare her for our visit and the reason behind it.

"Hi Mom."

"David! It's so good to hear your voice. When are you coming to visit your mother?"

"Actually, that's why I'm calling."

"You're coming home for a visit?"

"I am coming home for a while Mom."

"Are you OK?"

"I'm fine. It's Harold (Mom never liked "H.P."). He's sick. He has AIDS. It doesn't look good. I need help taking care of him."

Silence.

"Mom?"

"Of course." I can tell she's crying. "When are you coming home?"

"Tomorrow."

"See you then, son."

"Alright Mom."

"Take care of your brother."

"I will."

"I love you."

"I love you too."

Mom wanted us to move in with her, but I knew I couldn't deal with both my mom and my brother living under one roof. I rented a house for H.P. and myself in Danville despite having to work in Greensboro, North Carolina—50 miles away. H.P.'s condition was getting worse, and I tried to treat him with respect and dignity. We had never been very close, but I couldn't turn my back on him in his time of need. After buying a few items, we settled into our small home.

Happy Birthday: What a Drag

When I arrive home from work, H.P. is unusually nice, which always means that he wants something.

"David, do you know what Monday is?"

"Typically, the first work day of the week." I look at him and smile, knowing full well Monday is his birthday. "It's your birthday! Of course, I know what Monday is. You don't think I would forget your birthday do you?" H.P. shrugs his shoulders as if he is not sure of the answer.

"I really would like to go to Virginia Beach this weekend to see a drag show."

"First, how do you even know that there is a drag show in Virginia Beach this weekend? Second, how are we going to pay for the trip?"

"Please," he says, as he looks at me with big brown puppy-dog eyes.

"Sure."

What else can I say? He's dying. If seeing a drag show brings a few moments of joy to my brother's life, then, by God, we are going to see a drag show. Excitedly, H.P. calls for tickets, but I can immediately see the disappointment in my brother's eyes as he listens to the voice on the other end of the phone. The show is sold out. He hangs up the phone and goes straight to bed. He doesn't answer when I tell him how sorry I am that we can't go.

"I have to go by Mom's for a while or she says she's coming over here." I think that will get a response, but nothing. I leave and go to Mom's apartment.

Before she starts playing 20 questions about my brother's health, I tell Mom that I have to make a phone call. I call the bar that is hosting the drag show. I explain the situation and am told that there will be two complimentary tickets for us at the door. I thank the manager for his kindness and say goodbye. I visit with my mom for a while and give her my assessment of H.P.'s health. By the time I make it back home, H.P. is asleep. I wake him up the next morning and tell him that I have a surprise for him.

"Leave me alone."

I nudge him again.

"Leave me alone!"

"Damn it all to hell, there is just no surprising you. I got us tickets to go to the drag show, you sorry little shit. Now, get your ass out of bed and pack your bag. We're going to Virginia Beach."

"Thank you. Thank you. Thank you. You are the best brother in the world."

"Really? Wasn't it just last Tuesday that you told me that you hated my guts and wished I would leave you alone—forever!"

H.P. was as stubborn as they come. He was lying out in the sun without sunscreen. He thought a tan would make him look less sick. The poor guy cooked himself to the point that he could hardly move, not to mention that it was September and cold outside. I took the opportunity to act as his caregiver and gave him some new house rules to follow. That's when he told me that he hated my guts and that he wished I would leave him alone—forever.

"I don't recall saying that."

"Mmm mm."

H.P. throws a few things together, and we begin the four-hour drive to Virginia Beach. When we get to the bar, the performer headlining the show greets us. We are escorted to the front row. I had never been to a drag show before and found it fairly entertaining. After the show, H.P. was allowed to go back stage and meet the performers. I never realized he was such a fan. He knew all their stage names and apparently had seen them perform many times in other cities across the United States. That night, back at the hotel, H.P. was having a rough time sleeping. He was in a lot of pain, and he wanted to go back home immediately. It was 2 A.M., and I was too tired to drive, but I also knew that there was no way I was going to get some sleep when H.P. had other plans. I got up and prepared for our drive back to Danville. We ended up stopping along the way and sleeping in the car while parked on the side of the road. My anger was hard to contain, but H.P. kept talking about the show with a childlike abandon, which helped to reduce my anger over spending money for a hotel we hardly used and trying to drive home in the middle of the night only to sleep on the side of the road in my car.

It was cold outside when we stopped, so I kept the car running. The engine shut off at some point during the night, and we were met with frigid temperatures the next morning. The car would not start, and I had to flag down a motorist to help us jump-start the car. As we got back on the road, I reflected back to the evening and the drag show. It was not the best night of *my* life to say the least, but it *was* my brother's best night since returning to Danville.

Mommy Dearest

As H.P.'s illness worsened, I was not able to leave him alone while I went to work. Mom made arrangements to have H.P. move into her apartment. She emptied out a 7×10-foot room that she used for storage and placed a hospital bed in it for my brother. Mom took over the responsibilities of my brother's care and made him the same promise that I had—no hospitals. I tried to help as much as I could. Mom was already taking care of my terminally ill stepfather and maternal grandmother. She did all of this while putting in a 60-hour workweek managing the hotel that her apartment adjoined. This is the time when I began to have a deeply profound sense of respect for my mother. Over the years, that respect had faltered due to my perception of her feelings toward my brother, but I realized it was from a place of fear that her actions and statements caused me to question her love for my gay brother. She would tell me that she prayed that Harold would have a miserable life so that he could see the error of his ways. Despite these comments, she always welcomed him with open arms when he came to visit. It must have been hard for her to deal with my brother's in-your-face display of his sexuality. She did not approve of his life choices and feared for his soul on the on the basis of her religious beliefs. I think the hardest part for her was the fact that she was absolutely sure that it was his choice to live as a gay man (Reiter, 1989). In her eyes, it was not who he was; it was who he wanted to be.

After getting my brother situated in Mom's apartment, I gave up the house that I had rented and moved in with my paternal grandmother in Yanceyville, North Carolina. Living with my grandmother gave me some distance from everything that was happening. I had gotten so caught up in the responsibility that I lost track of how my brother's illness was affecting me. I was not sure how to react to H.P.'s illness. Looking back on the situation 15 years later, it was not so much that I was not sure how to react, but I think that I was not given the opportunity to react.

H.P.'s Final Words and
Mother's Final Act

On September 24, 1995, H.P. fell on his way to the bathroom and soiled his pajamas. For the first time, we put him in a diaper. During the majority of my brother's illness, we were fortunate that he was able to take care of himself. He had refused his medication close to the beginning of his illness. At the time, azidothymidine (AZT) was the only treatment available for patients with AIDS, and it left him feeling sicker than his illness did. We all tried to get him to take his medication; we tried to give him hope that some new drug might be easier on him than the AZT, but H.P. only took Marinol—a pill form of marijuana. He always had a good buzz, which helped his mood considerably after the cytomegalovirus retinitis reduced his vision to only dark shadows.

"Why don't you try taking your meds for a month or two and see if you can build up some of your strength?"

"I would rather live a week and feel good than to live a year or even two and feel like shit."

"I understand. It's just hard."

"Don't worry about me. I will be OK. Don't tell Mom I told you this, but I'm going to die tonight. It's time. I'm ready to go. I know I have not been the best brother to you, but you have been the absolute best brother I could have ever had. Thank you for always being there."

"You're welcome, asshole." H.P. laughs. I try to smile.

Around 2 A.M. that night, my grandmother's phone rings. We know that it's about Harold. During my visit that afternoon, Mom had moved Harold into a motel room that had a connecting door to her apartment. The room had two double beds, and she slept in the spare bed just in case H.P. needed something during the night. His breathing had become very forced and labored. It was the silence of his not breathing that woke her.

By the time I arrived, the police were there, and everyone was waiting for the coroner to come and take away H.P.'s body. When the coroner arrived she explained that she had to strip my brother of all his clothing and wash him down before she could take his body away. It was then that I witnessed the greatest display of love and loss that I have ever seen. It is this memory that constantly comes to surface every time I think about my brother's death.

As the coroner removed my brother's pajamas and he lay naked on the bed, my mother requested to wash his body. I watched the tears roll down her cheeks as she bathed his body and kept repeating these words, "My precious, precious baby." Watching this scene left me feeling as if I were invading an intimate moment that should not be shared. I felt so strongly that she should be alone during this process that I asked everyone in the room to leave, and then I removed myself from the touching scene. While waiting for this ritual to be done, I thought about the beauty of what I had just witnessed. My brother came into this world naked and connected to his mother, and that is how he left this world, naked and connected to his mother. Mom had been so adamant about her feelings of disgust toward my brother that I thought she could not stand the sight of him. However, it was at the moment that I heard her say, "My precious, precious baby," that I realized it was not my brother toward whom she had such hostility. It was his life that caused her conflict. Her love for H.P. had never faltered; she was with him until the very end—until he drew his last breath.

Family Response

I thought that H.P.'s death at the age of 34 would change some of my family's attitudes about AIDS, especially because my mother had allowed him to move in with her, but preparing for his funeral proved that there was still a great amount of shame. My grandmother told her friends that he had died of cancer. My father refused to allow the obituary to request that donations be made to the local AIDS prevention organization in lieu of flowers; my mother insisted on a closed casket due to H.P. looking "sickly." My brother did not want his child to come to the funeral and overhear any possible conversation about AIDS. These attitudes continued after the funeral, revealing a deep feeling of shame and secretiveness to keep the cause of an AIDS-related death from others (see Kadushin, 1999), such as the case with H.P.

The demonstrated attitudes of my family show the continuing effect of socially constructed views of people living with HIV and AIDS during the early 1990s and, for many, these attitudes continue today. The seemingly constant use of metaphors by the family describing AIDS as the "gay plague" or a punishment for sin escalated after H.P.'s death, bringing guilt and shame to other family members when mentioning H.P.'s name. This is because HIV was mainly viewed, during the time of H.P.'s death and into the 21st century, as affecting populations who are considered deviant by society at large (see Parker & Aggleton, 2003). The continued stigmatization by my family of H.P.'s death only reinforced the beliefs and biases that my family held. This familial stigmatization has played an important role in creating familial isolation of anyone who told others about H.P.'s AIDS-related death (see Parker & Aggleton, 2003).

My Turn to Grieve

Almost a year after my brother died due to complications from AIDS, I mourned his death. Looking back at his funeral, I think I had mourned my mother's loss more than my brother's death, but now I finally cried for *my* loss. As I think back to my brother's death, I realize that I was a witness to, rather than a participant in, my brother's death. I greeted the visitors at the funeral home, and shook the hands of friends at the gravesite. Occasionally, I would look over at my mom and wonder how she was coping at that moment. I felt I had to be strong for her. All of my focus was on her and the loss that she was experiencing. My mother told me that no one in the family could know the pain that she was experiencing except for my paternal grandmother, whose firstborn son Melvin died from the measles when he was five. I was so concerned that my mom would not be able to handle my brother's death that I did not have an opportunity to mourn or even realize my own loss (see Ellis, 1993). That my brother and I were not close was probably another contributor to my being able to focus on Mom.

As I revise, rethink, and rewrite this autoethnography (Ellis & Bochner, 2000), I now see myself as more of a participant in telling the story of H.P.'s death rather than an outsider voyeuristically observing the actions of my family in relation to H.P.'s death. I know it sounds cruel, but at the time I did not see myself as even having been affected by his death. This is a troubling realization, but now that I have put myself into the account of H.P.'s death, I have finally been *allowed* to take part in the grieving process (Soon, 2008). I am no longer an outsider; I am front and center. I grieved when I finally let myself feel *my* loss. In this chapter, I have revisited my loss, re-experienced it, and now I have a sense of reattachment to my brother. I am a part of my brother's life.

I keep my memory of H.P. alive through my celebration of his life. Every year on the anniversary of his death, I remember him by going to a bar and buying a round of drinks in his honor (Corr, Nabe, & Corr, 2006; Walsh & McGoldrick, 2004). This tradition is especially meaningful to me as it gave me a way to grieve the first anniversary of H.P.'s death without the judgment of my parents. I was able to think back on H.P.'s antics and smile regarding the memory for the first time since his death. You see, H.P. was known for not paying his rent; instead, he would go to a local bar and buy everyone drinks until he had no money and would have to bum a ride home from one of his fellow bar patrons. H.P. was always in need of assistance and support, and he will always be standing at the doorway of my life. I let him in from time to time and share new stories that I know he would have found interesting or humorous. Occasionally, he knocks unexpectedly, but I never say no. I learned my lesson that cold December day in Atlanta. I am my brother's keeper.

The continuing bond that I create each year through my celebration of H.P.'s life helps me to remember my brother in a positive and healthy manner. H.P. had always looked to me for strength and support, but it was his own strength that gave me courage every day. Each day, H.P. gave me proof for the meaning and existence of my own life (see Deremo, 2005).

The stigma associated with AIDS that arises out of ignorance of the disease itself and a lack of acceptance by friends and family of those infected (Eaves, McQuiston, & Miles, 2005; Gunzenhauser, 2006; Martin & Hetrick, 1988) shows a need for a continued dialogue about sibling loss as a result of complications from AIDS. Not only does the stigma associated with HIV/AIDS diminish the discussion of sibling loss due to death from complications of AIDS, but it also negates the value of the infected individual's life (Eaves et al., 2005; Parker & Aggleton, 2003). I hope that this personal narrative of sibling loss due to the complications of AIDS gives strength to others who find it necessary to manage a dialogue of rejection juxtaposed with a dialogue of grief and loss and the impact it has on other family members when they face struggles that require, or produce a desire for, familial support.

When I began this autoethnography, a peer asked if there was a need for this discussion. My peer considered awareness of HIV and AIDS to be already prominent, and that the stigma of HIV/AIDS was not as severe as when I had to deal with my family's rejection of my brother's life and their grief over his death. I was at a loss for words, but finally managed to say that there was still much hate, which in turn creates a stigmatized life that brings guilt and shame. Two months after our conversation, there were several suicides of gay teens. I asked my peer if she still questioned the relevance of my story. It seems nearly impossible to have the foresight to realize the pain that such treatment brings not only to the individual who is already suffering, but also to the individuals caught in the periphery, whether they be family, friends, or colleagues.

References

Bochner, A. P., & Ellis, C. (2003). An introduction to the arts and narrative research: Art as inquiry. *Qualitative Inquiry, 9,* 506–514.

Brown, W. (1989, September 10). Who to blame, who to forgive. *New York Times,* p. 53.

Corr, C., Nabe, C., & Corr, D. (2006). *Death and dying, life and living.* Belmont, CA: Wadsworth.

Deremo, D. E., & Meert, K. L. (2005). Grace's story. In D. E. Gelfand, R. Raspa, S. H. Briller, & S. M. Schim (Eds.), *End-of-life stories: Crossing disciplinary boundaries* (pp. 209–217). New York: Springer.

Eaves, Y., McQuiston, C., & Miles, M. S. (2005). Coming to terms with adult sibling grief: When a brother dies from AIDS. *Journal of Hospice and Palliative Nursing, 7*(3), 139–149.

Ellis, C. (1993). There are survivors: Telling a story of sudden death. *Sociological Quarterly, 34,* 711–730.

Ellis, C. (2009). *Revision.* Walnut Creek, CA: Left Coast Press.

Ellis, C., & Bochner, A. P. (2000). Autoethnography, personal narrative, reflexivity: Researcher as subject. In N. K. Denzin & Y. S. Lincoln (Eds.), *The handbook of qualitative research* (2nd ed., pp. 733–768). Thousand Oaks, CA: Sage Publications.

Frank, A. (1997). *The wounded storyteller: Body, illness, and ethics.* Chicago: University of Chicago Press.

Gelfand, D. E., Raspa, R., Briller, S. H., & Schim, S. M. (2005). Boundaries and bridges. In D. E. Gelfand, R. Raspa, S. H. Briller, & S. M. Schim (Eds.), *End-of-life stories: Crossing disciplinary boundaries* (pp. 209–217). New York: Springer.

Gunzenhauser, M. (2006). A moral epistemology of knowing subjects: Theorizing a relational turn for qualitative research. *Qualitative Inquiry, 12,* 621–647.

Kadushin, G. (1999). Barriers to social support and support received from their families of origin among gay men with HIV/AIDS. *Health & Social Work, 2,* 198–209.

Martin, A. D., & Hetrick, E. S. (1988). The stigmatization of the gay and lesbian adolescent. *Journal of Homosexuality, 15*(1), 163–183.

Parker, R., & Aggleton, P. (2003) HIV and AIDS-related stigma and discrimination: A conceptual framework and implications for action. *Social Science and Medicine, 57*(1), 13–24.

Reiter, L. (1989). Sexual orientation, sexual identity, and the question of choice. *Clinical Social Work Journal, 17*(2), 138–150.

Soon, S. (2008). *To care with passion: Walking a loved one through cancer and taking on the ministry of pain.* Singapore: Genesis Press.

Stroebe, M. S. (2001). Bereavement research and theory: Retrospective and prospective. *American Behavioral Scientist, 44,* 854–862.

Walsh, F., & McGoldrick, M. (2004). *Living beyond loss: Death in the family.* New York: W. W. Norton.

Chapter Nineteen

A Constant Resuscitation of Trauma
The Ties between Technology and Complicated Grief

Jason Barr

Complicated grief is an incredibly difficult concept to define, and try as they might, scientists, psychologists, doctors, and psychiatrists have wrestled with what exactly the term means. Complicated grief has been alternatively studied in parents who have lost children, people who have lost spouses or family members after long illnesses, people who have lost loved ones after a singular traumatic event such as an accident, and the friends and relatives of suicide victims. In other words, almost every conceivable manner of death can send someone down the path of complicated grief. The cause of death itself does not seem, necessarily, to matter to how those left behind begin and continue the grieving process. I argue, instead, that one of the determinants that merit examination in this new field is technology as a symptom or facilitator of complicated grief.

Much of the literature surrounding complicated grief attempts to understand who is more likely to go through the phenomenon. Essays ranging from studies concerning those with intellectual disabilities, certain personality types, and even "shattered worldviews" have all been identified as potential determinants for complicated grief. One aspect that has been overlooked, however, is the seeming access to the dead that many have through technology. More than ever, we can continue to "connect" to deceased friends and relatives through Twitter, Facebook, YouTube, and even online multiplayer games like Second Life. Mainstream technology—something as simple as a voicemail message—has the potential to spur, continue, or even exacerbate complicated grief.

It may sound clichéd, but everywhere we look, technology abounds. It chirps in our pockets, flashes bright colors all around us, even senses our presence or absence and reacts accordingly. News reports abound with a new trend: the ongoing preservation of departed loved ones through technological means. And I'm not talking about cryogenic freezing. Instead, people have found unique ways to seemingly circumvent the permanent nature of death.

Before the advent of digital technology, people used photographs, letters, and visits to graveyards as ways of maintaining contact with deceased loved ones. Augmenting these earlier practices are new waves of technology. As prices have dropped and devices have shrunk almost equally in size—but gained in processing power and the ability to store data—more and more people are finding ways to preserve sounds and images of their loved ones. Now, the deceased can be visited through video, online Web sites, and voicemail. Recently, in our household, the debate started to arise over our Nintendo Wii. Every Wii owner can make a cartoon-like "Mii" of themselves and their friends and family. Naturally, for the entertainment of the kids, we made Miis of everyone in our family, including the children's grandparents. But what do we do as the grandparents get older and eventually die? Should we allow the Mii character to continue a virtual afterlife, hitting monster home runs and flying airplanes around a resort island, or will the children (and we, for that matter) be overly upset by the image of our dearly departed relative—albeit in cartoon form—playing Frisbee golf?

It's a conundrum that has winnowed its way into the collective mindset, whether it is acknowledged or not. It's not just the young or technologically astute who face this problem. In 2008, the phone company Verizon did a fairly routine upgrade of 80-year-old pensioner Charles Whiting's phone service. Performing the upgrade required the deletion of any saved phone messages, however, and here's where the story got interesting. Whiting went to the press complaining that Verizon had deleted a phone message from his wife, Catherine, who had died in 2005. Claiming he listened to the message every day for comfort, Whiting demanded that Verizon do something, because "[n]ow they took her voice away." Eventually, after a round of media outrage, Verizon found the message in its archives and restored it to Charles Whiting's account. What was the message? I wondered. What did she say that was so profoundly touching that moved this elderly man to the somewhat radical notion of alerting the local press?

The message was actually a voicemail greeting. And all it contained was Charles's deceased wife saying her name: "Catherine Whiting" ("Lost voicemail," 2008).

Imagine, in this case of Charles Whiting, some small, cherished, probably less than five-second clip, was enough to grant comfort to someone on a daily basis. And, imagine, even more, that some small part of Catherine Whiting—just that small fragmented audio clip—was somehow still alive in the technological ether, a series of ones and zeros gallivanting about on Verizon's servers.

This isn't an isolated case, and, in actuality, such instances are becoming more and more frequent. A recent CNN profile of the deceased oil rig workers on the Deepwater Horizon oil platform—the one that exploded, killing 11 workers and spilling millions of barrels of oil into the Gulf of Mexico—revealed this same sort of cherishing of technological representations of the dead. In an article titled "'Daddy's in heaven': Rig victims' families share memories, mementos," a subsection titled "Listening to Daddy's Voice" reveals this somewhat heartbreaking passage:

> Sometimes, when their father's absence seems overwhelming, Shelley calls Jason's cell phone. She lets the kids listen to his familiar deep baritone, a message that lasts only seconds. "… I'll get back to ya …" The children tell him how much they love him, how much Daddy's missed. "It's just a way that we can hear his voice," Shelley says. (Drash 2010)

Like Catherine Whiting's ephemeral voice, this clip lasts only seconds. But is there a time to let go? Though these examples represent only the technological preservation of the disembodied voice of the deceased, Roger Rosenblatt (2010) wrote about a different phenomenon in his poignant memoir *Making Toast*. Throughout much of this memoir, which focuses primarily on the shift from grandparent back to parent when his daughter Amy dies suddenly, Rosenblatt fights hard to *not* listen to a recording of his deceased daughter's voice. During his struggles, it becomes readily apparent that many of the other family members and friends have listened to the message, possibly numerous times. The memoir is told in a series of vignettes as the newly-formed family goes through the holidays, getting ready for school, all of those little life moments that build into greater meaning over time. And then, with only pages to spare until the end, it is there. A transcript of Amy's voicemail, in italics. No introduction, no conclusion, no commentary attached to it. We are to assume that Rosenblatt has finally heard the voice of his daughter—who at this point in the narrative had been a few years deceased—but it is hard to say whether the act of listening to the message is hurtful or healing.

This form of potentially complicated grief has garnered more mainstream attention over the past few years. In a recent story arc of the popular AMC series *Breaking Bad*, a character named Jessie Pinkman loses his girlfriend to a heroin overdose as he, also passed out on heroin, sleeps beside her. For the next few episodes, Jessie's only movements and actions are to repeatedly call his girlfriend's phone number and listen to her voicemail greeting. It is only when her account is finally deleted that Jessie reluctantly begins to resume the regular habits of life. And in the British sci-fi series *Doctor Who*, an episode titled "Silence in the Library" briefly examines the psychological impact of "data ghosts," in which a person's consciousness continues autonomously in their technological devices for a brief period after their deaths.

When is this technological preservation damaging? Is it at all? Or does it create a lasting impact on someone's life as they attempt to interact with their lost friends and family? As a child of the late 1970s and 1980s, I'm frequently reminded of the *Puff the Magic Dragon* TV episode and song. I don't remember much about it, but I do remember little Jackie Paper leaving a deeply saddened Puff behind in Honah-Lee. The question becomes, are we now keeping our collective little Jackie Papers, our deepest friends, lovers, and confidants, artificially close to us in an effort to circumvent our sudden loneliness?

Of course, voicemail messages aren't the only method of sustaining the memories of the dead—they may even be among the worst methods, as the voice that is left behind is just that: a voice, disembodied, still somehow ghostly, still somehow not quite real.

Personal Tragedies and Technology

In the quest for a real resuscitation of the dead, people have begun to move toward social media, including Facebook and MySpace. Though I frequent Facebook throughout the day and sometimes share the mundane news of my life with a narrow set of friends and family, I was completely flabbergasted when I asked my students in one class how many of them visit with a dead person via Facebook. This has become such a popular trend that Facebook, in response, has created the concept of "memorial pages," places where a deceased person's profile is scrubbed of sensitive information and then reposted for their friends to visit at their leisure ("Facebook Memorial Sites," 2010). The question was asked somewhat in jest, yet, stone-faced, almost all of the 19 students in attendance that day raised their hands.

Curious, I prodded further. On Facebook, there are ways to write on a person's "wall," which usually takes the form of a vastly undersized e-mail. I asked the students how many of them not only visited the Facebook page, but also frequently posted to the person's wall. Around 12 of them raised their hands. When I asked what they were writing, if they wanted to share, some volunteered that they were simply writing "Happy Birthday," "Merry Christmas," or something of that nature. In later interviews, students elaborated a little more. One wrote to me that she shared

> some messages of some good times we shared and just saying i miss you and still think about you often [. . .] if something reminds me of him, ill go look at it. and i wrote on it the day of his death after the first and second year passed, and also on his birthday.

Another student wrote and told me that she, too, visited the Facebook page of a friend she had known for four years. Instead of sending messages, though, her view of Facebook appeared more utilitarian; she wrote that she "left pictures as requested by his parents. I have not left any messages," and that "I don't post anything; I just read what other people post."

Interestingly, neither student felt that visiting the Facebook page of a deceased person was traumatic or exacerbated their grieving; yet both shared that, especially in the early stages of grieving, they visited the deceased's memorial page 10 times a week or more.

One student, however, told me that she visited the site of a friend with whom she had just argued before the girl died in a car accident. At first, my student was crushed and left messages on the deceased friend's wall frequently—sometimes daily. As time progressed, however, she told the class that her visits tapered off, and she now visits the person's Facebook page only a few times a month.

This Facebook phenomenon, however, is no longer limited to just the young. A growing number of news articles shows that Facebook grieving is becoming common across all age groups. Calling Facebook memorial pages "living tombstones," *The Beaumont Enterprise* reporter Beth Rankin shares the story of Suzette Ratcliff, whose 19-year-old daughter, Rachel Clark, died in a car accident (Rankin, 2010). This article, like others, seems to overlook the potential for complicated grief, even among those being profiled. Though Rankin takes great care to quote a therapist and a funeral director about the supposed benefits of grieving online, Ratcliff appears to be wrestling with the notion. Almost a year after her daughter's death, Ratcliff "found herself engrossed, soaking up every video, every memory recounted publicly on Rachel's Facebook wall." Ratcliff continues, "I feel like I need everything that she was a part of. I need it [. . .] it makes some of the panic go away." Toward the end of the article, after discussing Ratcliff's Facebook visits and also her creation of a blog dedicated to her daughter, Rankin quotes Ratcliff again, who says, "Now I can't wait to get a message or a post on my wall. I see now how you can get caught up with it. I get it now." Ratcliff then reveals that visiting her daughter's Facebook page is part of an apparently stringent routine; her laptop rests on her nightstand, conveniently placed where she can frequently grieve online.

Another article discusses Erica Galbraith, who struggles with the loss of her 18-year-old son, Joshua. The article notes that it is 10 months after Joshua's death in a car accident, and that "his friends are still posting messages on his Facebook profile" ("Mourning," 2009). Like Beth Rankin, this unnamed journalist appears to unknowingly document factors that could lead to a greater complication of grief, including that Erica visits her son's Facebook tribute page "before dawn [at] 6 A.M. every day" ("Mourning," 2009).

Facebook's software is designed in such a way that the page will offer suggestions for people to "friend." Then, over time, users began to notice that the software was not only suggesting some deceased people as friends, but also telling users about the deceased person's birthdays and other information. Facebook spokeswoman Meredith Chin said, "It's a very sensitive topic, and, of course, seeing deceased friends pop up can be painful" (Wortham, 2010). No doubt. But what is interesting is the number of users who frequently continue to interact with the dead electronically, connecting with them via the magic of telephone wires and cable connections. And even though Facebook labels the process of seeing a dead person's page "painful," it hasn't stopped numerous people from creating memorial pages for their dead friends or family. The process has become so popular that Facebook even offers a form to fill out for those who would like to create or maintain a memorial page for someone who has died.

As I prodded my students about their Facebook-memorialized friends, I began to understand that this is simply a visit to the virtual cemetery for them. The older students in my class, however, were dismayed by the younger students' casual admission that they consistently interact with the dead. One student, the oldest in the class, accused the younger students of being exceptionally morbid, and suggested that they have become so used to interacting with their dead friends that they either can't heal the pain of the loss or have otherwise tricked themselves into thinking the person is alive. Then he told the students this story: It was the 1980s, and he and his friend were drunk and decided to go visit his friend's mother's grave. When they went to the cemetery, both of them were so drunk they couldn't orient themselves. After an hour or so of wandering around, his friend burst into uncontrollable sobbing, exhibiting drunken guilt over his inability to find his mother's grave and, in the words of my student, "give her respect."

"Now that," he told the class, "is true pain." The insinuation was that the Facebook-using young students were simply delaying their pain, or avoiding it altogether, creating a sanitized, unhelpful view of grief.

Interestingly, technology has thrown even this traditional process into confusion. For example, there is a Web site called World Wide Cemetery (www.cemetery.org), where families can post memorial tributes, poems, and photos in their growing database. The site's founder, Michael Kibbee, is "interred" on the main page. Visitors to the World Wide Cemetery can also leave virtual flowers for their loved ones—for a small fee. Other Web sites have followed World Wide Cemetery's lead, including Find A Grave (findagrave.com), Wild Rose Cemeteries (wildrosecemeteries.com), and Virtual Cemetery (virtualcemetery.org). There are even Web sites that now feature pet cemeteries (virtualpetcemetery.org), complete with user-uploaded essays, pictures, and poems ("We look forward to seeing you in Heaven" is an oft-repeated sentiment from owners to deceased pets).

With Facebook and, to a lesser extent, the virtual cemeteries, this grieving has changed dramatically, perhaps too dramatically for some. Now, it is possible to commune with the departed by visiting a Web page from the comfort of home, or by signing on to the page at a coffee shop or college computer lab. While on the page, one can post messages to the dead, view pictures or videos of them, and even communicate with mutual friends that one may never have met. But what about those who consistently visit the page out of a sense of guilt? Is technology helping or hurting them?

Technology, Complicated Grief, and National Tragedy

The explosions and the destruction of 9/11 were perceived as the endgame of technology for many people: Large skyscrapers, massive aircraft, numerous vehicles, cameras, camcorders, cell phones, and so on crowded the scene of both the Pentagon and New York City's World Trade Center Plaza. Americans had seen destructive force before; at the start of the Persian Gulf War, we tuned in to live wartime action as we would have a sitcom or drama. In the eerie green of night vision, the trails of missiles slammed into the outlines of nondescript buildings, all while the announcers and commentators provided real-time commentary. This process, unfortunately, would be repeated again, in the same country, during President George W. Bush's "Shock and Awe" campaign, also against Iraq. But these images were of people most of us had never met, people who existed only in our imaginations, if we dared to picture them running from the cruise missiles crisscrossing the sky, each of the weapons with tiny American flags painted on them.

From the moment something started to go wrong—that plane, was it a single prop or a jumbo jet? Did it really hit the tower on purpose?—technology governed our daily routines. Televisions and cable news channels bombarded us repeatedly with the same video frames over and over again, playing in slow motion, examined frame by frame, talking heads pausing only long enough for a commercial break (which, for once, provided respite), only to return again and again to the same themes: the planes hitting the World Trade Center, a massive, titanic technological explosion in which, at first, humans seemed to play only bit roles.

And then, the videos of people on the street as the towers collapsed, spewing toxic dust and debris in the air, the apocalyptic scenes of people picking through the rubble and calling for help. The technology, though, was endless, a facilitator in the recording of numerous moments: a doctor caught in the massive dust cloud; others just narrowly missing it as they dive into a nearby shop; people wandering the streets, coated in gray, calling for help, or loved ones, or both.

All of these scenes were recorded and replayed endlessly, pushing themselves into the collective American conscience. Unlike that other great American tragedy, the Japanese attack on Pearl Harbor, this event would be videotaped, photographed, recorded, and archived, ready to be relived practically on demand, causing a ceaseless cycle for anyone wanting to participate in the tragedy again. Two French filmmakers near the World Trade Center, Jules and Gedeon Naudet, turned the film into an on-the-ground, in-place documentary. With Pearl Harbor, all Americans have is grainy newsreel footage of partially sunken ships aflame. With 9/11, the documentary that would be released on DVD as *9/11: The Commemorative Filmmakers' Edition* (2002), viewers are not only at Ground Zero, but also inside the buildings, listening to the distant thumps of bodies, living or dead, hitting the pavement outside.

And then, in the days after 9/11, like a tide rolling back out to sea, the news cycle slowed, and the pictures of planes exploding abated, ever so briefly, as the camera lenses focused instead on the human loss. And here, we find grief memorialized and sustained by technology. In fact, it is here, I feel, that Americans discovered the power of technology (and media) to sustain the memory of the deceased.

What replaced the images of burning skyscrapers and dust- and rubble-strewn alien landscapes was the human element: long walls with pictures of loved ones pressed against almost any available blank space. In the confusing hours and days following the attacks, many people in New York City were without family members and were left with horrifying questions: did my spouse or brother or mother not come home because they perished in the attacks, or are they simply lost?

As a result, these walls became a form of communication. Citizens opened their doors for wandering folks who could not make it home on those first few days and, as such, these pictures of people's faces, coupled with information, and often, personal messages, became bulletins, announcing a lost relative to the rest of the world, and sometimes, sharing what would normally be private sentiments.

The resemblances, however, between Facebook's "wall" postings and the posters strewn across the walls of New York City in the days after September 11th are striking. "Please find my daddy," one says. Even with these resemblances, however, one great difference remains: on Facebook, a memorial posting can live forever (or at least until Facebook collapses). Yet, with the attacks, there are still millions of gigabytes of data preserved, most of it official, some of it personal. The huge amount of data floating in the electric ether is, and will be, preserved for many years to come. And yet, those most personal reflections seemed to have evaporated; our knowledge of the people associated with the tragedy has faded over time. As a result, as a memorial and new skyline arises out of the remains of the World Trade Center, most people in America seem to have moved on.

Even so, the Smithsonian Museum of American History soldiers on, and in a listing on their Web site, reveals a complete list of over 130 objects that have entered the museum's archives ("September 11: Bearing witness," n.d.). Some of the items found and stored, however, seem to be there simply because they could be: Whatever personal meaning that would be attached to them is mostly lost to the average viewer. A squeegee handle, some patriotic t-shirts, and some silkscreen prints have taken their place among the more personal posters and personal artifacts: cell phones, wallets, melted coins. People can even upload their own memories of the event. *Found*, a popular underground magazine that focuses on "the best lost, tossed, and forgotten items from around the world," has an ongoing archive online of "September 11th Finds" (see http://foundmagazine.com/tag/911/). Like the Smithsonian's choices, the site reprints an old invoice; a few memos from businesses; and some notes, some discussing the day's events, others not.

And yet, with 9/11, we see the nascent beginnings of the need to always remember, to never forget any singular moment, in an almost perverse wish to continue revisiting every detail, no matter how minor, of the event. Even as the staring faces plastered across billboards across New York City fade away and are consigned to the dustbins of museum archives, George Mason University has partnered with the City University of New York; they continue to collect information in the form of digital images and audio. The September 11 Digital Archive, as it has come to be called, not only maintains photographs and audio recollections of the event, but also contains copies of e-mails and other documents. Any researcher can access these archives; some of them have been made available online.

This user-friendly, on-demand digitization, however, can exacerbate trauma. Google, the owner of YouTube, attempted to perform an April Fool's joke on its user by allowing them to click on a "1911" button, which ostensibly showed how the 9/11 video would have looked in 1911: the video would become sepia toned, and jaunty ragtime music would play in the background. Unfortunately, Google found itself in the middle of a controversy, as many people were not amused by the idea that they could replay videos of the World Trade Center collapsing or other tragic events, such as the tsunami that struck Japan or the Rodney King beating. Google moved quickly to remove the 1911 button from certain videos, but by then, the inappropriate videos had done their damage. As the tech Web site Gawker dryly noted, "This joke is not appropriate for all videos" ("YouTube did not think," 2011).

In addition, there are numerous images of the World Trade Center collapse that can be found via a Google Images search that are tasteless and most likely traumatizing to those who see them. One set of images, particularly popular on the message boards of Web site news aggregators like Fark, shows professional wrestler Hulk Hogan, manipulated to be supersized, kicking the towers over and flexing his muscles in the rubbage as terrified people run from the site.

The massacre at Virginia Tech is a more contemporary example that features, in just a few brief years, a completely new and technologically advanced form of grieving. The shootings, orchestrated on April 16, 2007, by a mentally ill student named Seung-Hui Cho, cost 32 students and professors their lives. From the moments the massacre ended, however, the university was moving to create permanent memorials, both brick and mortar and virtual.

Brent Jesiek and Jeremy Hunsinger (2008) spoke at length about the April 16th digital archives in the article "The April 16 Archive: Collecting and Preserving Memories of the Virginia Tech Tragedy." They explain that the ultimate goal of the archive is to create "the digitization of memory, [and] the inscription of shared grief." Ultimately, the goal of the archive is to "collect the many digital artifacts qua memories" (p. 192) that came into existence after the massacre.

Interestingly, Jesiek and Hunsinger (2008) acknowledged the potential benefits of creating a digital archive. Some of them are practical: After all, a physical archive would require space and huge amounts of expenditure. Others, however, seem to indicate a capacity for complicating grief. In the few months after the shootings, the archive had already collected more than 60,000 items. Jesiek and Hunsinger acknowledge the problem with containing so much painful memory in one place; they go to great pains to argue that the memories and the archive itself would not be "machinic" memory that restricts thoughts and ideas, but instead is something else, which provides "a sense of space and time as plural, yet shared" (p. 192).

The difference is subtle, and Jesiek and Hunsinger (2008), ironically, are not immune to the effects of receiving so much memory. As conduits for the digitization of these various items, Jesiek and Hunsinger hoped, in one poignant passage, that

> By externalizing those parts of the event into the archive, the community assigns it a new register, a public register, and in that they might allow themselves to forget. Public memory projects enable forgetting through processes of memorialization, and forgetting is important for identity creation and continued existence. (pp. 194–195)

Essentially, Jesiek and Hunsinger hoped that digitizing and archiving memories and artifacts would lead to a letting go of grief. Unfortunately, the opposite could be true, as the phenomenon of complicated grief must be considered.

And here, we have a bit of a conundrum: The digitized items, which, though numbering in the tens of thousands, still represent only a small fraction of the complete materials relating to the event. Even despite their protestations to the contrary, the overwhelming nature of many of these artifacts took their toll on Jesiek and Hunsinger, who added that

> Our memory bank is located on Virginia Tech's Blacksburg campus, which largely eliminated the buffer between the immediate memories of the workers and the materials being submitted. Many of us responded by developing our own coping strategies—such as skimming text, working quickly, taking frequent breaks, playing music in the background—to help keep us from getting too tangled in the mass of memories that we encountered through our work. (p. 200)

Jesiek and Hunsinger seem to imply that technology reduces rather than complicates grief, but the very process they engaged in made their own lives and their work all the more difficult. Indeed, sifting through the remnants of these personalized archives and digitizing these memories instead seems to amplify grief rather than reduce it. The technology creates what could previously only be imagined. Had the tragedy occurred 20 years ago, around the time of the Columbine massacre, the only people who would have experienced the sorrowful ramifications of a personal note left at a makeshift shrine would have been the person who placed it there, and those that would have had the motivation to travel to the site. The Virginia Tech archive, however, now makes grief readily accessible to all those who seek it out. Though a majority of those who visit the archive Web site will no doubt encounter some sorrow at the items pictured, the question remains for those who are more deeply affected by the tragedy: the faculty, staff, and family members of those killed. A rudimentary browse through the site reveals a heartfelt typed letter to Erin Peterson; pictures of professor Liviu Librescu's funeral; and a handwritten letter to Michael Pohle, Jr., that reads, in part, "This letter is in away (sic) is a goodbye. It is a goodbye to the memorial I place it on." The letter is attached to Pohle's newspaper obituary. The author most likely did not know that their goodbye was never really a goodbye, but became a moment frozen in time and digitized for others to see.

In addition to the digital archive, there is also a Second Life memorial intended to honor the victims of the shootings. Second Life, of course, is a massive multiplayer online game, in which players create an avatar and wander about, meeting other avatars. Two videos of the Second Life Virginia Tech Memorial are posted online. One of them, posted by user BartHeart, was posted on the first anniversary of the shootings. The video is simple: It merely shows the viewer what the memorial entails: pictures of the deceased, screen captures of news articles about the shooting an eternal flame, and, most disturbingly, a statue that appears to weep blood (though it is possible the color is a close approximation to the Virginia Tech team color known as Chicago Maroon). The video, according to the description, is

> The VT Memorial in Second Life® on the sim "Memorial Park" is a quite[sic], peaceful place to remember those that were lost in the Virginia Tech tragedy. We remember those that lost their life last year on April 16th in the Virginia Tech tragedy. As we remember them everyday with our in world memorial on the sim of "Memorial Park". [sic]

Another video was posted by user WadaTripp less than a month after the massacre. In this video, the avatar visits the memorial (here, it is important to note that the Second Life memorial was created within three weeks). The video, bookended by images of the real Virginia Tech campus and memorials, shows the avatar walking around the memorial and finally bowing before the image of Dr. Liviu Librescu, who, according to WadaTripp, taught the user electrical engineering. On the surface, the video appears to be an appropriate measure of grief, even with such scarce details. But, a closer examination of the video reveals facets of the potentiality of complicated grief. After all, even though the video is three minutes long, the adding of a slideshow, a soundtrack, and even the recording of the Second Life avatar's visits, coupled with the editing of the video, and finally, the uploading of the video to YouTube, indicates several hours worth of effort merely to show a virtual person appearing at a virtual memorial and paying their virtual respects. Essentially, since the tragedy, people have set aside countless hours not only visiting the virtual memorial, but also creating it and adding their own materials to the site.

Facebook's debut didn't come until almost three years after the September 11 attacks; its user count started at a relatively puny million users by the end of 2004. By the start of 2010, Facebook had expanded to almost 450 million users. As the years have progressed, there has been a growing desire for technology, often for people to appear popular or trendy. As the prices of devices ranging from DVD players to MP3 players, cell phones, cameras, and camcorders have dropped and the devices have become even more user-friendly and miniaturized, almost every available human action can be recorded and transmitted. A quick browse through Twitter, for instance, the popular messaging service through which you can send text messages to all of your followers, shows quick snippets of normally mundane daily activity, now important enough to share: eating, traveling—and, in some disturbing cases, even defecating. And, even more, these interactions are recorded and repeated ad infinitum.

In other words, social media is becoming a large portion of the fabric of American society. Everything potentially can be shared, and it is little wonder that the grieving process is something that appears on Facebook or MySpace. What psychiatrists and psychologists need to examine, however, is the impact of online grieving on what would be considered a "normal" grief process. Is it acceptable, for instance, to spend a large amount of time each day on the Facebook page of the deceased? At what point in time does it become too much, and at what point in time have the visits moved from normal to, instead, a complication to the grieving process? "Nobody knows what's appropriate," says cultural critic Hal Niedzviecki, and this is a true statement. It is time now to examine how technology can potentially impact the grieving process; after all, as funeral director Tom Broussard (as cited in Rankin, 2010) pointed out, "We are not meant as human beings to carry grief infinitely forward (p. 3)."

References

Drash, W. (2010, August 1). *"Daddy's in heaven": Rig victims' families share memories, mementos.* Retrieved from http://www.cnn.com/2010/US/07/29/rig.victim.families/index.html

Facebook memorial sites taking hold. (2010, February 4). Retrieved from http://www.cbsnews.com/2100-501366_162-6172718.html

Hanlon, J., & Naudet, J. (Directors). (2002). *9/11: The commemorative filmmaker's edition.* United States: Columbia.

Jesiek, B. K., & Hunsinger, J. (2008). The April 16 archive: Collecting and preserving memories of the Virginia Tech tragedy. In B. Agger (Ed.), *There is a gunman on campus: Tragedy and terror at Virginia Tech* (pp. 185–206). Lanham, MD: Rowman & Littlefield.

Lost voicemail of man's dead wife restored by phone company. (2008, March 19). Retrieved from http://www.foxnews.com/story/0,2933,338992,00.html

Mourning in cyberspace. (2009, December 4). Retrieved from http://tvnz.co.nz/technology-news/mourning-in-cyberspace-3226488

Rankin, B. (2010, August 17). Loss and Facebook: How media affects grief. *Beaumont Enterprise.* Retrieved from http://www.beaumontenterprise.com/news/article/Loss-and-Facebook-How-social-media-affects-grief-729491.php

Rosenblatt, R. (2010). *Making toast.* New York: HarperCollins.

September 11: Bearing witness to history. (n.d.). Retrieved from http://americanhistory.si.edu/september11/

Wortham, J. (2010, July 17). *As Facebook users die, ghosts reach out.* Retrieved from http://www.nytimes.com/2010/07/18/technology/18death.html?_r=0

YouTube did not think through its April Fool's joke. (2011, April 1). Retrieved from http://gawker.com/5788078/youtube-did-not-think-through-its-april-fools-joke

Chapter Twenty

The Silent Grief of Women
An Emptying of the Soul

Annette Anderson-Engler

Introduction

The purpose of this chapter is to explore the process of grief among women. Women, as opposed to men, tend to linger in the past, remembering specific life events, whereas men often find ways of moving forward. According to Overbeck (2001), as parents, men and women process grief quite differently. Overbeck determined that a father who has lost a child will grieve for approximately six months, whereas a mother will continue to experience deep feelings of loss for as long as two years.

This distinction in how men and women grieve may stem from the idea of letting go and letting in. In other words, women may prefer to "empty out," even if they feel an unexplainable void, whereas men tend to hold onto their deep feelings of pain and internalize their suffering by simply not talking about it (Harper, 2001). Men are more apt to adapt to societal assumptions, which involve insensitive words such as "just get over it." Thus, they tend to deal with feelings of grief more privately. Most men prefer to avoid the social/public (societal) criticism associated with continuous grieving (Moules, Simonson, Prins, Angus, & Bell, 2004).

Martin and Doka (1999) asserted that although gender is a part of how we grieve, it does not always determine the pattern of grief. In other words, the grief process, whether among males or females, may be determined more by cultural identity and how well we are able to regulate our emotions. Martin and Doka suggested that women grieve intuitively, through feelings, crying, prolonged confusion, physical exhaustion, and anxiety, whereas men grieve instrumentally, through thinking rather than feeling, and problem solving, with only brief periods of cognitive dysfunction.

Patterns of grief among women may not be more problematic than those among men. However, the grieving process has a tendency to last longer in certain women, such as a mother who has just lost a young child. Studies have indicated that women have more difficulty dealing with and making sense out of feelings of loss. Some have reported taking prescribed medication for anxiety and depression in order to lesson feelings of grief (Raphael, Taylor, & McAndrew, 2007).

Moules et al. (2004) suggested that caregivers, especially nurses, need to allow for a fuller grieving process in their clinical work. In other words, clinical professionals should not focus primarily on helping clients get over, resolve, or end their grief but should encourage them to discover healthy ways to deal with deep, emotional suffering and sorrow. According to Moules et al., it is important "to make room for a relationship with grief that is livable, acceptable, creative and for a life that may be richer for its presence" (p. 100).

Hence, this begs the question of why women tend to suffer longer from the acute feelings of grief. In what ways do women actually grieve, and how can grieving women teach others about the complexities of grief? These and other similar questions are discussed in this chapter.

> For the beautiful child I was, I grieve. For the loss and betrayal of my innocence, I grieve. For the butterflies I never chased, for the softballs I never hit … for the little child who didn't enjoy life … for the death of my spirit, for all these things, I grieve—Adult survivor of childhood sexual abuse (Sofka, 1999 p. 125)

Although both men and women experience deep emotional grief, it is believed, in certain societies, that women and men do not process grief in the same way. In western cultures, boys are taught to abandon their emotions as they mature. They are taught that to express deep emotions, especially in public, is a sign of weakness and is therefore frowned upon. When examining the process of grief and all its complexities, it is also important to examine cultural identity. In many ways, men process grief by "doing," whereas women process grief by "being." In other words, women may oftentimes experience grief on a deeper, more intense level because they sit with feelings of sorrow longer. Traditionally, it is acceptable for women to linger in the residuals of grief and for men to get on with their lives.

Grief, which is sometimes a lifelong experience, can be viewed as the inability to resolve issues regarding the loss of a loved one, and in a large sense, a loss sense of self. Moules et al. (2004) suggested that there is a difference between grief and sorrow, and that sorrow resides inside of grief in the form of a deep sadness. Therefore, grief contains sorrow to the point where one struggles with having to relinquish the idea of loss itself. Intense sorrow, according to Moules et al., can end over time, but intense grief remains and is continuously being re-experienced throughout one's life. According to these authors, "In many ways, one could argue that loss becomes a part of our biological structure in the shape of grief" (p. 100).

The Silent Voice of Grief among Women

Grief has a voice that cannot always be heard among the smoldering ashes of sorrow—that sense of longing, a deep void that cannot be filled. Women in particular harbor unexpressed feelings of grief through physical touch, gestures, and inaudible expressions. This is especially true for women dealing with the loss or removal of a child from the home. For instance, women who are heads of households may experience the socioeconomic powerlessness often associated with not being able to care for their children. While working as a social worker for the department of child protective services, I once witnessed the removal of three small children from their single-parent mother. Within moments of the removal, the mother collapsed on the floor into a fetal position, trembling and shaking. Her grief had become so unbearable that she was unable to stand up or speak.

Some women who are unable to fully articulate feelings of deep loss often wander around in a dark place of silence not being able to recount any part of the traumatic event. These women feel like strangers to their own emotional experiences of suffering.

Unspoken grief place women at greater psychological risk due to the social and economic disparity that exists between women and men. In some cases, women who experience overwhelming feelings of grief fear that any expression of heightened emotional distress will make them more vulnerable to the social welfare system, which may deem them emotionally incompetent.

Understanding complexities of grief among women will enable doctors and mental health professionals to help women navigate more consciously through the grief process. This process can be achieved by helping women develop better ways to manage grief so that they may live a more productive life.

Displaced Grief: *The Un-telling*

Displaced grief is when one is unable to fully describe or articulate feelings of deep emotional loss. When grief becomes displaced, it is because painful stories have not been shared. These stories often are carried in the pockets of one's memories, tucked away in a drawer, pushed back behind dusty books on a broken shelf, always hidden somewhere in the subconscious mind. Displaced grief begs the questions: What feelings can you observe on the face of a grieving woman? What is hiding behind her eyes? What is her story of grief all about? Talking about painful events can often help make sense of the world we live in. Stories provide ways to articulate sorrowful emotions. For women, stories allow them to process grief by recalling episodes in their lives when they felt most lost and alone.

According to Lee (1997), women give personal meaning to their lives by sharing stories about painful events. As women share self-narratives, Lee asserted, they clearly identify social, cultural, and gender differences. Women share their stories differently from men in that women do not tend to speak or expound about the events in their lives in a linear, chronological fashion. Instead, women tend to frame their stories "episodically," relating to the specific occurring and reoccurring themes surrounding their lived experiences. Episodic narratives actually frame the social and personal identity of women, helping them to better articulate difficult points throughout their lives (Riessman-Kohler, 1987).

Narratives about important events can often be written, painted, or sung through artful expression. The use of artistic expression can be a viable outlet for women who find it difficult to articulate their grief process. Sofka (1999) referred to Alice Miller's essay describing the importance of integrating artwork as a way to "allow a client to actively channel energy into the creation of a tangible object to express an abstract idea or 'invisible' emotion" (p. 139). Hence, Sofka asserts that female survivors are more apt to release deep feelings of emotional loss through art.

Expressive art can be an important part of the grieving process for women. Raphael et al. (2007) have determined that women who have experienced sexual abuse and domestic violence might share a sense of grief through self-failure and the rejection of themselves by others. This leads to a sense of worthlessness and shame, which is linked to psychological maladjustment.

Grief is a reoccurring emotion that cannot be measured by space and time. It can surface at any time and place without any conscious awareness of its process. Through episodes of grief, women struggle to measure meaningful events from moment to moment. Thus, grief becomes a place of longing where harboring feelings of deep sorrow seems more meaningful and more sacred somehow. Hence, for women grief can be a silent process of unspoken emotion and deep pain that can linger in irretrievable parts of their memory.

Roaming in a Dark Place:
The Disbelief of Grief

Coming to terms with the loss of a loved one is not easy. The sting of loss can leave the heart dazed in a dismal feeling of unconscious awareness that something permanent has happened that has altered one's life forever.

Women who experience intensified feelings of grief are at a higher risk of developing physical and mental health problems. This is especially true for women who have lost a child as the result of infant death or miscarriage. It is believed that women who have experienced loss under these specific conditions are among those most affected by the grieving process and are more susceptible to experiencing prolonged grief (Kersting & Kroker, 2010).

According to Stroebe (2010), one of the distinguishing factors between how men and women grieve is that men are more affected by the loss of a partner, whereas women are more affected by the loss of a child, thus putting mothers at greater risk for complicated grief than fathers. Women who grieve roam in the dark, indistinguishable places, searching for both an exit from and entry into something familiar. The disbelief of grief can become internalized and thus affect the mental and physical well-being of women. Such grief may be described as a feeling of moving from the last place where you saw, heard, felt, or touched memories of a loved one so you can create a vacant place where your loved one cannot return to say good-bye.

Weeping from Within

The weeping from within among women can often be observed through their physical, inaudible expressions of grief. This can often be seen behind tear-filled eyes, quivering of the lips, the cradling of the head in the palm of open hands, and the grasping at the abdomen as if to hold in the intestinal innards of one's past. There are also outward appearances of grief such as buckling of the knees; clinching of toes; collapsing upon a cold, hard floor and just lying there.

Grief among men is described as having distinguishable differences from that of women. Harper (2001) refers to the work of Carol Staudacher on identifying four specific ways that men grieve: (1) silent, (2) secret grief, (3) physical and legal action, and (4) becoming immersed in activity. Because they are distinct from women, some men may not experience the bodily weeping identified in women. Unlike women, men may need to process grief in a more controlled fashion so that they do not lose themselves in the deep, uncontrollable emotion, which can sometimes become an inevitable part of the penetrating feelings of grief.

The Emptying Out: A Dry Heave

The Bellowing of Emotional Pain

For women, there is often an "emptying out" process associated with grieving. An emotional reflux, the toxicity of sorrow erupts deeply from within and bellows out. Women travail in birth as well as in death. They linger in places of ambiguity where they can no longer find their own voice. The travail of death and/or loss are indescribable emotions where thoughts outrace the mind's ability to think and rest. Piercing images begin to flood their minds with thoughts of what was and what will never again be. The fearful reality that tomorrow will not come today as it did yesterday. Death has beckoned to a loved one, and he has answered without consent. Then there is a wailing; a physical numbness; a slow, shallow burning that stirs from the inside where even hope cannot be retrieved.

Letting Go While Holding On

> *"I took off my rings and put them away."* Woman who lost her husband.
> —Moules et al., 2004

Moules et al. (2004) suggested that there is an underlying psychologically based assumption that learning how to grieve appropriately means learning how to say good-bye. Moules et al. attribute this theory to the early work of Sigmund Freud. According to Moules et al., "the idea of severing bonds and forming new attachments has stubbornly tethered itself to many grief models" (p. 101).

Letting go is believed to be an invaluable part of processing grief. Women are especially encouraged to embrace grief and learn ways to move forward. Yet, for many women who grieve, letting go can only be done by holding on. Relinquishing memories makes grieving more difficult. The expectation that this should be done makes women feel more separate from their losses and more connected to their grief. For women, loss must be inhaled naturally and not forced upon them as if they no longer had control over their ability to breathe in and out. Women need to know that it is okay to hold on to what was lost even when it no longer *seems* visible to others. It is through holding on that the letting-go process can occur. Letting go is often associated with "giving up," or ridding yourself of what was once yours. This only complicates the grief process, making it more turbulent and often fearful.

Grief: *A Healing Balm*

Grief hurts as well as heals, but in healing, grief must be understood as soothing oil to the wounds that have scarred the soul. Grief can be seen as healing if one is able to talk about it, feel it, and experience it over time and in her own way.

"When my grandmother died, I thought I would lose her but I didn't—I became more like her every day, so I did not lose her at all."—Family member (Moules et al., 2004, p. 101).

Societal pressures for women to heal only deepen the wound and lengthen recovery. Internal physical wounds are given time to heal and will often heal better if left undisturbed by the tampering of outside influence. Grief, like any other wound, may heal through the natural course of time. This cannot always be determined because life's circumstances may alter the grief process. For women, it is necessary to take a closer look at what is going on in their lives. Many women are raising families and suffer from an absence of nurturing relationships. When grief strikes at the heart of these women, it becomes the one last destructive thing in their lives. If women are allowed to process grief alone or in the company of a small group of other women, the healing balm of acceptance will begin to occur.

Dismembered Grief: The Reconstruction of Self

Ambiguity of Human Loss

Human loss entails a great deal of suffering. After all, how can we fully understand what it means to feel loss and to become lost in the midst of grief? The ambiguity of human suffering is something women have learned to live with. The loss of a child, spouse, parent, or sibling is often felt or experienced differently in women. Historically, women have been taught to endure long

periods of grief through childbirth and loss. Women as caregivers are culturally conditioned to be receptive of empathy and compassion and thus are
more likely to grieve the same way. Grief for some women is an integral part
of their cultural identity, especially in a matriarchal society.

Grief and Cultural Identity

According to Raphael et al. (2007), "evidence suggests that women's grief
is more intense, devastating and prolonged—seemingly un-ending" (p. 18).
Women who experience loss, specifically violent loss, are more at risk of
becoming stigmatized and discriminated against because they often do not
have the necessary resources to take care of themselves and their children.
Many of these women find they must endure extreme hardship for the sake
of their families and thus continue to face society's perception of social and
cultural worth as widows (Raphael et al., 2007).

Grief among various women may be processed differently. Women who
have suffered or have seen suffering as a daily part of life may grieve more
quietly than those who are not accustomed to experiencing suffering. It is
not unusual to see women who live in the grief cycle singing, praying, or
even sharing laughter while grieving. For some of these women, loss is a
necessary part of life; it is how they learn to move forward. It is not the end
of something, but rather its beginning. It is how they make sense out of what
has happened and how they make meaning of their lives. For some women,
to abandon the grief process would mean to suffocate their memories of
what has been lost and leave themselves in a valley of hopelessness. For
others, the grieving process may mean silence where there is an internal and
external restfulness, allowing them to linger without turbulent thoughts and
feelings of unrest.

Discovering ways that women grieve may help us better understand
the many complexities of the grieving process. In other words, we must
always take into account the distinct expressions of grief among genders.
Rosenblatt, Walsh, and Jackson (1976) conducted a study which indicated
that although there was little difference in the expectancy of crying between
men and women, women were allowed to express their grief more openly
and thus more fully.

The Peace to Release: *Permission to Grieve*

> *There is no love without loss. And where there is loss, there is grief.*
> —Anderson, 2010, p. 127

Both men and women often will deny the grief process of the other in order to feel some sense of control over the other person's pain. It is believed that men are taught early to deny their grief and simply not acknowledge painful feelings of grief. The denial of grief in men is often attributed to masculinity. Moules et al. (2004) suggested, "To talk about the sadness means to fall apart, to give voice and space would make it worse.... visible grief is an unhealthy grief and to make room for grief would be allowing it to take over altogether" (p. 102). Consequently, women are taught to freely express feelings of grief both privately and publicly. However, men are often taken aback by such overwhelming emotions and, thus, fear ways to respond to a woman's way of grieving (Anderson, 2010).

For women, the grief process is intrinsically linked to feelings of social acceptance, personal value, and self worth. Through unexpressed grief, silent, painful memories lay strewn across the floor, propelled by the winds of grief. Grief then becomes a self-deprecating process in which deep feelings of loss and total abandonment reside. When women disallow themselves to grieve, they also deny its gift of healing and spiritual restoration. Unexpressed grief becomes an encapsulated tomb of emotional trauma, lined with stolen dreams.

Disenfranchised Grief

Societal norms imply that loss should be dealt with over a reasonable amount of time, that emotions should resume their manageable state, and that conversations about loss should be dismissed. Disenfranchised grief occurs when society fails to acknowledge the grieving process. According to Doka (1989), if society does not recognize or validate that a loss has occurred, especially the loss of a child to a birthmother, grief becomes disenfranchised. Doka asserts that women who lose or give up their children at birth become "incapable" of fully grieving when the loss is unrecognized by others.

For many women, grief cannot be processed without permission, whether it is given by others or by themselves. There must be a way to expel deep feelings of pain, a way to share stories of grief by recalling memories, thoughts, and ideas. Granting permission provides women with the peace to release the harboring of pain, which cannot be fully endured. Such permission allows one to remain at the center of grief for a while. If allowed to walk through the difficulties of one's own pain, healing will happen over the natural course of time.

Doka (2002) asserted that women, particularly birthmothers, have difficulty letting go of intense expressions of grief, and thus the emotions become so intense that the complexity of grief is heightened and becomes disenfranchised. As a result, asserts Doka, these women will continue to experience acute problems in dealing with future losses. Thus, women are especially encouraged to find ways to release embedded feelings of grief.

Grief: *The Uninvited Houseguest*

Developing grief research defines grief metaphorically as an uninvited houseguest which Moules et al. (2004) suggested "arrives without invitation and remains in such a way that it touches all aspects of one's life, family, relationships and health" (p. 104). Grief in this aspect is described as being intrusive and difficult to either accommodate or rid oneself of. Moules et al. suggested that such grief sneaks into various "rooms" of our lives when we are most vulnerable or unaware. Eventually, we will become more tolerant of such intrusion by learning to live with unsolicited memories of loss. The uninvited guest provides a way of maintaining a conscious awareness of a person who is no longer a physical part of our lives. "Death does not mean the end of a relationship, but a change in the relationship" (Moules et al., 2004, p. 104).

The uninvited houseguest named grief may be especially problematic for women who are caregivers, responsible for clearing out the room and cupboards after the death of a child, or closets filled with clothes after the death of a partner. In some instances, many women may feel that it is easier to develop ways to live with, rather than without, feelings of loss. For some women, memories may be a source of comfort throughout the grieving process. Memories can represent not only feelings of "I didn't forget," but also "I will always remember" when others have forgotten. In other words, coming to terms with loss may simply mean coming to terms with oneself in relation to loss. It may mean not losing the things one can hold on to such as pictures, memorabilia, letters and other things that symbolize the life, rather than death, of loved ones. Forgetting or "getting over it" may not be a viable way to process grief for some women, but it may symbolize an emotional burial of life events, which still live and breathe inside one's memories.

Resolving Grief and Coming to Peace with Loss . . . Is it Possible?

Moules et al. (2004) asked, "Is resolution of deep grief possible?" (p. 102).

> When resolution is understood as the ending of something and when it is evaluated by the evidence of the absence of feelings of grief, then, as grief persists over time, people are subjected to a continual reminder they are not

able to complete the process in a competent way ... resolution may not be possible if you consider it as the absence of grief; but that there are other aspects of grief that are not all about suffering. Therefore, they will have good times again ... futures do not need to be tainted (Moules et al., 2004, p. 102).

For some women, the peace to release feelings of grief may mean forgiveness and reconciliation. For many women, forgiveness may simply be the ability to say, "I give myself permission to be invited to live in peace and am now able to reconcile with what I cannot go back and fix, but that's okay." The more a woman is able to access that peaceful place in her life, the better she will be able to process the cycle of grief. Without the peace to release, the complexity of grief among women becomes more mysterious, distant, and more inarticulate.

"*Grief does not need to disappear to resolve*" (Moules et al., 2004, p. 103). Grief can be defined as a "mapless" journey, allowing a deep, painful process to take its own shape in the form of each unique experience (Moules et al., 2004, p. 103). At the point in which loss occurs, women often feel the need to remember rather than forget. It is through a mixture of memories, anger, pain, sorrow, and blame that the reality of loss becomes more visible. Suddenly, the burden that comes with trying to make sense out of how we grieve begins to dissipate, and there are feelings of resolve and hope.

Conclusion

Understanding the process of grief carries with it the ambiguity of the emotional, social, and psychological meaning of one's internal and external worlds. It involves listening, interpreting, and reinterpreting the lived experiences of those most affected by deep sorrow and irretrievable loss. Grief in women becomes an integral part of their social and personal identity. Through shared stories, women are able to validate their grief by giving meaning to the idea of suffering loss. Some women share similarities with how men grieve in terms of silence. However, the internal sounds in women are often inaudible moaning, bellowing, and echoing of sorrow. Healing for women may come through allowing themselves permission to grieve without losing their sense of personal value and self-worth.

Finally, grief endured alone becomes an internalized disease of interminable feelings of loss that neither men nor women can fully endure. Coming to terms with loss does not mean losing oneself but finding the parts that, through overwhelming sorrow, have become embodied in the functioning of everyday life. This is especially true for women who, through death, have lost children and partners, yet have not found ways to navigate through the turmoil of grief. Resolution may not always be possible; peace may not always be attainable; but hope, through clinicians, medical workers, and family support, can be achievable.

References

Anderson, H. (2010, August). Common, grief, complex grieving. *Pastoral Psychology, 59,* 127–136.

Doka, K. J. (Ed.). (1989). *Disenfranchised grief: Recognizing hidden sorrow.* New York: Lexington Books.

Doka, K. J. (Ed.). (2002). *Disenfranchised grief: New directions, challenges, and strategies for practice.* Champaign, IL: Research Press.

Harper, J. M. (2001). *Grief and gender differences: Men and grief.* Retrieved from http://griefnet.org/library/griefgender.html

Kersting, A., & Kroker, K. (2010). Prolonged grief as a distinct disorder, specifically affecting female health. *Archives of Women's Mental Health, 13,* 27–28.

Lee, J. (1997). Women re-authoring their lives through feminist narrative. *Women and Therapy, 20*(3), 1–22.

Martin, T., & Doka, K. J. (1999). *Men don't cry, women do: Transcending gender stereotypes of grief.* Philadelphia: Taylor & Francis.

Moules, N. J., Simonson, K., Prins, M., Angus, P., & Bell, M. (2004, February). Making room for grief: Walking backwards and living forward. *Nursing Inquiry, 11,* 99–107.

Overbeck, B. (2001). *She cries—He sighs: Grief and gender differences.* Retrieved from http://griefnet.org/library/griefgender.html

Raphael, B., Taylor, M., & McAndrew, V. (2007, October). Women, catastrophe and mental health. *Royal Australian and New Zealand College of Psychiatrists, 42,* 13–23.

Riessman-Kohler, C. (1987). When gender is not enough: Women interviewing women. *Gender and Society, 1,* 172–207.

Rosenblatt, P., Walsh, R., & Jackson, D. (1976). *Grief and mourning in crosscultural perspective.* Washington, DC: HRAF Press.

Sofka, C. (1999, June). For the butterflies I never chased, I grieve: Incorporating grief and loss issues in treatment with survivors of childhood sexual abuse. *Journal of Personal and Interpersonal Loss, 4,* 125–148.

Stroebe, M. S. (2010, June). Bereavement in family context: Coping with the loss of a loved one. *Family Science, 1,* 144–151.

Part 6

Concluding Thoughts

The final chapter of this book, quite appropriately, is a concluding one reflecting on this anthology in its entirety. John Harvey does a superb job of highlighting the key themes of these readings (chapter 21). In fact, many of these points have been enunciated in some of my earlier commentaries throughout this book; for instance, that all grief is complicated to some degree and the notion of "closure" is somewhat absurd. Though Harvey concedes that some grief may be more severe, he adds that individuals often experience a "pile-up of losses," whereby one's grief is often a defining feature of one's existence. Harvey also makes it clear that loss and grief need to be understood within the larger social, cultural, and historical contexts of one's life. He also points out that sometimes grief reactions that seem illogical to some are perfectly sound to others.

Consistent with many of the chapters in this anthology, Harvey clearly argues that the writing and telling of one's stories of grief can provide psychological benefits to both survivors and outside readers. Perhaps this may be the greatest clarion call to those who hold some concern as to whether it is appropriate to view complicated grief as a disorder. By doing so, we may risk losing the potential for healing to occur through the stories told by those who are grieving. All are probably in agreement that no one should unduly suffer in the wake of loss and grief. The debate will likely continue as to the most effective ways to cope with serious grief. But again, as Harvey artfully contends, all of these stories highlight how the writing and sharing of one's grief are a path to such healing.

Chapter Twenty-One

Concluding Thoughts

John H. Harvey

In this collection, Eric Miller has done a great service to the field of loss and trauma by assembling an accomplished group of analysts who collectively and essentially hold up a mirror for the reader to behold. What the mirror shows is the complex web of feelings, thoughts, and behaviors that make up the phenomena of loss and complicated grief—phenomena that each human must confront.

Miller's technique of soliciting contributors who work and write in the area of bereavement either as scholars or practitioners, or both, via the Web, and who are willing to tell their own stories of complicated grief, is indeed unique. This technique has a number of advantages for future research on this and related topics. It can produce a large number of proposals, and as can be seen in the present papers, this method can produce in-depth personal accounts and accompanying analyses. As Miller suggests, such a technique was especially helpful in eliciting a cast of writers who are highly interdisciplinary and international in background.

These are invaluable commentaries on major losses in people's lives and the subsequent struggles with grief. Nevertheless, I would offer two reactions that challenge some of the logic found in the field of work on complicated grief. These reactions pertain to the use of the terms "complicated grief" and "closure."

Plain, Simple Grief?

First, I would contend that almost all grief is complicated, in the sense that it is difficult to understand well the particulars of the grief, its antecedents and consequences. Even what might be construed to be a "simple" loss (for example, the death of a pet) may have major implications for how the griever goes about living for some time into the future. It may affect self-esteem, motivation, interpersonal relations, and work–school activities. It simply is not that simple!

Such reasoning is not consonant with what is found in looking up the definition of complicated grief and its clinical equivalent term, "prolonged grief disorder." So-called "normal grief" is presumed to fade over a few months, whereas complicated grief does not (see http://www.mayoclinic. com/health/complicated-grief/DS01023). Prolonged grief disorder is associated with symptoms such as extreme focus on the loss and reminders of the loss; preoccupation with one's sorrow; bitterness about the loss; depression or deep sadness; withdrawal from social activities; and specific reactions to death of a loved one, such as intense longing or pining for the deceased, and problems accepting the death. This disorder also often is connected to feelings of hopelessness and difficulties in functioning at work and at home.

I think that it is useful to have a concept such as complicated grief and its equivalent clinical term, prolonged grief disorder. It facilitates people's decision to seek professional help when they are struggling with loss and, in turn, have major difficulties in navigating life's dilemmas. The existence of these concepts helps others reach out to people in crisis situations. However, built into the logic of this disorder connotation of complicated grief are untenable assumptions: It is not abnormal to grieve for a lifetime and still function quite well in one's various life pursuits. If you do not believe this is true, interview a few veterans of World War II or the Vietnam War. Similarly, all of the symptoms noted earlier may appear to varying degrees for all types of major loss, which I define as involving a reduction in a person's resources for which there is an emotional attachment (Harvey, 2002). Major losses include many types of loss other than the death of loved ones, including divorce and dissolution, chronic illness and loss of health, becoming disabled, tragic accidents, being physically or sexually assaulted, and on and on.

By asserting the earlier point, I also would admit that some grief is more complicated than other grief. Importantly, in this volume, the concept of prolonged grief disorder has been challenged in several of the chapters (for example, Houen, Cassity, Granek). The chief concern among these commentaries is that viewing the griever's long-term, intense grief as pathological is not helpful or fair to the griever. As these writers make clear, for many types of loss, that is just the way it is. In a completely normal way, the grief may last a long time and be dauntingly persistent. To paraphrase C.S. Lewis's (1961) depiction of his grief in his book, *A Grief Observed* (regarding his feelings of grief due to the death of his partner, Joy), it can be as high and wide as the sky. McDonald's essay about the loss of a child attested to such grief in a poignantly striking way. Similarly, Richards's chapter about the death of her mother spoke to the power of long-term, profound feelings of loss. These chapters are illustrative of grieving that, in my opinion, is natural; hardly pathological. The grief is about the abiding love for the lost loved one, a love that may not be dispelled in the lifetime of the griever.

Closure? The "Dark Elegy" Example

Second, the frequently contended notion that it is important to achieve closure via grieving is logically and psychologically absurd. We do not close off emotions, thoughts, and behaviors relevant to lost others. We may learn to live with these experiences and likely will change in major ways because of them, but these facts hardly constitute an act of closure.

"Dark Elegy" is a sculpture project developed by Suse Lowenstein to reflect the grief of mothers of children who perished December 21, 1988, in the terrorists' bombing of Pan Am Flight 103 over Lockerbie, Scotland. Most of these mothers had college-age children on this flight who were returning to Syracuse University after a period of study in Europe. The sculptures depict these mothers at the very moment they heard of the deaths of their children. Dark Elegy is a memorial to love in the context of the hate that led to the bombing. It is a powerful symbol of how grief and the sense of loss just do not readily fade away. They become part of the griever.

In a 1990s interview with the late CBS anchor Charles Kuralt, Suse Lowenstein spoke of the question people might raise about the benefit of keeping alive the grief inherent in the Dark Elegy project a decade after these children's deaths. Kuralt led into this topic by suggesting that Lowenstein was making grief palpable, when one might think that she should be "moving on," or seeking closure. As she has done in other interviews, Lowenstein did not hesitate in her reply. She said Dark Elegy was not her only pursuit in life. Like others who grieve, she said that every day she gets up and goes to work and goes about her normal family life. But she said that people should understand that this grief that she feels never goes away—it never, ever, leaves her mind and heart.

Richards's chapter in this volume reminds me of the folly of using the concept of closure as a sought-after state in dealing with loss and grief. She discussed the unexpected death of her mother in the wake of years of medical difficulties, financial crises, and family deaths. Then, she noted the many emotions that she had to work through in coming to terms with her mother's death. She indicated it took her 10 years to spread her mother's ashes, and she still experiences diverse, ambivalent emotions in thinking about her mother.

I would submit that closure is a media-hyped term that provides little if any benefit to our understanding of the grieving process. As Ellis eloquently states in her essay on loss and grief in this collection, "I suggest that it can be healthy to 'hold onto' grief as a way to maintain a relationship with a loved one."

Themes

Pile-Up of Losses

I learned some useful lessons from the stories in this volume that professionals told about their own experiences of complicated grief. A continuing theme of many of the chapters was the idea that complicated grief often is associated with a pile-up of losses in a person's life. In fact, a pile-up of losses almost seems to be a central, defining condition of complicated grief.

An illustration of a pile-up is the following: the death of a close other may be accompanied by health difficulties, financial challenges, the loss of esteem in one's community or profession, and difficult interpersonal relations with loved ones. Examples of these pile-ups are found throughout the chapters presented here. Russell discussed her father's death that was compounded by her experience of abuse in a personal relationship, that then was further compounded by the abduction of her child and related loss issues associated with the abduction.

Staples's essay was replete with multiple losses. At 36, she experienced a hysterectomy, a diagnosis of multiple sclerosis, and a divorce. Later, while battling multiple sclerosis, her second husband died. She said she was suicidal for many years. As she said with much justification: "My world was shattered, it imploded, and I did some crazy things."

Similarly, Navarro told of the death of her brother that occurred two years after the unexpected deaths of her parents. She indicated that these losses were made more difficult because she and her brother had battled over the family estate, leading her to feel shame and guilt upon his death.

Granek's chapter emphasized a pile-up occurring in 2006 when her mother died; in that same year, she lost an aunt, a close family friend, a woman who was close to her mother during her mother's cancer treatment, and a cherished professor. Granek used her experiences of a pile-up of losses to call into question the potential inclusion of the diagnosis of prolonged grief disorder in the next edition of the *Diagnostic and Statistic Manual of Mental Disorders*.

The pile-up concept also is illustrated by the fact that losses at one point in life can resurrect the hurt and emotions associated with losses at earlier points in life. Hanscombe's chapter described how being terminated from a professional position, which she had trained long and hard to achieve, led to the playing out in her mind of earlier childhood experiences of loss in the form of sexual abuse. In a related vein, Kerr wrote about how insecure attachment early in life, deriving from feelings of abandonment and/or other loss experiences, may presage the development of complicated grief when later losses mount (in her case, the loss of father and brother, after the earlier loss of her mother).

The idea of a pile-up of losses deserves much more attention in the literature. So often, not only is there a pile-up, but the pile-up may involve a convoluted causal sequence of events, involving different areas of a person's life. A divorce may lead to health difficulties, poorer work by children in school, financial difficulty, loss of feelings of self-esteem and self-confidence, reckless behavior, and more. The present chapters show some of these concatenations of events that spin out of a major loss in a person's (or family's) life.

Dialectics

For many writers, the yin and the yang of loss and grief included the extended, unquenchable yearning for a lost other paired with the joys of ongoing relationships and accomplishments. This dialectics concept is illustrated in Ellis's discussion of her brother Rex's death on the ill-fated Air Florida crash in the Potomac more than 25 years ago. As she said, it may seem as if grief has taken over the griever's life. Yet, in her case, her memories of Rex occur in the context of her joy and passion for living and relating to those currently in her life. She suggested that the complex of emotions attendant to her feelings for her brother deepened her overall experience of living, and that the stories she tells of her brother keep him alive in her memory.

The Relative Nature of Losses

As a teacher in the field of loss and trauma for more than two decades, I learned that relativity may be readily applied in helping us see how our losses stack up in a comparative sense, and to other people's losses. Losses do not stand on their own. Psychologically, they stand in context with other significant events in our lives. Our major losses seem to have a ranking in our minds, one that reflects devastation inflicted or the degree of coping needed to deal with them.

McDonald's chapter illustrates this relativity. Her indication early in her chapter that she is deaf set up an expectation that she would include that fact in her statement about complicated grief. Yet, this "loss," as it were, in making communication more difficult, soon paled and receded in her commentary as she described what it meant to loss her son of 22 weeks to sudden infant death syndrome. As is often the case, the loss of a child trumped other events and became a defining feature of the contemporary self, even as this loss, too, became part of the extended sequence of events, including some very positive ones for the writer (for example, taking up and becoming adept and quite regular at swimming).

Cultural and Historical Aspects

Antonelli's discussion of the losses that reverberated over the decades after her mother suffered and lost loved ones in a pogrom in Russia in the early 20th century suggests that complicated grief often is complicated because it involves a pile-up of related losses, sometimes accumulating over years and years. But it also is complicated because it must be seen in the context of cultural and historical factors such as the Holocaust, pogroms, and the countless atrocities of wars and conflicts since time immemorial. Further, these molar-level losses and the resulting grief just do not end anytime soon; they go and on in the minds of those who were and are affected.

Essentially, the same point can be made about how stigma associated with sexual preference (Purnell chapter), social identity and physical appearance (Sharma), or other conditions contribute to complicated grief. These chapters also make clear that such stigma is a product of particular cultural and historical forces and change with new sociocultural influences.

Grief Is Not Necessarily Logical

Grief often just happens without clear rhyme or reason. Sagan's essay is illustrative. She described how difficult it was for her family to live with her father, who suffered from Alzheimer's disease, for a long period before he died. One might think that such a death would bring relief to the family (relief being a concept often invoked by grievers who have observed the long-term suffering of a recently deceased loved one). Sagan mentioned that during her father's life, he had inflicted a harsh tyranny over her mother. Would her mother, therefore, be expected to feel relief at the death of her husband? Maybe on logical grounds she should. But as grief can be illogical, or psychological, her mother showed a grief that was "complete" and "unshakable."

Hope and Writing to Thrive

A final, overall theme in this book is that these professionals (most of whom are practitioners and/or writers and teachers) use their own life experiences, which include many major losses, in their present work with others. In fact, they often seem to cherish the hand that life has dealt them, however daunting, because it imbues them with greater knowledge, experience, and ability to help others. A related part of this theme is that writing and telling one's story is uplifting, life-preserving, and a powerful antidote to paralysis deriving from loss and grief.

Conclusion

I think that part of what we as authors in this collection have gained from this work must include a feeling of having had an opportunity to do some useful catharsis in thinking and writing about the concept of grief and our own experience of grief. We cannot run away from it. We can live with our own loss and grief, and probably with more grace, when we behold with care the suffering of our fellow human beings as they too struggle with their own loss and grief. Our stories of loss and the mourning of such loss, in turn, become precious gifts to those who read them and to those who, through these stories, try to walk a few steps in our shoes.

References

Harvey, J. H. (2002). *Perspectives on loss and trauma: Assaults on the self.* Thousand Oaks, CA: Sage Publications.

Lewis, C. S. (1961). *A grief observed.* New York: Farrar, Straus, & Giroux.

About the Editor

Eric D. Miller, PhD, is associate professor of psychology, Kent State University, East Liverpool, Ohio. He has published numerous papers examining various aspects of how adults cope with, and adjust to, loss and other adverse events. He was the sole author of the textbook *The Psychology of Adjustment and Coping* (BVT Publishing) and served as coeditor (along with John H. Harvey) of the book *Loss and Trauma: General and Close Relationship Perspectives* (Taylor & Francis/Brunner-Routledge).

About the Contributors

Annette Anderson-Engler, PhD, MSW, is a writer, academic, social worker, and mentor. Her area of focus is narrative analysis and the effects of grief, trauma, and loss on social, cultural, and collective identities. She developed the concept of "identity displacement" during her doctoral work, in which she examined the process of identify reconstruction through the shared meaning of stories. Dr. Anderson-Engler was awarded a three-year (2006 to 2008) scholarship from the Koerber Stiftung Foundation in Hamburg, Germany, where she participated in extensive research in story-telling dialogue and peace-building practices. She currently teaches in the Department of Social Work and Education at Salt Lake Community College in Salt Lake City, Utah.

Mildred Antonelli, PhD, practiced interpersonal psychoanalysis from the 1960s until 2000, when she belatedly discovered self-psychology and inter-subjectivity. She began training at, and graduated from, the Institute for the Psychoanalytic Study of Subjectivity. She has worked with adults, adolescents, and children of all ages in a variety of settings, including private practice. For the past three decades, she has been working intensively with victims of trauma, including the trauma of complicated grief and bereavement. She has taught in the framework of interpersonal theory in psychology and educa-tion, in graduate and undergraduate university programs, and she has taught interpersonal theory privately. She has presented papers in the United States and abroad.

Jason Barr is a member of the Department of English at Blue Ridge Community College, in Weyers Cave, Virginia.

Kathleen J. Cassity, PhD, is associate professor of English and coordinator of First-Year Writing at Hawai'i Pacific University, Honolulu.

Carolyn Ellis is professor of communication and sociology at the University of South Florida. She has published five books and four edited collections, the most recent of which are *The Ethnographic I: A Methodological Novel about Autoethnography; Revision: Autoethnographic Reflections on Life and Work;* and *Music Autoethnographies: Making Autoethnography Sing/Making Music Personal.* She has published numerous articles, chapters, and personal stories situated in autoethnography and interpretive representations of qualitative research, many of them dealing with grief and loss. Her current research focuses on interactive interviews and collaborative witnessing with Holocaust survivors.

Leeat Granek, PhD, is assistant professor, Department of Public Health, Faculty of Health Sciences, Ben Gurion University of the Negev, Southern Israel. She is a health psychologist with expertise in the areas of grief and loss, women's health, qualitative methods, and psycho-oncology. She has published her work extensively in academic journals, including *Archives of Internal Medicine, Social Science and Medicine,* and the *Journal of Health Psychology,* and in mainstream media publications, including the *New York Times* and *Slate Magazine.* Her current projects include examining the grief of oncologists over patient loss, bereavement follow-up care for cancer patients and their families, and the experiences of parents whose children have cancer.

Elisabeth Hanscombe, PhD, is a psychologist, a writer, and adjunct research associate, Swineburne Institute for Social Research, Melbourne, Australia. She completed her PhD in 2011 on the topic "Life Writing and the Desire for Revenge" and has published a number of short stories and essays in the areas of autobiography, psychoanalysis, testimony, trauma, and creative nonfiction in literary and psychotherapy journals and magazines throughout Australia and in the United States. She blogs at http://sixthinline.blogspot.com.au/

John H. Harvey, PhD, is professor emeritus of psychology, University of Iowa, Iowa City. He is a social psychologist with expertise in the study of loss and trauma and close relationships. He has authored nearly 200 papers or books throughout his career and serves as the current and founding editor of the *Journal of Loss and Trauma.*

Christina Houen, PhD, is an independent writer, researcher, and editor and adjunct research associate, Curtin University, Perth, Australia; she is reflections editor of the journal *Life Writing* (Routledge). Her thesis, being rewritten as a book, is a Deleuzian study of women's desire. The loss of her young children by abduction is the source of her passion for life writing as healing. She blogs at memoryandyou.wordpress.com, and her editing Web site is perfectwordsediting.com. She can be contacted at farthestnorth1@ westnet.com.au.

Laura K. Kerr, PhD, is an independent scholar training as a psychotherapist. She has interests in Jungian (archetypal) psychology and trauma-informed psychotherapies and has trained at the CG Jung Institute of San Francisco and several community agencies providing trauma-informed care. Dr. Kerr has also designed and led workshops on the topics of trauma and self-stigma and their impact on living full, authentic lives. She has been affiliated with the Beatrice M. Bain Research Group at University of California, Berkeley and the Institute for Research on Women & Gender at Stanford University, and she taught at Stanford University. With V. Y. Mudimbe and Godé Iwele, she is editor of *The Normal and Its Orders: Reading George Canguilhem* (Editions Malaïka, 2007). You can learn more about Laura at www.laurakkerr.com.

Rae Luckie, PhD, is a lecturer in education and coordinator of the Graduate Diploma in Education, University of Wollongong, Batemans Bay Campus, Australia, and teaches creative writing at Shoalhaven Campus. Dr. Luckie also works as a mentor and life writing consultant, facilitating projects in rural communities and schools. Her auto/biographical works are included in *What is Mother Love?* (2008), edited by Selwa Anthony; *Illness in the Academy* (2007), edited by Kimberley Myers; and *Best Australian Stories 2004*, edited by Frank Moorhouse.

Donna M. McDonald is an academic, social policy consultant, social worker, and writer. She is the convener for disability studies in the School of Human Services and Social Work, Griffith University, Brisbane, Australia, and undertakes consultancy projects in the area of social inclusion. Her publications on grief include *Jack's Story*, her memoir written in the wake of the sudden infant death of her son, and an essay, "I Am a Mother," published in *MotherLove 2*. She has also published several articles and book chapters about deafness and deaf people's lives.

Mary Lynn Navarro is assistant professor, English Department, Kingsborough Community College, Brooklyn, New York. She has mentored and taught high school students in New York University's Metro Center for Urban Education. Professor Navarro has also taught literature, composition-rhetoric, and English as a second language in many colleges of the City

University of New York. At Metropolitan College of New York, Professor Navarro has taught and developed programs in English, literature, writing, language and culture, and ethnography.

David F. Purnell, MA, is a graduate student, University of South Florida, Tampa.

Rose Richards, MA, PhD, has an MA in English Literature, and her PhD (psychology) dissertation was on narrative and identity in organ failure and transplantation. After a considerable period of ill health, she underwent a kidney transplant in 1991, and these experiences form the basis of her doctoral work. Her other research includes illness narratives, identity studies, and teaching writing. She has published academic work and short stories. Some of her writing has appeared in *Kunapipi: Journal of Postcolonial Writing, New Contrast, Qualitative Health Research, The South African Journal of Higher Education,* and *The Bed Book of Short Stories* (Modaji Press, 2010). She works with university students (at Stellenbosch University, South Africa) to help them develop academic writing skills.

Vanessa Russell, PhD, is a graduate of the English Literature and Creative Writing Program, University of Melbourne, Australia. Her first novel, *Holy Bible,* was published by Sleepers in 2013. She has a memoir coming out through Hardie Grant in 2014 about getting into, and getting out of, an abusive relationship and then being served with the Hague Convention.

Olivia Sagan, PhD, is academic co-ordinator for psychology, Bishop Grosseteste University, Lincoln, England. She has published widely on the subject of her research, the phenomenological narrative exploration of mental illness and artistic practice. Currently, she is preparing a book titled *Narratives of Art Practice & Well-Being: Connection and Reparation,* to be published by Routledge in 2014.

Parag Sharma is the pseudonym of an assistant professor of English at an American university.

Trish Staples, MA, MEd, is a qualified teacher and counselor living in the United Kingdom and has more than 35 years of experience working in education, health, and volunteer sectors. A diagnosis of multiple sclerosis in 1991 and other significant losses in Dr. Staples's adulthood led to her involvement with various organizations, in which she used learning, skills, and knowledge evolving from her experiences to inform and support others facing similar situations. Her master's dissertation embraced an integrative, qualitative exploration of wounded healers working with bereaved clients.

Paige W. Toller, PhD, is assistant professor, School of Communication, University of Nebraska–Omaha. She has published articles in the *Journal of Applied Communication Research, Sex Roles, Communication Studies, Iowa Journal of Communication,* and *Southern Journal of Communication.* She is on the editorial board for the *Journal of Applied Communication Research.* Her research primarily focuses on communication and parental bereavement.

Lynne M. Webb, PhD, is professor, Department of Communication University of Arkansas, Fayetteville. She previously served as a tenured faculty member at the Universities of Florida and Memphis. She has published articles in multiple journals, including the *Journal of Family Communication,* the *Journal of Applied Communication Research,* the *Journal of Health Communication,* and the *International Journal of Social Research and Methodology.* She is coeditor of *Communication for Families in Crisis* and *Computer-Mediated Communication in Personal Relationships.* Her research focuses on young adults' interpersonal communication in romantic and family contexts.

James A. Wren, PhD, DPhil, DSc, holds his PhD in comparative literature from the University of Washington, his DPhil in modern Japanese literature and cultural studies from Niigata University (Japan), and his DSc in immunogenetics from the Chinese University of Mining and Technology (People's Republic of China). Having widely published on the areas of modern Japanese and Indonesian literature, as well as in medical history and narrative, he has taught at Rhodes College and the University of Hawai'i. He retired from his post as professor of Modern Japanese Literature at San Jose State University to address the ravages of lupus and Parkinson's disease.

Index